LIVING HISTORY:
A FAMILY'S 19th CENTURY

Hugh Gault

Gretton Books
Cambridge

10010010013193

First published in 2010 by Gretton Books, Cambridge,
Cambridgeshire, England

A CIP catalogue record for this title
is available from the British Library.

ISBN
978-0-9562041-1-0

Set in 9/11 pt Arial

Printed in Great Britain
by the MPG Books Group
Bodmin and King

"It is the storyteller who makes us what we are, who creates history. The storyteller creates the memory [without which] surviving would have no meaning."

Chinua Achebe
'Things Fall Apart', 1958
introduction to 2001 edition

PREFACE

I first became interested in Spencer Perceval, his wife Jane Wilson and the lives of their twelve children in autumn 2007. He is best known, if he is remembered at all, for being assassinated. However, his legacy goes far beyond this, as do those of the Perceval children, all of whom are even less well-known. In October 2009 events were held in Ealing and Northampton to mark the 200th anniversary of Spencer Perceval becoming Prime Minister. It was a particular pleasure to meet descendants of the family at both. However, the focus of this book is of necessity one generation of the Percevals. Telling their stories has proved complicated enough, but perhaps one day the books will be written that the descendants and their histories often warrant.

No Perceval diaries have been found, and few letters, so this is a biography of public, rather than private, lives. They were political, but not always party political; their interests were extensive, and consequently the canvass has to be broad as well; in several cases their impact was both deep and lasting. Nevertheless, there are some personal tragedies included in these pages. This may be likely statistically across a number of lives, but these are real people rather than statistics, and it remains a shock all the same. Equally, however, there is ample evidence of action that improved the circumstances of their fellow citizens.

In preparing this book I have been dependent on many people who, in readily making available what they knew, often put me right as well. At the risk of omitting somebody who should be included, I thank Reverend Peter Wragg of St Dunstan's Church, Feltham; Paul Fitzmaurice a local historian in Ealing; Rita Boswell archivist at Harrow School; Celia Pilkington archivist at the Inner Temple; Nicholas Rogers archivist at Sidney Sussex College, Cambridge; many people in Uxbridge including Paul Davidson of Hillingdon Local Studies; Tony Reynaldson a Trustee of the Catholic Apostolic Church; Tim Bugby of the Forward in Faith organisation and other people at the Gordon Square Church of Christ the King; Reverend Erica Wooff and George Burton of St Luke's Church, Charlton; Archives and Local Studies staff in the Essex, Hampshire, Hertfordshire, Kensington & Chelsea, Kent, Warwickshire, Westminster and Worcestershire Record Offices; Rosemary Moodie and Sian Yates at Lloyds Banking Group Archives and Museum who hold the historic records of the Clerical, Medical and General Life Assurance Society; Geoffrey Martin archivist at Christ's

College, Cambridge; David Morrison librarian/archivist at Worcester Cathedral; Frances Bellis Assistant Librarian at Lincoln's Inn; the General Cemetery Company, Kensal Green cemetery; and archives staff at Brasenose College, Oxford and Westminster Diocesan Archives. As before, the librarians at Cambridge University Library have given invaluable help, and I remain fortunate to have this resource so nearby. The Cambridgeshire library service has enabled me to consult nineteenth century Census records, while the British Library has provided access to original letters written by the Percevals (as well as much else). Maria Perceval's handwriting is not always the easiest to decipher, being even smaller than mine, but her letters remain a delight - as well as a source of untapped treasure for the social historian.

I would also like to thank most particularly those who read a draft. They were: Anne Shellim, a direct descendant of Spencer Perceval junior and Anna Macleod; Jon-Paul Carr, Northamptonshire Studies Manager who helped co-ordinate the Perceval anniversary events in Northampton; David Poole, whose interest in history complements his housing and local government expertise; and Andrew Roberts, a Senior Lecturer in Sociology at Middlesex University with a special interest in mental health. The book has benefitted from their comments and advice.

If I have omitted to thank anybody for their assistance, this is inadvertent and I apologise.

Boyd Hilton at Trinity College, Cambridge, continues to set standards as a writer and historian to which I (and no doubt many others) aspire. His help with this book was less overt than with my previous one, but he provides a benchmark - as, in a different way, does the writing of George Dangerfield in the 1930s. Both bring history alive.

Ultimately, though, it is my family who have enabled me to realise my aim of a biography of some other remarkable lives.

Hugh Gault,
Cambridge,
April 2010

LIVING HISTORY: A FAMILY'S 19TH CENTURY

CONTENTS	Page

CONTENTS   **Page**

INTRODUCTION

This book is about the Percevals, but it is not just a book about the family. It is as much about the nineteenth century itself and the impact they had on it. The lives of the twelve Perceval children (six sons and six daughters) and their mother Jane Wilson illustrate many aspects of the century and in several cases were exceptional, sometimes tragic. This '**Family's 19th Century**' mirrored the experiences of many other people as well. They were, and this was, '**Living History**'.

Politics and religion feature in the lives of all the family, though not all belonged to the same religion nor held similar views of other groups. The army, civil service, empire and education are prominent in those of several. Mental health and disability were also significant, as were the impact of gender, marriage and family size on the lives they led. The family spread throughout much of the southern half of England and many parts of the west country; three of them lived in Europe at various times while five of the children retained their roots in Ealing. Between them, the children provide a record of many aspects of the nineteenth century and the communities they helped to forge.

The nineteenth century was a time of extensive change, to which people had to adjust if not adapt. In the view of John Maynard Keynes, "The power to become habituated to his surroundings is a marked characteristic of mankind."[1] But this is not always the case. The risks of change that were beyond the capacity of people to cope, that went too far or too fast, were recognised by many - politicians as well as philosophers and poets. William Gladstone towards the end of the century wrote, "I am for old customs and traditions [and] against needless change. I am for the individual as against the state. I am for the family and the stable family as against the state."[2] In 1827 George Canning saw it as his task as premier "to hold a middle course between extremes".[3] For Edmund Burke, "... the state of affairs which we seek to promote should be ... sufficiently better to make up for the evils of

---

[1] John Maynard Keynes, 'The Economic Consequences of the Peace' (Royal Economic Society edition, originally 1919), London, Macmillan, 1971, p1
[2] John Morley, 'The Life of Gladstone' (abridged and with a preface by CFG Masterman), London, Hodder & Stoughton, 1927, p56
[3] Wendy Hinde, 'George Canning', London, Collins, 1973, p466

transition."[4] For William Wordsworth, like Spenser before him, "Perilous is sweeping change, all chance unsound."[5]

It is often said that history speeds up as changes increase with the passing of time. But this judgement is largely based on hindsight. It is like being a bystander on a motorway: you are suddenly aware of how fast the traffic is going in a way that you were not when you were part of the flow. For those people living through change, this would have been significant whatever the period. This brings to mind GM Young's comment that the importance of history "is not what happened, but what people felt about it when it was happening".[6] The Percevals contributed to, and in some cases were the authors of, the changing times; all of them experienced the impact of these changes on their lives.

The national and international contexts

Everyday life in 1800 was as different from that in 1900, as the latter is from life in the twenty-first century. In 1800 education was rare.[7] Most children worked by the age of eight, though many families depended on some contribution to the family budget before then. For everybody employment conditions were harsh, the hours were long and leisure time was limited. There were few alternative sources of power to human toil. Communication was restricted for most people to others within walking distance and, while canals were developing, railways were still some time off. Britain was primarily an agricultural economy, with more than a third (35%) of the population working on the land.[8] Large towns had yet to develop, though neighbouring settlements were starting to join up with each other, and factories were just beginning to become a feature of the landscape. For example, Arthur Young writes that "About Wednesbury ... the whole country smoaks [sic] with coal-pits, forges, furnaces, etc. Towns come upon the neck of one

---

[4] John Maynard Keynes, 'The Political Doctrines of Edmund Burke', Keynes Papers at King's College, Cambridge, 1904
[5] Morley, op cit, p57
[6] GM Young, 'Portrait of An Age' in GM Young (ed.), 'Early Victorian England 1830-1865', volume 2, Oxford, Oxford University Press, 1934, Introduction to second edition 1952
[7] John Clarke, 'The Price of Progress: Cobbett's England 1780-1835', London, Granada Publishing, 1977 provides a number of insights into lives in the first half of the nineteenth century.
[8] Boyd Hilton, 'A Mad, Bad and Dangerous People?: England 1783-1846', Oxford, Clarendon Press, 2006, p8

another ..."[9] Housing was basic and often insanitary. Health and the importance of diet were not well-understood. Many children died in infancy, with the inevitable downward pressure on life expectancy - 36 or 37 years on average. For those people who survived the hazards of childhood and early adulthood, old age might be a realistic prospect,[10] but this brought its own difficulties and dangers - not least in automatic referral to the workhouse.[11] The Poor Law Act 1782 permitted the provision of outdoor relief and parishes joining together as unions. According to Colquhoun, more than 1m people were receiving relief in 1803 (with only 83,000 of them in workhouses).[12] The median family income was £55 a year, with 6m people (or two-thirds of the total of 9m people in England and Wales) living in families with an annual income less than £100 (a rough proxy for the subsistence level). For Arthur Young, writing of Hull in 1796, the average wage of an "industrious man" was about £40 per year, enough he says to support a man, his wife and "from two to three children, which it is conceived [sic] is about the average of families".[13]

In the next 100 years to 1901 the population of England and Wales had nearly quadrupled to 32.5m. Overall population density had increased by the same factor, from 152 people per square mile in 1801 to 558 in 1901,[14] with people from rural areas moving to urban ones.[15] However, the towns themselves increased in area as well as size,[16] so that population density in many urban areas did not increase substantially. It can be seen from Table 1 that by 1901 there were 33 urban districts with populations above 100,000 and

---

[9] Arthur Young, 'Tours in England and Wales', LSE Economic and Political Science Tracts, Reprint 14, London, Lund Humphries, 1932, p142. This quotation refers to a tour through the West Midlands in 1776.
[10] Patrick Colquhoun in his 'Treatise on Indigence', London, Hatchard, 1806 refers to 471 people aged 80+ in 55 workhouses he surveyed in 1805. These included 5 people aged 100+.
[11] See, for example, Pat Thane, 'Old Age in English History: Past Experiences, Present Issues', Oxford, Oxford University Press, 2002.
[12] Colquhoun, op cit, p54
[13] Arthur Young, op cit, p199
[14] See www.visionofbritain.org.uk/
[15] For example, John Langton & R.J. Morris (ed.), 'Atlas of Industrialising Britain', London, Methuen, 1986, p12: "The dominant nineteenth century trends were urbanisation and growth, and after mid-century increasingly extensive rural depopulation."
[16] Even, eventually, in London, though this was resisted initially with more people being crammed into the same increasingly over-developed areas. See Clarke, op cit, p58

75 with more than 50,000 people (with London being treated as one administrative district). FML Thompson points out that, while 11 towns had populations larger than 100,000 in 1801, this was the case for 44 towns by 1901.[17] London had increased its population by a factor of five over this period, with 960,000 people in 1801 growing to over 4.5m by 1901. By this date it accounted for 1 in 7 of the England and Wales population against 10% in 1801. However, the figure of 400 people per hectare in the City of London in 1801 had not been exceeded subsequently. Hogarth's images of

Table 1: Urban districts and populations at 1901 Census[18]

Population of Urban Districts	Number of Districts	Aggregate Population
Over 700,000	1	4,536,541
250,000 < 700,000	8	3,436,865
100,000 < 250,000	24	3,516,789
50,000 < 100,000	42	3,016,668
20,000 < 50,000	141	4,434,917
10,000 < 20,000	220	3,018,218
5,000 < 10,000	260	1,843,716
3,000 < 5,000	211	839,838
Under 3,000	215	414,803
Total	1,122	25,058,355

people living cheek by jowl, rubbing along as best they could in Gin Lane and other bustling parts of the city, belonged to the middle of the eighteenth century, but fifty years later areas such as St Giles and Seven Dials were just as notorious and were to remain so throughout the nineteenth century.[19] Cholera outbreaks were not unusual (for example, in 1832 and 1849). Henry Mayhew wrote of the poverty, slum housing and poor sanitation in London in the

---

[17] FML Thompson (ed.), 'Cambridge Social History of Britain 1750-1950: Volume 1 Regions and Communities', Cambridge, Cambridge University Press, 1990

[18] Amended from Vision of Britain website

[19] See, for example, Charles Dickens, 'Sketches by Boz', February 1836 (London, Penguin, 1995)

1850s.[20] Charles Booth found much the same at the end of the century.[21]

By 1901 Liverpool was the second largest city in the country with a population of 685,000 and Manchester the third with 544,000. A hundred years earlier they had both been smallish towns with populations of less than 80,000.[22] Their growth took place over a similar period, but for very different reasons and with different results.[23] Even by 1825 the contrast was apparent, giving another twist to the "condition of England question". William Huskisson, the MP for Liverpool from 1823, wrote to Robert Peel on 8th February 1827 comparing "commercial Liverpool with its thriving foreign trade to industrial Manchester with its grime and suffering humanity".[24] Liverpool was noted for its city centre architecture and boulevards, Manchester for its slums and factories, though Liverpool had its share of slums too. The social implications were equally stark. The poverty, poor housing, grim employment conditions and ill-health he found in the city led Engels to write 'The Condition of the Working Class in England' in 1844.[25]

By way of contrast Thomas Telford wrote on 26th February 1799:

---

[20] Henry Mayhew, 'London Labour and the London Poor', 2 volumes, London, George Woodfall & Son, 1851
[21] Charles Booth, 'Life and Labour of the People in London', London, Macmillan, 1902
[22] As early as 1700, though, they had been the largest towns not only in Lancashire, but in the north-west area. They retained this pre-eminence, with a rate of growth to match their growing role in the nation's life.
[23] Manchester became the symbol for laissez-faire and "immiseration of the working class", but it was not seen as a centre of wealth. For example, "Liverpool, as the greatest of northern commercial cities, followed the London pattern in producing more wealth-holders than Manchester." See p612 of W.D. Rubinstein, 'The Victorian middle classes: Wealth, occupation and geography', *Economic History Review*, 30 (1977 (a)), pp602-623. Robert Owen (1771-1858) drew some of his conclusions about the deleterious impact of machinery on man's environment, poor housing and character from his experiences in Manchester at the age of 17. See, for example, Vic Gatrell introduction p24 to Robert Owen, 'A New View of Society and Report to the County of Lanark', edited by V.A.C. Gatrell, London, Pelican, 1970: "With this increase nearly every feature of that grim environment ... had asserted itself: bad housing and bad factory conditions, labour exploitation, cyclical unemployment, poverty."
[24] Quoted in C.R. Fay, 'Huskisson and His Age', London, Longman Green & Co, 1951, p124
[25] Friedrich Engels, 'The Condition of the Working Class in England', (English translation 1892), London, Penguin, 1987

"Bristol is sinking in its commercial importance, it is not well situated, and its Merchants are rich and indolent. It will dwindle away. Liverpool is young, vigorous and well situated, it has besides taken Root in the country by means of the Canals - another port will arise somewhere in the Severn, but Liverpool will become of the first commercial importance."[26]

Writers such as Trollope and Dickens were illuminating the variety of human experience in the nineteenth century, while William Cobbett, and other journalists such as William Howitt[27] and George Borrow, were highlighting how the rural economy at the start of the century had its own hardships but these were as nothing to the consequences for many labourers as the Industrial Revolution took hold. Young contrasted the two worlds, with agriculture being left behind as industry forged ahead. For example, in writing of the removal of mud from the Humber at just over 2d per ton in 1796, he stated that

"Such facts are mortifying; they show how contented the whole race of agriculturists have slept for ages, while in manufactures and commerce every exertion of human abilities has been brought into full energy ..."[28]

Some workers were to benefit in time from improved pay and conditions, particularly where their employment required more than sweated toil and depended on skill or education. But this was far from the case for all,[29] with weavers and miners often the worst affected - though even here there were regional differences, and some employers were to prove themselves more enlightened than their colleagues (recognising the business benefits to be derived from, as well as the humanity of, improved employee welfare).

---

[26] Anthony Burton, 'Thomas Telford', London, Aurum Press, 1999, p56
[27] Considered by Daniel O'Connell as a potential editor (though a Quaker) of the Roman Catholic *Dublin Review* set up in 1836 to counter the Protestant *Quarterly Review* and *Edinburgh Review* (Tory- and Whig-supporting respectively). See Maurice R O'Connell, 'Daniel O'Connell: The Man and His Politics', Dublin, Irish Academic Press, 1990, pp37-38.
[28] Arthur Young, op cit, p179
[29] As JFC Harrison says in 'The Early Victorians 1832-1851', London, Weidenfeld & Nicholson, 1951, p35 "A vast amount of wheeling, dragging, hoisting, carrying, lifting, digging, tunnelling, draining, trenching, hedging, embanking, blasting, breaking, scouring, sawing, felling, reaping, mowing, picking, sifting and threshing was done by sheer muscular effort, day in, day out."

By 1901 average life expectancy had increased to 45 for men and 49 for women. In the previous 100 years, therefore, it had improved by a decade. Over the next century to 2001, when the comparable figures were 75 and 80, there was to be an increase of thirty years. This underlines that, while there was some amelioration in harsh conditions and poor diet during the nineteenth century, it took time for the major public health and medical advances of the Victorian period to have any substantial impact on the lives of most people.

"[1900] was a world of ... squalor and extreme poverty in the back streets, where the drab tenement houses were lit by gas or candles and where hot water was rare and hygiene was primitive ..."[30]

If you had money or land, however, the experience was very different. As it could be for those whose lives were transformed by education and other opportunities. It is worth noting, therefore, that while Britain was a divided society in 1801, it is a matter of opinion whether it had become more or less so by 1901.[31] The gap between rich and poor had become more marked, and inequalities had increased overall, but the base of social conditions and quality of life had generally improved for the majority. Although access to elementary education for 5-10 year olds had become an entitlement with the 1870 Act,[32] it was not until the Fees Act of 1891 that parents no longer had to pay to keep their children out of work.[33] The school leaving age was raised to 11 in 1893 and to 12 in 1899.

Few people had a right to vote at the start of the century. The 1832 Reform Act extended the franchise, but even so only 1 in 7 men were included in the ballot.[34] The basis was that they occupied

---

[30] John Montgomery, '1900: The End of An Era', London, George Allen & Unwin, 1948, p17

[31] Benjamin Disraeli, 'Sybil, or The Two Nations' provides a well-known illustration of the position in 1845. Wilkie Collins' novel 'No Name', 1862 is not so well-known and deserves to be more so. It stands comparison with any of his other books, including 'The Woman in White', and is very evocative of the impact of illegitimacy and the law at mid-century.

[32] WE Forster's Elementary Education Act, shortly to be followed by Cardwell's army reforms abolishing the purchase of commissions and then the Ballot Act of 1872.

[33] Gillian Sutherland, "Education", p145 in FML Thompson (ed.), 'Cambridge Social History of Britain 1750-1950: Volume 3 Social Agencies and Institutions', Cambridge, Cambridge University Press, 1990

[34] The number of qualified electors increased from 500,000 to 700,000, 1 in 7 men but 1 in 14 (7%) of the adult population.

property worth £10 per year in the new Boroughs, but more in counties. Liverpool had been represented in parliament for some time,[35] whereas constituencies were created for the first time for growing cities such as Leeds, Birmingham and Manchester. The 1867 Reform Act ensured that 40% of men (2 in 5) could vote[36] and gave additional MPs to each of these cities (including Liverpool). The third Reform Act of 1884 brought male suffrage for most of those over the age of 21. But even after these developments the female half of the population were still not allowed the vote in parliamentary elections in the nineteenth century. For those who could vote, the choice was between the Whig and Tory parties in 1800, between the Liberals and Conservatives in 1900. The names may have appeared similar, but nearly everything else had changed. In 1800 parties had only been identifiable as such at general elections, with the first national slogan being "no popery" in 1807. Between elections many MPs saw themselves as amateurs, fulfilling a duty and voting as their consciences (or, for some, other interests or influences) dictated. Parliament was usually in recess from July one year to January the next.

The co-operative movement had developed initially from Robert Owen and his initiatives at New Lanark in the first decade of the nineteenth century. It subsequently grew alongside trades unions from the late 1820s and during the 1830s. The "Rochdale pioneers" were established in 1844. The Labour party had yet to become a political force, with the first two MPs being elected in 1900[37] for the

---

[35] It was granted a charter as a borough in 1207 by King John. See, for example, Ramsay Muir, 'A History of Liverpool', Liverpool, University Press of Liverpool, 1907 or Alexander Brady, 'William Huskisson and Liberal Reform', (2nd edition), London, Frank Cass & Co, 1967, p18. The 800th anniversary of the city was celebrated in 2007.

[36] The Conservative Prime Minister the Earl of Derby had intended to go further than this to include the working class. Asa Briggs in 'The Age of Improvement: 1783-1867', 2nd edition, Harlow, Longman, 2000, pp451-452 says that Derby "professed 'the greatest confidence in [their] sound sense' ... They were not for the most part dangerous or revolutionary; they fitted into the social system rather than aimed at its destruction." Derby based this view on his personal experience of working with them in Lancashire to alleviate the worst effects of the 1860s downturn, a view that, according to Briggs, went beyond their tendency to deference and a corresponding inclination to vote Conservative in elections (Leonard's explanation in Dick Leonard, 'Nineteenth-Century British Premiers: Pitt to Rosebery', Basingstoke, Palgrave Macmillan, 2008, p230).

[37] One of whom was Keir Hardie for Merthyr Tydfil. There were fourteen LRC candidates (fifteen including Keir Hardie's other candidacy in Preston). Montgomery, op cit, p204, for example, says "At this time [1900] the labour movement was still in its infancy, but it was growing fast". It became the Labour

Labour Representation Committee. Pitt had been Prime Minister in 1800 (as he had from 1783) whereas Robert Cecil, the Marquess of Salisbury, was premier for a third time as the twentieth century dawned.[38]

Pitt's Act of Union 1800 between Britain and Ireland came into effect on 1st January 1801. It brought to an end the separate Irish parliament that had existed for eighteen years since 1782, replacing it with an expanded House of Commons that included the Irish constituencies. In 1901 the call for home rule for Ireland reverberated, rousing the "fiercest passions" and continuing to be an intractable problem for "successive governments"[39] - as Catholic emancipation had proved a century earlier. George III was King in 1800, as he had been for the preceding forty years. He was to celebrate his golden jubilee in October 1809, the first since Edward III over four hundred years earlier. The brand of executive monarchy that he had evolved was not to be repeated. His successor from 1810, first as Prince Regent and then as George IV from 1820, had a mixed relationship with the country, but never commanded the respect or affection shown to his father. William IV provided a more even-handed, but brief, interlude before Victoria became Queen in 1837. She has come to be associated with much of the nineteenth century, remaining on the throne to 1901 and presiding over a world in which the empire expanded.[40]

At the start of the period Malthus had just published his influential 'Essay on the principle of population' (1798). This was to let several governments off the hook as its deterministic view seemed to rule out the scope for human intervention in tackling poverty. A Dr. Edward Perceval, for example, accepted Malthus' initial propositions but said Malthus had "given the most gloomy and exaggerated view" where the impact of these on human happiness

---

Party in 1906, when 29 Labour MPs (including McDonald and Snowden) were successful in the general election that year.

[38] For an assessment of the twenty British Prime Ministers of the nineteenth century see Leonard, op cit. Leonard ranks them, putting Peel and Gladstone first equal and Rosebery last. He ranks Spencer Perceval 12th, ahead of Melbourne, Derby and Wellington.

[39] Montgomery, op cit, p20

[40] She became Empress of India in 1877. This proposal had first been put forward by Lord Ellenborough when he was the Governor-General over thirty years before. At that stage the Prime Minister Peel had "strongly deprecated it" (Leonard, op cit, p194). Disraeli clearly took a different view. (Perceval's grandson Horatio George Walpole subsequently became assistant under-secretary for India in 1883.)

and the progress of society were concerned.[41] In Perceval's view, public institutions in the rest of Britain should ameliorate vice and misery, as he claimed already happened in Scotland. He concluded that

"... surely no truth is better established than that in the manufacturing towns of Birmingham, Manchester, Leeds, etc. the injury done to the morals, the industry, and the prosperity of the lower orders by the precarious demand for labour in the different manufactories, is an evil incalculably great and pressing".

As the century went on, Malthus' views became increasingly discredited. The Catholic Emancipation Act was passed in 1829 and dissenter forms of religion, not least but not only Methodism, became increasingly popular alternatives to the orthodox Church of England. By 1859 Charles Darwin had begun to publish 'On the Origin of Species'. Along with geological developments, this was to turn human understanding on its head.

This provides some of the national context and social backdrop for the nineteenth century. Families such as the Percevals were far from being the poorest, but they were a long way from being the most privileged. Some of them moved in political and royal circles, but this was far from the case for all. 1807 had seen the abolition of the slave trade, but slavery was not finally abolished in Britain until the Slavery Abolition Act of 1833. It took at least another decade for this to happen in the colonies. Jean-Jacques Rousseau had said in the eighteenth century that "man is born free; and everywhere he is in chains".[42] For most people this was figuratively true in the nineteenth century, even if it was not literally the case for all.

At the start of the nineteenth century Britain had recently lost its empire in America and was under a real risk of invasion by a hostile France that was in the process of conquering much of Europe. By the close of the Victorian era much of the map was red, with Britain

---

[41] Edward Perceval, 'Remarks on a late publication, entitled, "An essay on the principle of population, or, A view of its present and past effects on human happiness, by T.R. Malthus, A.M. Fellow of Jesus College, Cambridge"', London, Bickerstaff, 1803, p4.
It should be said that this Perceval is not the Edward Perceval 1795-1840 who was one of Baron Arden's nine children, Jane Perceval's cousin and was to become her husband in 1821. See Chapter 3 below.
[42] Jean-Jacques Rousseau, 'The Social Contract', Amsterdam, Chez MM Rey, 1762, p2 (translated by GDH Cole)

controlling a vast empire and often being expected to provide leadership more widely. Indeed,

"Britain's colonial Empire was still expanding, and on January 4th the flag of the Royal Niger Company was formally lowered at Lagos and the Union Jack was hoisted over yet another sphere of British influence".[43]

Similarly, Richard Dowden follows Thomas Pakenham in describing how the unequal battle of Omdurman in 1898 reinforced British rule in the Sudan (with Egypt's flag conveniently flying alongside - symbolically, as well as perhaps literally, providing cover). For Pakenham "it seemed more like an execution" than a battle,[44] while for Dowden:

"The battle of Omdurman was fought at a moment when technology in the form of machine guns and breech-loading artillery gave the Europeans brief but total military superiority over African armies. ... The figures say it all. In one day the British counted 48 dead and 382 wounded. On the Mahdi's side 10,800 died and 16,000 were wounded. Afterwards the British general, Herbert Kitchener, had the body of the Mahdi dug up from its tomb in Omdurman and thrown to the dogs. British rule ... was firmly established."[45]

Africa (with the exception of Ethiopia and Liberia) was carved up by the European powers (mainly Britain, France, Germany, Belgium and Portugal) in the last quarter of the century. At the end of the century the India Office was still one of the top departments in the civil service. Individual colonies in Canada and Australia had been self-governing since the 1840s, while Canada achieved self-government as a single country through the British North America Act 1867 and Australia became a federal nation when the Commonwealth of Australia was formed on 1st January 1901. While Rosebery thought that "... the prestige of Britain stood higher [in 1900] than it had done since Waterloo",[46] this was rapidly unravelling as the Boer War unfolded.

---

[43] Montgomery, op cit, p15

[44] Thomas Pakenham, 'The Scramble for Africa', London, Abacus, 1992, pp542-546

[45] Richard Dowden, 'Africa: Altered States, Ordinary Miracles', London, Portobello Books, 2008, p161

[46] Montgomery, op cit, p16

Local circumstances

In 1801 Ealing (in the sense of the current London Borough) was spread out over a large area, but was essentially a series of villages with 4000 people in total. Ealing village itself was far enough from the centre of London to be seen as a retreat by people such as Soane and Perceval. A century later the population was over 105,000 as the area became increasingly accessible.[47] Similarly, Birmingham (an area Frederick Perceval moved to, and around, several times in his final years) grew from 85,000 people to 713,000 over the century becoming a key manufacturing centre at the heart of the "workshop of the world". These urban developments provide a stark contrast to rural areas such as Durham, Somerset, Worcestershire and Gloucestershire where other Perceval children made their homes. For much of the nineteenth century Ealing was one of the out-parishes within the Middlesex constituency, until 1885 when the Redistribution of Seats Act established a discrete parliamentary division.[48] Ealing became an Urban District Council (UDC) in 1894 and the first municipal borough in Middlesex in 1901.

The Perceval family: lives and legacy in the 19th century

Spencer Perceval came from the wealthy Egmont family,[49] but, as the second son of the Earl's second wife, he was not well off himself and frequently relied on his brother Lord Arden for financial

---

[47] The parish of Ealing itself grew from just over 2000 people in 1801 to over 33,000 in 1901. This rate of growth is lower, at only 16 times during the century, but is still very substantial and starting from a position where much of the land was already occupied by large estates. The grounds of some became parks, retaining an open and green feel for the area - i.e., a village. As well as Elm Grove and Pitzhanger Manor House, for example, other large houses were to be occupied by the Walpole family and by the Duke of Kent at Castle Hill Lodge. The latter was owned from 1795 by "Mrs. Maria Fitzherbert (1756-1837), morganatic wife of the Prince of Wales [the future George IV]. She sold it in 1801 to [his brother] Edward Augustus, Duke of Kent (1767-1820), who ... commissioned improvements by Wyatt but lived elsewhere from 1812". See 'Ealing and Brentford: Other estates', A History of the County of Middlesex: Volume 7: Acton, Chiswick, Ealing and Brentford, West Twyford, Willesden, 1982, pp128-131.
[48] This was to remain the Ealing constituency until further sub-division took place in 1945.
[49] Extracts from the Egmont family tree are included in Chapter 1 as Figure 2.

assistance. Arden left £700,000[50] when he died in 1840 - an enormous sum then and the equivalent of nearly £31m today. Spencer Perceval trained as a lawyer, developing his own legal practice and then becoming MP for Northampton in 1796. He was Addington's Solicitor General from 1801 and then Attorney General from 1802 to 1806. From 1807 he was Chancellor of the Exchequer and Leader of the House of Commons while the Prime Minister Portland sat in the Lords. From October 1809 Perceval was both Prime Minister and Chancellor of the Exchequer (after Palmerston had turned the latter post down). He was assassinated on 11th May 1812 before his 50th birthday. Perceval was well thought of by his political colleagues, if not necessarily by the general public, and had a happy marriage and family life. He was a prominent evangelical Anglican, but coupled this with very extreme views against Catholics and their emancipation.[51]

Jane Wilson married Spencer Perceval against her family's wishes when she was 21. In the seventeen years between 1791 and 1807 they had thirteen children, all but one of whom survived infancy. The family lived in several places in London including Lincoln's Inn Fields and Belsize House, Hampstead before settling at Elm Grove, Ealing from 1808. Almost three years after the assassination Jane married again in January 1815, becoming Lady Carr. She was presented to the Queen in May 1815 by her sister Margaretta (who had married Spencer Perceval's brother Baron Arden), but was widowed again from August 1821 when her husband Sir Henry William Carr, an equerry to the Duke of Kent and a mourner at George III's funeral, died in Southampton. He was eight years younger than Jane and had fought throughout the Peninsular War, being knighted in 1815 as a result of this. He had returned from the Peninsula only six months before their wedding, and the nature of their marriage raises many questions.[52]

The immediate family are set out in Figure 1. This shows the twelve Perceval children, the spouses of the eight who married and the number of grandchildren (who lived to become adults). Of the

---

[50] According to p56 of Rubinstein, W.D., 'The end of "Old Corruption" in Britain 1780-1860', *Past and Present*, 101 (1983), pp55-86. Arden's Dictionary of National Biography (DNB) entry says £800,000.
[51] For more detail see Hugh Gault, 'Spencer Perceval: Private values and public virtues', *The Historian*, Number 98, Summer 2008 (b), pp6-12
[52] See Chapter 2 below. John Quincy Adams kept a diary during his two years in Ealing from August 1815 and never saw them together, despite his attempts to meet Jane and meeting Henry Carr on his own.

children, only Jane and Spencer junior married before Henry Carr's death - in March and July 1821 respectively - and there was then a gap of almost five years before Henry's marriage in 1826. There were thirty-eight adult Perceval grandchildren, of whom Spencer and Ernest, the oldest and youngest sons, accounted for more than half.

The oldest child Jane was aged 20 when her father was killed, married her cousin Edward Perceval (Lord Arden's son) at the age of 29 and died less than three years later aged 32. All of her sisters lived into their 80s and only one of her siblings (Dudley) died before he was 60. Edward never recovered from her early death, gradually deteriorating over the next fourteen years until he was committed to a lunatic asylum in 1839. He took his own life a few months later.

The oldest son, also called Spencer, received a government sinecure before his 18th birthday and was an MP for seven years in three different constituencies between 1818 and the Reform Act of 1832. The first was in Ireland, the second in the Isle of Wight and the third the rotten borough of Tiverton. He was a Metropolitan Lunacy Commissioner for two years from 1830. By the end of his parliamentary career he was dismissed as "Saint Spencer" by his colleagues in the House of Commons, many of whom had been incensed by his religious mania. He was to become a fervent Irvingite and "apostle" in the Catholic Apostolic Church. He advocated fasting as a cure for cholera. This did not endear him to Londoners whose poverty often led them to starve but who suffered from the cholera outbreak in 1832 nonetheless. At least, unlike Lord Hertford, he did not run "like a rabbit".[53] He had 11 children, at least one of whom Jane was to feature frequently on the social circuit. He lived separately from his family in his final years and may have been contemplating a future in the Catholic Church when he died in Weymouth.

Four daughters (Frances, Maria, Louisa and Frederica) remained unmarried and moved to Pitzhanger Manor House in Ealing in 1843 from the family home at Elm Grove when their brother Spencer's family moved back. Pitzhanger had been re-modelled by Sir John Soane, a previous owner, and had been bought for them by their sister Isabella's husband. Frances and Maria were to live there for over thirty years, dying in 1877 aged 84

---

[53] Fay, op cit, p105

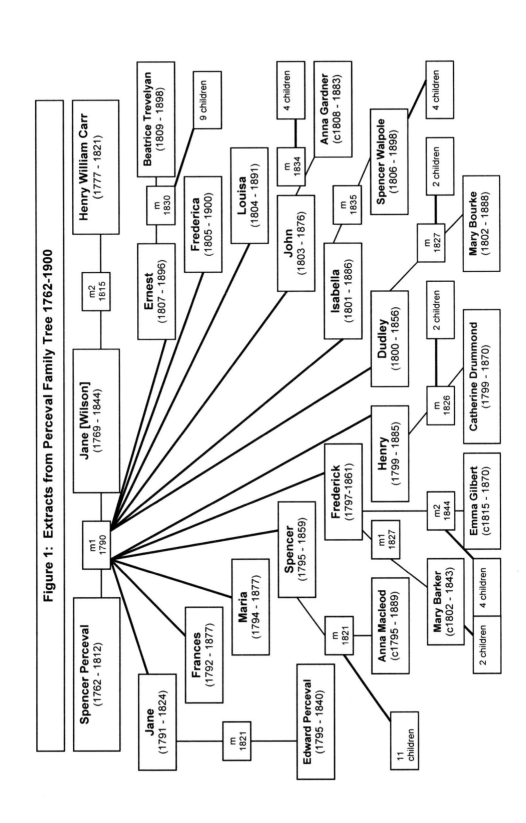

Figure 1: Extracts from Perceval Family Tree 1762-1900

and 82 respectively. (There was a gap of more than ten years between the two older sisters and the two younger ones. This provided another dynamic in their thirty-four years at Pitzhanger.) Louisa died in 1891 aged 87 leaving a large estate, as did her younger sister Frederica, the youngest daughter, who died in 1900 aged 95. She left money for a church to be built in memory of her father and All Saints Church, Ealing was consecrated in 1905.[54]

The second son Frederick is said to have been a semi-invalid[55] and he went to school in Rottingdean rather than Harrow like his father, all his brothers and several cousins. He was nearly thirty before he married Mary Barker in 1827. They had a daughter the following year and a son the year after, both born in Belgium. Mary Barker died in 1843 and he married Emma Gilbert the following year. They had five sons, four of whom survived into adulthood. After moving from Kent to Coleshill and then Warwick in his final years, Frederick died in Solihull in 1861 aged 63 and may have been buried in Birmingham (though he had a family vault in the churchyard at St Luke's Church, Charlton in which his first wife Mary Barker was buried). According to a now defunct Birmingham website, he claimed to be MP for both Westminster and Middlesex in the 1851 Census. However, the Census return shows him as JP for Middlesex and Westminster.[56] His deterioration in the last years of his life was real enough, without the story having to be embellished unnecessarily.

Henry Perceval was Head of School at Harrow and then went to Oxford University. Like his sister Jane before him, he also married a cousin and he and Catherine Drummond had a son and daughter born in Washington, Co. Durham where he was the vicar at Holy Trinity Church, Usworth. The church was built in 1831-1832, opened in 1832 and consecrated in March 1835. He was also the Rector at Elmley Lovett, Worcestershire, England for almost fifty years from 1837,[57] rebuilding most of the church about 1839. He died in 1885 aged 85. He had lived the life of a quiet reclusive country parson in an isolated rural area. Unlike his older brothers

---

[54] See www.allsaintsealing.org
[55] Denis Gray, 'Spencer Perceval. The Evangelical Prime Minister 1762-1812', Manchester, Manchester University Press, 1963. His biography refers briefly to the children up to the time of Perceval's murder in 1812. At this point Frederick was aged 14.
[56] *The Times* reported on 28th August 1843 that Frederick James Perceval of Notting Hill had been added to the list of JPs for Westminster.
[57] Crockford's Clerical Directories 1841-1890

Spencer and Frederick, he seems to have deliberately turned his back on society at large and a public life, making his parish and his family his world. But he remained vigilant and could be a vigilante when he thought it necessary.

His brother Dudley was a year younger, was to become a Companion of the Bath (CB)[58] and tried twice unsuccessfully to become a Conservative MP. The first time was in 1837 in Finsbury when he came third of three. The second was in 1853 when he was prevailed upon to stand against Gladstone for Oxford University. Gladstone had just become Chancellor of the Exchequer and was following the precedent of seeking re-election when appointed to Cabinet office, but he had made himself unpopular with some of the Fellows over University reform. Despite this, he was re-elected.[59] Dudley married Mary Jane Bourke[60] in 1827 after they had met in Cape Colony and they had a son and a daughter. He saw it as his filial duty to reiterate Spencer Perceval's religious views, for example repeating his father's stance against extra money for St Patrick's seminary at Maynooth and against Catholic emancipation. Dudley wrote 'Maynooth and the Jew Bill' in 1845[61] and was at the heart of the protestant backlash against increasing religious tolerance in the middle of the nineteenth century.

Isabella Perceval married the politician Spencer Horatio Walpole, dying at the age of 84 in 1886. Her husband, for whom Isabella was the leading influence, was an MP for over thirty-five years, twenty-five of them for Cambridge University, and was Home Secretary in three governments. Both their sons were civil servants and knighted. The elder one wrote a biography of his grandfather Spencer Perceval and proved a respected and reforming governor of the Isle of Man. The younger one was assistant under-secretary for India from 1883 to 1907. This was a relatively quiet period in India's history (certainly compared to the Indian mutiny in 1857 and events elsewhere at the time), but the administration of this part of

---

[58] A civil honour within the Order of the Bath.

[59] Gladstone had become Chancellor of the Exchequer for the first time from December 1852 in the Aberdeen coalition government that had taken office that month. This replaced the Derby government in which Disraeli had been Chancellor of the Exchequer.

[60] Her father Sir Richard Bourke was Governor of Cape Colony in 1825 and of New South Wales from 1831.

[61] Gladstone had resigned from the Cabinet in 1845 over the possibility of an extra grant to this Catholic seminary at Maynooth. He had found this incompatible with his Anglican beliefs.

the empire was extremely complex at what was recognised as one of the great offices of state.[62] When Keynes joined it in 1906, before Walpole's retirement, he found the complexity unnecessary, the bureaucracy stultifying and the routine boring. He left in 1908.

John Perceval the fifth son was committed as a lunatic at the age of 28 in 1831.[63] He attended two asylums (in Bristol and Sussex) for the well-off. By 1834 he had been discharged and had married. He was to have four daughters, one of whom married his sister Isabella's younger son. John himself published accounts of his experiences and was to become a leading mental health reformer. His self-help approach "sowed the seeds for today's user-survivor and mental health advocacy movements". He helped found the Alleged Lunatic's Friends Society in 1845 (becoming its secretary the following year) and campaigned to increase Parliamentary opposition to the Lunacy and Regulation of Lunatic Asylums Acts.

The youngest child Ernest was aged 4 when his father was murdered. He went on to become a Captain in the 15th Hussars and was aged 22 when he married in May 1830. Like Jane and Henry he also married a close relative. He and his wife Beatrice Trevelyan had twelve children in all, six of them in the seven years 1831 to 1838, the other six in the 1840s. He was a prominent civil servant in the Home Office, being private secretary to his brother-in-law Spencer Walpole on the first two occasions he was Home Secretary in the 1850s, and fulfilling the same role for Gathorne Hardy (1814-1906) in 1867-1868. It was Hardy who as Home Secretary set up the Royal Commission in 1868 that led to the major sanitation laws of the following decade. Ernest died in 1896 aged 88.

Implications and consequences

War proved to be one of the continuities of the century as conquest and colonial expansion were pursued, alliances and allegiances shifting as a result. In the early years of the century the war with France and the Napoleonic empire was of immediate concern, while Britain (along with France and Turkey) was at war with Russia in the Crimea in mid-century and with the Boer settlers in South Africa at its close. But turmoil of other sorts, as well as development and

---

[62] See Arnold P Kaminsky, 'The India Office 1880-1910', London, Mansell, 1986
[63] See Hugh Gault, 'An expert by experience', *The Psychologist*, vol. 21, May 2008 (a), pp462-463 for more detail

discontinuity in the course of the century, were as marked: for example, the 1870s were an "intellectual watershed",[64] while the 1880s were one of the periods of economic troubles and growing unemployment.[65] Hobsbawm refers to two bouts of the "great depression" in 1879-1880 and 1885-1887.[66] The first decade to 1810 was a world removed from that in mid-century, while the years 1851-1860 were very different to those of 1891-1900. The Perceval family often played a significant, if sometimes inadvertent or unintended, part in the political, economic and social developments that took place between 1800 and 1900.

In 1801 Spencer Perceval was just beginning to make his way on the national stage and eight of the twelve children had been born. By 1811 he was at the head of a government that had proved more effective than expected, and had won over the Prince Regent to its continuation despite the latter's previous preference for the Whigs. By 1821 Perceval's oldest son (Spencer Perceval junior) had ceased to be an MP for the first time and the oldest daughter Jane was to marry that March. His widow's second husband was to die in August shortly after "Queen" Caroline. George IV was on a state visit to Dublin and he remained out of England as Caroline's funeral procession left Hammersmith for Harwich, reaching Stadt on 20th August. Two men were killed by soldiers as the cortege passed through London in what the *Annual Register* described as a "struggle at Cumberland Gate".[67] The *Morning Chronicle* was to report their inquests in detail. 1830 saw George IV succeeded by his brother William IV, the last of the Hanoverians. In the middle of the nineteenth century four of the sons - Spencer (junior), Dudley, John and Ernest - proved the most influential. By the final decade several of the Perceval children (and some of the grandchildren)

---

[64] Asa Briggs in a review of 'The Victorian World Picture' by David Newsome in *The Times Higher Education Supplement*, 19th September 1977

[65] Robert Skidelsky, 'John Maynard Keynes 1883-1946: Economist, Philosopher, Statesman', London, Macmillan, 2003, p27. Skidelsky says that "The economic reversals of the 1880s caused the ominous word 'unemployment' to appear for the first time in *The Oxford English Dictionary* in 1888. The coincidence of economic troubles with the further extension of the franchise to the working-class in 1884-5, the terrorism and mass disaffection in Ireland, the revival of socialism, and the appearance of demagogues such as Parnell, Joseph Chamberlain and Lord Randolph Churchill, all pointed to a new and highly disturbing era in which ignorance and madness would take the place of reason in politics."

[66] Eric Hobsbawm, "Bernard Shaw's Socialism", *Science and Society*, 1947, vol. XI, pp305-326

[67] 'The Annual Register or a View of the History, Politics and Literature for the Year 1821', London, Baldwin, Cradock & Joy, 1822, pp119-128

had made their presence felt nationally. In the cases of John, Isabella and Frederica their contributions were to prove lasting. They had helped mould the future.

In summing up the century Robert Skidelsky says that

"The old gentlemanly culture, which had included learning and the arts, now stood sharply opposed to the much expanded world of business, money-making and politics. ... a generalised Puritan ethic had succeeded the morally more relaxed conditions of the eighteenth century; this made much greater moral demands on the individual in the name of social duty. On both counts Victorian civilisation paid a high price in cultural impoverishment and psychic strain for its material achievements and its social stability. Once theology ceased to provide for the thinking Victorian an axiomatic connection between morals and social requirements the tension between the ideals of civilised living and the 'needs' of society, between personal happiness and social obligation, came out into the open."[68]

Spencer Perceval has been described as a "Victorian born out of time",[69] often putting duty before personal preference, while Thompson is one of those who have drawn attention to the emergence of the middle-class in the latter half of the century, "respectable society"[70] as it has been termed. In this context purpose and zeal might be appropriate; discipline and hard work might well be necessary to avoid adversity or to secure progress in most circumstances. Several of the Perceval children exemplified this Puritan ethic. Some were to have their faith in evangelical religion challenged (though perhaps fortunately both Dudley and Spencer junior were dead by the time 'On the Origin of Species' appeared in 1859).

Needless to say, Skidelsky's overall view of society towards the turn of the century should not be confused with the position of all people all of the time. Most people were not middle-class and, even amongst those who were, public performance could differ from family behaviour in the privacy of home. Adherence to principles and values provided an overall code, but this could mean disputing the usual norms as well as adopting them unquestioningly. John

---

[68] Skidelsky, op cit, p23
[69] *Times Literary Supplement* in its 9th January 1964 review of Denis Gray's book, op cit
[70] FML Thompson, 'The Rise of Respectable Society', London, Fontana, 1988

Perceval was one of those who illustrated the importance of dissent, while several of the children followed the example of their parents in going beyond religion to improve people's welfare and support charities. For some people

"... the large-scale events from which 'world-pictures' were constructed were seen as largely irrelevant to the individual; 'history' was essentially individual experience and an accurate sense of this was only to be obtained by the close observation of individuals or small groups."[71]

Probably, though, the effects work both ways and certainly do for some of the people some of the time; individuals can have an impact on the wider world beyond their family, just as it may do for them. This study of the Percevals illustrates this two-way process.

For some commentators the nineteenth century epitomises a "vision and delusion of inevitable and humane progress".[72] But this may be no more than to point out that progress can be crab-like and circular, rather than linear and predictable. The Percevals illustrate how the lives of a single family often confound expectations, with difference as obvious and prominent as similarity.

---

[71] Martin Stannard, 'Evelyn Waugh: The Early Years 1903-1939', London, Dent, 1986, p291
[72] Christopher Sykes, 'Evelyn Waugh: A Biography', London, Collins, 1975 (quoted by Stannard, op cit, p291)

A 19th CENTURY CHRONOLOGY

Year	Perceval Family	Politics and Diplomacy	Legislation	People, Projects, Events	Publications
1800	Family living at Belsize House, Hampstead &/or Lincoln's Inn Fields 4th son Dudley born		Second Combination Act outlawing trade unions Act of Union with Ireland	Robert Owen's New Lanark model factory opens	Maria Edgeworth *Castle Rackrent*
1801	Spencer Perceval (SP) becomes Solicitor General 4th daughter Isabella born	Pitt resigns and Addington becomes PM Baron Arden re-elected at Totnes	Habeas corpus suspended First national census		
1802	SP becomes Attorney General	Baron Arden becomes British peer and ceases to be MP for Totnes General election	Robert Peel senior Factory Act Militia Act	William Cobbett's *Political Register* *Edinburgh Review*	
1803	5th son John born	Emmet uprising in Ireland			Robert Malthus *Essay on the Principle of Population (2nd edn)*
1804	5th daughter Louisa born Spencer junior at Harrow to 1813	Addington resigns and Pitt becomes PM again Baron Arden joins court (Lord of the bedchamber)		Martello Towers and other defences against French invasion	

Year	Perceval Family	Politics and Diplomacy	Legislation	People, Projects, Events	Publications
1805	6th daughter Frederica born	Battle of Trafalgar			Patrick Colquhoun *Treatise on Indigence*
1806	SP refuses to join Grenville's government	Pitt dies and Grenville becomes PM Delicate investigation of Caroline (wife of Prince Regent) General election		Britain and French empire begin trade war	
1807	6th son Ernest born SP becomes Chancellor of the Exchequer	George III dismisses Grenville and Portland becomes PM General election; 'no popery' slogan Copenhagen bombardment	British slave trade abolished	Joint stock boom in development of canals	
1808	Family move to Elm Grove, Ealing	Peninsular War starts Convention of Cintra		Manchester weavers' strike	
1809	SP becomes PM	Duke of York scandal Canning and Castlereagh duel Walcheren debacle	Curwen Bribery Act	Corunna and death of Sir John Moore as troops retreat Wellington victories at Oporto and Talavera George III royal jubilee	*Quarterly Review*

Year	Perceval Family	Politics and Diplomacy	Legislation	People, Projects, Events	Publications
1810		George III loses sanity		Bullion Report recommends resumption of cash payments	
1811		Regency introduced			
1812	SP assassinated	Regency confirmed Castlereagh returns to Cabinet Lord Liverpool becomes PM War against America starts General election	Orders in Council repealed	Luddite riots peak Baron Arden transfers to Windsor	Jane Austen *Sense and Sensibility*
1813	Spencer junior Teller of the Exchequer and to Trinity College, Cambridge				Robert Owen *A New View of Society* Jane Austen *Pride and Prejudice*
1814		Peninsular War ends Napoleon exiled to Elba War against America ends			Jane Austen *Mansfield Park*
1815	Jane and Henry Carr married Henry Carr knighted	Battle of Waterloo	Corn Law introduced	Samuel Whitbread suicide	
1816		Canning returns to Cabinet		Spa Fields riots	Jane Austen *Emma*

Year	Perceval Family	Politics and Diplomacy	Legislation	People, Projects, Events	Publications
1817			Clergy Residence Act	Pentrich rising	David Ricardo *On the Principles of Political Economy and Taxation* Jeremy Bentham *Plan for Parliamentary Reform*
1818	Spencer junior becomes MP for Ennis, Co. Clare, Ireland	General election	Habeas corpus restored Church Building Act	Samuel Romilly suicide	Jane Austen *Northanger Abbey* *Persuasion*
1819		Victoria's birth Peterloo massacre	"Six Acts" following Peterloo Act to resume cash payments by 1823		
1820	Spencer junior ceases to be MP for Ennis	Death of Duke of Kent (Victoria's father) Death of George III Cato Street conspirators apprehended General election "Trial" of Queen Caroline	Bill of Pains and Penalties abandoned after narrow victory in Lords		

Year	Perceval Family	Politics and Diplomacy	Legislation	People, Projects, Events	Publications
1821	Oldest daughter Jane and Edward Perceval married Oldest son Spencer and Anna Macleod married Death of Henry Carr	George IV coronation Death of Queen Caroline	Catholic Relief Bill defeated in Lords	*Manchester Guardian* Death of Napoleon Bonaparte	
1822		Castlereagh suicide Canning becomes Foreign Secretary			
1823		O'Connell founds the Irish Catholic Association	Gaols Act Warehouse Act	Anti-Slavery Society formed	
1824	Death of oldest daughter Jane		Repeal of Combination Acts against trade unions	Byron dies Robert Owen's New Harmony settlement in America	
1825	Henry becomes Rector of St Luke's, Charlton		Catholic Relief Bill defeated in Lords	Stockton–Darlington railway opened	William Hazlitt *The Spirit of the Age*
1826	Henry and Catherine Drummond married Henry becomes Rector of Usworth	General election		Edward Irving and others predict end of the world Thomas Jefferson dies	
1827	Spencer becomes MP for Newport, Isle of Wight and	Liverpool stroke and Canning becomes PM			

Year	Perceval Family	Politics and Diplomacy	Legislation	People, Projects, Events	Publications
	Under-Sec (Home Affairs) briefly Dudley and Mary Bourke married the day before Frederick and Mary Barker married	Canning dies and Goderich becomes PM			
1828	Spencer becomes clerk of Ordnance to 1830	Goderich resigns and Wellington becomes PM Canningites leave government O'Connell elected at Co. Clare	Repeal of Test and Corporation Acts extends civil liberties for dissenters		
1829			Catholic Emancipation Act Metropolitan Police Act	Manchester weavers riots	Honore de Balzac *Les Chouans*
1830	Ernest and Beatrice Trevelyan married	Death of George IV William IV coronation General election	Reform Act defeated in Lords	Death of Huskisson at opening of Liverpool-Manchester railway Swing riots start Simon Bolivar dies	William Cobbett *Rural Rides*
1831	Spencer ceases to be MP for Newport; becomes MP for Tiverton John committed to an asylum	Grey dissolves Parliament General election with huge reform majority	Truck Act		

Year	Perceval Family	Politics and Diplomacy	Legislation	People, Projects, Events	Publications
1832	Spencer ceases to be MP for Tiverton	Grey resigns; Wellington fails to form government; Grey resumes as PM General election	Reform Act Poor Law Commission	Jeremy Bentham dies Cholera outbreak intensifies and spreads to Britain	
1833			Abolition of slavery in British territories Factory Act	Catholic Apostolic church formed Brunel appointed chief engineer for Great Western Railway	
1834	John and Anna Gardner married	Tolpuddle martyrs transported Grey resigns and Melbourne becomes PM William IV dismisses Melbourne and Peel becomes PM	Poor Law Amendment Act	Robert Owen's Grand National Consolidated Trades Union	
1835	Isabella and Spencer Walpole married	General election Melbourne becomes PM		William Cobbett dies	
1836			Births and Deaths Registration Act		Charles Dickens *Sketches by Boz* *The Pickwick Papers*

Year	Perceval Family	Politics and Diplomacy	Legislation	People, Projects, Events	Publications
1837	Dudley stands for election at Finsbury Henry becomes Rector of Elmley Lovett	Death of William IV Victoria coronation General election			Charles Dickens *Oliver Twist*
1838			Poor Law extended to Ireland		Charles Dickens *Nicholas Nickleby*
1839		Melbourne resigns; Peel declines to form government; Melbourne resumes as PM Chartists' first petition rejected	Custody of Children Act	Chartist National Convention	
1840			Penny post introduced	Marriage of Victoria and Albert Houses of Parliament start to be re-built	
1841		General election Peel becomes PM	Names included in the census for the first time		
1842		Chartists' second petition rejected	Mines Act		Edwin Chadwick *The Sanitary Conditions of the Labouring Population*

Year	Perceval Family	Politics and Diplomacy	Legislation	People, Projects, Events	Publications
1843	Four unmarried daughters Frances, Maria, Louisa and Frederica move to Pitzhanger Manor House	O'Connell arrested at Clontarf	Patent theatres monopoly ends New Parishes Act	*The Economist*	Benjamin Disraeli *Coningsby*
1844	Death of Lady Jane Carr Frederick and Emma Gilbert married	Young Ireland founded	Bank Charter Act Joint Stock Companies Act Factory Act (Textiles) Dissenters' Chapels Act	Robert Owen's Rochdale Co-operative Society Death of Francis Burdett	William Thackeray *Barry Lyndon*
1845	John helps found the Alleged Lunatic's Friends Society	Peel resigns; Russell fails to form government; Peel resumes as PM	Maynooth grant increased Museums Act	Irish potato crop fails	Benjamin Disraeli *Sybil* Friedrich Engels *The Condition of the Working Class in England*
1846		Corn Laws repealed Peel resigns and Russell becomes PM		Irish famine worsens	Charles Dickens *Dombey and Son*
1847		General election	'Ten Hour' Factory Act Irish Poor Law Extension Act	Daniel O'Connell dies	Charlotte Bronte *Jane Eyre* Emily Bronte *Wuthering Heights*

Year	Perceval Family	Politics and Diplomacy	Legislation	People, Projects, Events	Publications
1848		Chartist riots Smith O'Brien uprising in Ireland	Public Health Act		Elizabeth Gaskell *Mary Barton* WM Thackeray *Vanity Fair*
1849				Cholera epidemic in London	
1850		Tenant League founded in Ireland		Papal bull restores Roman Catholic hierarchy in England	Charles Dickens *David Copperfield*
1851				Great Exhibition in Hyde Park Census of religious attendance	George Borrow *Lavengro* Henry Mayhew *London Labour and the London Poor*
1852		Russell resigns and Derby becomes PM General election Aberdeen becomes PM		Death of Wellington	
1853	Dudley stands in by-election against Gladstone for Oxford University	Gladstone's first budget			Elizabeth Gaskell *Cranford*

Year	Perceval Family	Politics and Diplomacy	Legislation	People, Projects, Events	Publications
1854		Crimean War starts		Battles of Balaclava and Inkerman Publication of Northcote-Trevelyan Civil Service report	
1855		Palmerston becomes PM	Metropolitan Management Act	*Daily Telegraph*	Elizabeth Gaskell *North and South* Anthony Trollope *The Warden*
1856	Death of Dudley	Crimean War ends		Bessemer steel-making process introduced	
1857		General election Indian mutiny	Matrimonial Causes (Divorce) Act		Charles Dickens *Little Dorrit* Thomas Hughes *Tom Brown's Schooldays*
1858		Irish Republican Brotherhood founded Derby becomes PM	Jewish Disabilities Act Public Health Act Local Government Act India Act	Robert Owen dies	
1859	Death of oldest son Spencer	General election Palmerston becomes PM		*Irish Times*	Charles Darwin *The Origin of Species*

Year	Perceval Family	Politics and Diplomacy	Legislation	People, Projects, Events	Publications
					Charles Dickens *A Tale of Two Cities* George Eliot *Adam Bede*
1860					Wilkie Collins *The Woman in White* George Eliot *The Mill on the Floss*
1861	Death of Frederick			Prince Albert dies	Charles Dickens *Great Expectations* George Eliot *Silas Marner*
1862				Distress in Lancashire caused by "cotton famine"	Wilkie Collins *No Name*
1863					Charles Kingsley *The Water Babies*
1864				Garibaldi visits England	Anthony Trollope *The Small House at Allington*
1865		General election Palmerston dies and Russell becomes PM			Lewis Carroll *Alice's Adventures in Wonderland*

Year	Perceval Family	Politics and Diplomacy	Legislation	People, Projects, Events	Publications
1866		Derby becomes PM	Sanitary Act		Charles Dickens *Our Mutual Friend* Wilkie Collins *Armadale* George Eliot *Felix Holt the Radical*
1867		Fenian rising in Ireland	Second Reform Act for England and Wales Factory Acts Extension Act	First Lambeth conference of Anglican bishops	Walter Bagehot *The English Constitution* Anthony Trollope *The Last Chronicle of Barset*
1868		Disraeli becomes PM	Second Reform Act for Scotland and Ireland	First Trades Union Congress meets Press Association founded	Wilkie Collins *The Moonstone*
1869			Trades Unions Funds Protection Act	National Education League founded	RD Blackmore *Lorna Doone*
1870		Home Government Association in Ireland founded by Isaac Butt	First Irish Land Act Elementary Education Act Army Enlistment Act First Married Women's Property Act	Civil Service reforms introduced	

Year	Perceval Family	Politics and Diplomacy	Legislation	People, Projects, Events	Publications
1871			Trade Union Act Army Regulation Act	Abolition of purchase of army commissions	Lewis Carroll *Through the Looking-Glass*
1872			(Secret) Ballot Act Scottish Education Act		George Eliot *Middlemarch* Thomas Hardy *Under the Greenwood Tree*
1873		Gladstone resigns; Disraeli declines to form government; Gladstone resumes as PM Home Rule League founded in Ireland			
1874		General election Disraeli becomes PM	Factory Act	First strike by agricultural labourers in England	Thomas Hardy *Far from the Madding Crowd*
1875		Minority interest purchased in Suez Canal	Public Health Act		Anthony Trollope *The Way We Live Now*
1876	Death of John				George Eliot *Daniel Deronda*

Year	Perceval Family	Politics and Diplomacy	Legislation	People, Projects, Events	Publications
1877	Death of Maria Death of Frances	Queen Victoria becomes Empress of India Transvaal annexed Gladstone visits Ireland	Prisons Act		
1878		British troops enter Afghanistan "Land War" in Ireland to 1882	Factory and Workshops Act	Roman Catholic hierarchy restored in Scotland Battle of Isandhlwana	Thomas Hardy *The Return of the Native*
1879		Irish National Land League founded Gladstone begins Midlothian campaigns		Flogging abolished in British navy	RL Stevenson *Travels with a Donkey*
1880		General election Gladstone becomes PM Parnell elected chairman of Home Rule Party	Employers Liability Act	Bradlaugh affair begins First South African War begins	
1881		Britain recognises the Transvaal Republic Parnell arrested and Land League proscribed	Second Irish Land Act	Flogging abolished in British army	

Year	Perceval Family	Politics and Diplomacy	Legislation	People, Projects, Events	Publications
1882		Revolt in Egypt led by Arabi Pasha Egypt invaded Murder of Chief Secretary in Dublin			RL Stevenson *Treasure Island*
1883	Henry ceases to be Rector of Elmley Lovett	Rebellion in Sudan led by the Mahdi			
1884			Third Reform (Representation of the People) Act	Fabian Society founded Mission mounted to rescue Gordon in the Sudan Royal Commission on the Housing of the Working Classes	GB Shaw *An Unsocial Socialist*
1885	Death of Henry	Salisbury becomes PM General election	Irish Land Purchase Act	Gordon killed in Khartoum	H Rider Haggard *King Solomon's Mines*
1886	Death of Isabella	Gladstone becomes PM First Home Rule Bill defeated General election Salisbury becomes PM		Unemployed riot in London	Thomas Hardy *The Mayor of Casterbridge* RL Stevenson *Kidnapped* *Dr Jekyll and Mr Hyde*
1887			Irish Land Act	Queen Victoria's golden	Bram Stoker

Year	Perceval Family	Politics and Diplomacy	Legislation	People, Projects, Events	Publications
1888			Local Government Act	jubilee "Jack the Ripper" murders Bryant & May matchgirls' strike	*Dracula*
1889				London dock strike	
1890			Housing of the Working Class Act		
1891	Death of Louisa		Factory and Workshop Act Fees Act (free elementary education)	Parnell cited in O'Shea divorce case	George Gissing *New Grub Street* Thomas Hardy *Tess of the D'Urbervilles*
1892		General election Gladstone becomes PM Second Home Rule Bill defeated in House of Lords			
1893		Foundation of Independent Labour Party (ILP)		National coal strike	
1894		Rosebery becomes PM	Local Government Act (parish councils)		

Year	Perceval Family	Politics and Diplomacy	Legislation	People, Projects, Events	Publications
1895		Salisbury becomes PM General election		Internal combustion engine invented by Daimler National Trust founded by Octavia Hill and others	Thomas Hardy *Jude the Obscure* HG Wells *The Time Machine*
1896	Death of Ernest			*Daily Mail* Marconi comes to England	
1897				Queen Victoria's diamond jubilee Tate Gallery opened	HG Wells *The Invisible Man*
1898				Curzon becomes Viceroy of India Battle of Omdurman Fashoda crisis	
1899		Second South African (Boer) War starts		Metropolitan Borough Councils established	
1900	Death of Frederica; money left in Will to build All Saints Church	Foundation of Labour Representation Committee General election		Relief of Ladysmith and Mafeking Boxer Rising *Daily Express*	HG Wells *Love and Mr Lewisham*

1. THE PERCEVAL BACKGROUND

The Egmont family

The Percevals claimed to be able to trace a direct line back to those who had accompanied William the Conqueror in 1066.[73] However, Vicary Gibbs[74] points out that the 1742 family history on which this claim is based contains very little that "is to be depended upon". Lord Dover described it as "a most remarkable monument of human vanity". Sedgwick in the History of Parliament 1715-1754[75] follows Horace Walpole in saying that it "incurred much ridicule". It is perhaps not surprising, therefore, that the etymology of the name is unclear.[76]

Although George Bernard Shaw was a fellow Irishman, it might be assumed that in all other respects he would stand in marked contrast to the Percevals. But before he turned to writing plays, he first tried his hand at novels. These were very poorly received, but the title of his final novel in 1884 was 'An Unsocial Socialist'.[77] Sir John Perceval (1683-1748), who became the 1st Earl of Egmont 150 years before this in 1733, could be described as a "social socialist".[78] Although this might seem a curious description for a peer, even an Irish one, there are several reasons why it is apposite in the Earl's case. For example, although he had to lobby to

---

[73] According to Ruth and Albert Saye, "John Percival, First Earl of Egmont" in Horace Montgomery (ed.), 'Georgians in Profile: Historical Essays in Honor of Ellis Merton Coulter', Athens, Georgia, University of Georgia Press, 1958, pp1-16.

[74] Vicary Gibbs, 'The Complete Peerage', vol. 5, London, St Catherine Press, 1926, p28

[75] Romney Sedgwick, 'History of Parliament: The House of Commons 1715-1754', London, HMSO, 1970, vol. 2, p339

[76] Ruth and Albert Saye, op cit, p2 refer to two possibilities: "le val de Perci" and military service on horseback, as in "per, or par, and cheval".

[77] Bernard Shaw, 'An Unsocial Socialist', London, Swan Sonnenschein, 1887 (reprinted London, Virago, 1988) It was first serialised in *To-Day*, a new "Monthly Magazine of Scientific Socialism" in 1884 and contains a description of Manchester exploitation on pp68-80 that amplifies page 5 and note 23 of the Introduction above.

[78] The Parliamentary Gazetteer of Ireland describes Egmont as an "old ruined Castle ... in the midst of a fine park and very extensive plantations". (Quoted in Gibbs, op cit, p28) This was in 1849, more than 100 years after Sir John Perceval had become the 1st Earl. Egmont is located three miles north-west of Buttevant, which itself lies on the main N20 route from Cork to Limerick. Ten miles south-west of Buttevant on the R580 is the market town of Kanturk (or "The Boar's Head" in Gaelic). Sir John was created Viscount Perceval of Kanturk in 1722/3, ten years before the earldom was conferred.

become an Earl, not least he said so that his children could "marry better", he then "used his influence not only to advance his personal interests, but also to secure government jobs and financial benefits for numerous friends".[79] More significantly, however, when Queen Caroline (1683-1737), wife of George II (1683-1760), suggested to him in 1732 that "May be you are for reducing people to poverty to make them honest", he replied that, this was "Not so ... [but] It were better if riches were more evenly divided."[80] He was in favour of law reform and thought it a "contradiction that law and equity should be different".   He was instrumental along with James Edward Oglethorpe (1696-1785) in founding the colony of Georgia, obtaining its charter in 1732 and becoming the first president of the trustees for the next ten years. In theory the colony was intended for imprisoned debtors,[81] but this seems to have been the case only infrequently, with Perceval describing most settlers from England as the "middle poor".[82] However, some colonists became discontented when it proved not to be the new opportunity they had been led to believe, let alone the promised land itself, even going so far as to compare it unfavourably with the neighbouring state of South Carolina that at least had the advantage, in their eyes, of permitting slavery. Disillusioned and ill, Perceval resigned from the trustees in 1742.

Sir John Perceval and the philosopher Bishop George Berkeley (1685-1753) became close friends after meeting in Ireland in 1708, writing regularly to each other from 1709 to 1731.[83] Bishop Berkeley had intended to found a college for potential colonists in Bermuda, even obtaining a royal charter, but never got further than Newport, Rhode Island where he made his home for two years from 1729.   However, his views were to prove influential in the arrangements for the Georgia colony, as well as in the development of colleges and universities elsewhere in America. He gave land and books to Yale University, where one of the colleges is named after him - as is Berkeley, California.

---

[79] Ruth and Albert Saye, op cit, p7
[80] Ibid, p9
[81] Sir John had first served from 1729 on the parliamentary gaols committee of which Oglethorpe was chairman.
[82] Ruth and Albert Saye, op cit, p11 See also RG McPherson (ed.), 'Journal of the Earl of Egmont: Abstract of the Trustees Proceedings for Establishing the Colony of Georgia 1732-1738', Athens, Georgia, University of Georgia Press, 1962
[83] Benjamin Rand, 'Berkeley and Percival [sic]', Cambridge, University Press, 1914

Sir John's interests and views stemmed in part from his strong religious faith. In 1731 he became a vestryman (a position of trust, as well as power and prestige, in the church) and the following year a trustee of a new church to be built at Woolwich (close to his country home at Charlton). Several of these characteristics were to be apparent in later generations of the family as well. (Extracts from the Egmont family tree are set out in Figure 2 below.) But, as is the case with many people, they were accompanied by less appealing traits. It is said that he could be "pompous and egotistical"[84] and, as he certainly lived in some splendour, aspects of his "socialism" may have fitted more comfortably with a "do as I say - not as I do" perspective. He was a leading light in the 1733 debate over the proper precedence of Irish peers compared to English ones. This went beyond a newly created Earl making his mark, and, while it might have been motivated by personal vanity to some extent, it was also an issue of principle for him given that he was always aware of threats to Irish authority. When the matter was not resolved satisfactorily, he and the other Irish peers demonstrated their obduracy by "boycotting" the royal marriage later that year.[85] This had the desired effect as their rights of precedence had been restored by the time of Queen Caroline's funeral in 1737. He was not above paying a large sum of money to become MP for Harwich in 1727[86] - though this was of course the usual practice at the time. On the other hand, he then "used his influence both in Parliament and in the Government to promote Irish interests",[87] such as opposing the imposition of an English tax on Irish wool in 1731, not least because of the message this would send of Ireland's subservient status.

As a friend of Sir Robert Walpole (1676-1745), generally acknowledged to be the first British Prime Minister from 1715-1742, his was not an influence that could, or was likely to, be ignored. In addition, Perceval was a Privy Councillor from 1704, maintaining this role even after George I (1660-1727) had become King in 1714, and was then made an Irish peer as Baron Perceval of Burton (also

---

[84] Ruth and Albert Saye, op cit, p9

[85] This was the marriage of the Princess Royal to the Prince of Orange. The word "boycott" entered general circulation nearly 150 years later in 1880 after Captain Boycott. There was subsequently a "Boycott Farm" close to the parish of Elmley Lovett, Worcestershire where Henry Perceval was the vicar from 1837 to 1883.

[86] £800, or the equivalent of £69,000 in 2009, according to Ruth and Albert Saye, but £1000 (£86,000 now) according to his DNB entry. Irish peers were able to sit in the House of Commons.

[87] Ruth and Albert Saye, op cit, p6

in County Cork) in 1715 before becoming Viscount Perceval of Kanturk. He had close connections as well to the Prince of Wales, the future George II, and was a favourite of the royal family generally. It was George II who ennobled him as the 1st Earl of Egmont.

In 1734 Sir John stood down as MP for Harwich in the expectation that his oldest and only surviving son John (1710-1770) would be elected in his place. However, this John was disliked by the voters, received insufficient support from the Walpole government and was defeated. To their mind he was unreliable and, in contrast to his father, they found him uncongenial and "unsocial". He has been described by Sir Robert Walpole's son, the diarist and historian Horace Walpole (1717-1797), as the unsmiling Earl - except at chess.[88] But, after failing to be returned by the 30 voters of Harwich, and subsequently by the 60 enfranchised voters at Haslemere, the younger John Perceval eventually found a seat at Westminster from 1741 - though only after the results of the original election had been overturned. He now represented 6000 voters. Like his father, he blamed Walpole for his defeat at Harwich, and condemned him in the House of Commons for his handling of the war with Spain (at a time when this was seen as particularly odious and unpatriotic as the country was also embroiled in the war of Austrian succession). When Perceval was subsequently rejected by Westminster in 1747, he then became MP for Weobley in Herefordshire with the support of Walpole's successor Henry Pelham. Although the government had got him elected, he soon proved a leading opponent in the House of Commons, allying himself with the Leicester House faction of Frederick, the Prince of Wales who made him a Lord of the Bedchamber. The following year he became the 2nd Earl of Egmont on his father's death.

By this stage Egmont was Frederick's most trusted adviser and between them they drew up plans for the new government that would take office once Frederick became king. These came to naught when Frederick died in 1751 and Egmont found himself out in the cold. A year later his first wife Catherine died, the day after her thirty-third birthday, sixteen years of marriage and seven children.

---

[88] "...he was once indeed seen to smile, and that was at chess. He did not dislike mirth in others but he seemed to adjourn his attention till he could bring back the company to seriousness." Horace Walpole, 'Memoirs of King George II', (J. Brooke, ed.), 3 volumes, New Haven, Yale University Press,1985.

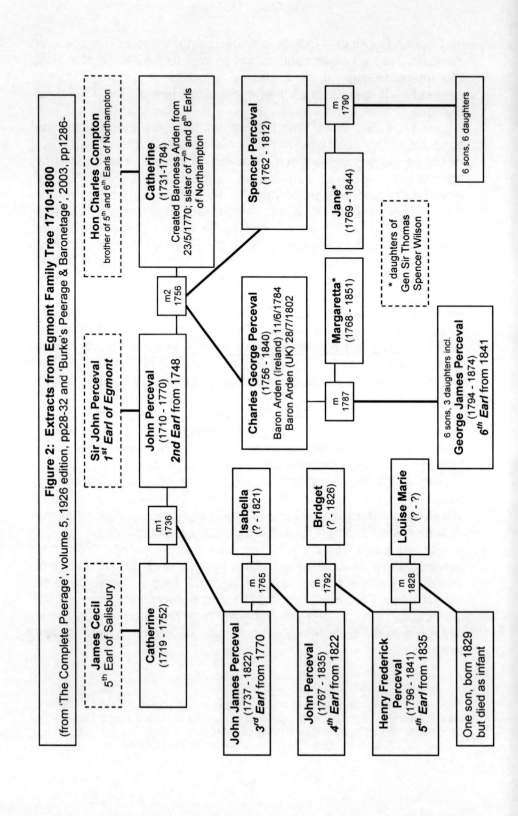

Figure 2: Extracts from Egmont Family Tree 1710-1800

(from 'The Complete Peerage', volume 5, 1926 edition, pp28-32 and 'Burke's Peerage & Baronetage', 2003, pp1286-

Hon Charles Compton
brother of 5th and 6th Earls of Northampton

Catherine
(1731-1784)
Created Baroness Arden from 23/5/1770; sister of 7th and 8th Earls of Northampton

Spencer Perceval
(1762 - 1812)

m 1790

6 sons, 6 daughters

Jane*
(1769 - 1844)

Margaretta*
(1768 - 1851)

* daughters of Gen Sir Thomas Spencer Wilson

Charles George Perceval
(1756 - 1840)
Baron Arden (Ireland) 11/6/1784
Baron Arden (UK) 28/7/1802

m 1787

6 sons, 3 daughters incl.

George James Perceval
(1794 - 1874)
6th Earl from 1841

m2 1756

Sir John Perceval
1st Earl of Egmont

John Perceval
(1710 - 1770)
2nd Earl from 1748

James Cecil
5th Earl of Salisbury

m1 1736

Catherine
(1719 - 1752)

Isabella
(? - 1821)

Bridget
(? - 1826)

Louise Marie
(? - ?)

m 1765

m 1792

m 1828

John James Perceval
(1737 - 1822)
3rd Earl from 1770

John Perceval
(1767 - 1835)
4th Earl from 1822

Henry Frederick Perceval
(1796 - 1841)
5th Earl from 1835

One son, born 1829 but died as infant

In the general election of 1754 Perceval moved from Weobley to become the MP for Bridgewater. The following year he was made a Privy Councillor, but otherwise resisted holding office until he was first made a British peer. On 26th January 1756 he married another Catherine, the daughter of Charles Compton. Two of her uncles were Earls of Northampton, as were two of her brothers thereafter. She was twenty-four years old, twenty-one years younger than him. Their first child, Charles George, was born eight months later on the 1st October and they were to have another eight children, including their second son Spencer Perceval. At this time it is said that John Perceval "respected himself rather more than the world respected him".[89] In 1758 he published 'Things As They Are' a diatribe against the war and the leadership of William Pitt the Elder (1708-1778), whom he loathed. Perceval justified the publication in the spirit of inquiry, which might mean the truth proved unpalatable:

"Public mistakes are always public misfortunes, and like misfortunes too rarely come alone; error follows upon error".[90]

He concluded that if his analysis was not 'Things As They Are', then it was certainly things as Britain would wish them to be. After George III (1738-1820) became King in 1760, Perceval eventually persuaded the Earl of Bute (1713-1792) to secure him the British peerage he had craved. This came in May 1762 when he was made Baron Lovel and Holland of Enmore.[91] The family had long-standing Somerset connections[92] and Bridgewater was only a few miles from Enmore. He was now at last ready to accept office.

From 1763 to 1766 Perceval was First Lord of the Admiralty with the two sons from his second marriage, Charles George and Spencer, as registrars of the court of Admiralty through reversionary grants.[93] Although the diarist Horace Walpole condemned Perceval for "pompous additions to the dockyards",[94] his reputation deserves

---

[89] Earl Waldegrave's judgement quoted in Lewis Namier and John Brooke, 'History of Parliament: The House of Commons 1754-1790', London, Secker and Warburg, 1985, vol.3, p267

[90] John Perceval, Earl of Egmont, 'Things As They Are', Dublin, S. Powell, 1758, p6

[91] Horace Walpole, 'Memoirs of the Reign of King George III', (D Jarrett, ed.), 4 vols., London, Yale University Press, 2000, vol.1, p59n

[92] Sedgwick, op cit, vol. 2, p336

[93] A reversionary grant is the right of succession to the post, or the emoluments, after the death or retirement of the post-holder. When Perceval took up post in 1763 these sons were six years of age and less than one.

[94] Walpole, op cit, vol.4, p200

to be more balanced than this. He took what was then the radical step of visiting the dockyards for which he was responsible in 1764 (the first such visit for fifteen years), and his subsequent administrative and practical changes speeded up the efficiency with which ships were repaired. He supported and funded the voyage that "discovered" the Falkland Islands, with Port Egmont being named after him in acknowledgement.[95] When his authority was undermined by the government disputing the necessity for the additional expenditure he had advocated, and took their concerns direct to the Navy Board over his head, George Grenville (1712-1770) found his ministry dismissed in 1765. It has to be said though that Grenville had irritated George III by his overall attitude, as well as over other issues apart from spending on the navy. When William Pitt the Elder refused to form a government, Perceval helped George III shape the Rockingham (1730-1782) ministry.[96] This was superseded in July 1766 when Pitt, by now the Earl of Chatham, did become first minister. Perceval resigned his post a month later in August 1766 when he was unable to reconcile his continuation in office, and his loyalty to George III, with his disdain for Pitt.

Perceval has been described as an eccentric in other areas of his life, but some of the examples that are offered to demonstrate this might simply be illustrations of his affection for the mediaeval period. He rebuilt Enmore as a moated castle, but in Horace Walpole's dismissive words:

"Lord Egmont was such a passionate admirer of those noble tenures and customs, that he rebuilt his house at Enmore ... in the guise of a castle, moated it round, and prepared it to defend itself with crossbows and arrows, against the time in which the fabric and use of gunpowder shall be forgotten."[97]

More extreme, though, was his proposal to George III in 1763 that he be granted St John island, Newfoundland to be settled on a

---

[95] Ibid, p184 Walpole describes "Falkland's Island [as] a desolate rock" and Britain's behaviour in taking possession of land that previously belonged to Spain as "piratical" - even Spain they had abandoned it. Spain took re-possession in June 1766 when the Port Egmont garrison surrendered.

[96] At one stage it was feared that Egmont would be asked to form a government himself according to Walpole, op cit, vol. 2, p162

[97] Walpole, op cit, vol. 2, p31 This was somewhat hypocritical, though, as Walpole said "I am building the castle of my ancestors" when asked to explain his house at Strawberry Hill.

feudal basis and that the scheme be extended to land elsewhere in Canada in order to levy troops.[98] Although the plan was set aside at the last minute, Egmont had anticipated Sir Walter Scott's romances and the Victorians' preoccupation with chivalry, knights and jousting by some years.[99] It might almost be said in his case that an eccentric is somebody whose time has yet to come.

Perceval's second wife Catherine had been created Baroness Arden in May 1770. The oldest son from his first marriage John James (1737-1822) succeeded him as MP for Bridgewater from May 1762 to March 1769, but never spoke in the House.[100] He ceased to be an MP after the Commons confirmed the Bridgewater franchise and clarified the boundaries of the constituency.[101] John James then became the 3rd Earl of Egmont on his father's death in December 1770. In Walpole's view, the 2nd Earl had

"... died the parent of the approaching war [with Spain over the Falkland Islands] ... a man always ambitious, almost always attached to a court, yet from a singularity in his turn, scarce ever in place!"[102]

In other words, not to be relied on - as the voters of Harwich had made clear was their view over thirty years before.

After the high profile mix of politics, principle and passion displayed by the 1st and 2nd Earls, their immediate successors were to lead less public, much quieter, almost withdrawn lives by comparison. John James was briefly Lord Lieutenant of Somerset in 1773-1774, but otherwise became the archetypal country squire indulging his preferences (particularly the "amusement" of fox-hunting). He died aged 84 in February 1822, five months after his wife. Their only child, yet another John (1767-1835), had failed to

---

[98] Ibid, where Walpole writes scathingly "While men were taken up with the politics of the age, there was a minister so smitten with the exploded usage of barbarous times, that he thought of nothing less than reviving the feudal system. This was the Earl of Egmont, who had actually drawn up a plan for establishing that absurd kind of government."

[99] See, for example, Tristram Hunt, 'Building Jerusalem: The Rise and Fall of the Victorian City', London, Weidenfeld & Nicolson, 2004, pp57-59 on the Eglinton tournament.

[100] Namier and Brooke, op cit, vol. 3, p269

[101] In other words, that the electorate were householders paying scot and lot, rather than the corporation as John James had argued. His opponent Anne Poulett was successful on petition in unseating him. Namier and Brooke, op cit, vol. 1, p367

[102] Walpole, op cit, vol. 4, pp202-203

be elected for Bridgewater in 1790 and became the 4th Earl at the age of 54.

Attention had switched by 1780 to the sons from the 2nd Earl's second marriage. Charles George Perceval was 24 and had yet to succeed his mother on her death in 1784 as Baron Arden. Spencer Perceval was 18 and, as the second son of his father's second marriage, was even less privileged than his brother.[103]

Lord Arden

The picture in Figure 3 shows Lord Arden, Charles Perceval, as one of the Lords of the Bedchamber, a position he held from 1804 after William Pitt's return as Prime Minister to 1812 when he moved to Windsor full-time for the remaining eight years of George III's life. The picture is dated 1806, when Charles Perceval was in his fiftieth year and, as it appears to show a younger man, may even have been painted to mark his fiftieth birthday. It identifies him as a Privy Councillor, a post to which Addington (1757-1844) had appointed him on 20th February 1801. These posts were only two of those that he accrued, and his apparently magnetic appeal seems to have extended to the rewards that went with prominent public life. This requires some explanation, particularly as the record nearly 200 years later is noticeably thin.

Although he was related to the Earls of Northampton, this was through his mother's side of the family (see Figure 2). His father had been created an English lord in 1762, less than six years after his birth, but both this and the title of Earl of Egmont would pass to his half-brother the 3rd Earl. Had it not been for inheriting the Arden

---

[103] Attention was to be re-focussed on the first marriage eighty years later when the 6th Earl of Egmont (Lord Arden's son) brought a legal case against the estate of the 5th Earl in the 1860s. The 5th Earl had been the last descendant of the first marriage to be Earl of Egmont, and in 1860 the last of his heiresses had died. The 6th Earl had succeeded to the title in 1841 but had waited twenty years, perhaps out of respect to his relatives, before bringing the case reported in *The Times* on 17th January 1863. This described the 5th Earl as "a man of reckless and intemperate habits, [who had] lived for many years in obscurity, and under an assumed name, without holding any communication with his family". He had died of consumption and delirium tremens, after allowing himself to be misled for many years over how badly off his estates were. He had retreated into isolation, no doubt thinking he could not afford any alternative, and had found solace in alcohol. The 6th Earl was correcting the record and confirming his inheritance.

Figure 3: Charles George Perceval, 2nd Baron Arden (by Georg Siegmund Facius, after Chandler stipple and line engraving, 1806 NPG D7086) © National Portrait Gallery, London

title from his mother, he might have remained Mr Charles Perceval throughout his life (as, indeed, his brother was to be Mr Spencer Perceval once he had turned down the customary knighthood on becoming Prime Minister). On the other hand, his family background was not only privileged, it was also well-connected (as the previous sections of this chapter show). This extended to royal and political circles, as well as aristocratic ones, he was to make the most of them and, at 83 when he died, should have had time to enjoy them. Being educated at Harrow and Trinity College, Cambridge may also have helped of course. Rubinstein makes the point that the Anglican religion and education in the nineteenth century, like "Old Corruption" in the eighteenth, were often fundamental determinants of wealth, and certainly of a notable career.[104] Arden straddled both centuries and both worlds. The importance of family connections is underlined in 'The Black Book', which exemplifies the inter-weaving (or "dovetailing" as it describes it) of the Castlereagh and George Canning families and their various branches. It then states:

"But to be serious; the aristocracy may be considered only one family, plundering, deluding and fattening on the people."[105]

It may also have been significant that Arden moved seamlessly to support Addington after Pitt's resignation in 1801 over George III's failure to endorse his Emancipation of Catholics Bill. Addington had also been aligned with Pitt, though not on the Catholic issue, and Arden was signalling that his allegiance to the King and the stability of his government was his paramount concern. Addington would have particularly valued this evidence of support when so many of the previous Cabinet had resigned along with Pitt.

Table 2 is drawn together from a number of sources.[106] It sets out the basic chronology of Arden's public career (and some

---

[104] For example, see page 621 in WD Rubinstein, 'The Victorian middle classes: Wealth, occupation and geography', *Economic History Review*, 30 (1977 (a)), pp602-623. Similarly, Bernard Cracroft in his analysis of the 1865 parliament points out that, of the 430 MPs who went to university and/or public school, 52 had been to Harrow and 110 to Cambridge University. See 'The analysis of the House of Commons, or indirect representation', pp 155-190 in G.C. Brodrick (ed.), 'Essays on Reform', London, Macmillan, 1867.

[105] John Wade, 'The Black Book, or Corruption Unmasked on Places, Sinecures, Pensions and Reversions', London, Fairburn, 1820, p94 Cracroft, op cit, p173 draws attention to the 1865 MP (an ex-governor of the Bank of England) who was related to 30 others in the House at the same time.

[106] The full list is:
A Aspinall (ed.), 'Later Correspondence of George III', 5 volumes, Cambridge, Cambridge University Press, 1970; 'Annual Register for 1783', London, J Dodsley, 1785; 'Boyle's Court Guide', London, Eliza Boyle, January 1816; 'Boyle's Court Guide', London, Eliza Boyle, April 1818; Buckle papers and family records held by West Sussex Record Office; Gibbs, op cit; AB Granville, 'The Royal Society in the Nineteenth Century', London, Churchill, 1836; Hansard House of Commons Debate 19 February 1813, vol. 24, cc655-6; 'List of the Society of Antiquaries in 1833'; Namier and Brooke, op cit; Victor Negus, 'History of the Trustees of the Hunterian Collection', London, E&S Livingstone Ltd., 1966; WD Rubinstein, 'The end of "Old Corruption" in Britain 1780-1860', *Past and Present*, 101 (1983), pp55-86; WD Rubinstein, 'Wealth, elites and the class structure of modern Britain', *Past and Present*, 76 (1977 (b)), pp99-126; RG Thorne (ed.), 'The House of Commons 1790-1820', 5 volumes, History of Parliament Trust, Secker & Warburg, 1986; Sidney Totman, 'A History of the Manor and Parish of Burgh, including Burgh Heath, Nork, Preston and Tattenham', Beaconsfield, Totman, 1970; Alan

aspects of his family life, but not those concerning his children or his siblings).

After concluding his education and training at Lincoln's Inn, Charles Perceval became MP for Launceston in 1780 at the age of 24. He had not stood in the general election earlier that year and Launceston became available when the previous MP James Cecil (1748-1823), Viscount Cranborne, succeeded his father in the House of Lords as the 7th Earl of Salisbury. The seat was in the gift of Hugh Percy (1742-1817), Lord Northumberland, who identified Perceval for it on the government's behalf. In illustration of the point stressed by 'The Black Book' that the aristocracy were essentially one family, it will be noted from Figure 2 that the 5th Earl of Salisbury, also called James Cecil, was the father of John Perceval's first wife. The connections continued through subsequent generations - as did the Northampton ones through John Perceval's second wife.

Perceval was a supporter of Lord North (1732-1792), speaking, for example, against the Bill introduced by Edmund Burke (1729-1797) to regulate the civil list. He argued that it would "reduce the Sovereign to humiliating dependency".[107] North was finally allowed to resign by George III in March 1782, being succeeded briefly by Rockingham and then by Shelburne (1737-1805). Perceval voted against Shelburne's early attempts at peace with America in February 1783, a month later George III replaced Shelburne with the Duke of Portland (1738-1809) and he in turn was dismissed in December of that year after the King had opposed the India Bill put forward by Charles Fox (1749-1806). Unsurprisingly, as staunch supporters of the monarchy, Lord Northumberland and Charles Perceval had also viewed the proposed Bill with "the utmost abhorrence", with Perceval voting against it in November 1783.[108] Portland's successor was William Pitt who, on forming his administration, made Perceval a Lord of the Admiralty, a post he was to hold to February 1801. As was then a requirement on being

---

Valentine, 'The British Establishment 1760-1784', Norman, University of Oklahoma Press, 1970; Victoria County Histories of Surrey and Sussex; Renee Wilcox, 'A history of the parish of St Paul, Nork, Banstead, Surrey', 1985
[107] Referred to in Valentine, op cit, p691
[108] Namier and Brooke, op cit, vol. 2, p266

Table 2: Key events in Charles Perceval's career

Year	Month	Day	Event	Age
1756	Oct	1	Born at Charlton, Kent - either very premature or conceived before his parents John and Catherine married on 26th January 1756	
1763			Father becomes First Lord of the Admiralty and Charles registrar through reversionary grant	6
1770	May	23	Mother becomes Baroness Arden (Ireland)	13
1770	Dec		Father dies	14
1771			At Harrow School to 1774 (Spencer at Harrow 1774-1779, aged 11-17)	14
1774			At Trinity College, Cambridge to 1777 (Spencer at Trinity College 1780 -1782)	17
1777			Entered Lincoln's Inn	
1780	Nov	28	Became MP for Launceston	24
1783	Dec		Appointed a Lord of the Admiralty	27
1784	June	11	Mother dies; succeeds as Baron Arden (Ireland)	27
1784			Nork House "let to Lord Arden on a long lease" after death of Matthew Buckle	
1785	April	18	Voted in minority for Pitt's motion for parliamentary reform	28
1786	Feb	19	Becomes Fellow of the Royal Society	29
1787	Feb	8	Took his seat in the Irish House of Lords	30
1787	March	1	Married to Margaretta Wilson (born 4th April 1768 and aged 18)	30
1790			Became MP for Warwick	
1790			"Obtained the lucrative reversionary sinecure of registrar of the court of Admiralty" (DNB). Holds this post for fifty years until his death in 1840.	
1796			Became MP for Totnes	
1801	Feb	20	Becomes Privy Councillor	44
1801	Mar		Master of the Royal Mint to July 1802	44
1801	May		Commissioner of the East India Board of Control to October 1803	44
1802	July	28	Created Baron Arden (UK)	45
1803			Became Trustee of the Hunterian Collection. Also, Fellow of the Society of Antiquaries	
1804	May		Became Lord of the Bedchamber, transferring to Windsor from 1812-1820 with	47

Year	Month	Day	Event	Age
			George III	
1812			Nork House sold to Lord Arden	
1830			Became Lord Lieutenant of Surrey (1820-1840 according to the Harrow School Register)	
1840	July	5	Died at St James' Place, London. Buried 11th July at Charlton. Widow Margaretta died 20th May 1851 (aged 83) at Nork and buried 28th May at Charlton.	83

appointed to office,[109] Perceval stood again in Launceston and was re-elected on 3rd January 1784 (as he was to be on 5th April that year when a general election was held). Perceval voted in favour of Pitt's motion for parliamentary reform on 18th April 1785, but it was defeated by 74 votes and Pitt never broached the subject again.

When his mother died on 11th June 1784 Perceval became Baron Arden in the Irish peerage. This did not prevent him from remaining in the House of Commons, and after almost ten years as MP for Launceston he became MP for Warwick "on Lord Warwick's interest" after "his erstwhile patron [by now] the 2nd Duke of Northumberland [from 1786] deviated from Pitt".[110] In 1796 he moved to represent Totnes on the "Duke of Bolton's interest", a change caused, according to Thorne, because he "... disliked the uncertain expense of Warwick elections ..." He remained the MP for Totnes for a further six years until 28 July 1802 when he became Baron Arden in the British peerage and moved to the House of Lords. As can be seen from Table 2, this was the fourth honour that Pitt's successor Addington had accorded him in less than eighteen months. He had been appointed a Privy Councillor almost as soon as Addington became Prime Minister, then Master of the Royal Mint a month later and two months after that a Commissioner of the East India Company Board of Control. Perceval was clearly an integral part of the inner circle. No matter that the Mint was largely a sinecure,[111] it was apparent to all that Perceval was trusted with the

---

[109] This requirement was standard practice until the Re-election of Ministers Acts of 1919 and 1926, with the latter finally abolishing the practice.

[110] Thorne, op cit, vol. IV, p763

[111] Thorne says that he received fees of £8000 in 1798 just as registrar of the court of Admiralty (a result of the reversionary grant he had received in 1763 and taken up in 1790). This is the equivalent of more than £250,000 today. His position at the Mint, brief though it was, would have added to this.

country's coin, as he had been with the navy and was with a major source of trade. In other words, he could be relied on to ensure that the country's mercantile income increased, imports and exports were protected and the country could pay - and, most importantly, that he would adhere to the government line in all matters.

Perceval had married Margaretta Wilson on 1st March 1787. He was 30 and she not yet 19,[112] a reader of William Cobbett and therefore "the only radical in the family".[113] He was already a Fellow of the Royal Society and was to become a Fellow of the Society of Antiquaries and in 1803 a Trustee of the Hunterian Collection. He retained this position until his death in 1840, and while this and the two Fellowships may have come about primarily because of his Admiralty office, he was expected to contribute to the annual Trustee meetings. However, he only attended twice in 38 years and was so inactive that he was listed as First Lord of the Admiralty at the 1805 meeting, and described in Negus' 1966 history as the sixth son of the 1st Earl of Egremont.[114] Once Pitt returned as Prime Minister in May 1804, Arden became a courtier.

Two further aspects of Arden's life deserving distinct attention are his houses in London and Surrey, and the sinecures he accrued as a pillar of the establishment, an issue on which 'The Black Book', as might be expected, is particularly scathing - as it is of other members of the family.

London and Surrey

In 1784, shortly after he had become an Irish peer, Arden took Nork House[115] on a long let. He was still single at this point, and Nork was a large property in the manor of Burgh near Banstead in Surrey. According to Wilcox,[116] the manor had originally been given by Edward I to his Queen in 1273. In 1550 a mansion known as Burgh House was built and sold sixty-four years later to Sir Christopher Buckle (1590-1660).

---

[112] They were married over 50 years until his death in July 1840 and had nine children.

[113] Gray, op cit, p433

[114] Negus, op cit, p117 - though in his defence it should be said that Egmont and Egremont are often confused.

[115] It is sometimes referred to as "York House" (e.g., by Gibbs) and sometimes as "North Park" (e.g., by the *Morning Chronicle*). These errors are understandable given that Nork seems an unlikely name and there is no obvious etymology.

[116] Wilcox, op cit, p1

"This became the centre of the Buckle estate ... Sir Christopher evidently spared nothing in his endeavours to build up the family fortunes, and is reputed to have sold his father's chain of office [as Lord Mayor of London] so as to buy a flock of sheep."[117]

In 1712 his great-grandson, another Christopher Buckle (1684-1759), succeeded him, building Nork House in 1740 and giving Burgh House to his eldest son. According to the National Archives account, "his fifth and youngest son, Mathew Buckle (1718-1784) ... was one of the most distinguished naval officers of the 18th century". Nork House passed to this son in 1759, before being leased to Arden on his death.

Although Arden was only 27, he could clearly afford such a property and as important was the prestige that went with it, with commanding views to Hampton Court and Windsor Castle.[118] The space would eventually be required for the large family he and Margaretta were to have. (Although she was only 16 at the time he leased Nork, they had known each other for some time in Charlton and he may have taken it partly in anticipation of, even to hasten, their marriage.) On 11th November 1807 he offered to purchase Nork House outright, but the Buckle family replied within the week declining to sell it as yet. It was eventually sold to him in 1812. In 1830 Arden became Lord-Lieutenant of Surrey and in 1837 Lady Arden granted both a site and the funds for an endowed Church of England school to be built in the village.[119]

"In 1846 the property passed to Lord Egmont[120] whose descendants held it until 1890. The old manor house had by now become ruinous and was demolished in 1886."[121]

On the 9th August 1821 the *Morning Chronicle* reported that Arden "had left town for his seat" at Nork. This notice appeared in its column 'The Mirror of Fashion' where those leaving town for the summer were featured. (The date was two days after the death of

[117] National Archives introduction to Buckle papers and family records held by West Sussex Record Office
[118] Wilcox, op cit, p3. Totman, op cit, p18 includes a picture of the house in 1790.
[119] Totman, op cit, p22
[120] This was the 6th Earl (1794-1874) not the 3rd Earl (1737-1822), as both Wilcox and the Victoria County History of Surrey (vol.3, p256) state. He died at Nork House, not "York House" as Gibbs claims. Similarly, it was his heir the 7th Earl who auctioned the site in 1890, with FE Colman being the principal buyer of 1320 acres.
[121] Totman, op cit, p10

Queen Caroline in somewhat mysterious circumstances in Hammersmith.) Even though he was by now in his mid-60s, Arden still felt the necessity for a base in London. George III had died the previous year, so he was no longer required at Windsor, and his only remaining duty was in the House of Lords. By January 1816 Boyle's Court Guide listed him as living at 26 St James' Place (alongside the Honorable Fred North) as well as at Nork House. In the 1818 version he was said to reside next door at 27 St James' Place, while number 26 had passed to DL North. The other occupants of 27 St James' Place were Sir Francis Burdett (1770-1844) and George Spencer (1758-1834), the 2nd Earl from 1783. The latter was also a Fellow of the Society of Antiquaries, had been MP for Northampton from 1780 to 1782 and spent much of his time at Althorp, his country house in Northamptonshire. Although Sir Francis Burdett had once been a Tory, was a baronet in his own right and was extremely well-off as a result of his marriage to Sophia Coutts (1775-1844), an heir to the bank, he had been a leading radical for many years. He was the MP for Westminster for thirty years from 1807, representing other constituencies before this and subsequently, and on almost every count his and Arden's views were diametrically opposed.[122] St James' Place was particularly convenient for those engaged in high politics or who wanted to be at the hub of events in London.

The "arch sinecurist"

Arden was one of the main examples chosen by Rubinstein to illustrate his points about patronage and place, "Old Corruption".[123] That Arden should be identified in this way is not all that surprising given that he had been singled out in 'The Black Book', which

---

[122] It might appear that sharing a house was extraordinarily enlightened behaviour by both of them, but it was possible that Burdett was effectively Arden's lodger, or used the property as a pied a terre in London, and that he and Arden saw little of each other. The alternatives are that Boyle's Court Guide has made an error, perhaps due to haphazard numbering, or is being mischievous. Both seem unlikely, but confusingly, Burdett's DNB entry says that he lived at 25 St James' Place from 1816-1844 and an 1825 map of St James Place identifies a different property entirely as Earl Spencer's. St James' Place, however, was the Arden address that others such as Spencer junior and Edward lived at and used for correspondence, and various sources record that Arden died there in 1840. .

[123] Rubinstein, 1977 (b), op cit, p118 Lord Eldon, the "celebrated" Lord Chancellor who died in 1830, is given as an example in both this article and an accompanying one 'The Victorian middle classes: Wealth, occupation and geography', *Economic History Review*, 30 (1977 (a)), pp602-623

reported that his gross annual income from the Admiralty sinecure was £38,574.[124] In 1812 the Sinecures Office Bill was debated by the House of Commons. This reflected widespread sensitivity when it stated that

"... no *existing interest* was to be touched; and it was only at the death of the possessors of sinecures that they were to be abolished".[125]

So, despite the Act of Settlement,[126] many MPs continued to hold sinecures during their lifetime. Arden was no longer an MP of course, but the practice was even more prevalent in the House of Lords. The twelve Lords of the Bedchamber cost the Civil List a total of £12,000 pa,[127] while the eleven East India Company commissioners received £1500 per head.[128] Arden had been the latter, with only a short interlude before becoming one of the former.

On 19th February 1813 there was a debate on the Admiralty Registrar's Bill (and, by implication, sinecures generally). Henry Martin identified that

"the average annual sum which was solely employed for the benefit of the noble lord (Arden) who now held the situation of Registrar, was £200,000 and for which no security was taken".[129]

---

[124] Wade, op cit, p15 On page 70 it refers to the £2000 annual pension Jane Perceval received after her husband's assassination, and to the £2700 sinecure her son Spencer held as a teller of the exchequer. It goes on "Of Mr Perceval [the son Spencer], it is enough to say, that his maiden speech, on the appointment of six equerries to the King, was rapturously applauded by the immaculate Castlereagh." See Chapter 4 below.

[125] Ibid, p93

[126] 'The Black Book' opens with this quotation from the Act: "That no person who has an office or place of profit under the King, or receives a pension from the Crown, shall be capable of serving as a Member of the House of Commons". However, the Supplementary Report of the Committee of Expenditure in May 1809 identified 76 who were, at an annual cost of £164,000.

[127] Wade, op cit, p134

[128] FML Thompson, 'English Landed Society in the Nineteenth Century', London, Routledge and Kegan Paul, 1963, p72

[129] Report in Hansard, vol. 24, cc655-6. This continues: "It had been conceded last session, by a late right hon. gentleman, who was certainly interested in the profits of the office, for the reversion of it was vested in him, he meant Mr. Perceval, that the situation required to be regulated, and indeed he proposed to regulate it much more extensively than it was the object of the present Bill to do, which merely went to assimilate the practice of the court of Admiralty in securing suitors' money, to the practice of the high court of Chancery." Perceval had not been able to regulate it

He received the following response from Castlereagh (1769-1822):

"he certainly should not oppose the Bill in that stage of it, but that if it should prove to be a similar one to that brought in last session, he should feel himself compelled to oppose it in every part of its progress."

And so it proved. There should be little wonder that 'The Black Book' was particularly contemptuous of Castlereagh and Arden.

Spencer Perceval

Arden was the "champion ... provider and confidant ..." of his younger brother Spencer Perceval.[130] They spent their early years at Charlton House,[131] which had been leased by their grandfather the 1ˢᵗ Earl of Egmont in 1720. It became the family's permanent residence after 1748 when their father became the 2ⁿᵈ Earl. The family continued to live there after his death in 1770, but in 1777 ownership passed to Jane Weller and her husband Sir Thomas Spencer-Wilson, Arden's and Spencer's future parents-in-law. In 1777 Spencer was a fifteen year old at Harrow School, while Charles, the future Arden, had just entered Lincoln's Inn after his years at Cambridge University.

Spencer went to Harrow School as an eleven year-old in 1774, remaining there until 1779. He was to repeat his academic success at Trinity College, Cambridge, leaving there with an MA in 1782 and

---

before his assassination, though it was most unlikely that he would have done so in any case.

[130] Thorne, op cit Some details of Spencer Perceval's life and career were set out in the Introduction and other aspects are referred to in the following chapters. For the moment his career is briefly summarised, with a few observations on his political legacy.

[131] The house has been owned by Greenwich Council since 1925. It is well-used, both as a library and for community activities, hosts a Japanese school on the second floor and rooms can be hired for a range of events, including wedding ceremonies and receptions. Many of the original features have survived, as have the grounds. It is described as "one of the finest surviving Jacobean manor houses in the country" in Beverley Burford (ed.), 'Images of Charlton House: A Pictorial History', London, Greenwich Council, 2002. The family church St Luke's dates originally from 1273 but was re-built in 1670. It is just across the road from Charlton House and is the location of the Egmont family vault. The church is steeped in history beyond the Percevals, as might be expected for a building that is more than 300 years old and has been the site of the parish church for Charlton village for more than 700 years.

entering Lincoln's Inn that December. He became a barrister in 1786 and was a junior counsel at the trials of Thomas Paine (1737-1809) and John Horne Tooke (1736-1812) for sedition in 1792 and 1794 respectively. In the latter year he was appointed Counsel to the Admiralty, his brother Charles having taken up the position of Registrar there in 1790. In 1796 he became a King's Counsel and a Bencher of Lincoln's Inn. In the same year his uncle Lord Northampton died, and with his son succeeding him in the House of Lords, there was a vacancy for an MP for Northampton. This was offered to Perceval who was unopposed because of the impending general election. A few months later in 1796 he fought the election as a Tory and was returned alongside the Whig Edward Bouverie. Perceval had become an MP only reluctantly. With a growing family and no independent means, he would have had to balance such considerations with his sense of duty and the chance to develop a political profile. At this stage Parliament only sat for six months each year, and it may have been that he judged the other six months sufficient to maintain his legal earnings and decided that he could not afford to ignore the opportunities offered by a political career. MPs were not paid, but his brother would provide some security if this proved necessary.

By 1800 Perceval was earning £1800 a year (£58,000 today) from the law. Like his brother he also benefitted from Addington's patronage, being appointed Solicitor-General in 1801 and Attorney-General a year later. Perceval's legal earnings rapidly increased to £10,000 by 1804 (the equivalent of £322,000 in 2009). As alarm about a French invasion spread, William Pitt returned as Prime Minister with Perceval remaining Attorney-General until Pitt's death in January 1806.

Perceval was now one of the leading lights in the Tory party - along with George Canning, Viscount Castlereagh and Robert Banks Jenkinson (later Lord Liverpool from 1808). All but Castlereagh were to become Prime Ministers, and all but Perceval were Foreign Secretaries during the Napoleonic wars. All four of them opposed the next government, William Grenville's so-called "Ministry of All the Talents". In Gillray's caricatures the ministers in this government were described as the "Broad Bottoms" - a coalition, but also an easy target. It was this government that abolished Britain's slave trade in 1807, a cause that both Canning and Perceval had espoused. Indeed, Canning had sought to persuade Pitt to make this a Government measure in previous years, but had failed to do so. It was only when Grenville adopted

Figure 4: Spencer Perceval © All Saints Church, Ealing Common

this course in 1807 that there was sufficient support for the law to be enacted. Perceval was an adviser to Princess Caroline, the estranged wife of the Prince of Wales, when her erratic behaviour led to the government's "Delicate Investigation" in 1806, and intrigued with George III and the other leading Tories to get Grenville's government dismissed. This happened in March 1807 when Grenville proposed to increase civil rights for Catholics - an issue to which Perceval, like the King, was deeply opposed.

In the next Government led by the elderly Duke of Portland from March 1807 Perceval was Chancellor of the Exchequer and Leader in the House of Commons. The main challenge facing him was to find the funding for the Peninsular War from 1808. Grenville when he had been Prime Minister had expected that revenues would only be sufficient for a defensive war, but Perceval raised enough loans to support the army offensive and managed to avoid increasing taxes to do so. From a disastrous start, the War began to improve when Wellington became the commander with victories at the Battles of Oporto in May and Talavera in July 1809.

Portland had a stroke in August 1809. Canning and Castlereagh had been at odds for some time and fought a duel in September 1809. Although neither was seriously injured, they both resigned - putting themselves out of the running to be the next Prime Minister. After lengthy consideration by George III, Spencer Perceval became Prime Minister on 4th October 1809. Only two members of his Cabinet were in the House of Commons - Perceval himself and Richard Ryder, brother of his friend from Harrow Dudley Ryder who had become the Earl of Harrowby earlier that year. Perceval also continued to be Chancellor of the Exchequer after others such as Palmerston had refused the post. From this unpromising start, the government improved - perhaps because it had to work as a team given the scale of the challenges at home and the war with France. By 1811 it had even won over the Prince Regent, a Whig supporter. The government went from strength to strength until Perceval was assassinated in the House of Commons on 11th May 1812. He was not necessarily the intended target, but was certainly a symbolic one - perhaps just in the wrong place at the wrong time. His assassin John Bellingham was tried and executed in the following week. Although he was thought deranged, he did not help his case by taking the witness stand and arguing that he should have killed Granville Leveson-Gower, his original target, rather than Perceval.

Perceval had sought to tackle the issue of non-resident vicars and the impoverished curates who often stood in for them, and had promoted new churches in the expanding towns. The Liverpool government extended the latter policy in 1818 by enacting the Church Building Act.[132] On the debit side, however, his opposition

---

[132] The Act followed a meeting chaired by Charles Manners-Sutton (1755-1828), the Archbishop of Canterbury and father of the Commons Speaker and MP for Cambridge University of the same name (1780-1845), on 6th February 1818. His DNB entry says "From at least 1809 he worked to secure government funds to build new churches to meet the needs of the rapidly expanding population. In the House of Lords he took an active part in the attempt to secure satisfactory legislation to provide adequate stipends for curates. ... he worked to secure the Additional Churches Act [sic] of 1818, which gave the Church of England £1 million to build new churches, although he was defeated by ministers in his wish that

to an increased grant for Maynooth, the Catholic seminary in Ireland, had almost brought down the Portland government in 1808. His religious views went beyond mainstream attitudes of the time, and his evangelical fervour was repugnant when deployed against Catholics rather than directed positively towards improving church stipends. He resisted parliamentary reform and the abolition of sinecures, and opposed the expansion of Lancaster's monitorial system that would have made free education more widely available. He certainly displayed repressive traits, some of which were abhorrent and delayed progress, but his motivation may have been primarily that of a traditional constitutionalist for whom change was not the priority at a time of national peril. His influence on the Prince Regent was clearly significant and beneficial, he gave Palmerston and Peel their first opportunities on the national stage and it was his government that secured success in the war with Napoleon.

The memorial to Perceval in St Luke's Church, Charlton states:

"Near this place are the mortal remains of
the Right Honourable Spencer Perceval
First Lord of the Treasury
and Chancellor of the Exchequer
who died on the 11th May AD 1812
in the Commons House of Parliament
in the 50th year of his age.
His noblest epitaph is the regret of
his sovereign and his country,
his most splendid mourner the glory of England
by his counsels maintained, exalted, amplified,
but the hand of the assassin
not only broke asunder the brilliant chains of duty
which bind the statesman to his native land
and made a void in the high
and eloquent councils of the nation

---

clergy should be in the majority on the subsequent commission for building new churches."
According to Hunt, op cit, p65, "To reclaim the godless streets of the expanding cities, new churches were desperately needed and in 1818 the Church Building Act allocated £1million (and in 1824 a further £500,000) to flood the urban centres with Anglican churches." Almost 4000 Anglican churches were built between 1835 and 1875, with the number in 1850 Birmingham three times what it had been in 1800.

it severed ties more tender and delicate,
those of conjugal and parental affection,
and turned a home of peace and love, into a house of
mourning and desolation."

This is a powerful epitaph, but such hagiography goes beyond even what might be anticipated in the family's traditional parish church - as, certainly, does such eloquence. A less partial and possibly more balanced view might be that of Lord Mulgrave, First Lord of the Admiralty at the time. In his judgement, Perceval

"... only wanted something more of the Devil to be a very good premier".

This is both a comment on Perceval's conscientious, but over-fastidious, personal competence and on actions that were sometimes driven by religious, and correspondingly blinkered, belief.

2.   MOTHER AND MATRIARCH: JANE WILSON (1769 - 1844)

Marriage to Spencer Perceval (1790)

Jane Wilson married Spencer Perceval on 10th August 1790 almost as soon as she was legally able without her father's consent. Her twenty-first birthday had been a month earlier on 7th July and, while she was now in a position to decide for herself, she would no doubt have preferred her family's blessing. Spencer was three months short of his twenty-eighth birthday. Her sister Margaretta had married Spencer's brother three years earlier when she was just eighteen, and although Jane and Spencer had sought to follow her example by marrying once Jane became eighteen, her father had refused to permit it. For him the differences were that Spencer was much less secure or well-off than his brother Lord Arden, with no guaranteed wealth behind him, and at an earlier stage of his career, barely beginning to make his way in the law. Lord Arden was already thirty when he and Margaretta married, and had been a Lord of the Admiralty for more than three years.[133]

Sir Thomas Spencer Wilson (1727-1798),[134] Jane and Margaretta's father, had bought the Percevals' manor house some years earlier and the families had got to know each other in Charlton during holidays. Even though her father soon accepted Jane and Spencer's marriage, he appears not to have done so in advance of the ceremony. Rather he probably decided subsequently to face facts and endorse a "fait accompli". One way or the other he made the adjustment rapidly. That August Spencer wrote to his lifelong friend Dudley Ryder[135] (1762-1847), later the Earl of Harrowby from 1809,

---

[133] See Table 2 above.

[134] MP for Sussex from 1774-1780. His parliamentary career is set out in Namier and Brooke, op cit, vol. 3, pp646-647

[135] See Chapter 4 below for the Ryder political dynasty in Tiverton, where Spencer junior was briefly an MP.
Dudley Ryder was born 22nd December 1762 and died at the age of 84. He and Spencer were at Harrow together between 1774 and 1779. He was aged 46 when created 1st Earl of Harrowby in July 1809, was Pitt's second in his 1798 duel with Tierney, a privy councillor from 1790, and owned the house in Grosvenor Square where the Cato Street conspirators planned to murder the Cabinet in 1820. He appears in four portraits held by the National Portrait Gallery (including Pitt addressing the House of Commons on the French declaration of war, 1793 and the Trial of Queen Caroline, 1820).

"[Jane and I] have been to Charlton, on Sir T's [sic] invitation, and were received with all the kindness and warmth that a very affectionate parent (as he certainly is) could bestow on his daughter. He also has told me that he will make up her fortune, just what it would have been had she married with his consent, and was not satisfied till he made us repeatedly assure him that we were convinced we had his full forgiveness."[136]

Jane and Spencer's mutual love was clearly matched by her father's for her, while their's was enhanced by a common devotion to religion and family life. In the immediate future, though, "As Jane's dowry was a frozen asset, the couple returned to London to live in lodgings over a carpet shop in Bedford Row."[137] However, this was probably not as bleak a prospect as Gray makes it sound. Although lodging over a carpet shop does not sound very salubrious, this would not be an unusual start for impecunious newly-weds in their twenties today. And carpets, of course, were a luxury item in 1790, only available to the well-off and well-heeled.[138] Most families would have no covering on their floor, and many others might be content with oilskin. Even more significantly, perhaps, Bedford Row is just north of High Holborn in the centre of London, though not a main road, between Gray's Inn and Lincoln's Inn. It was therefore at the heart of London's legal system and no doubt very convenient for Perceval, particularly when he was appointed a commissioner of bankrupts[139] in 1791, working for much of the time in nearby Chancery Lane.

Family and homes

Their first two children were born at Bedford Row - their oldest daughter Jane, named after her mother, on 19th October 1791 and

---

[136] Harrowby MSS, vol. VIII, fol. 146 cited by Gray, op cit, p10

[137] Gray, op cit, p10

[138] The word "well-heeled" was not used in this sense until 1880 according to the OED, and in America first.

[139] After, rather than before, his marriage as Gray indicates. These posts were in the gift of the Lord Chancellor. Perceval is listed as a commissioner from 1791 to 1798. On appointment he was one of 65 commissioners and shortly to be one of 70.

"The lists were composed of barristers, designated 'esq.' and attorneys, designated 'gent.'"

See C[harles] P[urton] Cooper, 'A Brief Account...of the Court of Commissioners of Bankrupt', London, J. Murray, 1828, pp242-402.

Frances, named after one of Spencer's sisters, on 27th November 1792.[140] According to Gray

"After the birth of their second child the Percevals decided that they could afford to move from Bedford Row. ... They chose as their first house 59 Lincoln's Inn Fields ..."[141]

Their next two children - a third daughter Maria and Spencer junior - were born at this house on 26th February 1794 and 11th September 1795. By the time their second surviving son[142] Frederick was born on 6th October 1797 the Percevals had also acquired Belsize House, Hampstead further out from town. Their ownership is described in the Hampstead section of Old and New London:

"After the lapse of many years, during which little or nothing is recorded of its history, Belsize came again to be occupied as a private residence, and among its other tenants was the Right Hon. Spencer Perceval, afterwards Prime Minister, who lived here for about ten years before taking office as Chancellor of the Exchequer, namely, from 1798 to 1807."[143]

The next two sons Henry and Dudley were probably born at Belsize House (on 2nd August 1799 and 22nd October 1800), but Isabella the eighth surviving child and the fourth daughter was born

---

[140] Spencer's sister Frances married Lord Redesdale in June 1802 and went with him almost immediately to Dublin when he was appointed Lord Chancellor in Ireland. He and Spencer Perceval had worked together on various legal cases in the past, including the prosecution of Horne Tooke, and Redesdale's letters to Perceval as Attorney-General from 1802 are addressed "Dear Attorney".
Another of Spencer's sisters Elizabeth became the children's favourite aunt. She remained unmarried and spent much of her spare time with them. See Gray, op cit, p433.
Mary, a third sister, was to marry Andrew Berkeley Drummond in April 1781. One of their daughters Catherine was to marry Henry Perceval, her cousin.
[141] Gray, op cit, p12 This property (along with numbers 57, 58 and 60) has been occupied by Garden Court Chambers since 2005. Their handout for London's Open House weekend says the Percevals lived there from 1791.
[142] Another son Charles had been born on 5th September 1796 but had died less than two months later on 3rd November. A tablet commemorating his brief life, and that of the Ardens' first son (Charles Thomas Perceval), is in St Luke's Church, Charlton.
[143] 'Hampstead: Belsize and Frognal', Old and New London: Volume 5 (1878), pp. 494-504. See www.british-history.ac.uk/report.aspx?compid=45253

at Lincoln's Inn Fields on 10[144]th December 1801.[144] In 1802 they purchased number 60 next door to accommodate the growing family and "thus re-uniting the old Lindsey House". It was Sir John Soane, their neighbour in Lincoln's Inn Fields, who carried out the work for them.[145]

John Thomas was born on 14th February 1803 and Louisa on 11th March 1804, both in the expanded house in Lincoln's Inn Fields. There were now 10 Perceval children, with the oldest only twelve. It was not surprising that such frequent births had taken their toll on Jane. In addition, Frederick, not yet seven and "always a delicate child", was another reason for Jane to move back to Hampstead in the hope that her health and that of all the children would improve away from central London.[146] There was then an interval, though a fairly brief one of seventeen months, before the youngest daughter Frederica was born on 27th August 1805 at Hampstead and a slightly longer one of nineteen months before the final child and sixth surviving son Ernest's birth on 17th May 1807. The oldest child Jane was not yet sixteen.

That summer the Percevals began "hunting for a country house to replace the unsuitable Belsize".[147] After a couple of false starts, they eventually settled on Elm Grove, Ealing in summer 1808 at a price of £7,500 and another £4,000 for decorations and repairs.[148]

---

[144] Gray, op cit, p52: Pressure of work meant that Perceval often had little time for his family and "Consequently Jane (who never liked Belsize House) brought her children to live with their father in Lincoln's Inn Fields."

[145] Ibid, p45 Soane had previously divided numbers 57-58 next door into two houses in 1795 "created two doors, and masked them with the current Roman Doric porch" (as the Garden Court Chambers handout says on the basis of Ptolemy Dean's 'Sir John Soane and London', London, Lund Humphries, 2006, pp156-157).

[146] Gray, op cit, p52

[147] Ibid, p141

[148] The equivalent figures in 2009 would be £255,000 and £136,000 respectively. In the Victoria County History, 'Ealing and Brentford: Other estates', A History of the County of Middlesex: Volume 7: Acton, Chiswick, Ealing and Brentford, West Twyford, Willesden (1982), pp. 128-131, the estate is described as follows: "Under an Act of 1808 the [Elm Grove] estate ... was sold ... to Spencer Perceval ... on whose assassination it was held by his widow Jane ... In 1821 the estate was settled on [Jane] and her son Spencer Perceval and on [her] death in [1844] it passed to her daughter-in-law Anna ... The house was occupied by Dr. W. R. Vines as a boys' school c. 1861, by the Revd. Charles Scott in 1864 and by the Royal India Asylum 1870-1892. After Leopold de Rothschild had bought the estate for building, Elm Grove was demolished in 1894." See www.british-history.ac.uk/report.aspx?compid=22578

At a combined cost of about £400,000 today this was clearly a substantial purchase and more than the Percevals could readily afford. Rather than accept the loan offered by his brother Lord Arden, however, Perceval borrowed from the trustees of Jane's dowry. It was a substantial investment, but the property came with 36 acres of land on the edge of Ealing Common. At this date Ealing was still a village and one with other distinguished residents who similarly wished to avoid the confines and pollution of London, but kept it within riding distance, only seven miles away, so that they could go up to town when necessary - even on a daily basis if required.[149]

Assassination of Spencer Perceval (1812)

Political assassination is not something usually associated with Britain, being more frequently thought characteristic of less tolerant or less democratic societies (or in the case of America and some mediterranean countries perhaps more hot-tempered ones). However, the situation in the twenty-first century should not be confused with that applying in the nineteenth. Britain was not notably tolerant or democratic at this period, and individuals who pressed for alternatives tended either to be seen as philanthropic (employers such as Robert Owen and Titus Salt (1803-1876)) or radical (such as William Cobbett (1763-1835) or Sir Francis Burdett). If they were fortunate, the judgement of posterity might be that they were enlightened; if they were less so, they might be derided as misguided, agitators or rabble-rousers. However, there was a long tradition of group disorder and riot, and it is not difficult to see how some individuals might decide to take matters into their own hands. If they felt sufficiently aggrieved, they might consider this the only way of removing an obstacle to change. If their reason was impaired, they may have engaged in even less justification and a more precipitate response.

That Jane's share of the estate passed on her death to Anna may suggest that Spencer junior was not living there.

[149] For example, Sir John Soane had purchased Pitzhanger Manor House in Ealing in 1800 and had re-modelled it by 1804, but then only used it as a weekend retreat never staying overnight before selling it on again in 1810. Another resident was the Duke of Kent at Castle Hill Lodge (see below). He had bought this property in 1801 from his brother the Prince of Wales' mistress Mrs. Maria Fitzherbert (1756-1837).

One of the few things widely known about Spencer Perceval is that he is the only British Prime Minister to have been assassinated. What is less well-known is that there were many other attempts at political assassination during this period. They included attacks on monarchs such as George III, George IV and Victoria (twice in the early years of her reign), as well as the Cato Street conspiracy in February 1820 that was designed to remove all the Cabinet at dinner as a prelude to establishing a republic, and the attempt on Sir Robert Peel in 1843 that led to the McNaughtan rules.[150] The difference is that they failed, while Perceval was murdered. The assassination was also unprecedented in that it took place in the House of Commons itself and the perpetrator John Bellingham was tried and executed within the week (despite being clearly deranged).[151]

Perceval's assassination on 11th May 1812 took place at the height of the Luddite riots and was accompanied by wild public rejoicing. This contrasted with the mourning of his colleagues and the grief of Jane and the family. If his brother Lord Arden was shocked, his wife and children must have been devastated: the bottom had dropped out of their world, and their lives had been transformed, in an instant. One moment they had been a happy family, with a prominent father at the height of a thriving political career, the next they were confronted with the trauma of a personal and family disaster - as well as a public one. They were left with a huge hole. Jane wrote a black-bordered letter[152] to her oldest son Spencer a few days after the assassination, enclosing the ten-pages his father had composed on 1st January 1809 to be sent only

---

[150] See, for example, Max Adams, 'The Firebringers: Art, Science and the Struggle for Liberty in Nineteenth Century Britain', London, Quercus, 2009, p284. Daniel McNaughtan (1802/3-1865) killed Peel's private secretary Edward Drummond instead of Peel, his intended target.
[151] The details are well-known and do not require repeating here. They are set out briefly in Gault, 2008b, op cit and Hugh Gault,'1809: Between Hope and History', Cambridge, Gretton Books, 2009, pp208-209, as well as in Gray, op cit and Spencer Walpole, 'The Life of the Right Honourable Spencer Perceval', 2 volumes, London, Hurst and Blackett, 1874. They are covered in depth in, for example, David Hanrahan, 'The Assassination of the Prime Minister: John Bellingham and the Murder of Spencer Perceval', Stroud, Gloucestershire, Sutton Publishing, 2008.
[152] British Library, Add. MSS 49191, f.23. This letter is not dated and addressed to "My dearest Spencer", whereas a previous letter to him eight months before on 22nd September 1811 had been addressed to "My dear Boy".

after his death.[153] In accordance with her husband's wishes Jane would not have read these in advance, but no doubt hoped they would help her son deal with his grief. As if the circumstances were not traumatic enough anyway, she would be aware that they might be worse for her oldest boy Spencer, a sensitive child, away from home at Harrow, and still only sixteen.

"I lose no time in sending you the accompanying ... invaluable papers and may the Almighty grant that it may have all the good affect upon you that your dear lamented Father wished. Keep it my dear Boy as the most invaluable Treasure read it frequently and dwell upon it and [...] the good feelings it will always excite in your mind to practise. Remember it is the voice of your dear Father ..."

Her son replied on 5th June, doing his best to comply with his father's instructions and support her:

"I hope my Dear Mother by the future to make up in some measure for the past, and in some small degree to compensate for the many pangs, which my inatention [sic] and neglect of his wishes, has occasioned to my dear Father, by never for an instant giving you reason again to think 'how sharper than a serpent's tooth it is, to have a thankless child'."[154]

To demonstrate his good intentions he allowed himself to be persuaded by his Harrow headmaster Dr Butler to stay at the school another year rather than go to "College" early as he had planned. He adhered to this resolution, but found it difficult to maintain other promises to his mother.

Perceval was buried in the Egmont family vault at St Luke's, Charlton five days later on Saturday 16th May, with few of the family present.[155]

"In the meantime Parliament had debated at some length the appropriate grant to pay to his wife and ... children ...
"Castlereagh had proposed to the House of Commons that 'The sum should be an handsome one, but still regulated by a regard to

---

[153] The instructions opened "If I were to die today ...", but the contents make clear that Spencer Perceval thought he was anticipating events years rather than months in the future.
[154] British Library, Add. MSS 49191, f.37
[155] Only Spencer junior according to Gray, op cit, p461

economy, and consistent with the present circumstances of the country'. Other MPs had their own views and the matter was not resolved until the 15th May when annuities were settled on his wife and eldest son (£2,000 and £1,000 per annum respectively), and a capital grant of £50,000 was made on behalf of the children.

"It is worth noting that some historians report that the level of support was decided on the day after Perceval's murder. Although the Prince Regent agreed on 12th May that provision should be made for the family, it was left to Parliament to decide the amount. **It took some time to achieve unanimity, a matter that was just as important to the family as the money itself.** [emphasis added] "Eulogies in Parliament and elsewhere concentrated on Perceval's principles as a public servant and his virtues as a family man. *The Times* even went so far as to compare him to Pitt and Fox. While inevitably it did not accord him the same political and debating skills, he did as well on the count of integrity and stood out for his private virtues."[156]

Perceval's brief Will left everything to Jane, with the one proviso that Arden become joint guardian of the children should she re-marry. In June 1812 Lincoln's Inn offered to provide free admission and legal training for whichever two Perceval sons Jane chose to nominate. She decided on Spencer and Dudley.[157] The following February the government appointed Spencer a Teller of the Exchequer (see Chapter 4 below). Jane wrote to the Prime Minister Lord Liverpool later that month to thank him and the Prince Regent for this "gracious" act.[158] She was no doubt relieved that this would help alleviate any financial concerns, and that these would not compound the impact of her husband's murder, but it must be of some doubt whether this compensation did, or could, numb her grief sufficiently. For many of the children, of course, there was not even this consolation.

The enigmatic Mr. Carr and a second husband

Henry Carr was born on 6th October 1777, the fifth of ten children and the second son of the Reverend Colston Carr (1740-1822) and Elizabeth Bullock (?-1826). His father was vicar of Feltham from

---

[156] Gault, 2008b, op cit, p10
[157] 'Records of the Honourable Society of Lincoln's Inn', vol. IV (1776-1845), London, Lincoln's Inn, 1902, pp125-127
[158] British Library, Add. MSS 38251, f.266

1771, but had left this post by the time Henry was born to move back to Twickenham and Brook House school which he had run since 1765.[159] From 1797 to his death in 1822 Colston Carr was vicar of Ealing.[160] He had a house at Putney[161] as well as the one in Twickenham, and the vicarage in Ealing from 1797.[162] Vicars did not always live in their parishes, and some were more interested in the collections and tithes, perhaps officiating at services, while impecunious curates resided there on their behalf on inadequate livings.[163]

Like the Percevals, the Carr family concentrated several births into a short period, with the ten children born in the 12 years 1773 to 1785. Henry Carr had six sisters and three brothers, of whom the

---

[159] In 1785 Brook House was "surrendered to Rev Colston Carr by the son of William and Ann Cowdrey", the owners. This may have been in recognition of 20 years as the schoolmaster there. See www.twickenham-museum.org.uk/house_detail.asp?HouseID=26

[160] 'Clerical Guide', 2nd edition, London, FC & J Rivington, 1822 (The first edition was published in 1817. In these five years the Ealing population grew from 5035 to 5361. By contrast the Feltham parish was much smaller, with a population of 620 in 1817 and 703 by 1822. These figures would roughly correspond to the size and attractiveness of the livings.)

[161] "On the 26th of May 1632, a chapel was consecrated in the house of the Earl of Portland [at Roehampton], then Lord Weston of Neyland, by Laud, Bishop of London. ... This chapel ... was pulled down in the year 1777 by Thomas Parker, Esq. who at the same time built a new chapel about a hundred yards from the house, which is now for a term of years the private property of the Reverend Colston Carr, who officiates there on Sundays." From: 'Putney', The Environs of London: volume 1: County of Surrey (1792), pp. 404-435.
Roehampton is within the parish of Putney, whereas Twickenham is on the other side of the Thames.

[162] "The vicarage house of 1315 was presumably where its successor stood in 4¾ a[cres] between the Park and Grange and St. Mary's roads in 1915. A red-brick house, said to be 250 years old in 1900, was improved by Colston Carr, vicar 1797-1822, and was commodious in 1816 and 1845." From: 'Ealing and Brentford: Churches: Ealing', A History of the County of Middlesex: Volume 7: Acton, Chiswick, Ealing and Brentford, West Twyford, Willesden (1982), pp. 150-153.

[163] Bills were promoted in the House of Commons in 1805, 1806 and 1808 by Spencer Perceval to reduce the poverty of resident curates. They were defeated each time and the issue of absentee ministers continued. (See, for example, Gault, 2009, op cit, pp58-59.)
It should be noted that on 2nd January 1821 the *London Gazette* reports the address sent by the inhabitants of Ealing to the uncrowned George IV (whose coronation had been postponed from August 1820). This address assured him of their continued loyalty at a time of national turbulence. It was transmitted on their behalf by the Reverend JL Young, who styled himself the Vicar of Ealing. It may be that this man had now taken over from, or was at least assisting, the 80 year-old Colston Carr, but he is not listed in the 1822 'Clerical Guide'.

oldest Robert James Carr (1774-1841) was to become Bishop of Worcester in 1831. He had been Vicar of Brighton from 1804, where he struck up a lifelong friendship with the future George IV who created him Bishop of Chichester in 1824. Alongside this, he was a canon in St Paul's Cathedral and held the honorary position of "clerk to the closet". He retained this latter post "until the accession of Queen Victoria [in 1837], when he was dismissed for his conservatism".[164] It can be assumed that these connections with evangelical Anglicanism, conservatism and the royal family were first forged by their father Colston Carr (though in his case the royal connections were with the Duke of Kent, a fellow resident of Ealing). They were to find a distinctive echo in Henry's life.

Robert Carr received his primary schooling in his father's school at Brook House and it is probable that Henry did so too. They were to follow the conventional career paths for the time, with Robert as the oldest son going to Oxford University in 1792 at the age of 18, before being ordained in 1798. Henry entered the army at the age of 16 in March 1794.

Henry first joined the 68th Foot as an Ensign and little more than two years later was a Captain in the 83rd Foot at the age of 18 (see Table 3).[165] He remained Captain for eleven years before being promoted to Major. The 83rd Foot were in the West Indies for much of this time, from 1795 to 1802, and then in Jersey from 1803 to 1805.[166]

Table 3: Henry Carr's initial army career

Year	Month	Day	Event	Age
1794	March	12	Ensign 68th Foot	16
1795	Sept	2	Lieutenant 68th Foot	17
1796	May	4	Captain 83rd Foot	18
1807	Sept	17	Major 83rd Foot	29

---

[164] See his DNB entry. This also says that "...the bishopric of Worcester [was] in fulfilment, as it was understood at the time, of a promise made by his late patron (Carr was the bishop who attended George IV during his last illness)".
[165] The information in Table 3 comes from John Philippart (ed.), 'The Royal Military Calendar or Army Service and Commission Book', 3rd edition, 5 volumes, London, Egerton, 1820. Henry Carr's entry is on p411 of volume 4, where he is the 1145th officer listed. All those of Major rank and above are included in order of seniority.
[166] 'Memoirs and Services of the 83rd Regiment, County of Dublin, 1793 - 1807', London, Rees, 1908, pp14-16

Peninsular War

Henry Carr was a Major in the 83rd Foot's 2nd Battalion, formed three years earlier. This battalion was part of Wellington's army that landed at Lisbon in April 1809, remaining to the end of the Peninsular War and the battles at Orthes and Toulouse in France in 1814.[167] The regiment had not been involved in Wellington's victory at the battle of Vimeiro in August 1808, nor in the debacle of the Convention of Cintra that followed, and it avoided the ignominy of Corunna in January 1809 only because the outcome became known before it could join Moore's troops there.

Table 4: Henry Carr's Peninsular War career

Year	Month	Day	Event	Age
1809	April		2nd Bn, 83rd Foot landed to end of Peninsular War	31
1809	May	12	2nd Bn, 83rd Foot at "Forcing of the Douro (Oporto)"	
1809	July	27-28	2nd Bn, 83rd Foot at battle of Talavera	
1810	Sept	27	2nd Bn, 83rd Foot at battle of Busaco	32
1811	April	3	2nd Bn, 83rd Foot at battle of Sabugal	
1811	May	3-5	Battle of Fuentes D'Onor - commanded 2nd Bn 83rd Foot	33
1811	Sept	25	2nd Bn, 83rd Foot at battle of El Bodon and Carpio	
1812	April	6	Capture of Badajoz after siege - commanded 2nd Bn 83rd Foot (- also previously at siege of Ciudad Rodrigo)	34
1812	April	27	Lieutenant-Colonel in the army	
1812	July	22	Battle of Salamanca - commanded 2nd Bn 83rd Foot	
1813	June	21	Battle of Vittoria - commanded 2nd Bn 83rd Foot	35
1813	Nov	10	Battle of Nivelle - commanded 2nd Bn 83rd Foot	36
1814	Feb	27	Battle of Orthes, France - commanded 2nd Bn 83rd Foot	

[167] Michael Glover, 'The Peninsular War 1807-1814: A Concise Military History', London, David & Charles, 1974. The 1st Bn 83rd Foot was not involved in the War at all, being stationed in the Cape of Good Hope from January 1806.

Year	Month	Day	Event	Age
1814	April	10	Battle of Toulouse, but HWC may not have been present	

Table 4 sets out the details of Carr's Peninsular War,[168] in which he was present at most of the well-known engagements of the war. In addition, it is worth noting that:

- at **Talavera**: "The regiment on their [the Guards'] left, the Eighty-Third, made a simultaneous movement, driving the enemy with immense loss before them; but the impetuosity of the Guards led to endangering the day ..."[169]

- at **Fuentes D'Onor**: Wellington's letter to Lord Liverpool of 8th May 1811 refers to being defended against enemy attack by several battalions, including "... the 2nd battalion of the 83rd regiment under Major Carr. These troops maintained their position ..."[170]

- at **Badajoz**: Wellington's letter to Lord Liverpool of 7th May 1812 written a month after its capture "The officers and troops in the 3rd division have distinguished themselves as usual in these operations. Lieutenant-General Picton has reported to me particularly the conduct of ... Major Henry William Carr of the 83rd ..."[171]

- at **Salamanca**: "in commemoration of the distinguished services of the battalion of the 83rd in this action, his Majesty has been graciously pleased to sanction ... Salamanca being inscribed on its colours and appointments."[172]

- at **Vittoria**: medal awarded to its commanding officer Colonel Carr for "gallant conduct" of the battalion. In addition, "Vittoria [was] inscribed on the colours and appointments of the 83rd, in commemoration of [its] distinguished service".[173]

---

[168] It combines the information provided by Glover with that of Carr's entry in the Royal Military Calendar. The former concentrates on the battalion, while the latter includes the battles at which Carr was in command.
[169] Lord Munster in 'Portugal and Spain campaign', 1831, i, pp145-146 referred to by Glover, op cit, p110
[170] Philippart, op cit, vol 1, p186
[171] Ibid, vol 1, p207
[172] 'Memoirs and Services of the 83rd Regiment', op cit, p30
[173] Ibid, pp32-33

-at **Orthes**: Lieutenant-Colonel Carr was wounded and Orthes was added to the regiment's colours.[174] Carr "received a cross and three clasps",[175] though this may have been for all his commands during the war rather than just Orthes.

When the battalion fought in the final battle of the campaign at Toulouse in April 1814, there is no indication that Carr was present. This may have been due to the wound he received at Orthes, but it is unlikely that he was invalided home before the whole army "embarked from Bordeaux" on 1st June 1814.[176] On their return Wellington was summoned to the House of Commons to be thanked personally, the troops were reviewed by the Prince Regent on 20th June and a summer of celebrations started.[177] A thanksgiving service was held at St Paul's Cathedral on 7th July.[178] On 22nd September 1814 Carr was formally promoted to Lieutenant-Colonel of the 83rd Foot.[179]

The 2nd Battalion had been out of England since 1807, quartered in the Channel Islands and Ireland prior to the Peninsular War. Meanwhile, the Perceval family had moved to Elm Grove, Ealing in 1808, and although Carr might have met the Percevals in the short period before Wellington's army sailed for Portugal in April 1809, there is no evidence that he did so. Nor is it likely that he returned to England before June 1814. Although some officers did return home while the army was in winter quarters, they were generally more senior than Carr. Apart from the effect this might be expected to have on the morale and performance of the troops, it became progressively more difficult anyway as the army moved inland and away from the coast. In addition, the army was engaged in other military activities during the winter, such as intelligence-gathering, even if they were not fighting. After Salamanca in July 1812 the army had to march across Spain before it fought again at Vittoria in June 1813. Even Wellington did not return to Britain

---

[174] Ibid, p35

[175] Philippart, op cit, vol 4, p411

[176] Memoirs of the 83rd, op cit, p36

[177] Herbert Maxwell (ed.), 'The Creevey Papers: A Selection from the Correspondence and Diaries of the Late Thomas Creevey', London, John Murray, 1905, p188

[178] 'The Annual Register for 1814', London, Baldwin, Cradock & Joy, 1815

[179] Philippart, op cit, vol 4, p411

between these campaigns.[180] A year later the army went into winter quarters in early December 1813 "on French soil".[181]

Colston Carr as the Vicar of Ealing would no doubt wish, and could be expected, to support Jane Perceval after her husband's murder.   Henry Carr, on the other hand, would have been superfluous in 1812 even if he had met her then. By June 1814, he was returning as part of a victorious army, and a high profile officer at that, and Jane had now been a widow for more than two years.

Further advances

Europe was once more at peace following Napoleon's abdication and exile to Elba.[182] It was not surprising that Jane and Henry Carr should get to know each other in these circumstances. But they might also be expected to take a hard-headed approach rather than be carried away on the tide of national euphoria. She was eight years older than him and at 45, the mother of twelve children, only four of whom were 18 or older by this stage. He had been a soldier for more than twenty years, on active service out of the country for most of this time, and, as far as is known, never previously married. Although he brought the allure of victory, she offered a settled and certain existence.   His father Colston Carr had supported her in the two years since Perceval's murder, and all three had prominent connections with the royal family, religion and, to some extent, high politics. What is not clear is whether their attachment developed for romantic or purely practical reasons. They both had much to offer the other, perhaps personally as well as socially, and it may be that Colston Carr helped to broker the arrangement.[183]

It is not clear exactly when they decided to get married, though this was by late November 1814. Jane approached Arden first given the condition in Spencer Perceval's Will that Arden would become joint guardian of the children should Jane re-marry. If not actually a necessity, therefore, it would certainly be prudent for her to obtain his consent in advance. Jane dictated a letter to Lord

---

[180] Charles Esdaile, 'The Peninsular War: A New History', London, Allen Lane, 2002

[181] Maxwell, op cit, note on p186

[182] Thomas Creevey moved to Brussels that autumn for his wife's health, and was to stay there during Waterloo in 1815 because his wife was an invalid and unable to move. He remained there for some years. In Maxwell, op cit, p218ff

[183] Henry Carr also had the same birthday as the Percevals' second son Frederick, whose disability had prevented him going to Harrow like his father and brothers. He was 17 in October 1814, twenty years younger than Carr.

Arden from Brighton where she was unwell seeking his permission for her re-marriage on 25th November 1814.[184] Since her letter refers to Carr's connections to the Duke of Wellington and other members of the aristocracy, it is clear that this was the first Arden knew of it. Jane concludes her letter by asking Arden to meet Carr and writing

"...if you will allow him that honour [of marrying me], but he ... [will] not do it without your permission."

Arden's reply from Nork two days later is worth quoting in full:

"My dear Mrs Perceval,
"There can be no disposition in my mind to be wanting in kindness towards you on account of your taking a step in which you have an unquestionable right to decide for yourself; or to diminish my esteem for you, if it is in the [...?] of reflection and person under all the circumstances of your situation, as I hope it is, and not of inclination only: you have I dare say called to mind all your duties before you engaged yourself to a second marriage, and I trust, well considered its many consequences.
"Being unacquainted with Col. Carr, I can only say that I have no doubt he fully merits the high character you give of him, and that I am ready to [avail myself?] of seeing him whenever he thinks proper, except Saturday, Sunday and Monday next when I believe I shall be in Windsor, and I wish to be informed whether I am at liberty to mention there what you have now communicated to me, which it will be my duty to do as soon as you give me leave.
"Your sister [...?] in concern to hear that you are indisposed, our sincere wishes for your welfare and happiness attend you.
"I am/ with great trust/ very affectionately yours/Arden"[185]

While this was as kind and understanding a reply as could be expected in the circumstances, Arden was also cautious and non-committal, perhaps properly formal and distant in some respects. It seems that not all Jane's children were inclined to accept the prospect positively.[186] By 17th December 1814, however, these

---

[184] British Library, Add. MSS 49188, f.70
[185] British Library, Add. MSS 49191, f.82
[186] A letter from his friend Edward Gambier to Spencer junior refers to the latter's absence from Trinity College, Cambridge in December 1814 as understandable in the circumstances and re-assures him that he has acted with forbearance. (See

concerns seem to have been allayed sufficiently for the *Morning Chronicle* to report that "We hear the widow of an unfortunate Prime Minister, Mrs Perceval, will shortly be led to the Hymeneal Altar by the gallant Col. Carr." This is clearly a singular way of describing their forthcoming marriage. It has echoes of the approach that some papers adopted at the time to Joanna Southcott (1750-1814),[187] though they could also report on her much more cruelly. The *Courier* on the following Monday 19th December is more circumspect in reporting that "A Morning Paper says, that the widow of the late Rt. Hon. Spencer Perceval will shortly be led to the hymeneal altar by Colonel Carr".[188]

Although there is no record of Carr and Arden meeting, they must have done (to the satisfaction of both) since the service was conducted by special licence[189] on 12th January 1815 at Arlington Street by the Rector of St George's, Hanover Square in whose parish the ceremony took place. Henry Carr had been back in the country for little more than six months. The following day the *Morning Chronicle* and the *Courier* carried the same report, under the heading of 'Marriage in High Life':

"... Henry William Carr to Mrs Spencer Perceval, widow of the late Chancellor of the Exchequer. After the wedding they left town for their seat at Ealing."[190]

Despite the headline, there is no mention of guests (though there may have been a number of reasons for the wedding to be low-key and the celebrations restrained). Nevertheless, the report raises

---

British Library, Add. MSS 49188, f.84) It also refers to Jane's illness being recounted in the papers (possibly brought on by anxiety and her children's reaction to her re-marriage?).

[187] The millenarian prophet and writer: The *Morning Chronicle* reported in November 1814 that she had been abandoned at the altar by the prospective bridegroom who had agreed to marry her ahead of her imminent (indeed overdue) confinement and the virgin birth of Shiloh as prophesied. Her DNB entry states that the marriage did take place on 12th November, though Shiloh had not yet appeared by the time Southcott died on 27th December 1814.

[188] Although Hymen is the god of marriage in mythology, this is a curious allusion for a mother, let alone the mother of thirteen children, given the word's other connotations. The Oxford English Dictionary (2nd edition, 1989) previously recorded the first use of "hymeneal altar" as being in James Grant's 'Sketches in London', published twenty-four years later in 1838.

[189] A licence is an alternative to the banns being read; a special licence allows the marriage to take place anywhere at any time, including in a private house.

[190] *Morning Chronicle* p2 and *Courier* p3, both 13th January 1815

several questions, not least why Perceval was not described as the former Prime Minister. Arlington Street is at the other end of the parish from St George's (next to where the Ritz Hotel now stands) and the marriage probably took place at number 18 Arlington Street, Henry Carr's residence in January 1816.[191] As was the case with their father's funeral, the children seem not to have attended. Whether this was through choice or convention is not clear, but there must have been a palpable and growing sense of exclusion - particularly perhaps for children such as John who were old enough to appreciate the circumstances, but may not have been old enough to accept them.

Meanwhile, on 3rd January 1815 Henry Carr was gazetted to receive a KCB (Knight Commander of the Bath) for his service in the Peninsular War (along with 179 other officers).[192] It might be supposed that this had some connection with, even if it did not necessarily cause, their marriage less than ten days later (though once it had been reported publicly, there would be little purpose in delaying it).[193] He was knighted on 12th April 1815 and became Sir Henry William Carr KCB. Jane became Lady Carr, the title that she was to use until her death nearly thirty years later. On 4th May 1815 her marriage was marked formally when Lady Carr was presented to Queen Charlotte by Lady Arden (her older sister Margaretta who had married Perceval's brother Baron Arden).[194] On 23rd May Henry Carr received the Portuguese Tower and Sword for "signal intrepidity" in the Peninsular War.[195] They were both coming to wider attention.

It was in 1815 that Carr gave up active military service after 21 unbroken years, going on to the half-pay of the 71st Foot. His

---

[191] Boyle's Court Guide for January 1816, London, Eliza Boyle, 1816. By April 1818 and the next issue of Boyle's Court Guide, number 18 Arlington Street had passed to the Marquess of Tavistock. Henry Carr was no longer listed as either a member of the court or one living in London. Possibly Ealing was by now his sole residence and his main attachment was as equerry to the Duke of Kent, who at this point was living abroad.

[192] *London Gazette Supplement* 3rd January 1815 This was within the military aspect of the Order of the Bath.

[193] They may also have taken the view that, to the extent that some of the children still viewed it negatively, they might be more likely to accept it after the event.

[194] *The Times* 5th May 1815 report of the Queen's drawing room. This acknowledgement would not have occurred if Arden had not reported favourably (or at least acceptably) on Colonel Carr.

[195] *London Gazette* 23rd May 1815. Carr's entry in the Royal Military Calendar states that "he is a Knight of the Tower and Sword of Portugal"; see Philippart, op cit, vol 4, p411

memorial in St Dunstan's Church, Feltham includes the words "...
Adorned by these distinctions [the KCB and Portuguese
knighthood], the fruits of his gallant services, during an
uninterrupted period of one-and-twenty years ..." It is not clear
whether he reached this decision entirely through choice following
his marriage, through necessity after his wound, or a mixture of the
two, but he no longer needed a soldier's pay.

John Quincy Adams was American minister in London in 1815,
remaining in this post until 1817 when he became Secretary of
State and subsequently the sixth President from 1825-1829. His
diary entry for 6th August 1815 refers to the house he had just
rented in Ealing. This came with

"...a pew at the church for the use of the house, and another for the
servants if we should think proper to use these. We accordingly
went to the church at Ealing. The church service was read by an
old clergyman, Dr. Carr, the father of Col. Carr, who married Mrs.
Perceval."

Adams lived in Ealing throughout his time in England and sought on
several occasions to meet his fellow resident Lady Jane Carr. He
never managed this, but does record in his diaries that he once met
Sir Henry Carr on his own. Even though Adams attended church in
Ealing throughout his stay, and sometimes heard Robert Carr
preach rather than his father, he never records meeting either
Henry or Jane Carr there. While it is possible that Jane Carr
remained at home much of the time with what was still a young and
large family, this seems unlikely given the nature of family life at this
time[196] - even in a family that had become used to the presence of a
mother, the absence of a father, and was not yet accustomed to her
re-marriage. While Adams and Carr might be more likely to meet
each other at social occasions which were not open to women,

---

[196] Only three girls were 21 or older by May 1815 and four of the children were
between 8 and 12. It might be expected that servants would look after the younger
children on a daily basis, along with their governess, before the boys were old
enough to go to school and while they and the girls were not there. Although five
of the six boys went to Harrow School, it is not known that any of the girls were
educated outside the home. "Parents between 1600 and 1914, born to the
assumption of gender roles and gender identity themselves, trained children to see
themselves as functionally and essentially different, according to their sex. Boys
and girls, they believed, had separate and distinct identities." (Anthony Fletcher,
'Growing Up in England: The Experience of Childhood 1600-1914', London, Yale
University Press, 2008, page xiv) This extended to the pattern of education.

Adams' failure to meet Lady Carr, or even see the Carrs together, raises an issue about the nature of the Carrs' marriage. Also, it must be questioned why Jane chose a husband who was eight years younger than herself. And it must have been a choice; regardless of whether her re-marriage was of benefit to the family, she is most unlikely to have just accepted it passively. The age difference between Jane and Henry would be noted as unusual today, but it was even more likely to be remarked upon two hundred years ago.[197]

Links to the Duke of Kent

Between 1815 and 1820 the Carrs are largely absent from the historical record - with three notable exceptions. On 5th November 1816 one of Henry Carr's sisters, Sarah, died suddenly at the age of 40 after attending a dance in Ealing. On 24th February 1819 *The Times* reported an attempt to extort money from the Carrs by a "poor Clergyman ... with a wife and large family" who had fallen on hard times. His appeal to the Carrs was set out in a letter that was given added authenticity by the seal of Lord Binning. It transpired though that he was an impostor and that Lord Binning's seal must have been obtained fraudulently. In November that year, a few months after her fiftieth birthday, Lady Carr and one of her daughters featured in a nasty carriage accident in Brighton:

"The following are additional particulars of the accident ... last week:- Her Ladyship was taking an airing in her chariot, accompanied by Miss Perceval. In passing the barracks, the carriage was met by three of the Lancers, who were returning from the inspection. The flags attached to their weapons so alarmed Lady Carr's horses, that they became unmanageable, and in the end overturned the carriage. Her Ladyship, who had let down the glass, and had her hand upon the edge of the roof of the chariot above, was very much hurt. The weight of the carriage falling directly across the hand, led, at first, to the supposition that the bones had been crushed; but this, happily, does not turn out to be the case. No bones were fractured whatever, but a severe cut was received above the right eye, and contusions of a very painful nature. Her Ladyship was removed to the hospital at the barracks,

---

[197] Although her initial response might have been a basic and instinctive one to a victorious soldier in uniform, the longer term implications would soon intrude. Once he left full-time service in the army, perhaps the attractions began to pall.

where a vein in the arm was opened; and soon after, in a kind of litter, to her residence on the South-parade. Her Ladyship has suffered much pain, and been entirely confined to her bed since, but the strongest assurances are now given of her desired and speedy recovery. Miss Perceval escaped almost unhurt."[198]

The explanation that her horses were frightened by flags sounds unlikely, and it might be supposed that she was leaning out of the carriage to talk to the soldiers or attract their attention. She had been in Brighton in 1814 when she first wrote to Lord Arden about marriage to Carr and was there again when her son Spencer wrote to her in November 1826.[199] Brighton seems to have been a frequent alternative to Ealing, and her addresses included Brunswick Terrace as well as South Parade.[200]

These were momentous years for Prince Edward the Duke of Kent, a fellow resident of Ealing from 1801 to 1812 when he lived at Castle Hill Lodge.[201] He retained the Ealing property, but no longer lived in it, after 1812 and subsequently moved to Brussels to economise.[202] The Duke would be expected to know Colston Carr as the local vicar of Ealing, but their acquaintance went deeper. In 1810 they acted jointly as character witnesses on behalf of a defendant in a criminal prosecution. They would have provided these statements only if they knew the circumstances.[203]

---

[198] *The Times*, 10th November 1819. There is no indication which of her daughters was with her on this occasion; they were all still unmarried, aged between 28 and 14. This was not the only carriage accident in which she was injured (see Chapter 10 below), with the latter incident in 1822 being taken to court.

[199] British Library, Add. MSS 49191, f.120

[200] The latter no longer exists by this name, whereas Brunswick Terrace is to the west and was only built after George IV became King in 1820. Antony Dale describes it as one of the "great architectural enterprises of Brighton" in 'Fashionable Brighton 1820-1860', Newcastle, Oriel, 1967, p70. In 1826 Jane Carr would have been one of the first occupants, moving with the times as well as the fashions.

[201] 'Ealing and Brentford: Other estates', A History of the County of Middlesex: Volume 7: Acton, Chiswick, Ealing and Brentford, West Twyford, Willesden, 1982, pp128-131

[202] Although the Duke was made a Field-Marshal in September 1805 after a successful career as a soldier, he had earlier been recalled from the Governorship of Gibraltar by the commander in chief, his brother the Duke of York, and never saw active service again, becoming the Keeper and Paler of Hampton Court from 1805. His DNB entry describes this as "the *reductio ad absurdum* of his career".

[203] Report in the National Archives of three individual petitions (the prisoner, Colston Carr and the Duke of Kent) on behalf of James Coxhead, journeyman baker and servant to Thomas Ashby, tried (with William House, former servant to

The Duke of Kent was the "most popular of George III's sons"[204] as evidenced by the House of Commons voting patterns on 15th April 1818 when additional allowances were agreed for the previously unmarried sons as the hunt for a royal successor got underway following the death of the Prince Regent's only child. The Duke's household was described in 'The Complete Peerage' as "modest" compared to those of his brothers and on 30th May 1818 an Act was passed enabling further provision to be made for him if his marriage (the day before) turned out to require it.[205] Sir Henry Carr was to become one of the Duke's equerries, possibly one of the last to be honoured in this way when the household was expanded in mid-1818 after the Duke's marriage.[206] At this point the household "... consisted of ... five Equerries (two of whom were Major-Generals, two Colonels, and one a Captain) ..."[207] There were also two Grooms of the Bedchamber, one a Lieutenant-Colonel and the other a Colonel. With the addition of Carr as an equerry, there were eight in total.[208]

The Duke of Kent won the race for the royal succession when his daughter Victoria was born in May 1819. He and his wife had returned to England only two months earlier so that Victoria could

---

Ashby) and convicted at the Old Bailey December Sessions [1810], for the theft of a sack and a bushel of flour, value 18/-, property of Thomas Ashby, baker on 27 November 1810.

[204] Gibbs, op cit, vol VII, 1932 edition, p184. Pages 179-185 cover the Duke of Kent and his household from 1799 to his death in 1820.

[205] *London Gazette* and Annual Register for 1818, p87

[206] 29th May 1818 at Coburg and then 13th July at Kew Palace. The Duke of Kent had speculated to Thomas Creevey in December 1817 that he would be required to marry to secure the succession, even naming the woman most likely to be chosen as his bride. See Maxwell, op cit, pp267-271 where Thomas Creevey reports their conversation in detail.

The Duke of Kent was one of the eight copyhold tenants listed as supporting the Carrs' petition to the Bishop of London for the rent of a small strip of land for a new road further away from Elm Grove than the existing one. See British Library, IOR/L/L/2/1708 This is archived with a date of 1812 but must have been submitted after the Carrs' marriage in 1815.

[207] Gibbs, op cit, pp184-185

[208] The other seven in addition to Sir Henry Carr were: Major-General Fred Hardyman, Major-General James Moore, Lieutenant-General Sir George Anson, Lieutenant-General Frederick Wetherall (another Ealing resident), Captain Sir John Conroy (later of Queen Victoria notoriety), Lieutenant-Colonel John Drinkwater and Colonel the Honourable George Stapylton. These are the ranks given by Philippart, op cit in 1820 so do not match exactly with those cited in 'The Complete Peerage' for 1818.

All apart from Captain Conroy have entries in the Royal Military Calendar (which does not include Captains), and several are covered by the DNB.

be born in this country. The Duke's entry in the Royal Military Calendar (and the subsequent Memoir by Sir John Philippart) says that they were unable to travel back any earlier because they could not afford it. Selling Castle Hill Ealing became the Duke's only option to fund his increased expenses, but this never happened in his lifetime.

The final two years ... but several more questions

1820 and 1821 were to prove eventful years - both for the royal family, and consequently for the country and even more directly for the Carrs.

On 23rd January 1820, eight months after Victoria's birth, the Duke of Kent died at Sidmouth from pneumonia. His funeral took place at Windsor on 12th February 1820, with six of his eight equerries/grooms present.[209] The Prince Regent did not attend, but the Dukes of York, Clarence, Sussex and Gloucester were there - as was Sir Henry Carr. He was also a mourner four days later at George III's funeral, again at Windsor.[210] Once again six of the Duke of Kent's household were present, but only Carr and three other equerries (Conroy, Moore and Wetherall) attended both funerals.

In February 1820 the Cato Street conspirators were apprehended at Earl Harrowby's house where they planned to murder the Cabinet as they were sitting down to dinner. An appeal fund was immediately instituted to reward the officers who had captured them. Sir Henry Carr and Lady Carr were among the contributors listed separately in *The Times* on 7th March, less than a fortnight later.[211]

The Prince Regent's coronation as George IV was first planned for 1st August 1820, but on 15th July 1820 the *London Gazette* announced that it had been postponed for "divers weighty reasons". This was a euphemism for the difficulties "Queen" Caroline's return to England on George III's death had stirred up. She was

---

[209] *London Gazette* 12th February 1820

[210] *London Gazette Supplement* 19th February 1820

[211] The fact that they were listed separately was unusual, but is unlikely to be significant given that Spencer Perceval and Jane Perceval had adopted the practice of being identified separately as contributors to the same charities. In this context it probably says more about their enlightened attitudes to equality for women (perhaps at Jane's insistence), as well as marking them out as prominent Tories.

determined to enjoy the privileges of being Queen; her husband, now King George IV, was equally determined that she should not. He had asked for her name to be removed from the liturgy in the Prayer Book,[212] and the matter had to be resolved before the coronation could take place. In these circumstances Lord Liverpool's government reluctantly introduced the Bill of Pains and Penalties in the House of Lords. As can be seen from Table 5, Queen Caroline's trial opened in mid-August and continued to early November. Sixty peers were excused from the trial, including those "professing the Catholic faith".[213] Of the remaining 250, 218 voted on 6th November with the majority for the Bill being a tiny 28 (123 for and 95 against). As Thomas Creevey wrote, "This is fatal", with such a slender majority making it impossible for the Government to take the Bill to the House of Commons where Caroline was even more popular. The chaotic atmosphere was compounded further by another vote on 8th November to determine whether a royal divorce was part of the Bill. The government accepted the inevitable and withdrew it.

Table 5: Henry Carr's last year

Year	Month	Day	Event	Age
1820	Aug	17	Queen Caroline trial in House of Lords to 8th November 1820	
1821	July	19	George IV coronation; Queen Caroline refused entry to Westminster Abbey	43
1821	July	31	George IV embarks on state visit to Ireland landing at Howth 12th August	
1821	Aug	7	Queen Caroline dies at Brandenburgh House, Hammersmith	
1821	Aug	16	Queen Caroline body arrives at Harwich en route to Stadt	
1821	Aug	18	Henry Carr dies in Southampton	43
			Monument in St Dunstan's church Feltham dedicated by Lady Carr	

---

[212] However, such an order could not apply to Scotland, so as Lord Cockburn writes "... the Presbyterians, who own no earthly head, kicked ... [and] prayed for her the more fervently that her husband's ministry declared that she was wicked". See Henry Cockburn, 'Memorials of His Time', London, T.N. Foulis, 1909 (orig. A&C Black, 1856), p351

[213] Maxwell, op cit, p306

Although the position of Queen Caroline was still unresolved, George IV's coronation eventually took place on 19th July 1821. Caroline tried to attend but was refused entry to Westminster Abbey on the King's orders, allegedly because she was "without a Peer's ticket".[214] She circled the Abbey, trying all the doors before she was forced to give up.

Shortly afterwards George IV set off on the first of a series of State visits, in this case to Ireland, sailing from Portsmouth at the end of July. He was still at sea when news of Queen Caroline's death on 7th August reached him four days later. The causes of her illness and death have been subject to much speculation - both at the time and since. She had been unwell since late July, and while there was some respite on the 1st August from an "obstruction in the bowels",[215] her condition deteriorated thereafter. Given the circumstances, it is not surprising that the worst was suspected: "Two hours after death, her body was black and swollen, which gave rise to rumours that she had been poisoned ..."[216] John Croker was part of the King's advance party to Ireland and his diary[217] provides a contemporaneous record:

"Dublin, August 5th. - We have an account of the Queen's being dangerously ill ...
"August 6th. - The Queen's disorder is said to be unabated. Some people think it is all a hoax, and others more charitable say that she is poisoned. **Certainly her death at this moment would be a most extraordinary occurrence.**" [emphasis added]

When the King disembarked at Howth the day after hearing of her death, Croker's diary for the 12th August records that he was "... gayer than it might be proper to tell ..." He may not have sought this outcome for Caroline, let alone planned it, but he must have welcomed it. It certainly got him off a hook.

If the circumstances of Caroline's death were extraordinary, those of her funeral procession through the centre of London to Harwich were equally so. This had not been the intended route

---

[214] John Adolphus, 'The last days, death, funeral obsequies, &c. of Her late Majesty Caroline ...', London, Jones & Co., 1822, pp3-6
[215] Ibid, p9
[216] Flora Fraser, 'The Unruly Queen: The Life of Queen Caroline', London, Macmillan, 1996, p461
[217] Included in Bernard Pool (ed.), 'The Croker Papers 1808-1857', London, Batsford, 1967 (from 3 volumes, London, Murray, 1884), pp58-59

from Hammersmith, but the government decided not to transport the body by river and consequently gave her supporters every opportunity to demonstrate her popularity along the route. At Cumberland Gate the Life Guards holding back the crowds lost their nerve after "Several were unhorsed by brickbats ..."[218] and fired, killing two people Richard Honey and George Francis. Despite the indecent haste with which the procession had started (perhaps under pressure from George IV so that the festivities in Ireland could get underway as soon as possible),[219] the funeral cortege took another couple of days before it reached Harwich on 16th August as it made its way back to Caroline's Brunswick homeland.

Queen Caroline had long been associated with the Percevals. For example:

- Spencer Perceval had been one of her closest advisers in the "Delicate Investigation" of 1806.

- his sister Frances, Lord Redesdale's wife, was a friend of one of Caroline's Ladies-in-Waiting Anne Hamilton. She wrote a letter to the *Morning Chronicle* in April 1813 pleading the Princess of Wales' case in the face of the Prince Regent's latest accusations of her adultery and misbehaviour. What was said by Frances, and what was then added by the *Morning Chronicle* in its subsequent reports, became a matter of dispute and the subject of an injunction.[220]

- Perceval's son (also called Spencer) attended her trial in 1820 as did others in London society that autumn.[221]

Such connections with the Percevals, long-standing though they were, would not be sufficient on their own to justify describing Caroline's death and funeral at such length. There were other links as well - possibly with the Carrs themselves. Most significantly, Adolphus in his account (published a year later) details the mourners in the funeral procession and identifies those who attended the arrival of the coffin in Harwich. The latter, though not the former, included "Lady Perceval's (the wife of Lord Perceval) carriage and pair".[222] While there are at least five possibilities for

---

[218] Adolphus, op cit, pp119-120; also see Steven Parissien, 'George IV: The Grand Entertainment', London, John Murray, 2001, p225

[219] Adolphus, op cit, p61; Henry Brougham letter to Thomas Creevey 14th August 1821 in Maxwell, op cit, p366

[220] *Morning Chronicle*, 12th, 22nd, 26th April and 5th June 1813

[221] See Chapter 4 below.

[222] Adolphus, op cit, p149 It might be thought prudent that some mourners should avoid the procession itself through London and other major towns, but wish to show their respects at some point. The convention was they could do this by sending their empty carriage, but Adolphus is quite explicit about this: "Lord Hood's

this person, the two most likely are Baron Arden's wife Margaretta, Jane's sister, or Jane Carr herself.[223]   Both of these might be referred to as Lady Perceval, though it was not strictly true in either case.[224]   On the other hand, Adolphus, as a supporter of Queen Caroline, and, therefore almost by definition an opponent of George IV, might wish, and might be wise, to mislead.   The connections were certainly to Lady Carr rather than her sister.

In addition, Caroline's final days, and then the public furore that followed the events of her funeral, might be one explanation why Henry Carr's death on 18th August was not more widely reported. For example, the inquests on Francis and Honey were extensively covered in the papers before a verdict of manslaughter was passed against the Life Guards on 12th September, the fourteenth day of Honey's inquest. There certainly needs to be some explanation as to why the death of an equerry to the Duke of Kent, a mourner at George III's funeral, a war-hero and Knight, not to mention the second husband of an ex-Prime Minister's wife, went largely unreported.   Both the *Morning Chronicle* and *Courier* carried the same terse notice on 21st August 1821, reporting the death in Southampton on 18th August of "Sir Henry William Carr, KCB, Lieutenant-Colonel of the 3rd Regiment of Guards". Quite why he was in Southampton, and why his regiment should have been inflated, are unclear.   There are no further reports until the much later notice in the Annual Register for 1821, which in the Appendix to the Chronicle gives his date of death as 20th August.   In

---

private carriage and four ... [followed] ...A mourning coach and six ... apparently empty." He does not indicate that Lady Perceval's carriage was empty.

[223] Although she was the wife of Lord Redesdale rather than Lord Perceval, the *Morning Chronicle* described Frances as "Lady Viscountess Perceval" in its 1813 articles. It is not clear why, though it may have been derogatory or to link her to the Percevals. Alternatively, it is conceivable that the Adolphus reference might be to Isabella, the wife of the 3rd Earl of Egmont, though she was to die a month later aged 83. It might also refer to Spencer Perceval's oldest daughter Jane who had married her first cousin Edward Perceval, Baron Arden's son, five months earlier. She was aged 29 and was to die a little over two years later in January 1824. However, none of these would usually be known as "Lady Perceval".

[224] Spencer Perceval had rejected the customary opportunity to be knighted on becoming Prime Minister, while Margaretta would usually be described as Lady Arden. Jane Carr's title, however, was 'Lady'. In addition, the introduction to JS Mill's newspaper articles refers to the riots that were characteristic of the first fifteen years of his life from 1806 and specifically to the Nottingham riot "... in celebration of the assassination of **Lord** Perceval." [emphasis added] See Ann P. Robson and John M. Robson (eds.), 'The Collected Works of John Stuart Mill, Volume XXII - Newspaper Writings December 1822 - July 1831 Part I', London, Routledge and Kegan Paul, 1986.

particular, there is not the obituary in *The Times* or other papers that might be expected. There appears not to have been a Will (perhaps not surprising for someone who died at the early age of 43), but no other records of his death have yet been found either.[225]

He was buried six days after his death on the 24th August at St Dunstan's church, Feltham, though the precise location of his grave has yet to be discovered. This could not happen so rapidly today, nor is it clear how his coffin was transported back from Southampton so quickly. His widow Lady Jane Carr dedicated a memorial to Sir Henry Carr in St Dunstan's church. This is extremely elaborate and in exceptionally good condition given that it is nearly two hundred years old.[226] As *The Gentleman's Magazine* for June 1825 says, it is in "marble showing the colours of the 83rd Regiment thrown over a sarcophagus". The first part of the inscription has already been referred to above. It continues:

"...but worn, alas! by his honourable exertions, he descended prematurely to the grave ... deeply and sincerely lamented by his family and numerous friends".

This might be entirely innocent of course, and refer only to his war service, but it is at least open to other readings given the other uncertainties about his life:
- The question of why he was in Southampton at all is unclear, though if Jane was in Harwich two days before, he might be keen to distance himself from this. Carr's regiment, the 83rd Foot, had been posted to Ceylon in December 1820 so this does not provide an alternative explanation. Nor does the Hampshire Archives Service

---

[225] Carr's death pre-dated the first Births and Deaths Registration Act in 1836. Although Coroners had been established since 1194, it was this Act that gave them a clearly defined responsibility for investigating sudden deaths. Compulsory registration of deaths was only enforced in England and Wales after more stringent conditions were introduced in 1875 (according to the National Archives). www.coronersociety.org.uk/wfBriefHistory.aspx explains that the 1836 Act was "prompted by the public concern and panic caused by inaccurate 'parochial' recording of the actual numbers of deaths arising from epidemics such as cholera. "There was also growing concern that given the easy and uncontrolled access to numerous poisons, and inadequate medical investigation of the actual cause of death, many homicides were going undetected.
"... [after] the Coroners Act of 1887 ... coroners then became more concerned with determining the circumstances and the actual medical causes of sudden, violent and unnatural deaths" rather than their previous tax-gathering responsibilities.
[226] Like the neighbouring monument to Colston Carr it may have been restored in 1936, but there is no indication of this.

have any records that would suggest other connections with the county.

- Quite why Feltham should have been acceptable to Jane for his memorial is unclear given that it is some distance from Ealing where she lived and where Carr's father had been vicar since 1797. Ealing was the place in England with which Henry Carr had been most closely associated since 1814 (especially after he ceased to live at Arlington Street).

- Even if Colston Carr insisted on Feltham, perhaps because St Dunstan's was the site of the family grave, it is not clear why he should have done. He had not been the vicar there since 1777, had been aged only 37 himself when he left and at that point six of his ten children had still to be born.

A final question might be why an emancipated woman such as Jane chose to be referred to as Lady Carr for the remaining 23 years of her life - even in her Will and even when Spencer Perceval had been the father of her children and they had enjoyed a demonstrably happy marriage. She remained Lady Carr despite her son John taunting her with this title when angry with her in later years.[227] There are three possible conclusions:

- Carr's death had been honourable, if unexpected, and Jane wanted to honour his memory as a public demonstration of her feelings
- Jane liked the status that the title brought
- and, perhaps, that she was either trying not to draw attention to something, or possibly to cover it up.

An alternative and more pedestrian explanation, of course, would be that she was insufficiently emancipated to defy convention. However, if she was certain enough of herself to marry Spencer Perceval in the face of her father's opposition and then to contract a second marriage after his assassination, despite the repercussions for her children, it is unlikely that the views of society would be sufficient to deter her on their own. On the other hand, if she now found it more difficult to resist society etiquette than her family, this may be a potent indication of how her attitudes changed as she got older.

In advance of any definitive evidence, it should be apparent that an atmosphere of mystery and intrigue surrounds the latter years of

---

[227] Gault, 2008a, op cit, pp462-463

Henry Carr.[228] The difficulty with enigmas is that it is impossible to reach firm conclusions. Henry Carr is no exception.

After 1821

Much of Jane's story after 1821 will become apparent in the following chapters. She was 52 when she became a widow for the second time, but with four of her children aged eighteen or younger was not yet in a position to restrict her role to that of family matriarch. Tragedies were to strike again in 1824 and 1831, when her grief was that of a mother.

She continued to support a wide variety of good causes. For example, in January 1832 she contributed to the fund to reinstate churches and schools torn down by a Barbados hurricane.[229] In 1840 she made a donation to help re-build Hanwell Church and in 1841 to the fund for boatmen whose families had been flooded out of their homes at Brentford.[230]

While she was still able, Jane made the most of Brighton. On 21st December 1830 *The Times* reported that Lady Carr and Miss Perceval had paid their respects to "Their Majesties [William IV and his wife since 26th June 1830] by leaving [their] names at [the] Palace" on the 20th December at Brighton.[231] On 28th December Lady Carr had attended a royal dinner and then a state party the following week.[232] Another week later *Freeman's Journal* recorded that Lady Carr and various Misses Perceval had been at Brighton while the new royals were at the Pavilion.[233] By this stage Jane was in her sixties, and was enjoying the company of her grown-up daughters. The report is not specific, but it may be that as many as

---

[228] It might not be too far-fetched to suggest that the inscription at least hints at mental health problems as much as physical ones. It may be that he had become unhinged by the Duke of Kent's death, removing as it did his primary purpose in life, and/or that some of the Perceval children had never come to terms with their mother's re-marriage and continued to treat him with hostility. While there is no evidence of suicide as the cause of Carr's death, this was not unusual among prominent people at this time. The MP Samuel Whitbread took his own life in 1815, as did the diarist Samuel Romilly in 1818 and Lord Castlereagh in 1822. Suicide should have precluded burial in consecrated ground, but this would depend on the particular circumstances. As the Carr family grave was in Feltham, burial there might have been more straightforward than in Ealing.
[229] *The Times* 4th January 1832
[230] *The Times* 28th August 1840 and 22nd August 1841
[231] *The Times* 21st December 1830
[232] *The Times* 29th December 1830 and 6th January 1831
[233] *Freeman's Journal* 13th January 1831

five of them accompanied her on this occasion. On 28th April 1831 Lady Carr presented her daughter Isabella at the Queen's drawing room.[234]

When the first Census to include names was carried out ten years later in 1841, a seventy-year old Jane and her four unmarried daughters were living at Elm Grove along with three other people. These were her brother-in-law Sir John Trevelyan (1761-1846), who was also the father-in-law of her youngest son Ernest, one of Sir John's daughters, 40 year-old Emma, and her husband Alexander Wyndham who was retired on army half-pay. Sir John's age is not given in the Census but he would have been about 80. There were also twelve servants, eight women between the ages of 15 and 35, and four men aged 30 or younger. At this point then Elm Grove accommodated some of the extended family most closely related to Jane, but her eldest son Spencer's family were living elsewhere. This was soon to change.

In August 1843, in almost her last appearance in the papers, Jane's butler Mr Ambrose was tried at the Central Criminal Court, the Old Bailey.[235] Jane had dismissed him, possibly because she was winding down her occupancy at Elm Grove, but perhaps because she already had her suspicions about his honesty. He had not been with her long (for example, he was not among the servants at Elm Grove in the 1841 Census). As he left her service he tried to purloin a number of items including a silver sauceboat and three pounds of wax candles. He claimed to have been unaware that the sauceboat was in one of his boxes, but made no attempt to explain the candles. Weighing more than a bag of sugar they could hardly have gone unnoticed. His arguments proved unconvincing and he was convicted of theft.

Jane's death in Ealing on 26th January 1844 was mentioned by a number of newspapers[236] but only briefly, and although they referred to her marriage to Spencer Perceval, their large family and her childless marriage to Sir Henry Carr, her Will seems not to have been reported and she was not accorded a full obituary. A life lived in the public eye, and at a heady social pace, had ended quietly. She was buried alongside Spencer Perceval at St Luke's Church, Charlton.

---

[234] *The Times* 29th April 1831

[235] *John Bull* 28th August 1843

[236] For example: *Freeman's Journal* 31st January 1844, *Caledonian Mercury* 1st February 1844, *Leeds Mercury*, *Bristol Mercury* and *Preston Chronicle* all 3rd February 1844

3. PROMISE UNFULFILLED: JANE PERCEVAL (1791-1824)

Early life

The first of the Perceval children Jane was born fourteen months after her parents' marriage on 19th October 1791, and was little more than a year old when her sister Frances arrived on 27th November 1792. They were the only two to live at Bedford Row, with their younger brothers and sisters being born in either Lincoln's Inn Fields or Belsize House, before the family moved to Ealing when Jane was 17.

Gray makes few references to Jane in the years before her father's assassination when she was 20. The first is to the dressing-up doll that her father purchased for her, and her sisters Frances and Maria, for Christmas 1800, with their gift to him being carved ivory shells.[237] A second is to her coming out presentation at the queen's birthday reception when aged eighteen. She was accompanied by the seventeen year old Frances, but Maria had to be content with being told about it afterwards.[238] A third reference is to the quizzing that the three "inseparable and irrepressible" sisters subjected everybody to, family and visitors to 10 Downing Street alike.[239] In addition to their natural exuberance, this was their opportunity to catch up with the latest gossip, as well as keep informed of current events, especially as, unlike their brothers, they were not educated outside the home.

Jane led an active social life, often accompanying her mother to various events once she was 17 in October 1808. There are several such references by Frances and Maria in their letters to their brother Spencer. For example, Maria wrote in February 1809 "Last Friday Jane went to a ball ... Jane was at the Opera the other night ..."[240] and on 1st March that "Mama and Jane are gone to the

---

[237] Gray, op cit, p45

[238] Ibid, p432 Maria reported the events to her brother Spencer at Harrow. Frances and Maria referred to Spencer as "My dear Pessy" until by early 1811 they were addressing their letters to "My dear Spencer". He had become 15 in September 1810 and perhaps felt that his childhood nickname was no longer appropriate.

[239] Gray, op cit, p431

[240] British Library, Add. MSS 49191, f.5 This letter from Maria, not dated but written between 19th and 25th February, also says that "Jane is at work" while her Mama and sister Frances were out visiting. It does not specify what Jane was working at.

Ancients",[241] while two years later on 21st February 1811 Frances explained that she had not seen much of her father and that "Mama is out dining at the Duchess of Brunswick's with Jane [now aged 19]".[242]

While her immediate response to her father's murder can be easily surmised, it might also fall to her to comfort her mother and to console the other children as best she could. Although this would not lessen her grief, it might have mitigated it and certainly provided her with something to focus on as an alternative to the event itself. It would not be surprising if almost immediately she became a surrogate parent for the younger children, and increasingly the main confidante and sole companion for her mother - as well as the social partner that she appears to have been for some time.

She soon felt obliged to admonish her brother and remind him of his intentions:

"My dearest Spencer,

"... My principal reason for writing to you is to induce you to write home. I must say that I think it hardly appears kind that you have not yet done it. ... I dare say if I were in your place I should find the same reluctance in doing it but one must not always consult one's own feelings alone without regard to those of others. I do not require of you my dear Brother to write to me but to write to our dear Mother. I know that it is your most earnest wish to do everything to gratify her and though she has not mentioned it I am sure that nothing would please her more than hearing from you. Believe me nothing but my affection for you and a desire that you should always act in such a way as to be worthy of him whose loss we so sincerely lament would have induced me to give you this perhaps not pleasant hint. I am the more anxious that you should write as Many [sic] people have asked if you had and appeared surprised when answering in the negative. ..."[243]

---

[241] British Library, Add. MSS 49191, f.7

[242] British Library, Add. MSS 49191, f.11 This is the first letter Frances signs as "Frances Eleanor Perceval", explaining to Spencer that she has taken such a fancy to the name Eleanor that she has adopted it as her own.
Spencer was to call his second daughter Fanny (1824-1850) and his sixth Eleanor (1831-1879), possibly reflecting his attachment to this sister in both cases. His daughter Eleanor's middle name was Irving (see Chapter 4 below) and she was the first of his daughters to marry, becoming the third wife of Alexander Matheson in April 1860.

[243] British Library, Add. MSS 49191, f.41

It is not apparent from the records that Spencer responded to this pressure, but Jane continued to correspond with him. Two years later in July 1814 she wrote to him from Old Burlington Street, giving him enthusiastic news of the round of parties and balls that she, Frances and Maria were going to as part of the celebrations for the end of the Peninsular War.[244]

However, another shock was not long in coming and, ostensibly because of her mother's illness in bed with measles in Brighton, it fell to Jane to inform the nineteen year old Spencer of impending events (and possibly to speak to many of the other children too and try to re-assure them). In November 1814 she wrote to him at Trinity College, Cambridge where he had been for a year. Her letter is undated but headed "Do not read this unless you are alone".[245] This was not an overly melodramatic warning, and may have helped Spencer to anticipate the contents:

"I never in my life sat down to write a letter more reluctantly than at this present moment. I hate to be the bearer of unpleasant intelligence ... /

[p2] "... and nothing but illness would have prevented [Mama] writing to you herself to make a communication which she is very much afraid you should receive from any other quarter. The certainty of not being able to write for several days has induced her very reluctantly to desire me to enclose you the copy of a letter ... to Uncle Arden.[246] Oh Spencer I beg and beseech of you for her sake for your sake for all our sakes[247] and I think I am [qualified?] in adding for the sake of your father's memory however disagreeable the circumstances may be to you do not allow yourself to feel any anger and resentment against her or make the least alteration/

[p3] "in your conduct to her; I [doubt?] not that you have before now guessed that it is her intention to make a second marriage. I believe in my conscience that if you could see as I have seen Colonel Carr's misery and anxiety about Mama's illness you would

---

[244] British Library, Add. MSS 49191, f.70
[245] British Library, Add. MSS 49191, f.134
[246] This is the letter of 25th November 1814 referred to in Chapter 2 above (i.e., British Library, Add. MSS 49188, f.70).
[247] These extracts are given as written. Standards of punctuation varied enormously: Maria's letters are carefully punctuated, as well as very newsy and amusing; other letters at this time have virtually no punctuation.

think him sincere when he told you he marries her for herself alone.
... /

[p4] "... I am afraid you will think that I express myself too strongly
as to my sense of Colonel Carr['s] honourable conduct but I am
sure you will consider it as such when you are told all he has said,
how considerate he is about our feelings how anxious he has been
that the communication should be made to you as soon as possible
and that it should be done in the kindest and most attentive manner
..."

As soon as Lord Arden replied on 27th November, his niece
Jane wrote to Spencer enclosing their Uncle's letter.[248] Jane may
have sent her two letters to Spencer at the same time, but in any
case they closely followed each other and she was obviously doing
her utmost to keep him abreast of the position. If the situation was
alarming for the children at home, especially given their mother's
illness, Spencer must have felt even more excluded (while those
brothers away at school seem to have been kept in the dark for the
moment). Jane's letter on the 29th November was much briefer:

"My dearest Spencer,
"Mama is going on as well as possible. I have not yet heard when
she is likely to return to Ealing [from Brighton]. She has been rather
agitated today by the kindness of the enclosed note which she
received from Uncle Arden. I send it to you thinking you would like
to see it. Isabella [just short of her thirteenth birthday and who had
measles too] is so well she is impatient to get up. My sisters great
and small desires their love to you.
"I am/your most affectionate/Jane Perceval"

adding underneath "Mama begs you will take care of Uncle Arden's
letter".[249] In other words, "make sure that nobody else sees it" so
that only the immediate family was privy to the information for the
present, decorum was preserved and protocol observed.[250]
    Despite Jane's attempt to placate him, it is not surprising that
Spencer felt the need to leave Cambridge before the end of term
and assess the position at home for himself. While his mother's re-

---

[248] See Chapter 2 above for the letter (i.e., British Library, Add. MSS 49191, f.82)
[249] British Library, Add. MSS 49191, f.80
[250] Informing the other brothers at the same time might have made it much more
difficult to keep the information private.

marriage was to become public knowledge within a couple of weeks when the newspaper announcements appeared in mid-December, Spencer's friend Edward Gambier seems to have been aware before this. Although Gambier's letter refers to Spencer's "forbearance", it is noticeable that he addressed it to Spencer at his uncle Lord Arden's in St James Place, London. While Spencer may have realised that he had no option but to make the best of it, he seems to have decided that recovering his equilibrium might happen more rapidly if he spent some time away from Ealing.[251] Although some of their brothers were not so sanguine, Jane's and Spencer's acceptance was also an important part of re-assuring Frances and Maria that their life would continue as before. No doubt they all helped each other, conscious that their reaction would be vital to re-assure Isabella and the younger girls as well. For example, Spencer's teasing exchanges of letters with Frances the following September elicited her tongue-in-cheek response that "I never knew such an impertinent boy ...",[252] while Maria replied to two letters from him that December informing her of his friends at Cambridge. "Pray let us know how Townsend is going on and whether he is in immediate danger", she wrote to him in Hertford.[253] They had clearly returned to their interest in others outside the family.

After leaving Cambridge with an MA in 1816, Spencer embarked on a continental tour that took in Naples in June 1817, Corfu in November and December, and Italy again by February 1818. By contrast, his sister Jane was living at home in Ealing, twenty-six in October 1817 and still unmarried. Spencer was six weeks younger than their cousin Edward, Lord Arden's fourth son, who had been born on 30th July 1795 at Nork House.[254] Both boys had left Harrow in 1813 on their way to Cambridge University, but the parallels ended there. Whereas Spencer had been at Harrow from the ages of nine to eighteen (entering in 1804 with two of Edward's older brothers), Edward was fifteen before he entered.[255]

---

[251] Spencer may have come to consider the St James part of London a refuge, as it was in this area that he was living separately from his family in 1851 - perhaps as he pondered the option of becoming Catholic. See Chapter 4 below.
[252] British Library, Add. MSS 49191, f.86
[253] British Library, Add. MSS 49191, f.88
[254] Joseph Jackson & Frederick Crisp (eds.), 'Visitation of England and Wales', vol. 6, privately printed, 1898, p90
[255] 'Harrow School Register 1800 to 1911', 3rd edition, London, Longmans Green & Co., 1911, p51 The Ardens' first son (of six) had died as an infant on 11th February

He was already the veteran of schools in Lewisham and Cheyne Walk, Chelsea,[256] and he may have been sent to Harrow at this point not only to complete his schooling but primarily because his younger brothers Charles (1796-1858) and Arthur (1799-1853) were entering at the same time. Although these five Arden brothers were all born between 1793 and 1799, the first four annually in the years to 1796, Edward seems to have been bracketed with the younger ones,[257] possibly because he stood out as more academically gifted than his older brothers.   He was certainly on a faster track than Spencer, taking his MA at Sidney Sussex College in two years rather than the conventional three, and being admitted to the Inner Temple on 23rd November 1815.[258]   He is listed in Boyle's Court Guide for January 1816 as the Hon Edward Perceval in Chambers at 8 King's Bench Walk along with a solicitor, a conveyancer and a barrister.[259]   The next edition in 1818 shows him at the same address, but with the Chambers almost having doubled in size.[260] He is supposed to have become a Doctor of Laws (LL.D.),[261] possibly by this time or shortly after, but no corroborating evidence has been found to support this contention despite extensive research.   He was never called to the Bar and never practised as a barrister.[262]

1793. This was two months before the next son was born. See Gibbs, op cit, vol. I, p191.

[256] JA Venn, 'Cambridge University Alumni Cantabrigienses', Pt. II from 1752-1900, vol. V, Cambridge, Cambridge University Press, 1953, p90

[257] Both of whom were to become vicars, Arthur eventually as Queen Victoria's Chaplain. Frederic Boase, 'Modern English Biography', vol. II, Truro, Netherton & Worth, 1897, p1461 notes that Arthur committed suicide by "taking laudanum, verdict temporary insanity".

[258] Venn, op cit, p90

[259] 'Boyle's Court Guide', 1816, op cit, p329

[260] 'Boyle's Court Guide', 1818, op cit, p360. Neither edition lists him as living at St James Place with Lord Arden as might have been expected.

[261] Drummond, 'Histories of Noble British Families', vol. 2, London, William Pickering, 1846, pp14-15 Since Oxford University's equivalent was, and remains, a DCL, this suggests that he received it from Cambridge University. However, Nicholas Rogers the Sidney Sussex College archivist has no record of this (personal communication, 26th August 2009). His LL.D. is not listed in Venn, op cit, and Edward Perceval is not named in G. D. Squibb, 'Doctors' Commons: A History of the College of Advocates and Doctors of Law', Oxford, Clarendon Press, 1977 though Squibb does say that not all Cambridge University records were available to, and therefore included by, Venn.

[262] Celia Pilkington, Inner Temple Archivist, personal communication, 19th August 2009

A brief marriage

Jane and Edward would have known each other as cousins from an early age as the families were always close. Jane also enjoyed a separate rapport with the Ardens. For example, Maria refers in a letter to "Aunt Arden sends for Jane ..." on 11th June 1817, while other members of the family went elsewhere.[263] Edward and Jane became better acquainted once Edward was in London. Jane would not have been short of sisters eager to chaperone her, and Ealing may have provided Edward with a respite from central London and the law. They were married on 20th March 1821; she was 29 and he was 25. It was the local vicar, and Jane's step-grandfather, the eighty year-old Reverend Colston Carr who performed the ceremony. At least three papers (though not it appears the London ones) carried the announcement of their marriage. The first appeared in the *Derby Mercury* on 28th March 1821 and the same notice was repeated in the *Caledonian Mercury* and the *Liverpool Mercury* on the following two days:

"Tuesday, at Ealing, by the Rev. Mr Carr, the Hon Edward Perceval, second [surviving] son of Lord Arden, to Jane, eldest daughter of the late Right Hon Spencer Perceval".

They moved to Felpham on the south coast soon after.[264] Felpham is a small settlement[265] between Bognor Regis and Middleton-on-Sea and, while Chichester is the nearest large town, it is seven miles away - as is Arundel. Somewhat isolated, Felpham had an eighteenth century history of smuggling that was only brought to an end after the Coast Guard, as it was first known, was formed in 1822. At the start of the nineteenth century, however, it was beginning to establish other reputations for itself. It had been home to some well-known residents, including the poet William Hayley (1745-1820) from 1791 to 1820 and William Blake (1757-1827) more briefly from 1800 to 1803 when he undertook a commission for Hayley. In 1819 the Prince Regent visited from Brighton to see Dr Cyril Jackson (1746-1819), previously the Dean of Christ Church, Oxford, who had moved to the Old Rectory in the

---

[263] British Library, Add. MSS 49191, f.92
[264] As well as uncertainty about the date of their move, it is not clear why they chose this spot so far from London.
[265] It had a population of less than 600 at this time according to the Victoria County History of Sussex, vol. II, London, Dawsons, 1973, p217.

village and died there in August. Felpham attracted those who preferred to take their leisure more discreetly than would be possible in Worthing or Brighton to the east or Bognor close by to the west:

"In 1796 the Hon. Mrs Anne Seymour Damer, sister-in-law of the Duke of Richmond and a famous sculptress was advised to take a rest cure for 'some plague' and chose to stay at Felpham."[266]

In 1824 the Duke of Richmond himself bought a farmhouse in the centre of the village and 170 acres of land.[267]

Edward and Jane moved into a large house - possibly the Turret House that Hayley had built or the Old Rectory.[268] They were to be married for less than three years before Jane died in Felpham on 13th January 1824 at the very early age of 32. As had been the case with her step-father, death certificates and coroners' inquests into sudden deaths were still some time off being routine. Her death was reported tersely in two newspapers: first, curiously,[269] in *Jackson's Oxford Journal* for 17th January which simply stated "At Felpham, near Chichester, the Hon Mrs Edward Perceval", and then in the local paper as "Died, on Friday, at her residence, Felpham, Jane, the lady of Edward Perceval, Esq."[270] It might be assumed that she died in childbirth, or shortly afterwards, but at this time of year the cause of her death may have been more prosaic. If, despite his retinue, the 52 year-old Duke of Kent could succumb to a chill in Sidmouth at the same time of year in 1820, Jane may have been even more vulnerable. She left no Will, and was buried in the family vault at Charlton with a monument in Charlton Church. This reads:

---

[266] Tim & Ann Hudson (eds.), 'Felpham by the Sea: Aspects of History in a Sussex Parish', Bognor, Hudson, 1988, p37

[267] See Sheila Gould, 'Felpham Matters: The Growth of a Sussex Coastal Village from 1800-1914', Felpham, Gould, 1996

[268] It must have been a large house to accommodate all the furniture that Edward Perceval sold by auction on 26th May 1825, *Hampshire Telegraph and Sussex Chronicle*, 23rd May 1825.

[269] Her brothers Henry, Dudley and John all went to Oxford University, but none of them were there in 1824. The main Oxford to London Road ran through the parish of Hillingdon, but as far as is known Edward's move to this area took place after Jane's death, and they had no connections previously. The Wilberforces might provide another connection but Samuel Wilberforce (1805-1873) did not become the Bishop of Oxford until 1845.

[270] *Hampshire Telegraph and Sussex Chronicle*, 26th January 1824

"Here rests
in the blessed hope of everlasting life
Jane
wife of the Honourable Edward Perceval
daughter of the Right Honourable Spencer Perceval
Nata 25 Oct 1791   Nupta 20 March 1821   Obit 13 Jan 1824

"Gentle lady may thy grave
Peace and quiet ever have
After this thy travail sore
Sweet rest seize thee evermore.
Who to give the world increase
Shortened hast thy own life's lease."

According to this inscription, she was born later than other sources record but the other dates are the same. The conclusion of the verse supports the supposition that she died in childbirth, but there must be some doubt as to whether her "sore travail" refers to other events as well - possibly her father's assassination and maybe also, in the light of future events, a marriage that had proved problematic.

Deterioration and demise

After Jane's death Edward moved back to London. In June 1824 he leased a meadow and 89 acres of land near Uxbridge Common together with the mansion Hillingdon House. The mortgage was paid to the previous owner Richard Henry Cox,[271] the banker who had bought it in 1810[272] and was a major player in the land market both in this part of London and elsewhere. The overall bond Edward posted was for £30,000 (more than £1.25m today), and the mortgage for £15,000 at 5%. At £750 pa in interest payments alone

---

[271] "I admire that family of Cox's at Hillingdon ..." as Charles Greville (1794-1865) wrote in his 'Memoirs', (edited by Lytton Strachey and Roger Fulford), London, Macmillan, 1938, vol. III, p238. Cox's daughter Charlotte was married to Greville's brother Algernon (1798-1864).

[272] Until the start of the nineteenth century the house and lands had been owned by the Dowager Marchioness of Rockingham. Edward Perceval was the third subsequent owner. National Archives, ACC/0503/083 Hillingdon House still exists and was bought in 1915 "by the fledgling air force [from a Cox descendant]. In 1919 it became RAF Uxbridge." (Audrey Wormald, 'Hillingdon Church and Parish 1770-1999', May 2008, p30) As a listed building, it will survive the current (2009) plans to re-develop the base, but its future use has yet to be determined and it will not be possible to visit before 2012 at the earliest.

this equates to £31,500 today. On any reckoning these were huge sums and it is not immediately apparent where the money had come from, nor why a single man should seek such a large property or choose to encumber himself in this way. It might be thought that his behaviour was becoming increasingly erratic, and at the very least he was clearly marking his return to London while keeping it at a distance (as he had done previously in Felpham). It would not be near enough to central London for him to practise there as a lawyer.[273] Nevertheless, Edward retained Hillingdon House for the remainder of his life, with the property and land only being sold back to Cox in 1843.[274]

In 1826 to 1828 Edward was in Italy. Four sonnets have survived from this period, all with Italian titles, one of which appears to be a translation and two of which were sent from Florence and Genoa.[275] The first 'Riso di Bella Donna' ('The Smile of the Beautiful Woman') is dated August 1826, with a chorus based on

> "We say earth smiles, and thus express
> Our sense of nature's loveliness,
> Using the image of the smile
> That plays on beauty's lips the while."

The sonnets become increasingly personal, with the final one in January 1828 referring to a dream in which he expressed his continuing misery after Jane's death. It is not too far-fetched to

---

[273] Wormald, op cit, p4 says that large houses in Hillingdon "were attractive places to live because they were near enough to London to commute ... but also far enough away to be considered country houses". However, she points out on the previous page that it took about two hours to journey from Hillingdon to London. This might be feasible, but surely would soon pall as a daily commute. Hillingdon is twice as far from central London as Ealing, in much the same direction, and neither Soane nor Perceval tried to commute on a daily basis even from there. William Wilberforce (1759-1833) was known to the Percevals and lived nearby in Hillingdon at The Chestnuts from 1824 to 1826. His house can still be seen on Honeycroft Hill with a plaque marking Wilberforce's residence between these years. This would have been subsequent to his move back to London in 1823 and before his purchase of "Highwood Hill, a house with a small estate at Mill Hill in Middlesex ... in 1826." (DNB entry)
The Reverend Robert Hodgson who had married the Carrs in 1815 had also been vicar of Hillingdon since 1810. He retained this post for 30 years, accumulating others as Dean of first Chester and then Carlisle during this period.
[274] National Archives, ACC/0503/101-104
[275] British Library, Add. MSS 47140, ff.94-97

suppose that it is she who invites him to join her in heaven, a foretaste of things to come as he became increasingly unhinged:

> "Wafted aloft by Fancy (while I lay
> Wrap't in soft slumber) to the realms of Day
> Methought I came where that bright spirit blest
> From earth releas'd now takes her heavenly rest.
>
> "Beauteous as erst, in angel radiance drest
> She met me, in her hand my hand she prest,
> Then softly smiling thus 'to thee the way'
> 'Lies here to join me if astray'
>
> "'Thou goest not wilful, - what in this bright sphere'
> 'I taste of bliss thou mortal canst not know,'
> 'But doubt not, - it shall crown thy faith sincere.'
>
> "She ceas'd and loosed my hand. Ah! wherefore so?
> While those lov'd accents sounded on mine ear
> In heaven I should - I woke to earth and woe."

For the moment he continued to resist this enticement, attractive though he clearly found it.

He made a Will on 30th December 1837, adding two codicils in the following eight months. These raise several issues, foremost of which are:

- His private secretary was removed as a legatee by the first codicil on 27th March 1838. Given that this was only three months after making the Will, and it was thought sufficient for the codicil to be witnessed by a servant, it must be assumed that this secretary had died.
- The second codicil on 3rd September 1838 removed his "supposed God daughter" Frances (1824-1850) and the eight thousand pounds annuities he had intended to leave her were redistributed to her father Spencer (Edward's cousin and brother-in-law). As she was still alive, something else must have caused Edward to reconsider.
- The second clause of this codicil adds his cousin Frederick as another legatee. Frederick was disabled and was bequeathed a lump sum equivalent to £23,000 today.

- It is perhaps significant that the next clause refers to Edward's own invalidity for the first time. It might be thought that this had happened in the months since the Will was first written, but it may also refer back to his original legacy to a Taunton surgeon Thomas Hare. He appears to have spent some time at his father's residence in St James Place, though it is not clear whether this was convalescence or a longer period. As he left twice as much to Mrs Anne Wood, a housemaid who had looked after him at Lord Arden's, as he had to Hare, it may be that he spent a lengthy period there (and/or that the two incidents were unrelated). What does appear clear though was that he was much more conscious of his own frailty in September 1838 than he had been only a few months earlier.
- It is not clear why this compassion did not extend to his remaining brother Charles George, the rector of Calverton, Buckinghamshire. The latter is not mentioned in the Will at all, and it must be assumed that whatever had happened to estrange these brothers it proved a chasm too wide to be bridged (even as other relatives came into the picture).

Towards the end of 1839 Edward was forcibly[276] admitted to a lunatic asylum near Uxbridge.[277] He took his own life there in the most grisly fashion on 11th March 1840, aged 44. There were eight newspaper reports of his death in the next few days. Even the briefest highlighted the circumstances:

---

[276] Though John Thomas Perceval claimed that Edward chose to be confined (see Chapter 10 below).

[277] This was Denham Park, a private asylum opened a year earlier in 1838 to cater for seventeen paying patients. The Royal College of Physicians in Edinburgh have "a number of reports and brochures for asylums around the country. The wording of one private institution is carefully euphemistic: **Denham Park** is not titled an asylum, but an 'Institution for the social and temporary retirement of invalids', aiming for 'the restitution of the mental faculties of persons in the upper walks of life when temporarily disturbed by disease or other causes' whilst making sure that these persons did not feel 'excluded from the ordinary privileges of society', such as horse and carriage, private servants if desired, and 'every recreation and amusement'. The leaflet points out that many private madhouses retain patients for financial gain, but that this one is subject to a Committee of Management and inspection by its Vice-patrons, drawn from the nobility and politics." See 1994 report by Joy Pitman, Archivist, at www.rcpe.ac.uk/library/history/reprints/improving-insane.pdf

"The Honourable Edward Perceval, son of Lord Arden, killed himself on Wednesday night, by leaping from the top of a lunatic asylum near Uxbridge, where he had been confined."[278]

There were four much longer reports, the last of which drew attention to the assumed verdict of insanity that the now mandatory coroner's inquest was believed to have delivered:

"Melancholy Occurrence at Denham Park
- Suicide of the Hon. EDWARD PERCEVAL
- On the night of Wednesday last, a melancholy occurrence, which has plunged several noble families into a state of poignant distress and grief took place at Denham Park, Bucks, about two miles from Uxbridge, the newly-opened private asylum for lunatics ... Every endeavour has been made to keep the matter as secret as possible, but our informant, from the inquiries he has made in the neighbourhood, has obtained the following particulars, which we believe may be relied on.
- For the last five or six months the Hon Edward Perceval, one of the sons of Lord Arden, a gentleman about forty-five years of age, has been an inmate of the above establishment. On the night in question the unfortunate gentleman managed, during the temporary absence of his keeper from the room, which was at the top of the house, to reach the window, raise it up, and cast himself therefrom, a height of about forty feet. His fall was heard by the domestics of the establishment, who instantly ran out and raised him in almost a lifeless state, from the frightful injuries he had received, and conveyed him into the house where he expired shortly afterwards. Information of this melancholy occurrence was on Thursday forwarded to Mr William Charsley, of Beaconsfield, the coroner for the eastern division of Bucks, who immediately issued his warrant for ... an inquest on that day. The inquest was held in the establishment, and some idea of the secrecy observed can be formed from the villagers being unaware of the melancholy occurrence, until they were summoned on the jury, and then only the jurymen were aware of it. What the exact verdict returned was we have been unable to learn, but we suppose it to have been that of insanity. Friday morning, at an early hour, the remains of the

---

[278] *Leeds Mercury*, 21st March 1840

unfortunate gentleman were removed from Denham Park to London for interment."[279]

Quite apart from the horrific circumstances of Perceval's death, this would not be welcome publicity for a private asylum that had been open for less than two years. An atmosphere of secrecy might be expected. The reaction of his parents can only be imagined. These events took place about four months before his father's death (and eleven years before his mother's). Although his father was an old man of 83, it would not be surprising if Edward's suicide pushed him over the edge. Edward was the third of his six sons to die before him.

Church regulations preclude the burial of suicides in consecrated ground. It might be expected that the rules would extend to the absence of monuments in church as well. However, above Jane's monument in St Luke's Charlton is an accompanying memorial to Edward. The brass reads:

> "Sacred to the memory
> of the Honourable Edward Perceval
> fourth son of the Right Honourable
> Charles George Lord Arden
> who departed this life
> on the tenth of March 1810
> in the forty fifth year of his age."

It must be assumed that the incorrect date of death was deliberately intended to mislead.[280] All the other details are correct and cannot refer to anybody else. Edward was indeed the fourth son of this Lord Arden, and was aged 44 when he committed suicide. The brass marks his life while concealing the circumstances of his death.

---

[279] *The Era*, 22nd March 1840
[280] It was certainly 1840 rather than 1810 and the majority of newspapers reported it, perhaps erroneously, as occurring on Wednesday 11th March.

4. A BROAD CHURCH: SPENCER PERCEVAL junior (1795 - 1859)

In September 1859 builders in Britain went on strike for a reduction in hours to nine a day and were then locked out.[281] The fate of John Franklin's expedition to find the North-West Passage in the Arctic had been made known the same month when a search party at last discovered the cairn confirming Franklin's death twelve years before. Charles Darwin saw 'On the Origin of Species' published that year, while in February a forty-year old George Eliot brought out 'Adam Bede', her first full-length novel. On 21ˢᵗ September 1859, *The Times* noted the death "On Friday night, the 16ᵗʰ inst., after a few hours illness, having joined his family on Thursday, apparently in good health, Spencer Percival [sic], eldest son of the Right Hon. Spencer Percival". There was no obituary and the same sparse information was later repeated in the Annual Register published the following year.[282] Isambard Kingdom Brunel had died the day before, just as boilers exploded on the SS Great Eastern's maiden voyage, an explosion that would have sunk any smaller ship.[283] Other luminaries to die that year included the writers Leigh Hunt and Washington Irving, the naturalist and geographer Alexander von Humboldt (after whom the ocean current is named), the historian Lord Macaulay and the Austrian chancellor Prince Metternich.

Spencer Perceval junior had celebrated his sixty-fourth birthday on the 11ᵗʰ September, but he had not been expected to survive infancy, let alone live to this age. When he was just a few days old, his "parents were told that he would not survive ... suffering extreme

---

[281] Though, as James Walvin, 'Victorian Values', London, Andre Deutsch, 1987 points out on p16: "... even though the ten-hour day was established in 1847 [by the Ten-Hour Factory Act], not until 1878 was that norm extended to all factories and workshops." Also see Henry Pelling, 'A History of British Trade Unionism' (5ᵗʰ edition), London, Penguin, 1992, p42

[282] 'Annual Register for 1859', London, J & FH Rivington, 1860. This terse statement was perhaps deliberately cryptic and might suggest that Spencer died at Elm Grove in Ealing. However, he died of apoplexy (i.e., a stroke) in Weymouth, as Boase, op cit, p1462 makes clear on the basis of a report in the *Weymouth Journal*. This is confirmed by Venn, op cit, vol. V, p90 for whom the source is *The Gentleman's Magazine*. This gives the same information as in *The Times* report (1859, vol. II, December, pp653-654).

[283] After a refit the following month, the ship continued in service to 1888. Brunel was 53 years old when he died.

pain"[284] from a bowel disorder. His father composed a prayer that he and Jane said together, not so much in the hope that their son would live but pleading that he should endure less suffering. But, as his father wrote, "... by the blessing of God our boy was restored to us".

Like his father and uncle, Spencer was educated at Harrow and Trinity College, Cambridge. He entered Harrow in 1804 at the same time as two of Lord Arden's sons, his older cousins George (1794-1874) and John (1793-1818). George left Harrow within the year to join the Navy and was in the crew of the Orion at the battle of Trafalgar that October. He was 11 years old. He was to stay in the Navy for nearly sixty years, retiring as an Admiral in 1863, and had briefly been the MP for West Surrey before becoming the 3rd Baron Arden on his father's death in 1840. He then succeeded his cousin as the 6th Earl of Egmont in 1841 (see Figure 2). Nork passed to him in 1846 and he was the President of the Royal Agricultural Society in 1847. His elder brother John was at Harrow for five years, preceding Spencer to Trinity College, but died a month before his twenty-fifth birthday.

Thorne quotes Lord Teignmouth's assessment that, after his father's assassination, Spencer became "the spoiled child of the nation".[285] John Shore (1751-1834), first Baron Teignmouth from 3rd March 1798, was the founder and first president of the British and Foreign Bible Society from 1798. He was a member of the Evangelical Clapham sect and shared many of the religious beliefs, as well as the work ethic and financial acumen, of the older Perceval. For example, his DNB entry refers to "his hard work, detailed knowledge of revenue systems, financial probity, and sense of justice" as well as to a "widespread judgement that he was a man of 'integrity, humanity, and honour'".[286] As such his assessment of the younger Perceval ought to have been informed and was certainly pertinent. However, there is some indication that his negative view should be attached to the country rather than necessarily to Spencer himself. It is the case that after leaving Harrow Spencer was showered with financial and educational compensation, and that his time at Cambridge was much less successful academically than his father's, but he would not be the

---

[284] Kenneth Bryant, 'The Spencer Perceval Memorial Church of All Saints, Ealing Common', Leominster, Orphans Press, 2005, p3
[285] Thorne, op cit, vol. IV, p764
[286] The latter points were made by J. Stephen in his article 'The Clapham sect', *Edinburgh Review*, 80 (1844), pp251–307

first young man (nor the last) who neglected his studies in favour of other attractions.[287] In addition to the £1000 annuity that Parliament had agreed (the equivalent of £34,000 in 2009), he received free legal training at Lincoln's Inn and was appointed a teller of the Exchequer in February 1813. This sinecure was worth £2,700 per annum (£92,000 today).[288] By the age of 18, therefore, he would have had no money worries, whatever his other concerns. As if to demonstrate his financial independence, as well as indicate where his priorities lay, Spencer was one of Lord Broughton's three friends who made a hunting excursion into Dalmatia in early October 1813[289] - even though he was due to start at Cambridge University. In November 1814 Lord Broughton visited Cambridge University and heard a debate at Trinity College in which Spencer spoke on the death of Charles I.[290]

The parliamentary years

1818-1820: Government placeman or radical re-alignment?

The custom of the grand tour had been revived after the defeat of France and the popularity of Byron's exploits, and Perceval travelled in Greece and Italy before he then followed his father into parliament as a 22 year old. Sir Edward "O'Brien and William [Vesey] Fitzgerald formed a coalition that took both [Clare] county seats and enabled Fitzgerald to return [Spencer as] a government nominee for Ennis"[291] on 26th June 1818. Spencer was still only 23 when he made his maiden speech as an MP in the House of Commons the following March. This was on the government's motion to economise by reducing from six to four the number of

---

[287] It was also at this time that his mother's re-marriage took place, with the attendant anxiety and consternation that it caused her children.
[288] Wade, op cit, p70 The post, one of four, was abolished in 1834 as a result of the Exchequer Receipt Act that modernised and rationalised the arrangements for dealing with the national accounts. Spencer's Exchequer return of the Teller's establishment dated 9th October 1834 includes his brother Dudley Montague as the Deputy Teller and First Clerk at a salary of £1000 pa. (British Library, Add. MSS 40409, f.130). It states that Dudley had been "Above six years at the Exchequer and nearly three years at the Cape of Good Hope".
[289] John Cam Hobhouse, (Lord) Broughton, 'Recollections of a Long Life', London, John Murray, 1909, vol. I, p56
[290] Ibid, p168
[291] Thorne, op cit, vol. II, p634 Ennis had a population of 6700 but 13 voters.

equerries attending an ailing George III at Windsor. Despite being a "government nominee", Spencer spoke against the proposal.

"But how would the country feel," he asked, "when they were told, that this [miniscule] saving was purchased at the expense of ingratitude and disrespect to the Crown - of cold and unkind treatment to the sovereign?" He continued, "... he would persuade them ... to resist the indecent conduct of those who would impair the dignity of the sovereign".[292]

The Leader of the House Lord Castlereagh, the promoter of the Bill, spoke next:

"Though they did not convince him, he had listened with the most pleasing attention to the arguments of the last speaker, and had witnessed with the utmost satisfaction the same enthusiasm of feeling exhibited by the son in defence of our revered monarch, as had formerly been displayed, so nobly and ably, by the father."[293]

Perceval's position in this instance might be put down to his allegiance to the monarchy exceeding that to his party, though it was still an exceptional attitude to express in a maiden speech. He was even more forthright in his opposition to the Seditious Meetings Prevention Bill on 6th December 1819, saying

"... he was fully convinced that the bill would be attended with the most evil consequences; that it would have an immediate and injurious tendency, and on this account he was called upon to oppose those with whom he generally acted".

After invoking Burke, he concluded that

"The people of England had too much understanding to be thus imposed upon by **those who affected to deprive them of their rights** [emphasis added], under the pretence that they would be injurious".[294]

---

[292] Hansard Parliamentary Debates, vol. 39, 16th March 1819, columns 1021-1023
[293] Ibid It should be noted that William Lamb (1779-1848), who was to be Prime Minister as Lord Melbourne from 1834 to 1841, also praised Perceval's speech from the Whig benches opposite "... he had listened with as much pleasure ..."
[294] Hansard Parliamentary Debates, vol. 41, 6th December 1819, columns 798-800

This was a principled as well as courageous stand, given that the Peterloo massacre had taken place the month before and this was one of the Six Acts with which the government had responded in order to clamp down on any further challenges to their authority. Some saw his attitude as foolhardy and it certainly provoked the government to react. He was replaced as the government's candidate in Ennis in the March 1820 general election,[295] and Croker noted that "his late unsteady conduct is not forgotten" when he unsuccessfully recommended him as an under-secretary at the Home Office in May 1821.[296]

Once again Spencer's speech was praised from "the other side of the House", this time by William Wilberforce, another Evangelical and member of the Clapham sect. A cynic might say that Perceval was doing the Whigs' work for them, naively undermining his fellow Tories. An optimist might say that he should have been on the Whig benches. Regardless of this, he was obviously not prepared to let his values be traduced by the immediate demands of party politics. Such considerations were of secondary importance. Whereas his father's lack of overt ambition and unassuming approach had not prevented his ascent to high office, Spencer lacked even his circumspection - as well as his legal, financial and, ultimately, political skills. (Although the shared views and support of George III had been critical to the older Perceval in 1809, it might be argued that his ability to win over the Prince Regent subsequently proved even more so.) At the end of the debate Spencer voted in the minority (153 versus 328, a government majority of 175) to limit the Bill to three years, though he had said in his speech that five years would forcibly demonstrate to the country how absurd and inappropriate the restrictions were. When the Seditious Meetings Prevention Bill reached the House of Lords, the 3rd Earl of Egmont also voted against it (as he did against the Press Restriction Bill), while Lord Arden voted along with Lord Liverpool, the Earl of Harrowby and the rest of the government side in support of it.[297]

---

[295] By Sir Ross Mahon who resigned three months later on 29th June to be replaced by Richard Wellesley who remained the MP for six years to 16th June 1826.

[296] Croker Papers cited by Thorne, op cit, vol. IV, p764 Perceval later held this post briefly from April to July 1827 in the short-lived Canning government when William Sturges Bourne (1769-1845), a lifelong Canningite, finally agreed to be a stopgap Home Secretary. Also, John Sainty, 'Home Office Officials 1782-1870', London, IHR/Athlone Press, 1975, p57

[297] Wade, op cit, p401 and p406

Spencer would not become an MP again until 25th May 1827 when his seat was Newport in the Isle of Wight. This was the constituency which George Canning (1770-1827) had represented since the general election the previous year after being MP for Liverpool for fourteen years. On becoming Prime Minister on 12th April 1827 Canning had to stand in a by-election, choosing Seaford in the Cinque Ports and relinquishing his seat in Newport. Canning died in August that year, but his distinctive brand of Toryism was to prove significant in Perceval's political rehabilitation. He too was not afraid to say what he believed, regardless of the consequences, and had also been a supporter of Queen Caroline, not least at the time of the "Delicate Investigation" undertaken by Spencer's father in 1806. Canning had offered to resign when Caroline returned to England in June 1820, and did so in December 1820 after the conclusion of her trial by the House of Lords, a trial that he found repugnant. Spencer had ceased to be an MP from March 1820, but Caroline's trial was the social spectacle in London that autumn and he was not unusual in attending it. Charles Greville (1794-1865) wrote in his Memoirs:[298]

"Oct 8th ... The town is still in an uproar about the trial, and nobody has any doubt that it will finish by the Bill [of Pains and Penalties] being thrown out and the Ministers turned out ..."

"Oct 15th ... Since I came to town I have been to the trial every day. I have occupied a place close to [Lord] Brougham, which, besides the advantage it affords of enabling me to hear extremely well everything that passes, gives me the pleasure of talking to him and the other counsel ..."

Greville was standing in this position when he heard Spencer Perceval suggesting to Brougham that referring to the ethereal shape in Milton's 'Paradise Lost' which "The likeness of a kingly crown had on"[299] might be one way of persuading Caroline's accuser to admit under examination that he was acting as agent for

---

[298] 'The Greville memoirs', 1814–1860, ed. L. Strachey and R. Fulford, 8 vols. (1938), cited by EA Smith, op cit, pp118-119

[299] John Milton, 'Paradise Lost', Book II, 673 Lines 666-673 refer to Milton's description of Death about to menace Satan. This is an interesting allusion given Perceval's later support for traditional conservative values and the existing constitution. It may be that in this instance he felt more sympathy for Caroline than the wayward and lecherous George IV.

the King. George IV was literally trying to keep his head down, but was clearly the principal and prime mover in the case.

The intervening seven years before Spencer was next an MP were largely taken up with personal and spiritual matters. While he had been a volunteer with the London and Westminster Light Horse,[300] this was for one year only in 1819. His father had served with them for nine years from 1794 to 1803, but the younger Spencer found their restraints too restrictive and the regimented approach did not have the compensations of religious fervour. The regular army did not attract him at all, as it did two of his brothers, John and Ernest.

1827-1831: Casting off the shackle?

Spencer did not speak in Parliament in 1827 on his return and only made one intervention in the first months of 1828 when he aligned himself with Peel on Lord John Russell's motion on the repeal of the Test and Corporation Acts.[301] Rather than require the House of Commons to vote on temporarily suspending the Acts, they suggested that discussion should be postponed until a time when repeal could be properly considered. In 1828 he had been appointed Clerk to the Ordnance, and this ensured that he would speak more frequently in following years as he presented Ordnance budgets and responded to the detailed line-by-line scrutiny of them in committee. Some of the questioning can only be described as pettifogging, but that is no doubt the proper role of such committees. It was ironic that one of the main scrutineers should be Joseph Hume (1777-1855), an MP in five constituencies including Middlesex from 1830-1837, whose first seat in Weymouth in 1812 had been arranged by the older Perceval and who had subsequently become friendly with the Duke of Kent.[302]

---

[300] Thorne, op cit, vol. IV, p764

[301] Hansard Parliamentary Debates, vol. 18, 28th February 1828, columns 828-829

[302] Part of Thorne's description of him (op cit, vol. IV, pp262-265) is worth repeating:

"When he re-entered the House in 1818 it was as an aggressively independent radical, with a political philosophy based on the ideas of Bentham and Mill and a working relationship with Francis Place ...

"Yet he was impervious to ridicule and, with his immense physical energy and stubborn perseverance, established himself during his long career as the foremost parliamentary champion of retrenchment and economy - a prominent figure in radical politics."

From April 1828 and into 1829, with Wellington as Tory Prime Minister, Catholic emancipation was the major issue facing Parliament. This was bound to be of huge significance to a Perceval, let alone the country. Then in 1830 Wellington was defeated on what was effectively a vote of no confidence on the government's proposed Civil List for William IV, the new King. This was the pretext, substantive evidence that political reform had become the critical issue facing the House of Commons, and that Wellington and the Tories could not be relied on to see it through. It would require the Whigs to lead it. Indeed, Wellington had amply demonstrated this himself when he had recently said "that he did not believe that the state of the representation could be improved".[303] This was a similar argument to that Perceval was to adopt in a later debate on 9th March 1831.

On Thursday 8th May 1828 Sir Francis Burdett proposed that a Committee should examine the laws affecting Roman Catholics with the aim of reaching "a final and conciliatory adjustment". In his view it was long since time to extend Catholic emancipation to representation in Parliament and to full civil rights, thus addressing Roman Catholic claims and removing all remaining disabilities. The debate continued through the evening until it was adjourned at 1a.m. on the Friday morning. Another full day of debate on the Friday was then adjourned to the following Monday, with Parliament eventually voting at 3.30a.m. on Tuesday 13th May. The issue had a long and passionate history and this was reflected in the predictably narrow outcome - a majority of 6 for Burdett's motion, with 272 for it and 266 against. Perhaps surprisingly, Spencer Perceval was in the majority supporting Burdett's motion.

Wendy Hinde (as well as writing biographies of George Canning and Castlereagh) has focussed exclusively on the events of 1828 and 1829.[304] The sub-title of her book, 'A shake to men's minds', demonstrates the strength of feeling that Catholic emancipation aroused. It had been the main domestic political issue for some time, a long-lasting and running sore. Thirty years earlier it had proved a dilemma for William Pitt as he contemplated France's designs on Britain through the back door of Ireland, the necessity for Union and the King's entrenched opposition to emancipation. For Thomas Pakenham:

---

[303] Briggs, 2000, op cit, p203
[304] Wendy Hinde, 'Catholic Emancipation: A Shake to Men's Minds', Oxford, Blackwell, 1992

"... the King's objections to giving Catholics the same political rights as Protestants was not mere bigotry. It was centred on a strange belief, shared by many of Pitt's cabinet, that this political concession would undermine the Established Church and so, indirectly, the safety of the State. This view ignored the fact that there was no Church Establishment in Scotland or Canada and neither had suffered political disaster. Pitt's own view, that of liberals in both political parties and in both countries, was that the Union of the two Parliaments would remove the last rational obstacle to full emancipation. The Catholic majority in Ireland could not abuse their political power in a United Parliament where the overall majority would be Protestant. Pitt had not, however, decided whether it was expedient to combine the two measures, or postpone emancipation till that dangerous anachronism, the Irish Parliament, had been safely merged with Westminster."[305]

In the end, at least in part in deference to George III's views, Catholic emancipation was excluded from the Union in 1801. When Pitt tried to introduce the Catholic Emancipation Bill subsequently, the King vetoed it and Pitt resigned.[306]

This question of the influence and authority of the Catholic Church, and whether it was thought to be for good or ill, was not just an issue for people in the nineteenth century. That it could produce effects that were far from benign is invoked by Tom Garvin as one of the explanations why Ireland remained under-developed (and largely undeveloped) and impoverished until the last quarter of the twentieth century.[307]

The three day debate in 1828 covers over 300 columns of Hansard. Spencer Perceval's speech on the first day accounts for five of them.[308] This is remarkable in a number of respects, not least because it summarises and dismisses many of the anxieties and concerns that the Catholic Church gave rise to. It also contains

---

[305] Thomas Pakenham, 'The Year of Liberty: The Story of the Great Irish Rebellion of 1798', London, Abacus, 2004, p242

[306] Gault, 2009a, op cit, pp34-35

[307] Tom Garvin, 'Preventing the Future: Why Was Ireland So Poor For So Long?', Dublin, Gill & Macmillan, 2005. In Garvin's analysis it was in the Church's interest to maintain an economy built on the pillars of small rural communities, primarily engaged in agriculture and comprising large families rather than to promote or permit a better educated, urban one. This concentrated and secured the power of the priesthood, and found expression in the politics of Eamon de Valera and Fianna Fail with which it accorded.

[308] Hansard Parliamentary Debates, vol. 19, 8th May 1828, columns 432-436

a most startling analogy. It shows that, however he was to be characterised by the time he finally left Parliament in 1832, the younger Perceval was very much his own man, foolhardy or fearless according to your view, but at this stage informed always by a closely argued logic that he had thought through. For these reasons his speech is treated in some detail.

First he drew attention to the fact that his views differed from those of his father:

"Mr Perceval said, that in rising to support the motion ... he felt himself bound, in duty to himself and to the House, to state the reasons which induced him to do so. The opinions which had been entertained on this subject by his lamented father were well known, and if he did not feel a reverence for that father's opinions, he should not only not be worthy of a seat in that House, but he should not be worthy to hold his head up in society. It might be well supposed, that the sentiments of his lamented parent had had a great influence in the formation of his opinions; indeed, from his habits and education, he was naturally biassed [sic] against the question ... But when he came to reflect upon the subject, he began to waver, and when he first had the honour of a seat in that House [i.e., ten years earlier], his mind had already been pretty nearly convinced that the fears and alarms which were excited upon the subject were not the offspring of sound wisdom, and had not any foundation in fact."

Secondly, he did not agree with Francis Burdett "that those who resisted [the motion] were chargeable with bigoted and intolerant motives". Rather

"This great question had been for years the chief, if not the only land-mark of those divisions which separated the two great parties in the state, and their respective leaders at least might be said to stand upon one common principle ... All of them [the proponents of the measure, including Grattan and Grenville] admitted that if ... the success of the question would endanger the Protestant establishment, they would not support it. [While opponents would support it if the concessions] might be granted with safety to the Protestant established church."

In Perceval's view, therefore:

"There was no difference ... of principle between the opponents and the advocates of this question; but there was a difference of judgment as to the future effect of an untried law." [emphasis added]

This was not to change his opinion that the Roman Catholic religion was "a foul pollution of the word of God". On the contrary, "she was controlled, mitigated and subdued by all that had taken place around her", particularly the vigilance of the Protestant faith.

"Notwithstanding the abominations and the enormities of the Roman Catholic church ... by the vigilance of the Protestant mind, and by the pressure of Protestant principles, it had been reduced to a state of comparative harmlessness."

This was not the time for that vigilance to be relaxed, therefore, but Perceval was certain that "there was no chance" of this probability arising. The analogy to his mind was

"If the sun by its rising did not alter the nature of the tiger, it drove him to his den, and mitigated that ferocity which it did not change." [emphasis added]

This is not only a very powerful, effective and indeed memorable metaphor, by extension it also provides clues to the ways in which Perceval viewed the two faiths at this time. One provided the world with light; the other was a wild beast that, while it might not be tamed, could at least be kept under control. In practice and, in Perceval's view appropriately, the two could and should co-exist. There could be little doubt for him about the predominance of the Protestant religion though:

"... how else ... to account for the fact, that while political storms had been harassing the rest of Europe - while every popish capital had been visited by calamity - while almost every popish royal family had by turns been banished from the land of their ancestors - England alone had been able to ride on her course secure and triumphant? As long as this Union continued, her greatness will continue; and he would rather drop down dead in his place at that moment than aid in dissolving such a Union. If the Protestant religion of England was now worth five years purchase, we could admit the Catholics with perfect safety. **There could be no danger**

with them, but there might be danger without them. The Protestant religion was the true religion, and no danger could accrue to it from the admission of Catholics to parliament."
[emphasis added]

To his mind if Parliament did not survive the entry of Catholics, it could only be because it was "rotten at heart". He deplored the "miseries and misfortunes of unhappy Ireland" that was "under the dominion of the priests", but he doubted that the system would be replicated given that it "produced such consequences". In conclusion, if Catholics in Parliament turned out to "weaken or endanger the religion or constitution of this empire", in other words if Perceval had "adopted a wrong course on this occasion, he could only ... say that he could not help it."

Perceval's position remained the same ten months later when he voted in the majority for the Catholic Relief Bill on 30th March 1829. In this instance the vote was more clear-cut: 320 for the Bill and only 142 against, a majority of 178.[309] Perceval even went so far as to support, though only grudgingly, an increased grant for the Maynooth seminary when this was considered as part of the Irish Education estimates on 22nd May 1829. He disapproved

"... of a vote to increase the power of the Catholic priesthood, and declared his determination never to give it his assent hereafter; although under the peculiar circumstances, he should on this occasion support the government."[310]

---

[309] Hansard Parliamentary Debates, vol. 20 - where virtually the whole volume from 6th February to 30th March 1829 is concerned with Catholic issues.

[310] Hansard Parliamentary Debates, vol. 21, 22nd May 1829, column 1555. The grant was to increase in 1829 to £8928 (over £440,000 in 2009). In April and May 1808 the Portland government had seen its majority reduced because Perceval's father had refused to agree any increase in funding.

An informative perspective on the setting up of Maynooth is provided by the Irish Professor of Politics at University College, Dublin. In Garvin's view (op cit, p164): "...British government money financed Maynooth regularly [after its inception in 1795], **the purpose being to use Catholic priests to ensure that Irish young men and women were shielded from the anti-Catholic and insurrectionist politics of the French revolution**. [emphasis added] A curious loveless alliance existed, in effect, between the Protestant British state in Ireland and the newly re-organised English-speaking Irish Catholic Church. London and Maynooth were united by a common terror of revolution, if by little else."

He was much less predictable than his father, therefore, or at least not as predictable in the same ways where Catholics were concerned.

He spoke once more in Parliament on the potential "inclosure" of Hampstead Heath on 19th June 1829, but was no doubt as relieved as other MPs that the House of Commons was then in recess from 24th June 1829 to 4th February 1830. This was a month longer than in the preceding year, but by no means unusual and certainly not unprecedented.[311] Ordnance estimates and their detailed scrutiny by committee occupied him from late March to early June 1830. After the death of George IV on 26th June, Parliament was dissolved on 23rd July and a general election held with the accession of William IV. Parliament re-convened on 26th October, with the new monarch's Civil List the first item on the agenda. Perceval was still MP for Newport (as he was to remain until the 1831 election, along with Horace Twiss) and voted in the minority (204 versus 233) against Parnell's motion on a committee to examine the Civil List. Wellington resigned on 15th November 1830 and Grey (1764-1845) formed a coalition government led by the Whigs. Perceval ceased to be Clerk to the Ordnance in December 1830.

By the time Lord John Russell's Bill to reform representation was debated in March 1831, Perceval seems to have reverted to type:

"He had pledged himself some days ago to offer his most decided opposition to the Bill, and to that resolution he adhered."[312]

Although many of the arguments are the same as, or similar to, those he had put forward in previous speeches, they are now expressed in a much more vehement and forthright, even extreme, fashion. This may have been partly because the issue of reform struck at some of the beliefs that Perceval held most dear, such as "the moment it passed a death-blow would be inflicted on the Monarchy", but it may also have been due to his increasing involvement in the Irvingite church.[313] He was also under pressure

---

[311] See Thorne, op cit, vol. 1, p388, though July to January was a more usual period for the recess.

[312] Hansard Parliamentary Debates, vol. III (new series 3), 9th March 1831, columns 256-268

[313] Some of his "speech" on 9th March 1831 reads more as a rant against the twin dangers of revolution and the overweening influence and threats of the press.

for a variety of reasons. His younger brother John had been admitted to a lunatic asylum in January 1831 (see Chapter 10 below) and it was Spencer who had brought him back from Dublin to Bristol. John had sought out the Irvingite church towards the end of 1830 as his sanity deteriorated.

Spencer reiterated that even in his first speeches in Parliament in 1819 he had been determined to "discharge his duty honestly and conscientiously", regardless of whether it was the rights of the people or the Crown that was at stake. Just as he had not betrayed these principles to toe the party line, so he would not be swayed by the threats of the press to expose MPs who voted against reform. The Constitution had withstood the tests of time in his view, and even the existence of rotten boroughs demonstrated its overall strengths. Mary-la-bonne (Marylebone) was an example of an area that was unrepresented, but this had not prevented its inhabitants from being well-off. He gave the example of a surgeon perplexed by an image upside down at the back of the eye. Understanding would not be enhanced by removing the eye; the system worked regardless of whether it was understood. The surgeon's knife, like reform, would destroy it. Nor did Perceval consider the proposals "gentle and gradual" as (Lord Bacon had suggested) they should be. In conclusion

"... he was humbly thankful that God had permitted him to do so much. He had done his duty and was satisfied."

As the atmosphere hotted up, on 21st March 1831 *The Times* was accused of a breach of privilege in its article on borough-mongering. On 22nd March Perceval was in the minority (312 versus 311, 168 of the latter representing closed boroughs such as Newport) on the second reading vote. Parliament was prorogued on 22nd April and a general election on the merits of reform followed.

1831-1832: The irony of Tiverton?

When Parliament returned on 14th June 1831 Perceval had been ousted from Newport, as had Horace Twiss who had expressed even more negative views of the reform proposals and was no

---

Compared to his 1828 speech considered on the preceding pages, he appeared to have "lost the plot". Spencer had been appointed as a Metropolitan Lunacy Commissioner from 1830 and it may be that this extra task had some impact too.

longer an MP at all. Perceval now represented the rotten and family-controlled borough of Tiverton.[314] Dudley Ryder (1762-1847), the 1st Earl of Harrowby, had been MP there from 1784 to 1803, as had his father Nathaniel (1735-1803) for twenty years from 1756 to 1776 and Dudley's brother Richard (1766-1832) from 1795 until he retired in 1830. Between them these three represented Tiverton for a total of 74 years, with at least one of them being MP for the borough almost continuously from 1756.[315] In 1831 another Dudley Ryder (1798-1882), Viscount Sandon, the future 2nd Earl of Harrowby, who had been MP there since 1819, chose not to stand,[316] but his brother Granville (1799-1879) maintained the family tradition as an MP from 1830 to 1832.

It would be seven months before Perceval spoke in the new Parliament. On 17th January 1832 the House of Commons was trying to deal with the enormity of the grave-robbing crimes of Burke and Hare, and to ensure that Schools of Anatomy were properly regulated in future. Perceval proposed that there should be a two-year moratorium before the possession and dissection of human bodies was again permitted. Parliament recognised that medical understanding could not be halted in this way and ignored the suggestion.[317] On 26th January Perceval called for a general fast in

---

[314] Palmerston (1784-1865) was later to be a Tiverton MP from 1835 to 1865, as he had previously been for Newport from 1807 to 1811. In this sense, therefore, he both preceded and succeeded Perceval. A twenty-five year old Palmerston had been offered the Treasury by Perceval's father in October 1809, but came into his Cabinet as Secretary of War instead.

[315] Prior to the 1832 Reform Act, Devon had elected 26 Members of Parliament, with 24 voters in Tiverton returning two MPs. The population was 6500 in 1801, and 9800 by 1831, yet it was not until the 1884 Franchise Act that Tiverton's representation was reduced to one MP in common with most other constituencies. There were then a total of 11 MPs in Devon.

[316] According to his DNB entry, "In 1827 Sandon was appointed a Lord of the Admiralty in Lord Liverpool's administration, but resigned next year, believing that the Duke of Wellington, who then became premier, would oppose Catholic emancipation. Though a Conservative, he held, like his father, many liberal opinions. He voted for the inquiry into the civil list which overturned the Wellington administration (1830). But on 18 December in the same year he again accepted office, as secretary to the India board. He voted for the Reform Bill on 20 April 1831, but resigned as secretary to the board a few days later. **Despite this resignation, his reforming position was unacceptable to his constituents and he did not stand for Tiverton in 1831, but was returned instead for Liverpool at a by-election in October 1831** and again at the general election of 1832, being supported there by the Gladstone family and the West India interest. **He thus moved from a backwater into the mainstream of commercial politics.**" [emphasis added]

[317] Hansard Parliamentary Debates, vol. IX, column 580

response to the outbreak of cholera sweeping the country. In Perceval's view cholera was God's judgement on human folly, but he was forced to withdraw the motion after other MPs became increasingly irritated by his over-pious and excessively religious speech. Diplomatically, Lord Althorp (1782-1845) said that Perceval's good intentions did not justify the motion.[318] The outbreak continued, however, and Perceval did not let the issue drop. On 31st January he accused *The Times* of breach of privilege by reporting his speech the week before, even though he had specifically asked that strangers be excluded from the debate. His bete noire Joseph Hume eventually admitted "himself the agent through whom the public had been informed of what had passed ..." Hume escaped sanction when Perceval withdrew the motion, concluding with a side-sweep at Daniel O'Connell (1775-1847), who had been particularly irritated by Perceval's over-zealous and "holier than thou" approach:

"[the] honourable and learned member for Kerry, who has expressed himself in his well-known tongue of sneer and irony ... I claim no peculiar mission to speak to the House on any subject, but I do claim the common right of a member of this House to speak on any subject that has reference to matters of common interest to the general well-being of this country."[319]

Although Perceval had supported Catholic emancipation, the subordinate position he had accorded the Catholic religion might be expected to jar with O'Connell's desire for equality, an essentially secular approach, irrespective of what the latter may have thought of the "saintly Spencer". Nevertheless, the fast day did take place on 21st March that year, with the Annual Register reporting the disturbance that resulted as a crowd of 25,000 took exception to what they saw as a pointless and misleading exercise.[320] In their view cholera was man's doing, rather than God's, even if it would be some time before the mechanisms of disease were properly

---

[318] Hansard Parliamentary Debates, vol. IX, columns 895-903 This was John Charles Spencer, the future 3rd Earl Spencer from 1834, whose father the 2nd Earl shared 27 St James' Place with Lord Arden in 1818 according to Boyle's Court Guide (see Chapter 1 above). He was a Whig MP for Northamptonshire, Chancellor of the Exchequer and Leader of the House of Commons. His DNB entry says "He [was known as] 'Honest Jack' because of his disarming truthfulness and the essential Englishness of his character."
[319] Hansard Parliamentary Debates, vol. IX, columns 1030-1048
[320] 'Annual Register for 1832', London, JG & F Rivington, 1833, p40 of Chronicle

understood, 1842 before Edwin Chadwick (1800-1890) produced his report and 1866 before the Sanitary Act became law.[321] It would be even longer before sanitary conditions began to improve. While the majority may have felt that a fast could do no harm in these circumstances, this was passive acquiescence while Perceval had promoted it as a necessity to ensure religious appeasement and deliverance from the plague.

On the day before the fast, the 20th March, the House of Commons resumed its debate on the third reading of the Parliamentary Reform Bill. Perceval's intervention proved so inflammatory that the debate had to be adjourned again. The increasing fury that he aroused in other MPs comes through clearly from the reports in Hansard. Perceval started by asking the House:

"In whose name do you sit here? In whose name do you sit here? In his [the King's] name, at the mention of whom, with bitter taunts *[cries of "Question"]*; and think ye, for one moment, that sitting here, in that forgetfulness of Him from whom alone all counsel, wisdom, and might proceed - think ye - think ye - think ye - *[cries of "Question", "Go on", "Divide"].*"[322]

This was not a good start, but it was to get worse. Once again Lord Althorp tried to be helpful, saying that if Perceval's aim was to propose an adjournment, he would not oppose it. Members supported the call with cries of *"Go on"* and *"Adjourn"*. But Perceval spurned this opportunity, launching into a further tirade:[323]

---

[321] Edwin Chadwick, 'Report on the Sanitary Condition of the Labouring Population of Great Britain', London, W. Clowes & Sons, 1842 Public Health Acts were passed in 1848 and 1858, but there was another cholera epidemic in London in 1849.

[322] Hansard Parliamentary Debates, vol. XI, column 577 His use of "Ye" reflects the Irvingite Church connection.

[323] It is worth noting that Hansard records each Perceval speech as a single paragraph. This is not necessarily unusual, given that verbatim reporting of proceedings had yet to be introduced, but it may say something about the cascade of ideas that flowed into each other and were difficult for the reporter to differentiate into separate paragraphs. By contrast, it is notable that well-regarded speakers such as Sir Francis Burdett are reported in Hansard as speaking in a series of brief paragraphs. While Hazlitt's profile of Burdett confirms that Burdett was a very clear speaker, in some instances, of course, this may be as much to do with a copy of the speech being made available as with their oratory. See William Hazlitt, 'The Spirit of the Age' (2nd edition), London, H. Colburn, 1825, pp337-341.

"Do you expect His blessing on this nation; do you expect His blessing on your counsels, whilst you are employed in the greatest of all works, establishing the basis of a Constitution - the greatest work of human counsel and human wisdom, which man is called on to perform? Do you believe for one instant, that you will experience that blessing, whilst in utter forgetfulness of Him who ought most to be borne in mind? ... How standeth the account of the House with its God at this time? Twice have ye, the Commons of England, been called upon, but twice have ye been called upon in vain, to humble yourselves before your God, and to seek his blessing in contrition and repentance *[loud cries of "Question", amidst considerable confusion, occasioned by a number of Members leaving the House.]* Ye depart, do ye, when the name of your God is mentioned? Ye would have sat till five o'clock, and till six o'clock in the morning, had not his name been mentioned, listening to the tongues of men tinkling like idle cymbals."[324]

There was to be more of this harangue, with Perceval clearly forfeiting any remaining sympathy from fellow MPs with every word. Despite two other MPs asking him to desist from mentioning God, Perceval's anxieties became clear:

"... I tell ye that this land will soon be desolate; a little time and ye shall howl one and all in your streets. I tell ye that the pestilence, which God is now holding in, will be let loose among ye, and that the sword will follow it. ... I tell the House more than this: the Church of the land shall be laid low, for she hath corrupted her way before God. ... trouble yourselves not with this Bill; for this which I have told you is your doom. ... God looketh into your hearts, and seeth that you care not for him. He seeth that ye think that ye have got your Sovereign into a net, but ..."[325]

When Perceval said "Ye may think me mad, and ridicule me as a man beside himself ...", he was still sufficiently in touch with the feeling of the House to put into words what most, if not all, the MPs still present must have been thinking. But he did not stop all the same. It was only when an MP said that there were strangers in the House and the Speaker ordered them to withdraw, that "Mr.

---

[324] Hansard Parliamentary Debates, vol. XI, column 577
[325] Ibid, columns 579-580

Perceval instantly ceased, and left the House". Hansard summarised:

"Indescribable confusion prevailed during [a] great part of the hon. Gentleman's speech. The Members stood grouped on the floor, or in the galleries eagerly observing him, and the cries of "Order", and "Adjourn", together with the noise caused by Gentlemen retiring, occasioned frequent interruptions, and rendered some of the hon. Gentleman's observations inaudible in the gallery."[326]

The debate on reform was adjourned for two days to Thursday 22nd March. The scene at the Tuesday session had clearly been pandemonium, but strangely it does not seem to have been interpreted as a breakdown on Perceval's part. MPs were not prepared to tolerate reform being hijacked by religion, least of all Perceval's particular apostolic mania, but perhaps they were right not to ascribe his prophecies to madness. It was not difficult to see why he had become known as "saint Spencer", a term that was dismissive, making clear that he should not be taken seriously. Ten days later Perceval was back, asking on 30th March about the proposal to abolish the payment of tithes in Ireland and the impact for the Established Church there. By the 2nd April he was describing it as "a conspiracy against the continuance of the Protestant Church as the Established Church of Ireland".[327] But he recognised that his protests were now in vain, and that the House was resolved on this step. It was to be his last intervention as an MP. The pre-reform Parliament had more than four months to run before it was prorogued on 16th August[328] and on 18th April 1832 *The Times* printed a spoof administration comprising twenty-one notable disaffected Tories. Under the heading 'List of the Buckingham Administration (Picked up on Monday night near the House of Lords)',[329] it included Aberdeen, Wellington, Sir Robert Peel, Henry Goulburn and Spencer Perceval as Chancellor of the Duchy of Lancaster. He had achieved a notoriety that was out of keeping with his ability and exceeded his status.

---

[326] Ibid, column 581

[327] Ibid, column 1244

[328] When the second reading of the Reform Bill was debated in the House of Lords on 13th April, Perceval's uncle Lord Arden continued to vote in the minority of "not contents" (175 to 184). Earl Grey moved that it be committed on the first day after the recess (i.e., in January 1833).

[329] *The Times* 18th April 1832

When the new House of Commons re-assembled on 29th January 1833, the MPs for Tiverton were James Kennedy (?-1859) and John Heathcoat (1783-1861).[330] Neither had been in the previous House of Commons and neither was a Ryder. Given the forbearance Perceval had shown just two years earlier in responding to the committee scrutiny of the Ordnance budgets, it must be questioned whether, or to what extent, his change from principle to pestilence, and to haranguing the House, was brought about by the millenarian predictions of the Irvingite church and his over-arching attachment to them. A further question would be whether this change had been gradual since entering the House in 1818, or more precipitate once reform became inevitable in 1831. For Greville, the link to the Irvingite church was clear:

"As to madness, [Lord] Dudley has gone mad in his own House, Perceval in the H. of Commons, and John Montague in the Park, the two latter preaching, both Irvingites and believers 'in the tongues'". [331]

Another large family

"Anna Eliza was the Fair one's claim;
But known by Nancy's more endearing Name:"[332]

These are two of the lines in Part 1 of 'A Morning at Porto Bello addressed to Miss Nancy Macleod by her Admirer and very faithful servant'. But not by her future husband Spencer Perceval, unfortunately, as he was only twelve when the poem was written in December 1807. She was thirteen - or so the poet claimed.

Spencer's step-father Henry Carr and Queen Caroline had died the month after Spencer and Anna Macleod married on 3rd July 1821 at Ealing.[333] Anna was the youngest daughter of the late Norman Macleod (1754-1801), the 23rd chief of the clan Macleod since 1772, and his second wife Sarah. Norman Macleod had been

---

[330] Inventor of the bobbin net machine, lace manufacturer and with a cotton mill in Tiverton from 1815. The latter escaped the attention of the Luddites though his mill in Loughborough was not so fortunate.
[331] Greville, op cit, vol. II, p274
[332] British Library, Add MSS, 49191, f.1-4
[333] 'Annual Register for 1821', London, Baldwin, Cradock & Joy, 1822, p211 of Appendix to Chronicle

on active service in India from 1781, attaining the brevet rank[334] of Brigadier-General with the East India Company, while Sarah was thirteen years younger than him at seventeen when they married in 1784, two months after Macleod's first wife had died in Britain. Sarah was the daughter of an East India Company administrator, Nathaniel Stackhouse of the Bombay Council.[335] When the East India Company rescinded the brevet ranks that had been awarded locally, Macleod was not prepared to countenance the reversion to Lieutenant-Colonel and loss of command that would have been required of him. He and Sarah returned from India in December 1789 to the Macleod ancestral castle at Dunvegan on Skye.[336] He became MP for Inverness-shire in 1790, and was closely associated with the reform movement, becoming a member of the Society of Friends of the People started in 1792 by Charles Grey (the future Earl from 1807 and Prime Minister from 1830). Pitt had previously been in favour of reform, but this was now seen as inappropriate and unpatriotic at a time when the French Revolution was entering a bloodier phase and threatening the rest of Europe. A letter from Macleod's mother dated 14th January 1793 regrets his devotion to Fox,[337] suggesting that he should align himself instead with the Duke of Portland (then the leading Whig in Pitt's coalition government from July 1794). He did not take her advice. Macleod had ceased to be an MP by 1796, standing down in Inverness-shire and then failing to be elected in Milborne Port in Somerset,[338] and was dead by 1801. The Macleods had lived in London from the mid-1790s,[339] and to the extent that her father's Whig views were perpetuated in Anna this may have been one reason why she and Spencer were drawn to each other (given the similar views he had expressed in his speeches while MP for Ennis).

---

[334] In other words, with the responsibilities and duties of the rank, but promoted without additional pay.

[335] According to RC Macleod in 'The Book of Dunvegan II 1700-1920', Aberdeen, Third Spalding Club, 1939, p65, the "jointure" settled on Sarah when they married was £500 (over £31,000 in 2009). On p134 it says that a further unspecified sum was paid out each year to widows, in her case from 1801 to her death in 1829.

[336] I.F. Grant, 'The Macleods: The History of a Clan 1200-1956', London, Faber and Faber, 1959, p517-518

[337] Macleod, op cit, p27

[338] Coming third out of four with 46 votes out of 100 at a cost of £15,000. He objected to 14 votes cast for the second placed Sir Robert Ainslie, who had received 55 votes from the 100 electors, and accused him of bribery, but the allegation was not pursued.

[339] Macleod, op cit, p27 includes a letter from Sarah on 13th April 1793 approving of the move to London.

Spencer was the second of the twelve Perceval children to marry, following three months after his older sister Jane. He was already well into his twenty-sixth year, while Anna was much the same age. She was from a fairly large family herself, with two brothers as well as three older sisters. Although they had made a comparatively late start on married life for the time, their first daughter was born almost exactly nine months after their marriage on 13th April 1822. A second daughter followed on 29th January 1824,[340] and they were to have another six girls. The oldest of their three sons was born in September 1828, with the other two following at five year intervals in 1833 and 1838.[341]

Saint and apostle

Just a few months before Spencer and Anna's oldest daughter was born, a relatively unknown Scottish preacher moved from Glasgow to the Caledonian Chapel in London on Christmas Eve 1821. Edward Irving (1792-1834) was not to be unknown for long, first becoming famous and then infamous. As Dr Stoughton the church historian reported,

"A singular phenomenon appeared in the religious world ... A Presbyterian minister came to an obscure place of worship in the metropolis and took all ranks by storm."[342]

By 1823 no less a figure than George Canning was referring to Irving as "a great orator" and doing so publicly in the House of Commons. Attendance at the services increasingly included the

---

[340] In both cases the 'Annual Register' reported in its Births column "Mrs Spencer Perceval, a daughter". See p240 of the Appendix to its Chronicle for 1822 and p182 for 1824. After this though no further births were reported. Perhaps the Chronicle could not keep up, or the Percevals had ceased thinking them worth reporting.

[341] Only the youngest son lived to the start of the twentieth century, while the second died in 1863 at the ago of 30 fighting the Maoris. Only three of the daughters were to marry, the first not till 1860 after her father Spencer's death. Their three sons in order of birth were called Spencer, John Spencer and Norman Spencer, with the first two being Home Office officials at various stages (See John Venn, 'Biographical History of Gonville and Caius College 1349-1897', vol. II (1713-1897), Cambridge, Cambridge University Press, 1898, Sainty, op cit and Jill Pellew, 'The Home Office 1848-1914: From Clerks to Bureaucrats', London, Heinemann, 1982, p210.)

[342] Quoted on p44 of Andrew Landale Drummond, 'Edward Irving and His Circle', London, Clarke, 1937

cultural and political elite, who were attracted by Irving's charismatic preaching, as well as others who may have thought of themselves as leaders of society, and for whom being seen in the congregation was a fashionable cachet.[343] By 1823 services in the chapel were packed. In 1824 William Hazlitt (1778-1830) included an assessment of Irving, alongside his judgements of Coleridge, Bentham, Southey and others, in his collection 'The Spirit of the Age'.[344] Hazlitt described Irving as "the Romantic in the pulpit" at a time when "Evangelicism was losing influence because it was unimaginative and prosaic".[345] Irving's sermons provided an uplifting tonic by contrast, "attracting by repelling"; in other words, sometimes, when he held his listeners spellbound, this was by castigating some of those among them. Those he had berated had to return to church the following week to show they didn't mind such open criticism; others were fascinated by the spectacle. In a sermon in 1823, for example, he preached against the views expressed by Southey, Byron, Cobbett, Hazlitt, Bentham and Godwin. Some of them were in the audience, while other prominent figures such as the current Prime Minister Liverpool, and future ones such as Canning and Peel, were keen to hear Irving. Evangelicals such as Wilberforce also attended, adding to his popularity and public acclaim. In 'The Argument' Irving protested against "two most nauseous and ill-formed abortions", the 'Visions of Judgement' put forward respectively by Southey and Byron.[346] It is difficult to escape the view that Irving had elevated his religion into a dramatic form, enrapturing his followers in the process.

While still a teacher in Kirkcaldy in 1816, Irving had begun a lifelong friendship with the historian Thomas Carlyle (1795-1881).[347] It was Irving who introduced Carlyle and his future wife to each other in 1821. She, as Jane Welsh (1801-1866), had been a pupil of Irving's and might have married him rather than Carlyle had Irving been able to extricate himself from his existing engagement to Isabella Martin (?-?).[348] Carlyle and Irving went on walking tours

---

[343] Ibid Drummond lists many of the famous people who attended on pages 49-50.

[344] Hazlitt, op cit, pp81-102

[345] Drummond, op cit, p53

[346] Ibid, p61: Southey's vision "was a panegyric of George III, the other [Byron's] a parody of that panegyric".

[347] He should not be confused with the Scottish advocate Thomas Carlyle (1803-1855) who was subsequently to become one of the apostles of the Catholic Apostolic Church alongside Spencer Perceval and Henry Drummond.

[348] According to Irving's entry in the DNB, although "[h]is marriage with Isabella Martin was a happy one, ... he might have benefited from a partner more prepared

together, one being "near Robert Owen's new mill"[349] at New Lanark. In 1818 Irving had resigned from teaching to prepare for the presbyterian Church of Scotland, first moving to Edinburgh and then assisting Thomas Chalmers (1780-1847) to introduce an urban ministry in a deprived area of Glasgow from October 1819. The Scottish clergy had been showing a "steady and marked descent" in the second half of the eighteenth century before Chalmers re-invigorated them. For Cockburn "Mouldering in their parishes was their general doom ... [until] Chalmers and his consequences arose".[350] In the case of Glasgow, as Drummond puts it,

"The year 1819 was a time of great hardship in Glasgow. Unemployment and underpayment were rife; industrialism was making for the most degraded conditions of labour and housing; discontent came to a head in the 'radical rising' at Bonnymuir ...Every reasonable reform was confused with 'sedition' by the authorities. The Town Council was a municipal oligarchy, self-appointed."[351]

Chalmers was in his element, but Irving was not ("feeling eclipsed by Chalmers and undervalued in Scotland", as the DNB describes his situation), and the move to the Caledonian Chapel in London at the end of 1821 must have seemed a calling, as well as an opportunity too good to be missed.[352] By July 1824 his

---

to exercise a critical influence. That was certainly the belief of Irving's early love, the strong-willed Jane Welsh."

[349] Drummond, op cit, p27 There was to be another connection later when the Irvingite church moved to a room at Gray's Inn Road "which at other times was occupied by the social reformer Robert Owen ..." (Ibid, pp214-215) after they had been ejected from the Regent Square church.

[350] Cockburn, op cit, p275

[351] Drummond, op cit, p34

[352] Irving was not the first clergyman to move from Scotland to London. Alexander Waugh (1754-1827), one of Evelyn Waugh's great-great-grandfathers, had much the same impact and enjoyed sustained success. As Stannard, op cit, pp11-12 describes it, "For most of his professional life he was based at the Wells Street Church in London ...

"He was a reformer, a founder member of The Dissenters Grammar School at Mill Hill and the London Missionary Society; he established the *Evangelical Magazine* and acted as a genial and benevolent spiritual guide to the Scots community in London. Carlyle remembered him with respect. His influence stretched far beyond the narrow bounds of his calling and attracted people of all religious persuasions. In the London of the late eighteenth and early nineteenth century a popular preacher enjoyed the prestige and influence of a politician. He agitated for the abolition of slavery and travelled widely. Wherever he preached in Britain he was

popularity had proved so sensational that a new church began to be built in Regent Square. But this was to prove the zenith of his appeal, with his uncompromising stance and lengthy sermons (sometimes more than three hours) contributing to a waning acclaim that was as rapid as had been his rise. Though his congregation remained large, it was increasingly down-market as the better-off and better-known were deterred from attending. By the time "the large Regent Square church was opened in May 1827, there were concerns about renting enough seats to pay off the debt".[353]

From 1825 onwards Irving became increasingly interested in prophecy and the second coming of Christ, or millenarianism, predicting this for 1868. Ever since the French Revolution, people generally had taken refuge, if not interest, in the study of prophecy,[354] with the scriptures providing an antidote to excessive and unpredictable outcomes. Laudable aspirations for equality and fraternity had been hijacked by events that had proved not so much to be a levelling as a levelling-down, and that were seen as the starting-point of human doom. Rather than human action being viewed as a critical building block on the path to communitarian, even socialist and humanitarian, agency, liberty had proved to be no more than a mantra, easily adopted as a slogan by those with other, less democratic, motives. In this context biblical prophecies, even the apocalypse, looked welcoming. As Ruotsila explains,

"The gradual germination of that empire [of the Anti-Christ] was taken to have begun during the French Revolution, and its culmination awaited the triumph of a false, man-centred faith ..."[355]

By October 1831, as the Reform Bill made its way through parliament and not long after Spencer Perceval's speech against it in March 1831, people began speaking in tongues in the Regent Square church. Although Irving opposed this practice to begin with, he gradually allowed it to develop. The result was inevitable, with the church attracting all manner of attention-seekers and crackpots as well as genuine believers. The trustees took fright at the growing

---

met with crowded congregations and ... It was a distinguished career for a minister of a small and, until his time, relatively obscure denomination."
[353] Irving's DNB entry
[354] Columba Graham Flegg, 'Gathered Under Apostles: A Study of the Catholic Apostolic Church', Oxford, Clarendon Press, 1992, pp298-299
[355] p78 in Markku Ruotsila, 'The Catholic Apostolic Church in British politics', *Journal of Ecclesiastical History*, 56 (2005), pp75-91

ridicule in the press, and they banned the church from Regent Square. Glossolalia was heresy as far as the Church of Scotland was concerned and in March 1833 the authorities put Irving on trial and defrocked him. As Jane Welsh (Jane Carlyle from October 1826) said, "There would have been no tongues, had Irving married me."[356]

When Irving returned to London and the larger premises that had been found at Newman Street, it was as pastor to the emerging Catholic Apostolic Church.

"The origins of [this] Church lay ... in [the] *glossolalia* ... [and] in separate prophecy investigations concurrently undertaken by a group of Anglican[s] ... at Albury, Surrey. The latter were organised by Henry Drummond ... a London banker ..."[357]

Drummond (1786-1860) had briefly been an MP from 1810 to1812, and was to be again from 1847 until his death in 1860. For Ruotsila,

"Drummond was one of [the most extreme and anti-modernist] conservatives, and he set the terms of [the] Catholic Apostolic Church discourse on so-called secular politics."[358]

He had been connected to the older Spencer Perceval during his first period as an MP, partly owing his seat at Plympton Erle to Perceval's intervention on his behalf.[359]   Although he is said to have left parliament at the dissolution in September 1812 because of ill-health, Perceval's assassination may have had something to do with it. It is possible to speculate but there is little indication why Drummond then returned to the House of Commons in 1847 after a gap of 35 years, other than perhaps out of a sense of duty (or mischief[360]), but it was as MP for West Surrey, the constituency where Lord Arden's son, George Perceval, had been MP previously from 1837 to 1840.   It was close to both the Arden (and

---

[356] Drummond, op cit, p273

[357] Ruotsila, op cit, p76

[358] Ibid, p81 Andrew Landale Drummond, op cit, p239 describes "Henry Drummond as a "crack-brained enthusiast" in politics and religion.

[359] Thorne, op cit, vol. III, p622

[360] "... he was an original; no other definition of him can be given" according to J. Ewing Ritchie, 'British Senators: Or, Political Sketches, Past and Present', London, Tinsley Brothers, 1869, pp395-396

subsequently Egmont) country home at Nork and the estate at Albury Drummond had purchased in 1819. At the time of the Albury conferences from 1826, however, Drummond had no formal political role, though his wealth and contacts ensured that his influence was no less strong.

Drummond had many other connections to the Percevals. Like several of them he was educated at Harrow School - not at the same time, but with contemporaries such as Byron and Peel. He left in 1802, going on to Christ Church at Oxford University and leaving after two years in 1804, the same year in which Spencer junior entered Harrow. Although Spencer and his father both attended Cambridge University, three of the younger Percevals, Henry, Dudley, and John Thomas went to Oxford University.[361] Drummond had proved himself a staunch Tory and high Anglican in the 1810 to 1812 period, and went on subsequently to become a close friend of John Wilson Croker (as had the older Perceval) and to endow a village church like Arden.[362] Both Thorne and Flegg cite Irving's anxiety in 1825 that Drummond "... was in the chair; he is in all chairs - I fear for him". By this time they were well-known to each other. The following year the first of the Albury conferences took place. These

"... were called for the purposes of examining the Scriptures - and especially the prophetic writings - with a view to interpreting the political and social events of the day, [as well as] determining the extent to which biblical prophecies had already been fulfilled in the life of Christ and the history of the Christian Church ..."[363]

Flegg goes on to list the participants, approximately forty at any one meeting, of whom about two-thirds were clergy and about the same proportion Anglican. From March 1829 the proceedings were published in the Church's own publication *The Morning Watch*, edited by John Tudor (1784-1861), subsequently an apostle. In August 1831 Thomas Carlyle (the historian) attended a dinner party

---

[361] Henry went to Brasenose, Dudley, like Drummond, to Christ Church and John Thomas to Magdalen Hall (now Hertford College). See, for example, the 'Harrow School Register 1800 to 1911', op cit, pp51, 59 & 72

[362] See Thorne, op cit and Flegg, op cit, as well as Drummond's entry in the DNB (written by Flegg), for further detail on the period between 1810 and 1826. This includes his travels abroad and an interest in land reform, endowing the Chair of Political Economy at Oxford University from 1825.

[363] Flegg, op cit, p36

at Drummond's house in Belgrave Square. The other attendees were Irving, Tudor and Perceval, and to Carlyle "They were all prophetical, Toryish, ultra-religious".[364] In 1832, after the general fast sanctioned by the government on Perceval's motion against the cholera epidemic, it was said that "Neither Cockney crowds nor police regulations damped the ardour of disciples like Spencer Perceval."[365] In this respect it might not be too surprising that Perceval's religious faith got the better of his parliamentary scruples, spilling over and showing itself in his "un-parliamentary language" in his speech on Reform in the House of Commons.[366] Perceval was voicing his opposition, and also that of the Church and high Anglican conservatives, to social change that was clearly seen as man-driven rather than God-given.

The Catholic Apostolic Church was well on the way to being formed at this point, with Perceval as one of the leading figures. By 26th December 1832 the Church had decided its order of ministry of apostle, angel and an evangelist. Each apostle would oversee the traditional three-fold structure of bishop, priest and deacon. The first apostle, and one of the most influential, was a lawyer JB Cardale created in November 1832. He was followed by Henry Drummond in September 1833, with King-Church and Spencer Perceval junior being the next two apostles created by the end of 1833. The next two followed in 1834, and another six (making up the agreed twelve in all) in 1835.[367]

Greville records in his 'Memoirs' for 2nd December 1833:

"I went yesterday ... to hear [Irving] preach, and witness the exhibition of the tongues. ... After these three Spencer Perceval stood up. He recited the duty to our neighbour in the catechism, and descanted on that text in a style in all respects far superior to

---

[364] Quoted in Drummond, op cit, p126

[365] Ibid, p215

[366] Ruotsila on p79 notes that "Drummond fought hard, first of all to prevent all proposed extensions of the suffrage". Both here and on p84 he makes clear why the Church supported the traditional constitutional and monarchical arrangements, and opposed naturalist, rationalist, socialist and scientific progress. A view echoed in Greville, op cit, vol. II, p220 when he described Drummond as "... mad, but very clever, and a Reformer, though for saving the rotten boroughs ..."

[367] The Church was subjected to the criticism that there was an unacceptable and inappropriate circularity in the initial ordinations (e.g., Drummond anointing Cardale initially, and then the latter ordaining Drummond). However, they were quite open about this, arguing that it was inevitable and should be expected with a new Church.

the others. He appeared about to touch on politics ... when suddenly a low moaning noise was heard, on which he instantly stopt [sic], threw his arm over his breast, and covered his eyes, in an attitude of deep devotion, as if oppressed by the presence of the Spirit. ... [When all was finally still] Spencer Perceval, in slow and solemn tones, resumed, not where he had left off, but with an exhortation to hear the voice of the Lord which had just been uttered to the congregation, and after a few more sentences he sat down. Two more men followed him and then Irving preached."[368]

Greville clearly had a mixed view of Perceval. In an entry for 19th August 1834 Greville recorded that

"As I rode into London yesterday morning I fell in with Spencer Perceval, and got off my horse to walk into town with him. He talks rationally enough till he gets on religious topics ..."[369]

and in January 1836 that Perceval had approached all the Privy Councillors asking them to repeal all the legislation of the last five years that in his view were "evidences of a falling off from God".[370] He was given short shrift, as was Drummond who had approached the Anglican Bishops.

Flegg includes a summary of the apostles as a precursor to considering their social status and backgrounds.[371] Interestingly,

---

[368] Greville, op cit, vol. II, pp424-426

[369] Ibid, vol. III, p73

[370] Ibid, vol. III, p274

[371] Flegg's summary (in the order in which the apostles were created) is:

"John Bate Cardale (1802-1877): solicitor

"Henry Drummond ...

"Henry King-Church (1787 - 1865): Clerk in the Tower of London

"Spencer Perceval ...

"Nicholas Armstrong (1801-1879): Anglican priest, formerly Rector of St Dunstan-in-the-West, London

"Francis Valentine Woodhouse (1805-1901): barrister and eventually 'Father of the Bar', son of the Dean of Lichfield

"Henry Dalton (1805-1867): Anglican priest, formerly Church of Scotland minister, incumbent of St Leonard's, Bridgenorth, Shropshire, later Vicar of Frithelstock, Devon (whilst retaining his apostleship)

"John Owen Tudor ... author, artist, editor ...

"Thomas Carlyle (1803-1855): advocate at the Scottish Bar, defended Irving before the General Assembly [when the latter was tried for heresy in 1833]

"Frank Sitwell (1797-1864): of Barmoor Castle, Northumberland, brother-in-law of Archbishop Campbell Tait of Canterbury

however, his analysis almost leaves Perceval out of account other than to mention his father's assassination when Prime Minister. In the case of both Perceval and Drummond, Flegg describes them as Members of Parliament. Both had been, Perceval only recently, but neither was when they became apostles and Drummond had not been an MP for over twenty years.

Flegg continues:

"The social status and backgrounds of the apostles are worthy of note. With one exception [Mackenzie] they came from either the lower aristocracy or the professions [with Perceval presumably being in the former group rather than the latter]. Of those who had been previously ordained, two were Anglicans and one a Presbyterian [though Perceval and Sitwell also had extensive Anglican connections]. Most were in their thirties at the time of their call [as was Perceval]; Drummond (at 47) was the oldest and Woodhouse (at 29) the youngest."

It has generally been assumed that the origins of the church were mainly Presbyterian, but the Anglicans were in the majority (as they were amongst the apostles). Where the Irvingite congregation with their Presbyterian background were influential was in the move from Newman Street to a new church in Gordon Square in 1853. This was the movement's "Central Church", had been built specifically for it and is of magnificent design and cathedral-like proportions.[372] The apostles had backgrounds in Scotland, Ireland and Wales, as well as in various parts of England, though the first six to be created were based in or near London. Cardale had been educated at

---

"William Dow (1800-1855): formerly Parish Minister of Tongland, Dumfries, deposed like Irving
"Duncan Mackenzie (1785-1855): wholesale chemist, and elder at Irving's church; later (1840) withdrew from apostolic work." Flegg, op cit, pp64-65
It should be noted that Irving was not among the apostles, even though he had been present from the first of the conferences in 1826, indeed had provided the record of it, and lived to see the initial six apostles created. His position in the Church as pastor was less elevated.
[372] While the attached chapel is still open to the public each day, the church is not. It is used very occasionally for services conducted by the Bishop of Fulham and an organ recital is held on the first Friday of each month in order to preserve the instrument. The church is now known as Christ the King, and while the Forward in Faith organisation is based on the premises, as are the trustees of the Catholic Apostolic Church, the movement itself no longer exists in the UK. The church includes an In Memoriam window to the apostle Carlyle who died in 1855, and a more recent stained glass window by the celebrated Archibald Nicholson.

Rugby and Woodhouse at Eton, while Harrow had two representatives (Perceval and Drummond). There were five graduates among them (Woodhouse from Oxford University, Armstrong and Dalton from Trinity College Dublin, Carlyle and Dow from Edinburgh University), while Perceval and Drummond had been to Oxbridge.

Two decisions were soon taken that were to have a lasting impact on the Church's future development: to proselytise the movement worldwide by allocating "tribes" and territories for the apostles to evangelise; and not to replace apostles when they died, thus preventing the future ordination of bishops and ensuring that congregations would shrink as they became leaderless locally. Flegg, as he acknowledges, has a slightly different list of tribes and territories from that given by Davenport.[373] In both cases, however, the lists agree that Perceval was allocated Italy which was thought to have the key characteristics of "civic virtues and faithful citizenship" (which supposedly determined the assigned tribes as well, though Flegg ascribes the tribe of Asher to Perceval while Davenport identifies Manasseh).[374] In 1838 all the apostles visited the countries they had been allocated with the aim of developing allegiance to the Church and building congregations in those countries. Cardale had been assigned England and remained there. Carlyle and Woodhouse had considerable success in Germany and Austria (particularly the former in North Germany), Drummond less so in Switzerland and Scotland. For Perceval and Sitwell, however, the Roman Catholic countries of Italy, Spain and Portugal proved to be very difficult. They were "almost completely closed",[375] so despite Perceval's high Anglican background, and even had he and Sitwell been better linguists, it is doubtful that they would have made more headway. The uphill nature of their task would make a record of their experiences and travels particularly interesting. However, the British Library has no Perceval papers from this period, even though this is where the Church records (apart from a few registers) are now held.[376]

---

[373] Flegg, op cit, p71 Rowland Davenport, 'Albury Apostles', Birdlip (Glos), United Writers, 1970, pp132-133

[374] Boase, op cit, p1462 agrees that Perceval represented Manasseh.

[375] Davenport, op cit, p138

[376] Tony Reynaldson, Trustee of the Catholic Apostolic Church, personal communication, 14th July 2009 However, James Fenimore Cooper (1789-1851) did publish 'Excursions in Italy' in 1838 (2 vols., London, Richard Bentley). This gives a flavour of the times, as do other reports of the grand tour. Even though Perceval's own grand tour twenty years earlier had included Italy this was still the

According to Davenport, Drummond and Perceval gave Cardinal Acton (1803-1847) a copy of the Church's testimony in July 1838 for forwarding on to the Pope.[377] Perceval had been particularly prominent in the preparation of this, as he was generally in the early years of the Church, but after his experience as an apostle to Italy "... little is heard of him during the last twenty years of his apostolate; no doubt he did his duty faithfully and unobtrusively".[378]

However, it may be that this comment indicates how little is documented for the remaining twenty years of Perceval's life. He was still only 44, with a third of his life before him. His mother-in-law had died ten years earlier and his mother was now aged 70, but Spencer and Anna were the parents of eleven young children (the oldest of whom was seventeen). With his four unmarried sisters having moved to the nearby Pitzhanger Manor House from 1843, relative seclusion and a more private domestic life must have been an attractive prospect for them - though they may have achieved this separately rather than together.

The first three apostles died in 1855, four years before Perceval, and by 1869 there were only three left. From 1879 Woodhouse was the sole remaining apostle, and though he lived until 1901, the decision not to replace them (as there was no authority in the scriptures to do so) meant that the Church was bound to decline. New ordinations (first of bishops and then of priests) could not take place and, other than in Germany, the few active people and the smaller congregations remaining then returned to the religions with which they were most familiar.

After 1839

When the 1841 Census was carried out the residents of Elm Grove did not include Spencer, Anna or their children, and there would not

---

age of city states before Cavour and unification from 1848. This would not have helped Perceval either. Cooper points out that "I was told that the disposition to force their own opinions and habits on the strangers they visited rendered the English unpleasant, and that there was a general feeling against receiving them." (vol. II, p171) Although this was not true of the majority, as Cooper underlines, Perceval's performance in parliament makes it unlikely that his visit to Italy could just be passive. He would be expected to voice forthright opinions and to do so forcefully.

[377] Davenport, op cit, p136, though Acton did not become a Cardinal until 1842. His father John Acton (1736-1811) had been the Prime Minister of Naples

[378] Davenport, op cit, p172

have been room for them anyway. In late 1826 and early 1827 Spencer and Anna had been in Edinburgh with their first three children Anna (1822-1895), Fanny (1824-1850) and Emily (1825-1826).[379] By June 1827 Spencer was writing from an address in Whitehall[380] and by 1833 he was living at 6 York Street in St James.[381] There is no record of any of the family in England, Scotland or Wales in the 1841 Census, and, while their omission from the count may have been an error, it must be supposed that they were outside the country, perhaps living in Italy with all eleven children.

It is probable that they moved to Elm Grove either shortly before Jane Carr died or after her death in January 1844. Spencer's unmarried sisters, and the other residents, would have to move out in order for his family to move in, and this would have been signalled to them in advance. Pitzhanger Manor House would have been purchased for the sisters in order for this change to take place at Elm Grove. It is not certain that Spencer ever lived there with his wife and eleven children, but may have done so briefly, perhaps maintaining the York Street address as an alternative residence. By 1851, the year of the Great Exhibition, however, Elm Grove was occupied by Anna, seven of her daughters and three servants,[382] while Spencer appeared to be living separately, still at 6 York Street, where he retained a coachman and a female servant.[383] At this time he was being visited at this address by Father Basrelli, a Roman Catholic priest from Lucca in Italy. Basrelli may just have been a friend, of course, but there seems an inherent improbability

---

[379] British Library, Add. MSS 49191, f.120 & f.121 for Spencer's letters from Edinburgh to his mother Jane at 2 Brunswick Terrace, Brighton.

[380] British Library, Add. MSS 49191, f.129

[381] British Library, Add. MSS 49192 consists largely of letters from other apostles to Spencer at this address. In April 1837 his aunt Elizabeth Perceval wrote to him at the same address (f.139).

[382] Her other daughter Fanny had died in 1850, while her oldest son Spencer was at Caius College, Cambridge, the next John Spencer was at school in Hampstead, and the youngest Norman Spencer was at school in Iver. All three boys attended Harrow, but John had done so for only four terms in 1846/7 and Norman was to attend even more briefly for one term only in 1852. 'Harrow School Register 1800 to 1911', op cit, pp183, 193 & 252.

[383] York Street runs from Jermyn Street to St James' Square which then links to Pall Mall. This would have been very convenient for Spencer when he was at the Ordnance Office on the other side of Pall Mall. He may also have thought this part of London a refuge ever since he had gone to stay with Lord Arden in St James' Place in late 1814 as his mother's intention to re-marry became apparent. It had become somewhere he could get his thoughts in order.

about this as a likely or sufficient explanation given their religious backgrounds.

There are two other possible, but diametrically-opposed, explanations for his visit. The first is that Basrelli was one of the "growing band of anti-Catholic lecturers who toured Britain in the 1850s and 1860s"[384] as part of the Protestant backlash against 'papal aggression'.[385] In this instance Spencer might have met him in 1838 during his own attempt, largely unsuccessful, to attract people in Italy to the Catholic Apostolic Church. If this was the case, however, it would be expected that Basrelli would have renounced his vows. The Census form makes it clear that he was still a Roman Catholic priest. The second, and more likely, explanation is that Spencer was at least considering converting to the Roman Catholic Church himself. Father Dominic Barberi (1792-1849), the Italian Passionist missionary who received Newman into the Roman Catholic Church in 1845, had been rector of the seminary at Lucca from 1831 to 1833. Barberi had then established foundations in Belgium and England, and in 1844 two new priests from Lucca added to the mission in England.[386] More were promised. Spencer's visitor Basrelli was aged 40 in 1851, and might well have been training at Lucca when Barberi was the superior there twenty years before. In addition, a year earlier in 1850 the Pope had appointed a full hierarchy of Roman Catholic bishops for England and Wales for the first time for nearly three centuries. This may have been a further reason for Basrelli's visit.

Not only had attitudes shifted a long way within the Perceval family since his father's time, but this was apparent also within the country. At the start of the century some evangelical Anglicans such as the older Perceval took an extreme view of Catholics almost as a matter of course, perhaps still seeing their Church as a threat.[387] By mid-century some high Anglicans had begun to align themselves with the Roman Catholic Church, while some went so far as to convert. Dudley Perceval and Manning were in

---

[384] K Theodore Hoppen, 'The Mid-Victorian Generation 1846-1886', Oxford, Clarendon Press, 1998, p445

[385] Spencer's brother Dudley Perceval was one of those at the forefront of defining a growing threat to the established Anglican Church, the union of church and state, as such. See Chapter 8 below.

[386] Urban Young, C.P., 'Life and Letters of the Venerable Father Dominic Barberi, C.P., Founder of the Passionists in Belgium', London, Burns Oates & Washbourne Ltd., 1926; Denis Gwynn, 'Father Dominic Barberi', London, Burns Oates, 1947

[387] Some, such as Spencer's brothers Dudley and Henry, still did of course - see Chapters 7 and 8 below.

correspondence at this time (see Chapter 8 below), even if Dudley's purpose was to convince Manning not to convert, and it may have been that Spencer junior knew Newman as well. They had all moved in similar high Anglican, evangelical, and sometimes Wilberforce, circles. Spencer junior's disillusionment with the Anglican Church by this point seemed to have gone beyond what he had once hoped the Catholic Apostolic Church might offer. This may have been why little was heard of him after 1838, but he would now be interpreting his faithful duty differently.

Eight years later Spencer was buried at St Mary's Church, Melcombe Regis on 22nd September 1859[388] after his death in Weymouth. In effect this was an ecumenical church, rather than just an Anglican one, with

"... places of worship for Independents, Baptists, Wesleyans, and Roman Catholics."[389]

It remains possible, therefore, that Spencer had converted to Catholicism.

---

[388] See www.opcdorset.org/WeymouthMelcombeFiles/MelcombeSM-Burs1851-1860.htm

[389] www.british-history.ac.uk/report.aspx?compid=51394

5.   CHASTITY, CHARITY AND THE UNMARRIED DAUGHTERS

In the first quarter of the nineteenth century an average family might have six children, the aristocracy slightly fewer.[390]   Although as a twenty-one year old when she married, Jane Wilson might be likely statistically to have more children than the average, the Percevals were unusual nevertheless in having twelve surviving children. Although their first three children were girls, the next five were boys, four of whom survived, and it seems improbable that gender was a factor when they then went on to have another five children. It may be that they interpreted the size of their family as God's blessing on their union, and that they felt they were affirming the biblical purpose of marriage.   They were also exceptional in that four of their six daughters never married, compared to about one in eight women nationally.   (The same was true for five of the eight daughters of Spencer junior.) While this might be due in part to their eligibility, and the availability of potential partners outside the family, it seems likely that the trauma of their father's assassination and their mother's re-marriage had at least something to do with it. Although they did not lead cloistered lives (as the references to Jane Perceval's social life in Chapter 3 make clear), they may have preferred flirtation within regimented, and predictable, formal situations to any longer-lasting commitment.   Aspects of their mother's example may have deterred them, their sister Jane's death may have disillusioned them further, or possibly the opportunities may not have arisen in time.

Irrespective of these factors, though, it will be apparent that the Percevals did not lead straightforward, "ordinary lives", a description that is often misleading, but spectacularly so in their cases. Rather they were subject to twists and turns that were more extreme than most of us would expect to experience. These were due to events or circumstances for which they had not bargained, let alone planned, a characteristic of the children as well as their parents. They were living in extraordinary times; their lives proved equally so.

Some people would ascribe the unexpected to chance or providence, while others attributed it to divine intervention. Religious belief and a reliance on religious explanation were much more   widespread   in   the   nineteenth   century   -   perhaps

---

[390] Thompson, 1988, op cit, p57

understandably when the realities of daily life were grim for most people and even this depended on unremitting toil. When infant mortality was high and life expectancy low, ascribing the consequences to God's will must have been comforting. However, it was also a recipe for resignation if not fatalism, an acceptance of the status quo. If results depended less on human agency than on other forces, this could be a formula for inaction, for removing the responsibility for amelioration and improvement from individuals. This resort to determinism was one of the main reasons why Malthus' views on population gained currency, though they were unpopular with some people at the time and became increasingly discredited as the century went by. They contrast markedly with those of others such as Robert Southey (1774-1843),[391] for example, who was one of the first to ascribe "increasing misery of the poor to the manufacturing system".[392] Fortunately, there were reformers who refused to accept the implication of social impotence, while dissenting forms of religion grew, scientific explanation and understanding advanced, and the fundamental roles that education and public health had to play in raising the quality of life were increasingly recognised. Without such initiatives, and an accompanying determination in the face of commonly-held beliefs, progress would have been pursued less assiduously and the outcomes less beneficial.

Against this background, three phases can be distinguished in the children's lives. The first was in the period up to their father's assassination in 1812 - their childhood for most, an age of comparative, even blinkered, innocence for all; the second was the time between this event and their independence; and the third their years after this. For eight of the children the second period ended with their marriage: nine years in the case of Spencer junior and Jane who were the first to be married in 1821, fourteen or fifteen years for Henry, Frederick and Dudley, and into the 1830s for Ernest, John and Isabella, the last to be married in 1835. All, apart from Ernest, were at least 25 before they married, and many were much older than this, with the two daughters to marry, Jane and Isabella, being 29 and 33 respectively. For the other four daughters this period lasted until 1843 and their move together to Pitzhanger

---

[391] Robert Southey, "On the state of the poor", 1812, collected in 'Essays, Moral and Political', 2 volumes, London, John Murray, 1832
[392] Donald Winch, 'Riches and Poverty: An Intellectual History of Political Economy in Britain 1750-1834', Cambridge, Cambridge University Press, 1996, p324

Manor House.[393]   They had always lived in the same house and this, provided it could be afforded, must have been a natural step. Once their brother Spencer, sister-in-law Anna and their eleven children decided to live at Elm Grove it would be clear that there was insufficient room for them. But they were almost bound to have different priorities to a growing family in any case. Although they had little option, living separately must have been an attractive prospect at their ages, with Frances older than 50, Maria close to it, and Louisa and Frederica coming up to 40.   They may have welcomed the opportunity, even if they did have to move out of their home of thirty-five years to realise it.

The map on the opposite page shows Ealing in 1822.[394] Elm Grove stood at the south-west corner of Ealing Common, while Pitzhanger Manor House and the Walpole home, both at Ealing Green, lie north-west of this (closer to what is now Ealing Broadway).

Frances (1792-1877) and Maria (1794-1877)

Frances and Maria were indeed "inseparable" as Gray described them.[395]   They lived in the same places for just short of 83 years, and in the two houses in Ealing for nearly 70 of them. They died within three months of each other. A few of their letters still survive in the British Library, written for the most part to their brother Spencer in the years up to 1818 when he was in Italy. (Some of these have been referred to in Chapter 3 above.)   There is one further letter, which is unusual in being from Spencer to Frances (rather than to him), dated ten years later in June 1827.

---

[393] Known at this time as the Manor House, Sir John Soane had been one of the previous owners of this property (see Chapter 2 above) and it was bought for them by Isabella's husband, their brother-in-law Spencer Horatio Walpole (1806-1898), after standing empty for a few months in 1843 (Emmeline Leary, 'Pitshanger Manor', London, Pitshanger Manor Museum, 1990, p27). Walpole's DNB entry is incorrect when it implies that he resided "at Ealing Manor, in part of which he lived with his family while letting his Perceval sisters-in-law occupy the wing now called Pitshanger Manor at a nominal rent. Bought as a country retreat in 1844 for the sake of his elder son's supposedly weak constitution ..." He did not live in the same house as he had bought earlier for his sisters-in-law. St Mary's Church, Ealing refers in a pamphlet to Walpole's large house on Ealing Green, where Ealing College now stands.

[394] Victoria County History of Middlesex, op cit, vol. 7, p112 where it is juxtaposed with the 1876 and 1914 maps to show how the area evolved over the century.

[395] Gray, op cit, p431

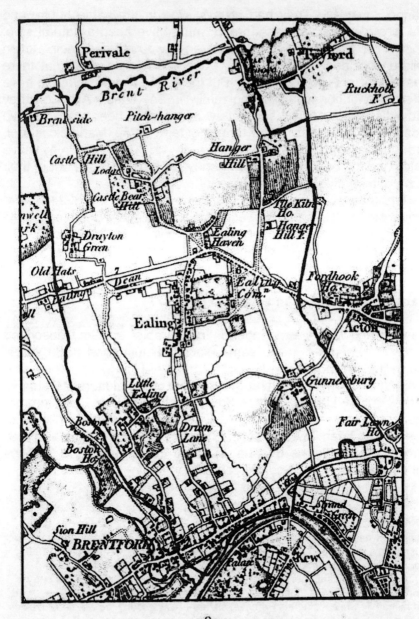

1822

Figure 5: Ealing in 1822 (from 'Victoria County History of Middlesex', vol. 7, p112) © and database right "Crown Copyright and Landmark Information Group Ltd" (All rights reserved 2009)

But despite the accuracy of Gray's comment, and Frances' claim that she thought alike to Maria "so wonderfully alike [that there may be] great similarity in letters",[396] their differences were just as apparent. Indeed, one interpretation of this assertion by an eighteen year-old Frances is that she may have copied some of Maria's letter and was trying to convince her brother of another explanation in case he had spotted this. She had been forced to admit to copying much of a previous letter to him from the newspapers. She knew she was not as good a letter writer as Maria, "not being very profuse" as she explained. Frances was more conventional, or at least more modest about her accomplishments.

By contrast Maria was genuinely interested in current affairs, and as a consequence her letters are more newsy, and spicy, even from a young age. Some of them remain fresh, even original and evocative of the period and the people about whom she wrote. She was not afraid to make her views known. For example, at the time of the Duke of York inquiry in early 1809 she wrote as a fifteen year-old of two of the main protagonists, the Duke's mistress and the MP who had made the allegations of corruption, "... that I hate and detest Mrs Clarke, a nasty toad, and that I am not overpartial to the Honourable Gentleman Mr Wardle".[397] These may have been the traditional views a conservative monarchist such as her father might express, but the language was her own and she was equally prepared to express contrary opinions. A month later she was commenting on Lord Granville Leveson-Gower, a dinner guest, in whom she was as disappointed as she had been with Sir Arthur Wellesley (the future Duke of Wellington). As far as Maria was concerned, he was too slim, slouched and was not as handsome as her teenage infatuation (described in her letters as <u>Him</u>) to whom her mother had teasingly compared him:

"... instead of his beautiful legs he has sticks ...
"... there is no more comparison between them than between light and darkness or to name two things still more unlike one another between the King and Bonaparte".[398]

A couple of months later she provided her brother with an early report of Wellesley's success at Oporto, and of George III's

---

[396] British Library, Add MSS 49191, f.11 (21st February 1811)
[397] British Library, Add MSS 49191, f.5 (February 1809)
[398] British Library, Add MSS 49191, f.7 (1st March 1809)

temporary recovery from insanity when she referred to the King riding out for the first time, with good accounts of his health from her father who had seen him a few days earlier.[399] His improvement was not to last.

She also commented on other events that struck her, such as her sorrow at the fire that had burned the Drury Lane theatre to the ground "for I had a very great affection for it". She pointed out that she would have seen the fire better from their house in Lincoln's Inn Fields than was possible from Downing Street, underlining the wider threat the fire posed when she highlighted the families who had posted servants on their roofs to keep the burning embers off their homes.[400] Spencer must have felt he was there rather than miles away at school in Harrow.

On 25th May 1811 Frances wrote to him that Mama would not be able to go to the forthcoming Harrow School speeches because she expected to be too tired to get up early enough after attending the Prince Regent's the previous day. Frances suggested that Spencer ask his Headmaster Dr Butler to put the speeches back. But, Frances explained, she and her father still planned to attend "if Mama will let me".[401] This letter gives some insight into Frances' relationship with her parents, their sense of priorities, and illuminates the place in society she assumed would be accorded the premier and his family. She may have been right. She continued

"I am going to Ealing to Mama. Tell Henry [her eleven year-old brother, also at Harrow School from January 1810] I am quite miserable till I receive his gracious pardon."

These were her own words, but it is possible to hear her father speaking when she comments in the same letter that the Duke of York "has at last had justice done to him" now that he has been restored as commander-in-chief of the army.[402]

---

[399] British Library, Add MSS 49191, f.15 (21st May 1811)

[400] The fire had taken place a few days earlier on 24th February 1809. British Library, Add MSS 49191, f.7

[401] British Library, Add MSS 49191, f.17 All these letters f.5 to f.17 were written from Downing Street; as were Jane's for some time after Perceval's assassination. In other words, the Government allowed the family to continue to live there for a while as well as in Ealing.

[402] By his brother the Prince Regent more than two years after he had resigned as the pressure mounted over the Mrs Clarke affair and the possibility that he had connived in her sale of army commissions.

Their mother had been scrupulous in leaving the same to all four unmarried daughters in her Will.[403]   There is no record of Frances after the move to Pitzhanger and her mother's death in 1844; even Frances' Will has not been found.[404]

Maria's Will has not been found either and the last two letters from her held by the British Library are dated 1817. Both of these use Maria's own shorthand and abbreviations over four pages of dense handwriting (presumably reflecting the cost of paper and perhaps increasing the likelihood that the letters would reach Spencer intact). Maria wrote the first over several days from the 7th June to keep her brother in touch with family news, gossip and events in Parliament while he was in Italy. As an illustration of the latter she opens the letter with references to papers considered by the secret committee on sedition. She disagreed with this secrecy, despite the justification one MP had offered for it:

"I [should] have thought [the] more knowledge, the less chance of delusion."[405]

She was writing this letter at the time of the Pentrich crisis, with uprisings sparked by a public push for reform. The Industrial Revolution and the Prince Regent's extravagant lifestyle contrasted with the absence of improvement for most people as their expectations had been confounded. On the 11th June Maria wrote that

"The trial of the Traitors began yesterday but Lord Ellenborough forbade any part of it being published till it was over."

She also referred to a plot in Yorkshire that had resulted in ten arrests and to a less than well-attended meeting in Hertfordshire

---

[403] Her Will is dated 20th November 1841 and attached two codicils: the first, dated 8th March 1839, referred back to an earlier Will of 20th July 1821 and a subsequent codicil of 17th August 1837, while the second was dated 26th August 1843 and left the contents of her wardrobes to these four daughters.

She prepared the earlier Will the day after George IV's coronation and a month before Henry Carr's death. To the extent that the events were connected, the contents may make interesting reading if they can be found.

[404] After Spencer's letter in 1827, and the proving of her mother's Will on 19th April 1844, no references have been found in newspapers, periodicals or Ealing Parish magazine.

[405] British Library, Add MSS 49191, f.92 (June 1817)

against the Act suspending Habeas Corpus. "Gentlemen" in particular were noticeably thin on the ground in her view.

These tense times would explain "Mama [putting] off her journey till tomorrow, because she could not sleep last night after packing", and a day later on the 12th Maria recorded that

"The Malvern party Mama Sir Henry Fanny Isabella set out this morning to proceed as far as Woodstock today".

There are references to family members spitting blood and recovering shortly afterwards. As these are to real people (e.g., Aunt Frances and her husband Lord Redesdale), they may be entirely accurate. However, as the people seemed to recover in a day or two, even though the illness may have been some time gestating, they may also have been symbolic of the parlous state of the country.

Subsequently, there are two tantalising references that may relate to her. The first, in *The World of Fashion and Continental Feuilletons* magazine on Saturday 1st November 1834, was supposedly a fiction entitled 'A Belle in a Village', but this may have been a disguise to avoid libel. The story concerns Percival, then Perceval, Paragon who thinks he will add another female conquest while staying in the village. Maria Homely seems the most likely candidate, but she is not taken in by his bluster and charm, and bests him. Maria may have been "homely", but she was clearly a woman of the world, used to men's advances and far from naïve. Maria Perceval was then aged 40, did live in a village, as Ealing then was, and her letters of twenty years earlier make it apparent that she was alive to the ways of the world and not easily impressed. What is most intriguing, however, is that the story ends by referring to Sir R. H__ who could tell the readers more had he not become a hermit as a result of Maria's upbraiding him. Without identifying Sir R. H__, the "Paragon" of the story, there can be no certainty that the drama referred to Maria Perceval, but the circumstantial evidence is intriguing and the story was clearly not fiction. On the second occasion *The Times* and the *Morning Chronicle* both refer to Miss Maria Perceval as attending Queen Victoria's drawing room on 3rd June 1853. Maria was not presented to the Queen, but her sister Isabella Walpole was there (as she often was) presenting two other people. Maria was now aged 59 so it may not have been her. On the other hand, her niece Maria had been presented at a drawing room two years earlier, along with her sister Eleanor, by their mother Anna, Spencer junior's wife. Rather than this niece Maria re-appearing at the Queen's drawing room two years later, but remaining in the crowd, a more attractive conclusion may be that this was the older Maria as close to Victoria as her sister Isabella could arrange.

Louisa (1804-1891)

While documents for Frances and Maria, such as early letters, have been found, there are no such in the British Library for their sister Louisa. She was ten years younger than them, and while they always lived in the same places, this gap would have been sufficient to separate her from them - at least until the 1820s. This age gap also meant that the same life-events had a different impact on her. Unlike them, for example, she would have had only a limited recollection of her father and family life before his assassination. She was then eight, and would have experienced the trauma of his death rather differently. On the other hand, she was a seventeen year-old when her step-father died and still under twenty at the time of her oldest sister Jane's death, and it might be expected that these events would have assumed a different importance for her at these ages.

Nor does it appear that she was as prominent as her sister Frederica became after their move to Pitzhanger. Indeed, the first records for Louisa refer to the last ten years of her life. She was already seventy-eight when the *Daily News* reported on 17th June 1882 that

"Mrs Spencer Walpole [Isabella] is seriously ill at the Manor House, Ealing, where she had gone to attend on her sister Miss Louisa Perceval who has been suffering from congestion of the lungs and bronchitis."

Fortunately, both recovered, with Isabella living to 1886.

After Louisa's death on 13th September 1891, however, she featured in a number of newspapers due to the large amount left in her Will. This included personalty of £10,078, the equivalent of £604,000 in 2009, and substantially more than most people left - such as, for example, the successful writer Harriet Martineau (1802-1876), the landscape painter Thomas Creswick (1811-1869) or Lord William Pitt Lennox (1799-1881). It was enough to see Louisa feature in 'Wills of the Year' in the *Leeds Mercury* on 30th November

1891 - even if she was the last to be listed. Other stories on the same page included 'The Gateshead Disaster' when eleven people died in a theatre collapse, a convict "mutiny" at Wormwood Scrubs prison, a stabbing at London docks, and two murders, one of a sweetheart who had been drowned by her lover. Louisa's estate was not thought to be out of place among this sensationalism. In the three days beforehand the size of her Will ensured she had featured in the *Birmingham Daily Post* and *The Newcastle Weekly Courant*, as well as in *The Belfast News-Letter* report that

"The will (dated June 19, 1889) of Miss Louisa Perceval ... late of the Manor House, Ealing ... was proved on November 13 by Horatio George Walpole, C.B., and Cecil Henry Spencer Perceval, the nephews [Isabella's and Ernest's sons], the executors, the value of the personal estate amounting to over £10,000."[406]

The *Leeds Mercury* added the same day that "The only legatees under the will are the testatrix's brother, sister, nephews, and nieces." Her two younger siblings, Ernest and Frederica, were the only ones to outlive her, dying in 1896 and 1900 respectively. According to *Hearth and Home*, "Miss Perceval ... was in receipt of a generous pension from Government",[407] a euphemism, if not an explanation, for "well-off".

Frederica (1805-1900)

St Mary's, the parish church in Ealing, stands half way between Elm Grove and Pitzhanger Manor House, and members of the family worshipped there for most of the century. Lasting testaments to this are the two windows given by these four daughters, with Isabella and her husband funding the Baptistery in memory of the Walpole and Perceval families when the church was extended in 1866. While Frances, Maria and Louisa concentrated their benevolence on the Ealing community, the youngest daughter Frederica also looked further afield. Frederica was almost eighteen months younger than Louisa, and, similarly, no letters from her are held at the British Library. Unlike her, however, she was both noticed at the time and ensured that she left a memorial that outlasted her.

---

[406] *The Belfast News-Letter* 27th November 1891
[407] *Hearth and Home* 1st October 1891

The *Daily News*, one of the national papers most obviously interested in social improvement, refers in its obituary to her good works, describing her as "a friend of the poor". It concludes:

"She remembered perfectly her father's assassination in the House of Commons by Bellingham in 1812, the victory of Waterloo, the festivities which followed it, the Thames being frozen over [the last Frost Fair being in 1814], and numberless other events of interest in the early part of the century. These she could recount with much detail to her intimates. She had lived for a long time at Ealing in a house next to that of her brother-in-law, Sir Spencer Walpole, so long member for the University of Cambridge, and thrice Home Secretary, who died in 1898. There she devoted herself to good works, and the poor will lose in her a great friend."[408]

She had died on the 12th May, three months short of her 95th birthday, the last of the Perceval children. Her Will included a share of a house at Hove, as well as Pitzhanger Manor House, and amounted to an estate of £15,891 (£907,000 in 2009), of which £13,057 (£745,000) was personalty (rather than unsettled property)[409] - even more than Louisa had left. Frederica had been particularly close to her younger brother Ernest and to her companion Lucy Alice Simpson (aged 27 in the 1891 Census). As well as leaving some furniture and the substantial sum of £1100 (£63,000 today) to her, Frederica added a further bequest of 490 shares in the Artizans, Labourers and General Dwellings Company. Assuming these were ordinary rather than preference shares, they amounted to almost one-twentieth of 1% of the £545,000 share capital in 1891[410] (more before then, as another 20,000 shares had been issued at the start of the year). Although this might not sound a huge amount, it does mean that 2000 shareholders such as Frederica accounted for all the share capital and therefore owned the Company. Lucy Simpson now became an equally significant shareholder. The shares stood at 110.5d in September 1892,[411] so they would have cost Frederica something like £225 to purchase (£13,500 today), not a negligible investment. The Company's aspiration was to show an annual return of 5%, as they had in 1890, amounting to a dividend of over £11 per year - indeed, "philanthropy

---

[408] *Daily News* 14th May 1900
[409] *Daily News* 26th June 1900
[410] *The Economist* 28th February 1891
[411] *Birmingham Daily Post* 20th September 1892

at five per cent" was the marketing slogan that sold shares in companies such as this, holding out the prospect of a better return than many other investments. At a time when £100p.a. was a reasonable working class family income, this and the capital bequest would have put Lucy Simpson well on the way to this level in interest alone.

Most pertinent, however, is Frederica's philanthropic interest in the Company itself. It was one of the model dwelling companies that developed in the second half of the nineteenth century to improve working class housing. There were five Artizans Dwellings Acts between 1868 and 1882, as well as two Select Committees in 1881 and 1882. The Company was founded in 1867 by "a self-made ... [but] illiterate, building contractor, William Austin (?-?)",[412] with the legendary reformer and philanthropist Lord Shaftesbury (1801-1885) as its first president. The involvement of Lord Shaftesbury would have been sufficient to convince Frederica and many others to invest in the Company. Although she was not a member of the British and Foreign Bible Society herself,[413] Shaftesbury had become president in 1851 as Lord Ashley (Anthony Ashley Cooper MP) just before his father's death and remained so until 1883. This was only one of his pre-occupations with social reform and, as Canton's history describes him in 1851,

"... he had rescued women and children from the horrors of brute labour of mines and collieries, had regulated the hours of work in factories, had done much to alleviate the misery of homeless and destitute children, had helped to assist convicted thieves to an honest livelihood."[414]

Shaftesbury's bona fides were impeccable and were to be vital to the Company getting off the ground initially and benefitting from the association thereafter.

By 1900 the Company was the largest in London, housing 42,000 people.[415] Although it did not operate in Ealing itself, it

---

[412] Anthony S Wohl, 'The Eternal Slum: Housing and Social Policy in Victorian London', London, Edward Arnold, 1977, p151

[413] George Bourne, 'The History of the British and Foreign Bible Society From Its Institution in 1804 to the Close of Its Jubilee in 1854', 2 vols., London, Bagster & Sons, 1859 W. Canton, 'History of the British and Foreign Bible Society', 5 vols., London, John Murray, 1904

[414] Canton, vol. II, pp168-169

[415] Wohl, 1977, op cit, p147

developed three major housing estates in other London suburbs, with its Shaftesbury Park development in south London near Clapham Junction being opened by Benjamin Disraeli (1804-1881) when he was beginning his second term as Prime Minister in 1874. The other estates were Queen's Park in north-west London and Noel Park in north London. The purpose of the Company was to offer "workmen the alternatives of renting or purchasing the freehold of their houses",[416] thereby being both a building society and a housing association. In Wohl's judgement, however,

"[a]s a means of encouraging the London working classes to think in terms of house ownership ... [it] cannot be said to have been as successful as the building societies operating in the north of England."[417]

Nor was it free from financial scandal. After his recommendations the previous year had been ignored, the auditor issued a written warning to shareholders as early as 1877 that dividends were being paid out of estimated, rather than actual, profits.[418] His lengthy statement provided illustrations of nepotism, graft and corruption. The Company attempted to deflect the criticisms, issuing an erratum slip saying that liabilities exceeded assets (as they would in these early days) by less than the auditor had claimed, adding

"... unfortunately, as the reader may infer from the subsequent parts of the Pamphlet, this by no means represents the total deficiency existing in [the auditor] Mr Pearce's judgement."[419]

But this proved insufficient to convince some of the most influential shareholders, a number of whom had not been notified of the original meeting (if, according to Pearce's statement, they had "opposed the Directors in previous years"). They were far from being re-assured, let alone mollified, and insisted on calling an Extraordinary General Meeting. As Wohl says, the Company did not

---

[416] Ibid, p152
[417] Ibid, p153
[418] John Pearce, 'The Artizans', Labourers and General Dwellings Company Limited: A statement addressed to the shareholders', London, 1877
[419] Ibid

"establish a sound relationship with the Public Works Loan Commissioners [on whom it depended for much of its advance working capital], and drifted off into middle-class housing ..."[420]

Although Frederica may have purchased her substantial shareholding after this scandal, it is much more likely that she did so when the Company was first floated or in its early days, and then stuck with them thereafter. She would already have been in her sixties when the Company was founded and, as well as matching her interests in public welfare and social improvement, its approach would have appealed to her.

In addition to better housing for the working classes, Frederica was supportive of other charities as well. In 1844 the fund for building a Hospital for Consumption and Diseases at Royal Brompton, Chelsea benefited from three Perceval donations of £10 each, including by Miss Perceval and Miss M. Perceval,[421] while a similar donation was made by a Miss Perceval to Charing Cross Hospital some years later.[422] Frederica also followed, and in some senses surpassed, her father's Anglican zeal. In 1874, for example, she attended the Mildmay conference in Islington called to establish a protestant preacher at Spa in Belgium.[423] There were many such conferences organised at Mildmay Park in Islington. In 1874 alone, for example, they included a week of Universal Prayer in January organised by the Evangelical Alliance,[424] while in July an offer in the *Glasgow Herald* included both the magazine 'The Christian' and afternoon conference meetings at Mildmay. One of these was held by the Association of Female Workers, addressed by Maria Charlesworth and Mrs Pearsall Smith who emphasised that on both sides of the Atlantic women had much to offer through the mundane hard work that often led to more significant influence.[425] In 1894 a Miss Perceval, most likely Frederica, was listed as a contributor over three years to the Church Defence Institution. Headed 'The

---

[420] Wohl, 1977, op cit, p152

[421] These would almost certainly have come from Maria and her sister as the next generation was not yet old enough. It is not clear who the third, a Miss J. Perceval, was, as Spencer junior's daughter Jane was only aged ten. *The Times* 13th July 1844

[422] *The Times* 17th April 1858

[423] Boase, op cit, p1461

[424] *Daily News* 6th January 1874 and *The Graphic* 10th January 1874

[425] 'Words of Truth and Trust: being addresses at the meetings of the Association of Female Workers held after the Mildmay conference', London, SW Partridge & Co, 1874

New Attack on the Church', an advertisement in *The Times* stated the organisation's mission was to ensure the "permanent provision for religious worship and teaching in every parish of the land".[426] This would have chimed with her determination to protect the established church.[427]

Despite these echoes of a more traditional, conservative and repressive time, progress and diversity were increasingly evident. It is unlikely that Frederica would have resisted them, even though they would have been anathema to her father - particularly on his doorstep. A new congregational chapel opened in September 1860 on Ealing Green where she lived.[428] One of the adverts carried in the Ealing parish magazine was for the local British School "No Sectarian Religion taught", and described later as "Free to all denominations". This was based in Lancaster Road, Ealing, named after Joseph Lancaster (1778-1838) the founder of the monitorial system that bore his name. In 1810 Spencer Perceval had prevented such a school being established in Northampton, had encouraged the Church of England to set up the National Society in opposition and eventually persuaded the Prince Regent to withdraw his patronage from Lancaster. But, as Robert Southey concluded in 1812

"What we are obliged to Lancaster for is ... frightening the Bishops who ... would never have exerted themselves if they had not been impelled to it."

As well as various family bequests, the main purpose of Frederica's Will was to leave sufficient money for the building of All Saints Church, Ealing Common in memory of her father. The Daily News reported that

"... having the intention to build a church and tower on the Elm Grove estate in memory of her father, Miss Perceval authorised the executors, if she should have entered into a contract for the building

---

[426] *The Times* 15th June 1894

[427] See www.victorianlondon.org/dickens/dickens-r.htm where the objects are described as "To combine persons of all classes, without reference to political or religious opinion, in defence of the established Church of England; to circulate correct information about it; to resist, in the House of Commons and elsewhere, attempts to weaken or destroy it."

[428] 'Ealing Parish Magazine', numbers 1 to 39, January 1860 to March 1863. After this date it was incorporated by the publisher Acworth in his *Ealing Post and General Advertiser*.

of the church, to apply a sum of £5,520 and the ultimate residue of her estate in completing the contract, and in fitting up and beautifying the church, but if, at the time of her death, she should not have entered into such contract, they are to invest £5,000 and her residuary estate, and to accumulate the income therefrom for 21 years, or until such time as the capital will be sufficient, to build the church and tower in accordance with the plans prepared for her, which are not to be altered, and a tablet is to be placed on the church, bearing the inscription, "Erected by Frederica Elizabeth Perceval, last surviving daughter of the Right Hon. Spencer Perceval, to the glory of God, and in memory of her father, who was assassinated in the House of Commons, in the year one thousand eight hundred and twelve". The patronage of the church is to be in St Mary's Ealing."

She had left nothing to chance and the church was consecrated in 1905.[429] The land, building and fitting out had cost just under £16,000.[430]

---

[429] This took place on 1st November, All Saints Day and the anniversary of Spencer Perceval's birth, as had the laying of the foundation stone two years before. *The Times* 2nd November 1903 and 2nd November 1905

[430] Bryant, op cit, p25

6.   RECEDING HOPE: FREDERICK PERCEVAL (1797-1861)

Disability and difference

Frederick was a singular child in several ways.   Because of his delicate health he was the only one of the sons not to attend Harrow, effectively the Perceval family school.   He must have felt separate, as well as separated, from the rest of the family at an early age.   He lived in many places in England, and while only the four unmarried daughters remained in Ealing all their lives after 1808, he was the one child to lack fixed roots.   He turned out to be a geographical nomad - though his brother Spencer was certainly an intellectual one.   Moving around as frequently as he did was unusual at this time, and in his case was evident as early as 1817 when his sister Maria wrote that "Frederick left us this morning for Billericay".[431]   He was to live in Ramsgate, Ghent in Belgium, Notting Hill and other places in London, Herne Bay, Coleshill near Birmingham and Warwick.   By contrast, his brother Henry, was vicar of Elmley Lovett in Worcestershire, twenty miles due west of Warwick, for nearly 50 years.   Frederick was less rooted in ways other than place as well - and, of course, "less rooted" can also mean more flexible, primed to grasp opportunities as they arise and possibly to generate them.   In his situation this may have been a necessity.

There were several reasons why Frederick was sent to school in Rottingdean (at what proved to be the start of the family's long-standing links to Brighton, four miles away, and the south coast generally).   Although it was still a small village, 550 people in 1811, and not yet a seaside resort, it was already developing a reputation for its sea air and healthy climate:

"By the beginning of the 19th century Rottingdean had become celebrated for the salubrious properties of its wells ... Baths were then established, and machines provided for sea bathing."[432]

---

[431] British Library, Add MSS 49191, f.92 (June 1817) This is the first unambiguous reference to Frederick in his siblings' surviving letters. His oldest sister Jane wrote in June 1812 that "little Freddy is still better today" (op cit, British Library, Add MSS 49191, f.41), but this might possibly refer to another relative.

[432] Victoria County History of Sussex, vol. VII, London, Dawsons, 1973, p233

Dr. Hooker, the vicar of Rottingdean from 1792, ensured that the school he had established in the vicarage also became well-known, often preparing pupils for Harrow and Eton. The future Cardinal Manning and Lord Lytton

"... were among his pupils. The latter [as Edward Bulwer-Lytton] was at Rottingdean from about 1810 to 1818, and showed such great promise that Dr. Hooker recommended that he be sent to a public school."[433]

In the event, though, Edward Bulwer-Lytton (1803-1873) received private tuition from a Reverend Charles Wallington in Ealing from 1819 until he went to Cambridge University in 1822.[434] Frederick and Bulwer-Lytton had attended Rottingdean for some of the same time, while a nephew of the Duke of Wellington was among other pupils at the school. At the end of the century the painter Edward Burne-Jones (1833-1898) and, more briefly, Rudyard Kipling (1865-1936) were among those to take advantage of the peaceful surroundings by living in the village.

After his years at Rottingdean and Billericay Frederick virtually disappears from public view in England until his marriage ten years later to Mary Barker on the 25th July 1827 at St Mary's Church, Lambeth. He was two months short of his thirtieth birthday. *The Derby Mercury* reported that she was the "eldest daughter of William Barker, Esquire of Eyam in this county".[435] Her age is not recorded, and nor are the names of her mother or siblings here or elsewhere, but she was born in about 1802 in Bakewell, Derbyshire.[436]

In 1812-1814 Britain and America had fought a war they should have been able to avoid over trade grievances and the impact on American shipping of the Orders in Council Britain had instituted in 1806 in its war with France. The Treaty of Ghent in 1814 ended the

---

[433] Ibid, p234 Henry Manning (1808-1892) went to Harrow in 1822 (Harrow School Register 1800-1911, op cit, p101). From about 1841 he was to oppose John Newman (1801-1890), another person with Ealing connections, believing that the Anglican church was sufficiently broad to accommodate his Catholicism rather than require him to convert. Eventually, however, he was to follow Newman into the Roman Catholic church in 1851.

[434] Bulwer-Lytton's DNB entry

[435] *The Derby Mercury*, 1st August 1827 The same notice had appeared in *John Bull*, 30th July 1827. The Barker family lived at Burn House in Derbyshire according to Burke's Peerage.

[436] See www.familysearch.org/eng/Search/frameset_search.asp

American war, as did the Treaty of Vienna in 1815 with respect to the Napoleonic one. Castlereagh, brought back into government by Spencer Perceval in early 1812, was the Foreign Secretary (as he remained until his suicide in 1822) who oversaw the negotiation of both treaties, the latter agreeing the boundaries for European countries and confirming Britain's status as a great power. Henry Goulburn (1784-1856), a future Chancellor of the Exchequer when both Wellington and Peel were Prime Ministers and the recipient of a letter from Frederick Perceval in 1846, had been a "key ... negotiator at Ghent ... charged with [agreeing] the final arrangement of frontiers, fisheries, and maritime rights".[437] Yet, despite the connections between the Ghent Treaty and Frederick Perceval, it is much more likely to have been the new opportunities in Europe after Napoleon's defeat that attracted him to Belgium.

One conclusion from the Congress of Vienna was that Belgium, the Netherlands and Luxembourg should be united, and from 1817 Belgium was under Dutch protestant rule. To characterise it crudely, Belgium was itself an uneasy alliance between the French-speaking and predominantly Catholic south and the Flemish-speaking, largely protestant, north. Despite these language and religious differences though, Dutch rule went relatively smoothly until 1821 when the Netherlands attempted to recoup some of their debts by imposing a financial burden on Belgium. Belgian grievances began to build and by 1830 the country was in revolt, with pitched battles being fought on the streets of Brussels and elsewhere. There were large numbers of casualties on both sides, with even the garrison in the protestant stronghold of Ghent being attacked. In November 1830 Belgian diplomacy sought to persuade the Duke of Wellington of the justness of their separatist cause, despite Britain's close links to the Dutch. It was clearly sympathy and moral support that they sought, with perhaps some hope that the British would intercede on their behalf. Whether the mission to London was successful or not the overall campaign was, with the new King Leopold entering an independent Belgium in July 1831 and choosing to do so via Ghent in order to confront the large number of Orange supporters there head on.[438]

In the late 1820s and early 1830s, therefore, Belgium was a very turbulent country. But in the first ten years after Waterloo, and after independence in 1831, the opportunities would have been

---

[437] Goulburn's DNB entry
[438] Demetrius Boulger, 'The History of Belgium 1815-1865', London, Pitman, 1913, pp64-177

more apparent than the drawbacks. There was already an English community in Brussels[439] and there was one in Ghent from 1816 too.[440] Billericay in Essex had been a rural agricultural area, but by the early nineteenth century the developing leather and particularly silk industries were adding to the area's long-standing reputation for wool.[441] Silk mills were becoming a feature of this part of Essex, with a silk manufacturer trading in Billericay by 1832.[442] As Bragg says, Ghent was one of the first towns in Belgium to industrialise and attract skilled textile workers from England. It would be most surprising if Frederick, an entrepreneur manqué, did not see the potential and try to make the most of it. He had the political and manufacturing connections that made this a real option. Ghent may also have been attractive as a bastion of non-Catholicism.

Clerical, Medical and General Life Assurance Society

He was to grasp rather different possibilities in Britain too when he became a Director of the newly-formed Clerical, Medical and General Life Assurance Society. Frederick had been nominated on 29th March 1826 to replace Dr Sutherland, thereby reducing the number of medical practitioners on the Board to eight, the new minimum.[443] The Society had been founded in 1824 and Frederick was one of the eighteen Directors from 1826 to 1840.[444] At the time of its inception there were several competitors, including names that have remained familiar such as the Equitable and the merged Sun Alliance, but also several pirates out to fleece the public. All the latter had to do was "issue tempting terms and, after collecting the

---

[439] See, for example, reference to Thomas Creevey in Chapter 2 above.

[440] Rosemary Bragg, 'The Anglican Church in Ghent', Maidenhead, Bragg for St John's Church Ghent, 1980 The first English chaplain in Ghent was appointed in 1839 by the Bishop of London at an annual stipend of £200.

[441] Victoria County History of Essex, vol. II, London, Dawson & Sons, 1977, pp381-2, 408 & 463

[442] Ibid, p468

[443] It had been nine previously: Arthur Digby Besant, 'Our Centenary: Being the History of the First Hundred Years of the Clerical, Medical and General Life Assurance Society', London, Clerical, Medical and General Life Assurance Society, 1924, p10 and information from Lloyds Banking Group Archives and Museum, personal communication, 10th November 2009.
The HBOS Group Re-organisation Act 2006 states in its preamble that "The Clerical, Medical and General Life Assurance Society was formed by a Deed of Settlement dated 14 February 1827 for the purposes of making or effecting assurances on lives and survivorships and other related activities".

[444] Besant, op cit, p322

money from the victims for a few years, fail to fulfil the stipulated contracts".[445] There were no safeguards of course, and it was by no means certain that the Clerical, Medical and General would survive, especially as another seventeen life assurance companies had also been formed in 1824, a boom year for Joint Stock companies.[446] Looking back in 1832, the Society's founder and Bloomsbury physician George Pinckard (1768-1835) reflected on these troubled times eight years earlier:

"... The Scheme of the Society was novel, the public opinion was adverse; the times were disastrous; speculation in Joint Stock companies was carried to a fearful extreme; Assurance Societies, almost numberless, were projected, many failures occurred; and it may be said, in the language of the Society, that our success was *doubly hazardous*."[447]

The Society paid its first dividend of 4% in 1827, 363 policies were in force by 1828, bringing in income from premiums of more than £11,000 (the equivalent of over £560,000 today), and the Directors were confident enough to hold their first Society dinner in 1829, but it was not until 1830 that success looked certain. In this year the Directors showed their appreciation to Dr Pinckard with the gift of 100 guineas worth of plate, and doubled their own fees to one guinea per meeting. Even in 1832, however, the outbreak of cholera had a major impact, removing the Society's scope to add bonuses to policies that year.[448]

Early in 1828 adverts for the Society listed Frederick as one of the Directors.[449] Although he had written the previous August a month after his marriage to Mary Barker offering to resign as he was going to the Continent,[450] this was not accepted. He had attended three Board meetings in the month after their wedding and

---

[445] Ibid, p4

[446] The Society did survive, merging with the Halifax in 1996 and subsequently becoming part of HBOS in 2001 and then part of the Lloyds Banking Group.

[447] Besant, op cit, p6

[448] Ibid, pp97-99 &124 See Chapter 4 above for Spencer Perceval's call for a fast in response to this cholera outbreak. Greville (in Strachey and Fulford, op cit, vol. II, pp169-170) highlighted in his diaries how threatening this outbreak was, particularly on the continent where it overshadowed Belgium's independence. By contrast Britain escaped relatively lightly.

[449] *Ipswich Journal*, 12th January 1828; *Liverpool Mercury*, 25th January 1828; *Hull Packet and Humber Mercury*, 8th April 1828.

[450] Lloyds Banking Group Archives, 29th August 1827 letter, LD0299 - item 23

at the Board on 22nd August 1827[451] had proposed that his life be assured for £1000 (almost £50,000 in 2009). This was agreed,

"... taking his life at 37 instead of 30, on account of a lameness, arising from a paralytic affection [sic] which occurred during his infancy."[452]

This clarifies the nature of Frederick's ill-health and disability, and helps explain why he was treated differently to the other children. It also justifies Besant's assertion that, in contrast to some companies, nobody was excluded by the Clerical, Medical and General; rather premiums were adjusted to take account of underlying conditions, such as the examples Besant cites[453] of gout and asthma but extending to afflictions such as Frederick's.

Frederick may have gone to Ghent ten years earlier, but in 1827 he and Mary Barker certainly did so. In 1828 their first child Frederica Mary Jane (1828-1903) was born there. On 24th November 1829 they had a son Spencer Frederick John (1829-1887), also born in Belgium.[454] He was named after his paternal grandfather as well as his father so was yet one more in what, it might be thought, was proving to be a *surfeit of Spencers*.

On 22nd August 1831 Mary's mother died at Frederick's house at Ramsgate (as the newspaper report described it).[455] This may have been a holiday home or it may have been their permanent residence in England. In 1832 he was listed in the Poll Book for

---

[451] This was to be his last attendance at the Board for over ten years until 21st March 1838.

[452] Lloyds Banking Group Archives, Clerical Medical Minute Book No.3 1827

[453] Besant, op cit, p12

[454] Frederica Mary was the third wife of the painter William Waterhouse (c1817-1890), marrying on 18th April 1860 and moving to Kensington. They had children but Burke's Peerage does not specify how many nor whether they lived into adulthood. The 1861 and 1871 Censuses record six. These Censuses also confirm Frederica's place of birth as Ghent, and it may be that the International Genealogical Index records Hampstead because this was a convenient place for both Frederica and her brother to be registered as British citizens.
In the 1881 Census Spencer J. (as he called himself, having dropped the Frederick) was a married man living at 2 Bolton Road, Eastbourne, Sussex. He and Ellen Norton had married on 30th March 1867 and had one daughter according to Burke's Peerage.

[455] *The Derby Mercury*, 31st August 1831

East Kent as a Ramsgate freeholder.[456] Although it is not clear when the family returned permanently to England, they had certainly done so by 21st March 1838 when Frederick began re-attending Clerical Medical Board meetings after a gap of more than ten years.

In 1843 Mary herself died on 24th April at their home in Ladbroke Terrace, Notting Hill. She was buried at St Luke's, Charlton. They may have been out of the country again after Frederick ceased to be a Clerical, Medical and General Director in March 1840 as there is no record of them in the 1841 England, Scotland or Wales Censuses.[457] In August 1843 Frederick was added to the list of JPs for Middlesex[458] and on the 6th April 1844 he and Emma Gilbert were married at St Mary's, Lewisham. There was an age-gap between them, possibly as much as twenty-one years, though this would not be a huge one for the time. She was born between 1815 and 1818, so would have been much the same age as his first wife had been at her wedding. She was the "eldest daughter of the late Ralph Gilbert Esq."[459] and they were to have six sons in the eight years 1846 to 1854, four of whom survived into adulthood.

A peripatetic life

From the information that does exist, including addresses on the few surviving letters at the British Library, it is possible to construct a picture - though not necessarily a comprehensive one - of Frederick's movements. This is set out in Table 6. It should be stressed that this combination of being a JP, life assurance company director and a gentleman[460] pillar of the community while

---

[456] 1832 Poll Book for East Kent, Centre for Kentish Studies, Kent Archives. His name does not appear in the other three Poll Books for East Kent (covering Ramsgate and Herne Bay) for February 1852, July 1852 or 1857.
The 1851 Census twenty years later recorded Frederick as living at Herne Bay, just along the Kent coast. Herne Bay was almost certainly their permanent residence at that time as this Census was counted on the night of 30th March.

[457] The 1841 Census returns for Ladbroke Terrace are missing from those held by the Royal Borough of Kensington and Chelsea's Local Studies. However, the 1841 Rate Book shows that the Percevals were not living in the street at this point: 3 Ladbroke Terrace was occupied by someone else, while number 12 was empty. This ties in with their move to the latter property by November 1841 while living elsewhere earlier that year.

[458] *The Times*, 28th August 1843; *The Era*, 3rd September 1843

[459] *The Court Magazine & Monthly Critic*, 1st May 1844

[460] Yet he is not listed for either Ramsgate or Herne Bay in any of the Kent directories that preceded the first Kelly one in 1862: Pigot's Directory 1826/27, the

moving home many times is out of the ordinary. This makes his mother's 1841 Will even more significant as a source of information. After her death in 1844 he moved first to Herne Bay and then to the Birmingham area, eventually to Warwick. While he lived in Notting Hill for over ten years, and for much the same time in Herne Bay, there is a sense in which each subsequent decade represents a decline in his fortunes compared with the previous one.

Table 6: Frederick Perceval - key moves and other events

Year	Month	Day	Location	Event	Age
1797	Oct	6	Born at Belsize House, Hampstead		
1801	Dec		59 Lincoln's Inn Fields (60 added in 1802)		4
1804			Belsize House, Hampstead		6
1808			Elm Grove, Ealing		10
			School at Rottingdean, Sussex - probably to 1815		?-17
1817	June	11		Billericay, Essex - sister Maria reports him leaving Ealing	19
1826	Mar	29		Nominated as Director of CM&G Life Assurance Society	28
1826	Apr	19		Attends CM&G Board meetings until 18th July 1827	
1826	Nov	6		Letter of apology for non-attendance at CM&G Board sent from Ealing	29

Post Office Directory 1851 or Melville's Directory 1858. Gentry and traders are listed for each settlement. Pigot's may have been too early and Melville's possibly too late, but it is more difficult to explain why Fred. Jas. Perceval, Esq. does not appear in the Post Office one for Herne Bay either.

Year	Month	Day	Location	Event	Age
1827	July	25		Marriage to Mary Barker in Lambeth	
1827	Aug	8		Attends CM&G Board meetings for fortnight to 22nd August 1827	
1827	Aug	22		Proposal for assuring own life accepted by CM&G	
1827	Aug	29	Notting Hill	Letter resigning as CM&G Director	
1828			Ghent	Daughter Frederica born	30
1829	Nov	24	Ghent	Son Spencer born	32
1831	Aug	22		Death of mother-in-law Mrs Barker in Ramsgate, Kent	33
				In 1832 Poll Book as Ramsgate freeholder and elector	34
1835	Feb	11, 13	3 Ladbroke Terrace, Notting Hill	Letters to Sir Robert Peel, Prime Minister (9th December 1834-8th April 1835)	37
1838	Mar	21		Re-attends CM&G Board meetings to 4th March 1840	40
1840	Mar	5		Retires from CM&G Board along with three other Directors	42
1840	May	6		Cousin Edward Perceval's Will proved	
1841	Nov	8	12 Ladbroke Terrace, Notting Hill	Letter to Sir Robert Peel, Prime Minister (30th August 1841- 27th June 1846)	44
1843	Apr	24		First wife Mary dies at Ladbroke Terrace, Notting Hill	45
1843	Aug			In list of JPs for Middlesex	
1844	Apr	6		Marriage to Emma Gilbert in Lewisham	46
1844	Apr	23		Letter from "Lower

Year	Month	Day	Location	Event	Age
				Steigne", Brighton four days after his mother's Will was proved and three months after her death on 26th January 1844	
1845			Hampstead	Son James born*	48
1846	Apr	22	12 Ladbroke Terrace, Notting Hill	Letter to Treasury	
1847	Mar	7	Sydenham, Kent (Herne Bay, Kent or Hampstead)	Son George born	49
1847	May	1		In list of JPs for Kent	
1848	July	19	3 High Street, Herne Bay, Kent	Son Charles born	50
			High Street, Herne Bay	In 1848/49 Electoral Register for East Kent as occupier of house and stables	
1850	Jan	25	Herne Bay	Son Montague born	52
1851	Mar	30	Herne Bay - Census return for High Street.	Residents include Frederick, Emma (said to be aged 33), two children from Frederick's first marriage as well as their first four sons, four servants	53
1852	Jan		Hampstead	Son James Francis born*	54
			Herne Bay	In 1853/54 and 1854/55 Electoral Register for East Kent as occupier of leasehold houses. (Freeholds of 1, 2 and 3 High Street belong to James Dolman.)	
1854	Mar	20	Herne Bay	Son James Wilde born	56
1857	Feb	23		In list of JPs for Kent	59
1858	Sept & Nov		Coleshill, Birmingham	Letters to Edward Bulwer-Lytton	60-61

Year	Month	Day	Location	Event	Age
1860			Gerrard Street, Warwick	In rate book for St Nicholas Parish, Warwick, renting property	62
1861			Warwick - Census return for Gerrard Street.	Residents include Frederick, Emma (said to be aged 43), son from Frederick's first marriage as well as their four surviving sons, two servants	63
1861	July	22	Died at Solihull and buried at Charlton		63
1870	Dec	23	Acock's Green, Birmingham	Second wife Emma dies	

*One of the two sons who did not live into adulthood.

By 1800 Ramsgate was known as a seaside resort. William Powell Frith's painting (see Figure 6 below), purchased for the Royal Collection by Queen Victoria after it had thrilled the crowds who flocked to see it at the Royal Academy, shows how popular it had become by mid-century. A population of just over 3000 in 1801 had increased to nearly 8000 in 1831 when Frederick had a house there and by another 50% to almost 12,000 in 1851. An 1849 map of Ramsgate by GM Hinds demonstrates how extensive and substantial a settlement it had become. The largest house was The Elms belonging to the brewer Richard Tomson. It has not proved possible to establish where in the town Frederick's house was.

Three of the surviving letters from Frederick are to Sir Robert Peel (1788-1850) when he was Tory Prime Minister. Two are dated February 1835 during Peel's first brief premiership, and the third in November 1841 shortly after Peel had begun his more substantial second term as Prime Minister. Peel had been preceded on both occasions by Melbourne, a Whig, and was to be succeeded in 1846 by Russell (1792-1878), a Liberal. Frederick could expect no help from them and he almost certainly did not write to them, for his letters to Peel were not raising political issues or commenting on topical matters of the day, but begging him for his assistance in finding employment. The first two were addressed from 3 Ladbroke Terrace, while the third six years later was from number 12, further along the street. The letters are obsequious but they are not excessively fawning, and it may be questioned whether Frederick

Figure 6: William Powell Frith, 'Ramsgate Sands' or 'Life at the Seaside', 1854 The Royal Collection © 2005, Her Majesty Queen Elizabeth II

was genuinely seeking employment or going through the motions. He may have felt obliged to pursue it, possibly even was being pushed and persuaded to do so, and he only gave Peel a couple of months as Prime Minister before he laid out his case each time. Alternatively, his motivation may have been clear but he may not have been sufficiently skilled to construct a convincing letter. Perhaps this partly accounts for Frederick's apparent lack of expectation even before the initial rebuff he received in 1835, let alone the foregone conclusion that was to be the outcome of his approaches in later years.

Frederick's first letter on 11th February 1835 opened by referring to an attempt to secure a personal interview with Peel, who had been Prime Minister for two months since 9th December:

"Sir,
"In answer to the note I had the honour to receive from you yesterday, I beg to observe that the principal object I had in view, when I requested the favor [sic] of an Interview, was to lay my case before you.

"I am the second son of the late Right Honble Spencer Perceval, without any ostensible employment, and, having a young family to provide for, am <u>wholly</u> dependent upon [an] annuity paid me by Lady Carr.

"I am consequently most anxious to obtain an employment, and very desirous to be of use to his [sic] Majesty's Government in any capacity in which my humble talents can be made available.

"I beg most humbly to observe, that I consider myself, as being the son of the late Mr. Spencer Perceval, to have some claim on your favourable consideration and I trust, that any applications backed by the recommendations of my friends Messrs. Goulburn and Herries,[461] may <u>eventually be attended</u> with success.

"Should I be so fortunate as to meet with this object I have in view, through your assistance, I will strive by a diligent application to the duties of whatever situation I may obtain to justify a continuance of your disposition to [serve?] or repose trust in a son of <u>my Father</u>.

"I have the honor [sic] to remain ..."[462]

Fred Perceval, as he signed himself, had invoked his father's name twice, an appeal that might be expected to have some impact given that Peel had entered parliament in 1809 and the older Perceval had quickly spotted his promise, indeed made him his protégé. But it was to no avail. The draft of the Prime Minister's acknowledgement a day later on 12th February is on the back of Perceval's letter in pencil. Peel "saw no possibility", not least because he had recently received a similar "application for employment ... from your brother Mr Dudley Perceval". Peel was unlikely to be prevailed on anyway, but he was certainly not about to become the benefactor of the entire Perceval family.

Interestingly, Frederick professed to be unaware of this approach by Dudley, and indeed probably was, as he lost no time in making clear to Peel on the 13th February:

---

[461] By "friend" Frederick was referring to his father's relationship rather than necessarily, or solely, his own. Spencer Perceval had represented Goulburn's mother as a lawyer free of charge when she was in financial difficulties, then found Henry Goulburn his first seat in parliament and brought him into the government from 1809. John Charles Herries (1778-1855) was a civil servant in the Treasury, and Spencer Perceval's private secretary at one stage, long before becoming an MP and eventually Goderich's Chancellor of the Exchequer. He too benefited from Spencer Perceval's patronage, and all three men had similar religious views.
[462] British Library, Add MSS 40414, f.103

"Sir,

"I have the honor [sic] to acknowledge the reply of your's of the 12th Inst., in which you express your regret at being unable at present to comply with my wishes. I trust you will excuse the liberty I take in further troubling you on the subject, but I hope that, in the event of my being able to point out any situation that may fall vacant in your gift, that you will <u>bear me in mind</u>, and not forget this application I have made for employment, the more so, as I am totally unoccupied, and have no professional occupation. I regret much having troubled you, after an application made by a <u>younger brother</u> [underlined twice in the original], and should not have done so, had I not been compelled by sheer necessity, and by my great desire to obtain employment under His Majesty's Government.

"Begging you again to excuse the liberty I take in further addressing you ..."[463]

His third surviving letter to Peel was sent nearly seven years later on 8th November 1841. Frederick wrote:

"Sir,

"I hope you will excuse the liberty I take in addressing you, but being anxious to obtain employment in a civil capacity under her Majesty's Government, I venture to make my request known to you, and I trust that in case of a vacancy occurring in the Commissionerships of Stamps, Customs or Excise my claim as the second son of my late ever to be lamented Father, who lost his life, while discharging the duties of Prime Minister, may be taken into favourable consideration by you.

"I have already applied to the Chancellor of the Exchequer who has promised to speak to you on my behalf. Should I be so fortunate as to obtain the object of my wishes through your kindness, I will endeavour by a diligent attention to the duties of the office to show myself worthy of it.

"I have the honor to be ..."[464]

The Chancellor of the Exchequer throughout this government was Frederick's "friend" Henry Goulburn. It is not known whether he did approach Peel on Perceval's behalf, but the Prime Minister's reply

---

[463] British Library, Add MSS 40414, f.182
[464] British Library, Add MSS 40494, f.173

the following day was clear enough. Peel was "still unable to hold out to him the expectation of an appointment".

Other surviving letters in the British Library are dated 1844 and 1846, and are not addressed to Peel specifically. The first was sent from Brighton, a black-bordered letter presumably as he was still in mourning for his mother who had died almost three months before:[465]

"My dear Sir,
"Perceiving that the County Courts Bill has passed through the Committee of the House of Commons I venture to renew the application I made last year[466] to you to recommend me to Sir Robert Peel for one of the <u>Treasureships</u> which are at his Disposal ..."[467]

It is difficult to gauge what reaction such a letter would have evoked in the Civil Service. While Frederick may have been hoping for sympathy, it is possible that it had the opposite effect. Any remaining credibility may have been in shreds. As the civil servant who dealt with it contented himself with erroneously noting on the letter "4th son of the late Spencer Perceval", it can be assumed that it made no impact on the higher echelons of the Service.

Just before Peel resigned in June 1846, Frederick was reduced to writing even more speculatively to the Treasury on 22nd April 1846:

"My dear Sir,
"Perceiving by the Paper this Evening that the Receiver Generalship of the Customs is vacant, though I am not sanguine enough to think that I have a chance of obtaining the employment, I venture to address you for the purpose of reminding you, and through you Sir R Peel of my [....] to obtain employment. At the

---

[465] Victorian mourning etiquette for upper class families was twelve months "of a parent for a child and vice versa ... while six months was stipulated for a brother or sister" according to Pat Jalland, "Death, grief and mourning in the upper-class family, 1860-1914", p183 in Ralph Houlbrooke (ed.), 'Death, Ritual and Bereavement', London, Routledge, 1989. The extent to which this period was observed, and whether it extended beyond dress to other matters such as letters, obviously depended on the people concerned.

[466] This letter, no doubt like others, has not found its way into the British Library collection.

[467] British Library, Add MSS 40543, f.82

same time I beg to observe that I am not ambitious of a very high appointment, but should gratefully accept a moderate one.

"Believe me/ My dear Sir/Y^{rs} very truly/ Fred Perceval

"P.S. I hope to hear a more satisfactory account of the health of Mr Goulburn."

Across the corners of the letter a Treasury functionary has written dismissively

"Let Mr Stephenson know this to be habit [i.e., Perceval's plaintive letters seeking employment].   Tell Mr Perceval that I have forwarded it to him."

James, the first son of Frederick's second marriage, was born at Hampstead on 20th October 1845.[468] On 1st May 1847 Frederick was listed as a JP for Kent (as he was in the subsequent list ten years later on 23rd February 1857).[469] By 1848 the family had moved to Herne Bay, with the third son Charles being born at 3 High Street according to the *Morning Chronicle*.[470] Frederick is included in the 1848/49 Electoral Register as the occupier of a house and stables at High Street, Herne Bay.[471] Like Ramsgate, Herne Bay was off the recently built Canterbury to Margate road.[472] Whereas Ramsgate lies on the eastern extremity of Kent, Herne Bay was north of this road, and is closer to London on that part of the Kent coast that faces north. Herne Bay was a much smaller settlement than Ramsgate, and grew at a slower rate, but nevertheless more than doubled in size in the first half of the nineteenth century with the population increasing from 1200 in 1801 to 3100 in 1851.[473] The town developed to the west first (comparing Keen's 1876 map with one in 1898), with the High Street running from the Town Hall to the Brunswick Hotel by 1898. The Perceval home on the High Street was a substantial property. As well as Frederick and Emma, there were six children living there (the son and daughter from his first marriage both now in their twenties, and

---

[468] *The Era*, 26th October 1845

[469] List of Justices of the Peace, Kent Archives, Centre for Kentish Studies Q/JC 66-67

[470] *Morning Chronicle*, 21st July 1848

[471] However, he does not appear in any of those from 1840/41 to 1847/48 for Herne Bay, nor in those from 1840/41 to 1844/45 for Ramsgate.

[472] Frank W Jessup, 'A History of Kent', London, Phillimore, 1974, p129

[473] Victoria County History of Kent, op cit, vol. III, p358

four of their sons aged five or under), and four servants: a cook, a nurse maid, an errand boy and a housemaid. Their sixth and youngest son James Wilde was born in Herne Bay in March 1854.

In the 1853/54 and 1854/55 Registers Frederick is described as the occupier of leasehold houses in Herne Bay. These may or may not have been in the High Street, but the freehold of numbers 1 to 3 High Street now belonged to a James Dolman. Frederick may have sold the property to him, perhaps occupying it on a leasehold basis instead, or been persuaded to exchange the freehold for leaseholds elsewhere in the town.

By 1858 the Percevals had moved to Coleshill, Birmingham. Frederick was now in his 60s and keen to find a post for his oldest son Spencer Frederick, still at home and soon to be thirty. Edward Bulwer-Lytton had become a Tory MP in 1852 after being out of parliament since 1841. Frederick wrote to him on 21st September 1858[474] shortly after the Prime Minister Lord Derby had made Bulwer-Lytton Secretary of State for the Colonies:[475]

"Dear Sir,
"I do not know whether ... you will recollect so humble an individual as myself who was constantly meeting you at Ealing when you were a Private Pupil with Mr Wallington ... If you should, perhaps you will excuse my taking the liberty of asking you if you can assist me in obtaining an employment in British Columbia or elsewhere for my son who is anxious to emigrate as an agricultural student.[476] Begging to apologise ..."

It may be that Frederick thought the Ealing connection more pertinent rather than that he had forgotten their Rottingdean schooling; though he may have feared Bulwer-Lytton had, given the difference in their ages and the limited overlap in their time there. Frederick's hand-writing was now that of an old man, and there is no indication that he received a reply, with an official noting on the back simply "Perceval/21 Sep 58/Appt for his son".

---

[474] Hertfordshire Archives and Local Studies, D/EK 026/149/1

[475] According to his DNB entry, Bulwer-Lytton's "...brief period of office was marked by two notable achievements: the establishment in 1858 of the new colony of British Columbia, and the separation from New South Wales in 1859 of the new colony of Queensland ... Ill-health forced him to resign his office in December 1859 but he retained his seat [in Hertfordshire] until 1866, when Lord Derby offered him the peerage he had long coveted ..."

[476] George, the oldest surviving son from his second marriage, was now aged 11 so the letter might conceivably refer to him but this seems unlikely.

Two months later Perceval was seeking a judicial appointment in British Columbia for a barrister acquaintance who was "very anxious to go out there".[477] His association with Bulwer-Lytton was becoming known and perhaps Frederick was trading on this, even boasting of it as a way of maintaining some sort of reputation. Once again, though, his approach seems to have been fruitless.

At some point after this date and before 1860 Frederick and his family had moved to Warwick. By this stage the picture was one of decline, not quite to penury or destitution, but certainly the optimism of the 1820s was long gone - perhaps precipitated by his mother's death in 1844, when Frederick's annuity was replaced by a capital sum for him to manage himself. He had of course also been left £23,000 by his cousin Edward in 1840. This sum may have helped fund the move to 12 Ladbroke Terrace by November 1841, perhaps from a rented property to one Frederick purchased or at least to a larger property, while his mother's legacy no doubt assisted Frederick and his new family to move out of London to Herne Bay. A large house in Herne Bay had become a smaller one in Warwick with only two servants. Their house in Gerrard Street was close to St Nicholas Church, with a Baptist chapel, Methodist meeting house and burial grounds all in the same block bounded by Gerrard Street and Back Hills.[478] The parish had had an active workhouse since at least 1851.[479] On one side of the Percevals' house were six almshouses according to the 1861 Census enumerator, while the house next door was to let. One of the neighbouring houses was occupied by a dressmaker, her son (or grandson) who was an errand boy and their lodger a pupil teacher, and another by an upholsterer and cabinet maker and his wife. The Percevals' house with nine occupants would have been very unusual.[480] It was rented from Mrs Catherine Cookes, who owned seven of the properties in Gerrard Street and lived in the neighbouring St John's in some opulence, owning a "house, garden, lawn and stable" and renting a pantry, and "close garden and plantation" next door for her own use. The total rateable value of her St John's properties was

---

[477] Hertfordshire Archives and Local Studies, D/EK 026/149/2

[478] Back Hills is now called Castle Hill. Gerrard Street is in the centre of Warwick, near the Castle, and for the most part the properties that can be seen today are those that existed in the mid-nineteenth century.

[479] Victoria County History of Warwickshire, vol. II, London, Dawsons, 1965, p192

[480] As houses in Warwick were not numbered until 1870, it is not possible to tell either from the 1851 map of the town or by visiting which one it was.

£61.[481]   The house Frederick rented from her included premises, although it has not proved possible to establish what these were, let alone whether the family used them.   There is no indication in the 1860 Warwickshire Directory, where Frederick and Mrs Cookes are among the few private residents listed in Warwick.[482]   Only one other person in Gerrard Street is identified as such, though Henry Cooke the upholsterer living next door but one to the Percevals appears in the commercial list.   While the Percevals' property was smaller than the one in Herne Bay, and much smaller than Mrs Cookes', having a rateable value of £32, this was the highest figure in Gerrard Street and was only just exceeded by the Three Tuns Inn (£33 RV) among other properties in the block.   These were the highest figures in the area of Gerrard Street, Back Hills and Smith Street apart from one other, which eclipsed all properties in this part of Warwick (including Mrs Cookes') with a rateable value close to £79.

As well as Frederick and Emma, the son from his first marriage, Spencer, still lived with them as did their four surviving sons.   The four servants they had employed in Herne Bay had been reduced to two, a housemaid and an eighteen year old manservant.   The latter would have been employed to look after Frederick who was becoming increasingly frail.   He was to die a few months later at Solihull.   Although Emma lived another nine years to 1870, she was still only in her early fifties when she died at Acock's Green.[483]

Three months after Frederick's death the *Birmingham Daily Post* reported that:

"Frederick James Perceval, Esq., of Gerrard Street, Warwick, **and** [emphasis added] Herne Bay, Kent, died at Solihull, Warwickshire, on the 22nd July last, having executed his will in 1847, and has added thereto three codicils, dated respectively 1849 and 1860, nominating his brothers, John Thomas Perceval and Ernest Augustus Perceval, Esqrs., executors and trustees, to whom probate was granted by the London Court on the 23rd ult., the personalty being sworn under £12,000.   ...   The testator was twice married, and has left a large family.   This will is entirely of a family

---

[481] '1860 Rate Book, St Nicholas parish, Warwick', Warwickshire County Record Office, CR1618/W33/61-89

[482] 'Warwickshire Directory 1860', Warwickshire County Record Office, C910 KEL

[483] Given this picture of decline, it would be useful to have the family perspective on it from Frederick's siblings or children. Unfortunately, however, no records or commentary have been found.

nature. To Mrs Perceval, the relict, is bequeathed a life interest in the testator's entire property, with the power of disposition over a portion of it. On the decease of Mrs Perceval, the property is bequeathed to four of the sons of the testator, George, Charles, Montague and James. There are no other dispositions contained in the will. Mr Perceval, the testator, filled the office of magistrate for the counties of Middlesex and Kent. He appears to have led a retired and quiet life, and died at the age of 63."[484]

In addition to the assertion that the Herne Bay property was still in the family and part of the estate, possibly was virtually the entire estate, it should be noted that there were no bequests to either of the children from his first marriage and that the newspaper report does not specify the size of the personalty. The lack of any bequest may have been the reason why his son Spencer subsequently ceased to use the name Frederick. As £12,000 in 1861 is the equivalent of almost £520,000 in 2009, Frederick was in Louisa's league - though not in Frederica's - if the estate was as large as this. However, there are reasons to conclude that it was less, perhaps much less. In current parlance, Frederick may have been "property rich, but cash poor", but it must be doubtful if even this was the case if his interest in the Herne Bay property was now a leasehold one. Employment was, in his words, a "necessity", not just a matter of occupying his time. If this was the case in 1835, it would have become more so twenty-five years later, when he had long ceased to have an annuity from his mother to fall back on - or even the fees for attending Clerical, Medical and General Board meetings.

Given that Frederick was a magistrate in Kent, and especially if he still owned property in Herne Bay or elsewhere, a move to Coleshill in his late fifties or early sixties with four young children, and then for the family to move again to Warwick shortly after, requires some explanation. It may be that Emma's "power of disposition over a portion" of the property meant very little by this stage, but if nothing else Frederick must have expected the term of the lease to outlast her if anything was to pass to their children after her death.

---

[484] *Birmingham Daily Post*, 4th November 1861

7. THE VIGILANT AND VIGILANTE VICAR: HENRY PERCEVAL (1799-1885)

Henry was less than two years younger than Frederick and about four years younger than Spencer. While Frederick and Spencer had led markedly different lives to each other, these had largely been determined for them from the outset. As the oldest son, and having received free legal training at Lincoln's Inn (as would his younger brother Dudley), Spencer was expected to maintain the Perceval name in politics. He approached this in his own fashion and was to adopt a different attitude to religion from his father, coming first under the influence of Drummond and the Catholic Apostolic Church, and eventually aligning himself with Roman Catholicism as his disillusionment increased. Frederick was treated very differently, enjoying none of the inherited or educational advantages that fell to Spencer. The course of his life reflected a mounting struggle to be recognised and rejoin the elite society into which he had been born.

Henry's life, by contrast, was emblematic of a third approach to the circumstances in which he found himself. He was twelve and a half when his father was assassinated, and while this event would have had a major impact on him at this age, he was also protected to some extent by his five older siblings and by the Harrow School environment he had entered a year earlier with three of his Arden cousins, Edward, Charles and Arthur. As he was aged fifteen when his mother then re-married, it might have been understandable if Henry had gone "off the rails". However, he seems not to have taken the opportunity to make a drama out of a crisis, instead immersing himself more deeply in the life of the school, choosing to conform rather than rebel. According to Gray, who cites Harrowby at this point, Henry was industrious and "vastly proper", showing an "unaffected simple heartedness".[485] Like both his father and brother Spencer before him, and Dudley and John (but not Ernest) subsequently, Henry became a monitor (prefect) at Harrow in 1815. Unlike any of his other relatives, however, he then went on to be made Head of School in 1816, his final year. This must have reflected the respect in which he was held by teachers and fellow pupils alike, in part no doubt because of the way he had responded since 1812. He obtained a BA from Brasenose College at Oxford

---

[485] Gray, op cit, p431 contrasts Henry with Dudley on the basis of Harrowby MSS, vol. IV, fol. 56. Dudley entered Harrow two years after Henry in 1812-13.

University in 1820 and then an MA in 1823 as the Reverend Henry Perceval.[486]

A country parson

His first clerical post was as rector to St Luke's Church, Charlton in 1825. This was the Perceval parish church and already contained memorials to his father and older sister. According to the Brasenose College Register, he was also at this time the Vicar of West Hoathley in Sussex.[487] A few months later in March 1826 he married his cousin Catherine Drummond (1799-1870).[488] She was 25 as well, having been born the same month as Henry in August 1799, and was related (though more distantly) to the Henry Drummond who had been instrumental in starting the Catholic Apostolic Church and had so influenced her brother-in-law Spencer in this. Her father Andrew Berkeley Drummond (1755-1833) and Henry Drummond's father, another Henry, were also cousins and from the same banking dynasty. Catherine's mother Mary (?-1839) was a daughter of the 2nd Earl of Egmont and therefore a sister of Lord Arden and the older Spencer Perceval.[489]

Later that year they moved to County Durham when Henry became rector of Washington. Their son Henry Spencer (1827-1876) was born there in January 1827 and their daughter Catherine Mary (?-1923), who was to die aged 94, followed in 1828 or 1829. While his father and brother Spencer were Tory MPs, and his brother Dudley sought to be a Conservative one, Henry was clearly a conservative in daily life. Of the four occasions he was referred to in the newspapers during his tenure at Washington, all of them between 1828 and 1833, three of them concerned the 'Washington Association for the Prosecution of Felons'. There were several such organisations in this part of Durham, an area that depended on agriculture and mining, though the Washington group may have been one of the first. To give a positive description, they might be glossed as self-help community organisations, but they were also

---

[486] *Jackson's Oxford Journal* 24th May 1823
[487] 'Brasenose College Register 1509-1909', 2 volumes, Oxford, Blackwell, 1909, vol. I, p450
[488] *Jackson's Oxford Journal* reported on 1st April 1826: "Married - At St Mary's Church, Marylebone, the Rev. Henry Perceval, son of the late Right Hon Spencer Perceval, to Catherine Isabella, second daughter of Andrew Berkeley Drummond, Esq. of Bryanstone-square and Cadland, Hants."
[489] Gibbs, op cit, vol. X, p494 and Burke's Peerage pp 3109 & 3112

vigilante associations that went beyond the passive protection of their members. For example, the *Newcastle Courant* included the following advertisement after the 1828 Annual Meeting:

"... it was resolved to enforce, with the utmost Rigour and Effect, the Resolutions of the Society for detecting, apprehending, and prosecuting to Conviction, all Persons who shall molest or injure, in any Respect, the Persons or Properties of any of the Subscribers. This Association have also determined to exert every legal Means within their District for bringing to Justice ... [robbers, burglars, receivers of stolen goods, etc.] Liberal Rewards [for information] preventing ... any Scheme of Fraud and Villainy."

adding

"This Association having established a Night Patrole [sic] for the Detection of Sheep-stealers, hereby invite such Associations as are in their immediate Neighbourhood, to join in apprehending this Class of Offenders." [490]

Thirty-seven people, often farmers or others in scattered and out-of-the-way properties, are listed as members. The first name on the list, as it was in the advertisements that followed the Annual General Meetings of 1829 and 1833, was that of "Rev. Henry Perceval, Washington".[491] This was an isolated and rugged part of the country, people had to look to their own resources to protect their properties and the lives of their families, and there was no reliable law enforcement agency to depend on.[492] The local vicar's name would be important to promote the scheme, assuring others of its value and encouraging them to join. That Henry Perceval appears first on the list, however, suggests that he may well have played a prominent role in developing it.

Henry Perceval was also mentioned in the *Newcastle Courant* when he established a local Diocesan Committee in Aid of the

---

[490] *The Newcastle Courant* 2nd February 1828

[491] *The Newcastle Courant* 24th January 1829 and 2nd February 1833

[492] "County [police] forces were gradually established [after 1830] until the [County and Borough Police] Act of 1856 required every County to provide its own constabulary." (Edward Troup, 'Home Office', London, GP Pitman & Sons, 1925, p45) Prior to this, areas had been dependent on local watchmen in some towns or special constables appointed by, and answerable to, the Justices of the Peace (JPs).

Church-Building Society.[493] This saw a church built in Usworth by 1835, an example of the growth in church-building that his father had set in train, and, though it remained part of the Washington parish for the moment, Usworth had a separate "Perpetual Curate" assigned to it.

After eleven years in Washington the Percevals transferred in 1837 to the parish of Elmley Lovett in Worcestershire where Henry was the rector of St Michael's for 46 years to 1883. This is a remote area today, more or less equidistant from Bromsgrove, Droitwich and Kidderminster which form a triangle of large settlements at least five miles away. There are a few other villages in the area, and the isolation is no doubt heightened by the contrast nowadays with the densely populated parts of the Midlands that lie to the east and north-east. Although it would have been remote in the 1830s, it would not necessarily have seemed so at the time and was at the heart of a thriving agricultural community. A map prepared in 1918 for the sale of the Elmley estate gives some idea of its secluded rural position. The corollary of this, of course, is that the community would have been self-sufficient. The area is little changed today, still with the church and a few scattered farms and cottages. The population never exceeded 400 after 1831, and by 1891 had declined to 300. About 20 children on average attended the village school during this period.[494]

Edwin Chadwick's 1842 report concluded that, with the exception of the most densely populated counties of Lancashire and Middlesex, Worcestershire had the highest death rates per 1000 population in England and Wales in 1838, both for the four classes of disease that he examined specifically and overall.[495] Rates of 16 and 29 respectively per 1000 of the population compared with 13 and 21 in Durham and Kent, 13 and 20 in Gloucestershire and Warwickshire, and 11 and 18 in Sussex. These figures doubtless say something about standards of reporting, with the lowest rates being recorded for areas such as Cumberland, Herefordshire, Lincolnshire and the North Riding of Yorkshire, but Worcestershire was far from being a rural idyll. The standard of cottage

---

[493] *The Newcastle Courant* 7ᵗʰ January 1832
[494] Victoria History of the County of Worcester, 4 vols., London, Dawsons, 1971, vol. IV, pp467 & 536 Horace Monroe, 'Elmley Lovett and the Moules of Sneads Green', London, Mitchell, Hughes and Clarke, 1927, p9
[495] Chadwick, op cit, p2 The highest rates in Lancashire and Middlesex reflected the most densely populated and unsanitary urban areas that lay within their boundaries.

accommodation occupied by labourers was generally poor. Following the second report of the Health of Towns Commission in 1845 a branch of the Metropolitan Health of Towns Association had been established in Worcester by 1846, as it had in some other places.[496] But, as Fay puts it,

"The regulation of ordinary sanitation did not become the duty of local authorities until the passing of the Public Health Act of 1848, and until that date the provision of water supply and sewage disposal was scanty...
"Unfortunately the spirit of the age did not believe that public welfare should be a public concern."[497]

Rural areas might fare better than urban ones in their overall environment, but individuals were still subject to the effects of their poverty. Diet was also important:

"The agricultural labourer was in fact the worst fed of all workers in the nineteenth century".[498]

The patronage of the Church living had been sold to Christ's College, Cambridge in about 1840.[499] The seller was Bryan Sneyd Broughton (?-?), and he and Henry Perceval swapped, with Broughton concluding the sale from Washington Priory in April 1840[500] (though it was not finalised until 1841, as a letter in October 1840 makes clear[501]). It was a comparatively well-paid living, with a

---

[496] Anthony S Wohl, 'Endangered Lives: Public Health in Victorian Britain', London, Dent, 1983, p145

[497] C.R. Fay, 'Round About Industrial Britain 1830-1860', Toronto, University of Toronto Press, 1952, pp69 & 72

[498] Wohl, 1983, op cit, p49

[499] 1837 according to the Victoria History of the County of Worcester, op cit, vol. III, p110, but 1840 or 1841 according to the records at Christ's College, Cambridge (Geoffrey Martin, Archivist, personal communication, 13th November 2009). See also the 1900 College history at www.archive.org/details/christscollege00peiluoft which says on p282 "... in 1841 the rectory of Elmley Lovett was purchased for £3,320 exclusive of costs. That is the last living which the College bought; it will probably remain so."

[500] Christ's College, Cambridge Archives, 'Conveyance of the Advowson of Elmley Lovett to the College and Abstract of Title', April 1840. Consulted with thanks to The Master, Fellows and Scholars of Christ's College, Cambridge

[501] From Bryan Sneyd Broughton to Christ's College's solicitors: Broughton had been prepared to sell since March but "Mr Lynes' Solicitor has been the cause of further delay ... Mr Lynes ... and myself have been much annoyed by the delay".

gross value of £607[502] (the equivalent of more than £25,000 today). By comparison, the neighbouring parish of Elmley Castle and the nearby one of Salwarpe both had larger populations, and bigger churches to serve them, but smaller livings. The contemporary local historian John Noake makes a number of disparaging comments about Elmley Lovett compared to Elmley Castle, referring only to the former's "Rev. H. Perceval rector" while Hugh Bennett is described as an "excellent vicar" for Elmley Castle, who had lectured on the history of the parish in 1864. Perhaps Bennett shared Noake's interest in local history, but Henry Perceval had clearly made little impact on him in his initial thirty years as vicar. Possibly Henry relished the prospect of a reasonably paid backwater; a smallish parish would allow him to spend more of his time as he chose.

The first Elmley Lovett church was built in 1274 when the list of vicars in the Church lobby starts. St Michael's Church itself is described as "of little architectural interest".[503] It was rebuilt in 1840 shortly after Henry became vicar and "consists of a chancel, nave, west tower with spire, and south porch".[504] It is undecorated inside, but this plain and simple approach is all the more affecting, at least to the extent that the message, rather than one of neglect, is that this is a house of worship, dedicated not to the fripperies of religion but to God's word.

Noake takes a more critical view:

"The church accommodation, 284; free seats 120. With the exception of the tower and spire the church was rebuilt about 1839 in the debased Gothic, fashionable at that time, and what is the worst feature of the business is that the expense of re-building (£1,500) was taken from the funds of the local grammar school, or rather the income is appropriated to paying off the mortgage on the church, and so the school is in abeyance; but this was done under the guidance of the Court of Chancery. Estates had been left for

---

[502] John Noake, 'Noake's Guide to Worcestershire', London, Longman, 1868, p143
According to David Morrison, the Librarian/Archivist at Worcester Cathedral, on the basis of Crockfords for 1865, "The tithe was £545, Glebe 30 acres; Rector's income £605 and a house" (personal communication, 6th November 2009).
However, the value of the Washington living was substantially more at £953 with a population six times as large. See the forerunner of Crockfords, 'The Clergy List for 1841', London, Cox, 1841, pp65 & 201 in the list of benefices.
[503] Victoria County History of Worcester, op cit, vol. III, pp. 106-110
[504] In 'A History of Worcestershire Churches' the only comment is that "it survived the re-building"

the three-fold object of repairing the church, paying a schoolmaster, and relieving the poor, but **the Elmley people of 1839 saved their pockets by sacrificing the school children and the poor of the parish** [emphasis added]."[505]

It can be assumed that Henry would have been involved in these decisions at the start of his tenure. Indeed, part of the attraction for any Bishop of Worcester may have been Henry's previous experience of building the church at Usworth. At the time of Henry's appointment, the Bishop of Worcester was still Robert James Carr, the brother of Henry's step-father, and this connection was no doubt germane, as may have been the fact that they were both educated at Oxford University. Elmley Lovett was close to the Bishop's palace at Hartlebury, and therefore the vicar appointed to the parish would be of even more moment than would ordinarily be the case.[506] It might be expected that the Bishop would give it substantial attention since the last thing he would want was an incompatible incumbent. It is not surprising, therefore, that they took a similarly conservative line on most questions. At a Vestry meeting on 25th August 1837, two months after Henry had transferred,[507] an architect reported on the "impossibility of repairing [the Church] and the absolute necessity of taking down greater part thereof."[508] This was the course agreed, which was just as well as the architect had already written more than a month before in early July to the solicitor for the Charity Trustees to tell him so.

Noake's sarcasm may have been sparked in the first place by a letter from George Griffiths of Kidderminster that appeared in the Daily News in June 1853. In Griffiths' view, Worcestershire was no worse than elsewhere in the abuse of authority, but even it "teems" with examples. One of those Griffiths cited was the Elmley Lovett school whose

---

[505] Noake, op cit, pp143-144

[506] As his entry in the DNB states, Carr "... died on 24 April 1841, at Hartlebury Palace, near Worcester, from paralysis, and was buried on 3 May in the churchyard of Hartlebury parish." His successor Henry Pepys was created Bishop of Worcester 20th May 1841.

[507] 'Bishop's Register', Kidderminster Deanery, Elmley Lovett institution folios f.25-f.40, Worcestershire Record Office, 716.093/2648/12b/ii f.40

[508] 'Elmley Lovett Vestry Minute Book 1824-1887', Worcestershire Record Office, 850/9845/5(ii)

"... rents [were] mortgaged to pay for interest on the money borrowed to rebuild the church, and no one dare seek restitution because of the dread of Chancery".[509]

Noake provides further instances of the parish's chequered history, incidents which he describes as "blots and misfortunes".[510] These included the attempted humiliation in church at the end of the eighteenth century of a young mother and her seducer, though the latter stayed away and the girl had to face her public disgrace alone. Not surprisingly, she "... afterwards became a zealous Methodist". In the first decade of the nineteenth century the squire and the parson

"... made the parish infamous by their ruinous squabbles and lawsuits about the estate. ... Both parties were imprisoned repeatedly, and at length died in most evil odour ..."

In 1805 a Colonel Passingham and his friend Mr Edwards were indicted by a Mr Forester:

"The Colonel had debauched Mr Forester's wife and carried her off; Edwards became a bankrupt, and Forester was his opposing creditor. The Colonel and Edwards conspired to oblige Forester to make a large settlement on his wife, and he was terrified into doing so by charges of the most horrible crimes. These facts having been proved on the part of the prosecution, the defendants brought eleven witnesses to swear that Forester had actually been guilty of the said crimes, but they utterly broke down, and were sentenced to three years' imprisonment and the pillory. The latter part of the penalty was abandoned, from an apprehension that the criminals would have been killed by the popular fury. Forester afterwards obtained a divorce from his wife, she having contrived to visit the Colonel in prison and assumed his name."

In 1809 a churchwarden was gaoled for posting libellous texts on the walls of the church against the then rector. In 1831 a local lad of "weak intellect" was hung for setting fire to a rick of wheat,[511] while in 1832 the Reverend John Lynes (?-?), the rector who is

---

[509] *Daily News* 2nd June 1853
[510] Noake, op cit, pp144-145
[511] *Jackson's Oxford Journal* 12th March 1831; *Derby Mercury* 30th March 1831; *Caledonian Mercury* 11th April 1831

supposed to have sold the living to Christ's College a few years later,[512] was sued for £270 (or "one-third of his annual income") for non-residence under the Clergy Residence Act of 1817, but was found not guilty of "the entire three months absence".[513] Lynes seems to have been a disputatious character who in one instance sought to enforce a milk tithe on a parishioner by taking him to court.[514] He was no doubt as pleased to sell the living on as some parishioners were to see him depart. He was succeeded in 1835 by the Reverend Bryan Sneyd Broughton,[515] who recorded several comments on his new parish and some of the parishioners in his 'Curate's Memo Book and Parochial Visitor's Guide'.[516] Broughton welcomed the opportunity this gave him to marry that July, but had moved on himself by 1837 changing places with Perceval.

Henry had been elected Guardian of the Parish in March 1838 "there being no opposition" and seems to have adopted a low-key role.[517] From 1841 the Vestry only met twice a year, once in March to elect officers and once in April to agree the accounts.

Elmley Lovett's small population had clearly proved no deterrent to a pattern of colourful events. Indeed, its isolated nature may have been responsible for stimulating some of them and encouraging others to extremes once they had started. The parish was no doubt ready for a low profile and a period of tranquillity. However, this respite was shattered in 1849 when it was thought that a wealthy farmer who had left his substantial estate to strangers might have been poisoned. It was claimed that the only way to test whether he had been murdered was to dig up his remains, though it is not clear that a definitive conclusion was

---

[512] According to the Victoria History of the County of Worcester, but as is often the case, the story is more complicated, as Christ's College records show. Reverend John Lynes had been installed as vicar while the living belonged to his father. Lynes subsequently inherited it in 1831 and sold it on to his successor Broughton in 1836. It was Broughton who sold it to Christ's College. Christ's College, Cambridge Archives, 1831 Will of John Lynes; Letter from Reverend John Lynes to Reverend Bryan Sneyd Broughton re the Conveyance of the Advowson of Elmley Lovett, 29th September 1836; and 'Conveyance of the Advowson of Elmley Lovett to the College and Abstract of Title', April 1840 (as above).

[513] *Jackson's Oxford Journal* 24th March 1832

[514] *John Bull* 19th August 1833

[515] *Derby Mercury* 10th June 1835; *Jackson's Oxford Journal* 13th June 1835

[516] A standard format had been published in 1833 by JH Parker of Oxford, leaving space for a vicar to record his comments in various pre-determined categories. Worcestershire Record Office, 850/9845/5 (i)

[517] Elmley Lovett Vestry Minute Book, f.137 (later folios are not numbered)

reached. It no doubt provided a topic of interest for some time.[518] As if to indicate that the hiatus had only been temporary, the exhumation was the precursor to a number of events in the 1850s that put Elmley Lovett back in the news. The conservatism Henry had previously exhibited at Washington mirrored that of the parish itself, which was not only anti-change, almost regardless of the form this took, but was determined to make its opposition to progress known to the outside world.

In March 1853 the Jewish Disabilities Bill[519] was being considered in Parliament. Various petitions were presented in support of the legislation, such as by the Corporation of London, while one Catholic MP made the point that in supporting the Bill he would be

"... acting in accordance with the opinion of every individual in the large Catholic constituency which he had the honour of representing."[520]

This was not just a matter of minorities sticking together. He continued, quoting the Duke of Wellington's intervention in a debate on the Maynooth College Act in 1847:

"This is not a religious question, it does not involve any religious principle, but it involves the great Christian principle of abstaining from persecution."[521]

But this did not deter the rector and churchwardens of Elmley Lovett who presented one of the petitions in opposition to the Bill.[522] It was likely that Henry Perceval was the prime mover in this, not least given his father's views in the past and his brother Dudley's current opposition. No doubt Henry had also opposed the earlier proposal in 1845 to make the Maynooth grant recurrent rather than annual.

---

[518] *Freeman's Journal and Daily Commercial Advertiser* 4th October 1849; *Trewman's Exeter Flying Post or Plymouth and Cornish Advertiser* 4th October 1849; *John Bull* 6th October 1849; *The Lady's Newspaper* 6th October 1849; *Lloyd's Weekly Newspaper* 7th October 1849; *The Hull Packet and East Riding Times* 12th October 1849

[519] It is considered further in the following Chapter where Dudley Perceval was in the vanguard of opposition.

[520] Vincent Scully (1810-1871), Liberal MP for Cork, quoted by the *Morning Chronicle* 12th March 1853.

[521] Ibid The second reading was then agreed by a majority of 263 to 212.

[522] *The Times* 12th March 1853; *Morning Chronicle* 12th March 1853

This had been equally, if not more, contentious. In the Worcester Diocese, however, Robert James Carr had been replaced as Bishop from 1841 by Henry Pepys. In a decisive intervention

"Bishop Pepys explained to the clergy of Worcester that, in opposition to their declared views, he had voted in favour of the grant because he did not believe Catholicism was 'so full of errors, so corrupted from its original purity, as to make it a sin in a Protestant State to contribute towards the education of its ministers'."[523]

Pepys did not come into direct contact with Henry Perceval and Perceval outlasted him. Pepys' Visitation Act Book 1841-1878 makes no mention of either Perceval or Elmley Lovett - an omission for which both parties were no doubt greatly relieved.[524]

In 1854 Lord Elmley led the Elmley Lovett parishioners in petitioning against the Parliamentary Oaths Bill,[525] while in 1856 he had the Agricultural Statistics Bill in his sights. On this occasion he was at the head of a petition from the landowners and occupiers of 62,000 acres in Worcestershire and Gloucestershire, 209 people in all.[526]

In 1819 Henry had contributed five guineas while an undergraduate to the Old Harrovian fund for an additional school building.[527] After the Duke of Wellington died in 1852 a fund was established to build a national memorial to him. Queen Victoria headed the list of subscribers with a donation of £1000 (nearly £60,000 in 2009), while Henry Perceval made the more modest, but still substantial, contribution of £5.[528] In June 1853 the Morning Chronicle reported an Old Harrovian meeting to determine the

"... tribute [to] be paid to the memory of the late George Butler, Dean of Peterborough, and for twenty-four years Head Master of

---

[523] E.R. Norman, 'Church and Society in England 1770-1970: A Historical Study', Oxford, Clarendon Press, 1976, p118 quoting from 'A Charge Delivered to the Diocese of Worcester by Henry Pepys, D.D., Bishop of Worcester', London, 1845, p23

[524] Worcestershire Record Office, 716.011/2657

[525] *The Times* 8th April 1854

[526] *The Times* 3rd May 1856

[527] *Morning Chronicle* 27th December 1819 As the building was for the purposes of developing declamation and public speaking, it was presumably a hall or theatre.

[528] *The Times* 10th January 1853

Harrow School, by the erection of a monument in the parish church of Harrow."[529]

It was this Dr Butler who had persuaded Spencer Perceval junior to remain at Harrow another year after his father's assassination.[530] Spencer was at the meeting and seconded the formation of a committee to decide the most appropriate monument, joining it himself. Four of the Percevals subscribed: Spencer gave £5, while Henry, Dudley and Ernest added £2 each. The only Old Harrovian brother missing from this list was John Thomas, though none of his Arden cousins featured either.

In October 1859 the Elmley estate was put up for sale.[531] The 1250 acres had an annual rental of £2600 per annum (£112,000 today) and included farms, cottages and other manors as well as Elmley Lovett itself. By early November the *Daily News* and the *Morning Chronicle* reported that it had been sold for £77,200 (over £3.3m in 2009).[532] By this time the Oxford, Worcester and Wolverhampton railway had opened up the general area, with a station at nearby Hartlebury, but the Severn Valley line was still being built and the overall impact on the parish was minimal. It may have made it easier for people to leave, but did not entice others in for there was nowhere to live and no jobs. The population trend remained downward.

Henry's wife Catherine died in early 1870,[533] but he continued in the parish for another thirteen years, becoming one of the longest serving vicars. According to the *Leeds Mercury* report in May 1882, a hale and hearty Henry was still officiating in his eighty-third year.[534] He retired in 1883 and was succeeded by John Sharpe who was vicar to 1896. John Sharpe already had an established reputation and the *Birmingham Daily Post* reported on 1st June 1884 that he preached the sermon at the Worcester ordinations that year.[535] Henry was not all that healthy and fit though, with his signature to the Vestry meeting minutes deteriorating markedly after

---

[529] *Morning Chronicle* 4th June 1853

[530] See Chapter 2 above

[531] *Morning Chronicle* 19th September 1859; *Daily News* 27th September 1859; *The Times* 8th October 1859

[532] It was put up for sale again in the 1890s and then in 1918 as separate lots.

[533] See *John Bull* 19th February 1870 for the death notice of "Mrs Henry Perceval".

[534] *Leeds Mercury* 20th May 1882

[535] His 'Notes and dissertations on the prophecy of Hosea' appeared the same year. He may have been a favourite of the then Bishop.

1880.[536]   He also seems to have neglected the Church for some time, with John Sharpe's first Vestry meeting on 29th February 1884 agreeing that he could apply for faculty to re-arrange and ornament the chancel.

On 18th September 1874 the Will of George Perceval, the 6th Earl of Egmont, was proved.[537]   He made a number of very substantial family bequests, including to his Perceval cousins: £10,000 each to Henry and John Thomas, £8,000 to each of the four unmarried "Misses Perceval" and £15,000 to Ernest.   This totals £67,000 (over £3m in 2009).   Isabella's husband Spencer Walpole was left £20,000.   The families of those cousins who had pre-deceased him, Spencer, Frederick and Dudley,[538] received nothing with the exception of Frederick's son "Frederick" Spencer, the only member of the next generation to be remembered, who was left £5000.   This may well have been charity and stands in marked contrast to the lack of any legacy from Frederick Spencer's own father.

One of Henry's last public acts in January 1885 was to contribute to the relief fund set up after an earthquake disaster in Spain.[539]   His contribution was £5, while his largest charitable donation - perhaps fittingly, if ironically - had been £10 in November 1870 to the Poor Clergy Relief Fund.[540]   It is worth noting that this is over £450 in 2009.   On 1st April 1885 *The Times* recorded his death in a straightforward notice:

"... at Hill End, Salwarpe, Worcestershire in his 86th year the Rev. Henry Perceval, eldest surviving son of the late Right Hon. Spencer Perceval, formerly rector of Elmley Lovett in the same county."[541]

There was no obituary.   His Will, dated 6th September 1882, was proved on 28th May 1885 with his two Walpole nephews as the executors.[542]   His son had pre-deceased Henry and was buried in

---

[536] Elmley Lovett Vestry Minute Book, op cit

[537] *John Bull* 3rd October 1874   George Perceval had entered Harrow with Spencer junior in 1804 and had brought the extraordinary legal case against the estate of the 5th Earl.   See Chapters 1 and 4 above.

[538] His other cousin Jane Perceval had died 50 years earlier but had left no family.

[539] *The Times* 20th January 1885

[540] *John Bull* 26th November 1870

[541] *The Times* 8th April 1885   The *Pall Mall Gazette* 8th April 1885 carried the same notice.

[542] See www.archive.org/stream/visitationenglan06howa which records the 1893 visitation of England and Wales (Jackson and Crisp, op cit).

Reading, while Catherine Mary, Henry's daughter, did not marry and is listed as living at Chobham House, Surrey.[543]

Henry and Catherine are buried in the churchyard at Elmley Lovett. The Church contains the following inscription near the altar:

"Here sleeps in Jesus
Catherine Isabella
The Beloved Wife
of the
Rev Henry Perceval
Born August 19 1799
She Lived
the Faith of the Son of God
Blameless and Harmless
Child of God Without Rebuke
And Died
In the Hope of Eternal Life
Feb 11 1870.
+
"Also the Said
Henry Perceval
46 Years Rector of this Parish
Born Aug 2 1799 Died April 1 1885
The Memory of the Just is Blessed."

Compared to his testimony to Catherine, Henry's memorial is relatively simple - though with an intriguing last line. He may well have found himself in opposition both to some of his parishioners and Bishop Pepys, as well as out of step with the national trends towards increasing liberalisation in politics and religion. He no doubt viewed his conservative approach as not only appropriate but necessary in order to put off if not prevent, to hold back if not disperse, the forces of change.

---

[543] www.british-history.ac.uk/report.aspx?compid=42998 clarifies that she owned the house: "The [Aden] manor was sold to General Broome, and then to Mr. Jerram the vicar of Chobham in 1808. It passed through four more owners to Miss Perceval, the present owner. The house was rebuilt on another site, and is now called 'Chobham House'."

8. THE CONSCIENCE OF DUTY: DUDLEY PERCEVAL (1800-1856)

Many people might be described as "the conscience of the nation", but Dudley Perceval would not be one of them - even by the partisan *John Bull* magazine. He was, however, the conscience of the Percevals, guarding his father's reputation and religious beliefs zealously, and spending much of his adult life in devoted duty to his father's memory. But, while his zeal developed early, it took some time for his intelligence to catch up. According to Denis Gray, Dudley was fourteen when he "... got mixed up in a fight between Harrovians and Anabaptists which resulted in one death."[544] Needless to say, this is not mentioned in his entry in the Harrow School Register; nor did it prevent him becoming a prefect in 1815.[545] But these "early signs of his violent religious opinions" cannot have been quite as early as Gray suggests. Dudley relates the incident in a letter to his sister Maria:

"A party of Anabaptists, about 100, came down here ... Well, as they went down the hill, the fellows, about 60 or 100 **of us** [emphasis added], being enraged at some impudence ... pursued ... and pelted those baptists with great zeal for the Church, till they were at the bottom, and returned very much delighted at the exploit."[546]

The Anabaptist who died had his skull fractured by a stone. Dudley claimed not to be involved (despite the circumstantial evidence in his reference to "us" fellows) but was singled out when the case was taken to court. The Harrow headmaster Dr Butler was furious, not least because of the discredit it brought the school. Dudley took a more dismissive line, which even for a teenager writing to his sister was surprisingly blasé:

---

[544] Gray, op cit, p431 from Harrowby MSS, vol. IV, fol. 56

[545] Harrow School Register 1800-1911, op cit, p59

[546] British Library, Add. MSS 49193, f.1 The letter is dated 10th November and the British Library has tentatively added "1817?". Dudley's 17th birthday was on 22nd October and he left Harrow School that term. He ended the letter by saying "Henry and Ernest send loves". This complicates the dating further as Henry had left Harrow in 1816 and Ernest did not enter until 1817. However, the event must have taken place later than the 1814 date Gray suggests.

"Now the riddle's read I expect to be arrested some day and carried to town ... but as I can prove an alibi I don't care."[547]

The case seems to have been quietly dropped, and in time he learned to channel his passions more productively into cerebral, rather than physical, confrontations, expressing his religious views in ways that he hoped would convince others. After his early death at the age of 55, the impact, and to some extent the effectiveness, of this strategy was recognised by the *Morning Herald* in his obituary:

"... The death of the lamented gentleman was very sudden, having taken place after a few hours' illness. ...
"After holding high office at the Cape of Good Hope, he returned home some years ago, and attracted public attention by his able and elaborate pamphlets on great constitutional questions. The peculiar characteristic of Mr Perceval's mind was his undeviating adherence to high honour and principle. Every opinion which he avowed, every act which he performed, were always tested by him by this standard. His writings afford the strongest evidence of this assertion. Mr Perceval took a first class degree [in Classics at Christ Church College, Oxford[548] in 1822] ... and renewed his connection with that university by his memorable contest with Mr Gladstone for its representation four years ago [actually 1853]. On that occasion Mr Perceval did not succeed. He was, comparatively with his opponent, an untried man; but it was highly honourable to him to have sustained such a contest, and to have obtained so many votes on the strength of his individual character in private life. He failed because he was too good a churchman to excite enthusiasm in the minds of either of the extreme parties in the church."

This was repeated by the *Manchester Times*, but as Manchester was probably the last place one would expect to see Dudley Perceval remembered in glowing terms, there are aspects of it, the last sentence in particular, that were probably sarcastic.[549] Dudley

---

[547] Ibid

[548] This was the College Gladstone later attended from 1828-1831 (the sister college of Trinity College, Cambridge according to the DNB).

[549] *Manchester Times* 13th September 1856
See, for example, www.historyhome.co.uk/peel/refact/refmod2.htm: "The 'Manchester School' emerged in the 1820s and newspapers such as the

had been nominated for the 1853 contest by a High Churchman and by an Evangelical. These may not have been the two "extreme parties" referred to, but they were at least two of them.[550]   In addition, and even though Dudley was a vestryman at St George's, Hanover Square, he would have had to be "a very good churchman" indeed to better Gladstone. But this apart, if this eulogy otherwise sounds familiar, it probably is. Of all the twelve children, Dudley followed his father's views most closely. Others adopted some of his opinions, some of the children demonstrated their adherence at certain times though not invariably, while most, perhaps all, revered his memory, but it was Dudley who best fitted the mould - a mould he modernised as circumstances required. Hansard described him in effect as a "chip off the old block" in 1851, but a similar line might have been taken in 1829 with regard to 'Quietus Optabilissimus', his first venture into print at the time of Catholic emancipation.[551] Goaded by the prospect, and galvanised by a Wilmot Horton[552] (1784-1841) pamphlet the previous year on 'Protestant Securities', he felt compelled to publish his views. 'Quietus Optabilissimus' appeared on 9th February 1829 (two days before his first child's birth)[553] and was promoted from the family home at 2 Wilton Street, London.[554] The puff at the start of the pamphlet says

"These remarks were ready for the press some time before the purport of the King's Speech was surmised. The Author, through

---

Manchester Times and the *Manchester Guardian* were founded and spread the doctrine of the middle class industrialists. The idea of free trade was particularly strong in this area because of the cotton industry."
[550] The *Morning Chronicle* reported on 8th January 1853 that many Evangelicals would have nothing to do with Dudley Perceval's candidature. However, as the paper favoured Gladstone and strongly opposed Dudley, their report was not impartial: they were talking up Gladstone's chances at a time when the outcome looked uncertain.
[551] Dudley Perceval, 'Quietus Optabilissimus: or, The nature and necessity of real securities for the United Church, with a liberal and lasting settlement of the Catholic question', London, Ridgways, 1829
[552] Horton was a cousin of Byron, an inveterate proponent of emigration and pamphleteer on many subjects, and Governor of Ceylon 1831-1837.
[553] Advertisement in *The Times* on 9th February 1829 on the day of publication
[554] This is between Belgrave Square and Grosvenor Place. The family had moved to 16 Wilton Street by 1835 and were there for the 1851 Census. Although Dudley gave his address as Wilton Crescent in adverts for the National Club in 1845, and the family were not recorded in the 1841 Census, the Post Office London Directory (London, Kelly, 1841) places him at 16 Wilton Street in 1841, as does the Rate Book for St George's, Hanover Square (Westminster Archives, C660, 2291) on 31st March 1841. The rateable value of the house was £80.

diffidence of the soundness of his views, had not decided on their publication. As it now appears that they are substantially confirmed by the high authority of those distinguished Statesmen, upon whose firmness and prudence the Country has the happiness, at this juncture, to depend, he can no longer hesitate to bespeak the indulgence of the Public for his feeble endeavours in so good a cause."

Like many puffs it was disingenuous, if not actually misleading.

Dudley's pamphlet sought to steer between the "Scylla and Charybdis of our political navigation" as he represented it,[555] between dismembering the Empire on the one hand, and civil war and domestic insecurity on the other, that he argued would follow from Catholic emancipation if steps were not taken first to protect the constitution and the established Anglican Church. He adopted the same mechanism as Horton had advocated of a "Standing Committee on Religion" but claimed his was to a different end. Rather than prevent Catholics from voting on Church issues, his version of the Committee was to provide an additional defence by determining whether any motion in the House of Commons was "consistent with the safety and interests of true religion and of the Established Church".[556] If not, the motion could not proceed. In Dudley's view,

"... the powers of such a Committee, though great, would be merely and solely *conservatory*, and therefore could never become unconstitutional."[557]

Another perspective might be that, as long as this repressive conservative end was achieved, in other words the preservation of the status quo, any means was acceptable. For example, since the Committee could not adjudicate on a motion if it was inquorate (less than twenty MP members), and could not deal with contentious issues requiring a division unless more than forty of the sixty Members, all Privy Councillors and certificated Anglicans, were present, it could be stopped in its tracks and held to ransom by a few rabid Members. Dudley was clearly alive to such anxieties and proposed that there should be annual renewal by ballot to prevent such cabals. It might be argued, however, that a year would be

---

[555] Perceval, 1829, op cit, p3
[556] Ibid, p14
[557] Ibid, p16

more than time enough to organise alternative opposition or disarm the original intention. In line with his "belt and braces" approach, Dudley further proposed that the Coronation Oath be extended so that laws could only be altered or repealed with the Committee's sanction. He was clearly not prepared to leave anything to chance, but it would be difficult to see any monarch abrogating their rights, not in favour of Parliament as a whole, or even just the House of Commons, but of a specially selected and no doubt self-perpetuating oligarchy. Doing so in private might be one thing; affirming it in public quite another.

Dudley's pamphlet proposed two additional securities that he argued were vital for the Establishment's safety. These were to reverberate in future years. The first was to open the universities to Roman Catholics, not as a desirable end in itself, but in order to avoid the separate education of priests at Maynooth and their consequent disaffection with the current constitution:

"There they will learn to respect our Church, if they cannot in conscience accept her ministry, - to wish her no evil, if they cannot bid her 'go forth and prosper'."[558]

This would not only do away with the annual arguments over grant, but with the necessity for Maynooth at all. His second proposal was to prevent the Catholic Church hierarchy associating itself with particular sees such as Kildare or Armagh. Dudley saw titles such as the "Roman Catholic Bishop of Armagh" as an "insolent assumption" that "implied equality" with the Established Protestant Church in Ireland which "makes it an evil".[559] This was similar to the issue that Lord John Russell's Ecclesiastical Titles Bill sought to tackle in 1851 in the midst of the Protestant backlash against Catholicism. Russell's Bill was

"... designed to punish any cleric outside the established church who assumed a British territorial title ... The bill ... was passed with large majorities. The new Catholic bishops ignored it."[560]

---

[558] Ibid, p19

[559] Ibid, pp19-21

[560] Hoppen, 1998, op cit, p444 In effect this re-stated the position that had applied since 1829 when the "Catholic Relief Act ... forbade non-Anglican ecclesiastics to take the title of sees already occupied by bishops of the established church" (p145).

Dudley's pamphlet received similarly short shrift in 1829, even though he sought to leaven it with some apparently enlightened proposals. For example, he wrote that the real cause of Irish disturbances was Irish misery not Catholic emancipation. The solution in his view was to provide for the poor of Ireland from the land of Ireland "avoiding the abuses of the English poor laws".[561] Some would argue that it was implementing policies such as these that led to the famines less than twenty years later; others that they were never adopted as intended, and that neglect by some landlords, and a focus on financial gain rather than their tenants by others, were just as significant factors. It is arguable whether Dudley was putting these proposals forward as a sop to Catholicism, or was already aware that the consequences could be double-edged. The Poor Law was extended to Ireland in 1838 after this had been recommended by the 1833-1836 Commission, but the remedial measures they proposed were not.

His pamphlet asserted that

"... the [electoral] barriers which are now proposed will excite no small hostility from those members ... whose real and half-avowed object is not the attainment of their own rights - but the overthrow of ours."[562]

Like Spencer junior in Parliament the previous year, Dudley concluded that, if the enemies of the established Church triumphed, at least this would not be due to any lack of effort by people like himself who had sought to defend the constitution.

Administrator abroad

After graduating from Oxford in 1822, Dudley took up the free legal training offered by Lincoln's Inn but, like Spencer junior, was not called to the bar.[563] The *Derby Mercury* stated some years later that "weak health [had] induced him to give up the law",[564] but there is no other evidence for this. Dudley then went to the Cape of Good

---

[561] Perceval, 1829, op cit, p27 By this he may have been referring to outdoor relief (which was abolished to widespread condemnation in 1834) and a belief that the Poor Law created dependency.

[562] Ibid, p26

[563] Frances Bellis, Assistant Librarian, Lincoln's Inn, personal communication, 26th November 2009

[564] *Derby Mercury* 12th January 1853

Hope where he was Clerk of the Council between 1826 and 1828.[565]   The Colony's acting Governor from March 1826 to September 1828 was Major-General Richard Bourke (1777-1855) who had been appointed to stabilise the Colony after the disastrous governorship of his predecessor Lord Charles Somerset (1767-1831). Somerset's despotic and arbitrary behaviour in the

"... later years of his administration were marked by distress and discontent among the Colonists and many complaints were laid before the Secretary of State and the British Parliament, as a result of which he was eventually recalled."[566]

Sir Rufane Donkin (1773-1841), a distinguished army officer and acting governor in the Cape in 1820-1821, was one of those who complained most vigorously about Somerset.   Donkin first sought a personal interview with the Secretary of State Earl Bathurst (1762-1834)[567] in 1826, but when he was refused then spent the next four months carefully compiling a letter that documented his concerns at length.[568] It was not surprising that he was so incensed with Somerset, who had countermanded Donkin's orders, overturned his decisions "without any reason at all",[569] put the safety and well-being of more than 5000 British settlers at risk and then mounted a vendetta against him. Donkin felt his integrity

---

[565] Joseph Foster, 'Alumni Oxonienses: The Members of the University of Oxford 1715-1886', 4 volumes, Bristol, Thoemmes Press, 2000 (reprint of Oxford, Palmer and Co., 1888), vol. III, p1097 This was the Council that had been set up from 1825 to advise the Governor.
Dudley Perceval was not Colonial Secretary (Secretary to the Colony) as his entry in the Harrow School Register, op cit, states. This was Sir Richard Plaskett.
[566] G.E. Pearse, 'The Cape of Good Hope 1652-1833', Pretoria, JL Van Schaik Ltd., 1956, p151
[567] He was Secretary of State for War and the Colonies in Lord Liverpool's government from 1812 to 1827, resigning when George Canning became Prime Minister and asked him to move to the Home Office. He subsequently returned to government as Wellington's Lord President of the Council in 1828-1830. His London home was 16 Arlington Street, next door to Henry William Carr's house (in 1816).
As Bathurst was in the Lords, the Government's main spokesman for the Colonial Office in the Commons was Wilmot Horton, the future author of the pamphlet on 'Protestant Securities' already referred to.
[568] Sir Rufane Donkin, 'A Letter on the Government of the Cape of Good Hope, and on certain events which have occurred there of late years, under the administration of Lord Charles Somerset: Addressed most respectfully to Earl Bathurst', London, Carpenter & Son, 1827
[569] Ibid, p37

had been impugned and that Somerset's tyrannical behaviour had made the Colony a human as well as a financial disaster. In Donkin's view, he had no option but to adopt Burke's saying that "when bad men conspire, honest ones should unite".[570] He was pleased that

"... my truly honourable and excellent friend General Bourke ... is endeavouring ... by every means in his power, by economy and good management, to carry on the financial operations of the Government."[571]

At this point Bourke was acting Governor while Somerset had been given leave of absence to defend himself against the charges in England. Donkin was one of those determined that he should not be allowed to return; Mr Bishop Burnett was another.[572]

Somerset's conduct was debated several times in the House of Commons during 1825, 1826 and 1827.[573] The first of these included a petition presented by Joseph Hume (the MP who harried Spencer Perceval junior)[574] in which the MP said

"Such was the tyranny of Lord Charles Somerset that if any man ventured to open his mouth to object to his conduct, he was liable to be deprived of his liberty and his property, and to be persecuted even unto death."

The second debate had included a call for Somerset's impeachment. However, there seems to have been no final parliamentary censure once the advisory council to put a check on the governor's most tyrannical behaviour had been established. The Commission of Inquiry set up in 1822 eventually reported publicly

---

[570] Ibid, p23

[571] Ibid, p79

[572] Bishop Burnett, 'A Reply to the "Report of the Commissioners of Inquiry at the Cape of Good Hope, Upon the Complaints Addressed to the Colonial Government and to Earl Bathurst by Mr Bishop Burnett"', London, Sherwood, Gilbert & Piper, 1826

[573] Hansard Parliamentary Debates, vol. 13 (new series 2), 27th May 1825, columns 903-909; 16th June 1825, columns 1166-1173; 22nd June 1825, columns 1274-1275; 5th July 1825, columns 1483-1485; vol. 15, 19th May 1826, columns 1277-1282; vol. 16, 7th December 1826, columns 303-313; 8th December 1826, columns 320-321; vol. 17, 17th May 1827, columns 883-895; 8th June 1827, columns 1168-1175; 29th June 1827, columns 1427-1438

[574] See Chapter 3 above

about four years later, and may well have provided Bathurst with a private report and a definite conclusion on Somerset's excesses. He did not return to the Cape of Good Hope and was replaced as Governor by Lieutenant-General Sir Lowry Cole in late 1828.

Dudley Perceval had worked closely with Bourke for two and a half years and, to nobody's surprise, he and one of Bourke's daughters Mary Jane (1802-1888) married in the Cape in July 1827 by special licence.[575] They had not long returned to England when their son Charles Spencer (1829-1889) was born in February 1829. Their daughter Isabel Jane (?-1921) was to be christened on 27th April 1831 at St Peter's, Eaton Square (according to the International Genealogical Index), and was aged 19 at the 1851 Census, but her precise date of birth is not available.[576]

Benefits of bureaucracy

Dudley was a Deputy Teller of the Exchequer from 1828 to 1834 in his brother Spencer's section.[577] His employment as a public servant prevented him from running for office but, far from silencing him, seems to have added to his opportunity to express his views, and possibly his credibility in doing so. It was after the closure of this section that Dudley wrote to Robert Peel seeking alternative employment.[578] Unlike his brother Frederick, however, Dudley had some relevant and recent experience to offer. Although he soon obtained another post in the Treasury as Deputy Comptroller to Thomas Spring Rice[579] (1790-1866), there was no immediate pressure to do so. Some months after the event *The Times* reported the Treasury Minute of 27th February 1835 setting out the compensation to be paid to employees on closing the Tellers'

---

[575] Their marriage settlement included a £2000 bond from her father and Dudley's share of the £50,000 grant that had been settled on the Perceval children in 1812. This amounted to £1000, with £250 in accrued interest, but, as the Cape Town notary recorded, "he is uncertain whether the exact amount of his share has been definitively appointed under the powers by the Act of Parliament vested in his mother ..." See British Library, Add. MSS 49193, f.4 and f.21

[576] According to Burke's Peerage she was aged 91 when she died in December 1921, so would have been born in 1830, but it does not specify her date of birth either.

[577] See Chapter 4

[578] See Chapter 6

[579] Subsequently Lord Monteagle from 1839. He was a Trustee in Dudley's marriage settlement (and would have been known to Richard Bourke from Limerick), as was Andrew Berkeley Drummond of the Bank at Charing Cross, Henry Perceval's father-in-law.

section. Dudley's salary had been £1000 and he was to be granted an allowance of £600 pa. At the equivalent of about £28,000 in 2009, Dudley was exemplifying the adage "To those that have shall be given". The justification for this largesse, according to the Minute, was

"... as the case of a son of a Prime Minister of this country, whose career was abruptly terminated by so melancholy an accident, [he is] entitled to greater consideration than that of an individual in ordinary circumstances, and ... therefore, [we] propose that an allowance of £600 per annum should be granted to him, to which he is particularly entitled, as having used his best endeavours to advance the success of the measure which has deprived him of a lucrative situation."[580]

For doing nothing, therefore, he was to receive sixty per cent of what he had previously been paid as an employee. Even a 73 year old Teller, Mr Manningham, who was senior to Dudley, more than twice his age and had twenty-five years service, only received £700 pa. The annual saving from closure was alleged to be £37,000 (about £1.7m today), but it may be apparent why the Treasury Minute often uses the word "eventually" to qualify this.

Protecting reputations

In 1835 Dudley took vigorous exception to a section in volume IV of Napier's history of the Peninsular War that denigrated his father Spencer Perceval.[581] Dudley's first letter of complaint was written on 25th March seeking evidence for three passages in which

"... you have thought proper, directly to impute, or sneeringly to insinuate, motives degrading to my Father's [sic] personal and private character."[582]

He continued:

---

[580] *The Times* 5th December 1835
[581] Dudley Perceval, 'Remarks on the character ascribed by Colonel Napier to the late Right Hon. Spencer Perceval', (2nd edition), London, James Fraser, 1835
[582] Ibid, p10

"The good name of my Father [sic] is the only inheritance he left to his children. You cannot wonder that I should seek to defend it from such charges."[583]

There were three passages that Dudley objected to in particular:

"... Mr Perceval, who sought only to maintain himself in power."
"... His religion did not deter him from passing a law to prevent the introduction of medicines into France during a pestilence."
"... his crooked, contemptible policy was shewn, by withholding what was necessary to sustain the contest [the Peninsular War], and throwing on the general [Wellington] the responsibility of failure."[584]

Dudley took offence at the use of the word "only" in the first phrase, and Wellington eventually provided him with support in relation to the last.[585] With respect to the second, Napier reminded Dudley of the Jesuit's bark Bill that had been passed in 1808, though he accepted that there had been no general pestilence in France. Napier argued that the charge had been directed at the Anglican religion, rather than at followers such as Perceval, since no religion should permit a "war against hospitals". He acknowledged that Perceval may have been a good private man ("I neither knew nor inquired about his social conduct"), but emphasised that "I thought him a bad public man".

Napier made it clear that he felt entitled to reach these conclusions as a historian, provided he could justify them, but Dudley did well to keep his temper all the same. Dudley replied on 23rd April that Napier's view was at odds with the speeches from both sides of Parliament after Perceval's assassination:

"... which speeches are in fact the justification of Parliament, in making, on the express ground of that character, a public provision for his family, far too large to be defended on the score of compassion alone."[586]

---

[583] Ibid, p11
[584] Ibid, pp12-15 for Napier's initial reply to these points on 5th April 1835
[585] Ibid, pp57-59 where Wellington's reply on 6th June 1835 to Dudley's letter the day before includes the statement that "... I should have been ungrateful and unjust indeed, if I had excepted Mr Perceval [from his praise for Ministers' support], than whom a more honest, zealous, and able Minister had never served the King."
[586] Ibid, p19

The £50,000 grant Parliament voted the children in 1812 equates to nearly £1.7m in 2009.

It was probably for the best that the dispute was conducted by letter allowing time for reflection and depending on reasoned argument. Dudley's views were as forthright as ever, and the correspondence went on to July 1835, before Dudley brought it to a close when he realised that Napier would hold his ground regardless of the evidence put forward to the contrary. This was essentially a courteous, though heartfelt and increasingly heated, skirmish compared to some of the acrimonious arguments in which Dudley would engage in later years. Dudley sent a copy of his pamphlet to Robert Southey who replied on 9ᵗʰ July 1835:

"I thank you for your pamphlet ... You have completely refuted a slanderous accusation, and have done it in a manner every way worthy of your Father's [sic] son.

"Mr Perceval was in my judgement the best minister we have ever had. I looked upon his Death, at the time, as the greatest misfortune that could have befallen this country; and subsequent events have shown that it was so."[587]

Three years after leaving the Cape, Dudley's father-in-law Richard Bourke was appointed the governor of New South Wales in 1831. The population almost doubled during his time to 100,000 before he resigned in December 1837 when compelled by the Colonial Office to retract a dismissal. Bourke had been knighted in 1835, and was to be offered other posts in later years, but his governorship had proved controversial as early as 1832 when he found himself trying to balance the interests of former convicts and other immigrants. In 1836 the disputes intensified and Dudley sprang to his defence with a letter to *The Times* that October. But it was clear where the paper's sympathies lay. In their account, Bourke's regime had so relaxed convict discipline that it supposedly threatened the safety of other settlers. In leading articles in October and December *The Times* thundered that this was "misgovernment" that had occasioned a "melee".[588] However, given that the colony erected a statue in Bourke's memory and seemed genuinely distressed when he left, it appears that his enlightened measures, such as the introduction of civil juries in criminal cases, had mainly

---

[587] British Library, Add. MSS 49193, f.22
[588] *The Times* 8ᵗʰ October, 19ᵗʰ October and 13ᵗʰ December 1836

threatened the vested interests represented by *The Times*. It was to Dudley's credit that he supported Bourke even though the colony's Church Acts in 1836 provided public funds for all the main denominations, thereby preventing domination by the Anglican Church. There had been local opposition to the measure, and while Dudley would have found it hard to stomach otherwise, it was outweighed in this instance by his respect for, and loyalty to, his father-in-law.

An aspirant MP

At the 1837 general election following Victoria's accession to the throne, Dudley first attempted to become an MP, standing for Finsbury. The constituency had been created by the Reform Act and was well-known as a radical stronghold. The *Morning Chronicle's* view was:

"It appears that the Tories have started Mr Dudley Perceval, a son of the late Mr Spencer Perceval, as a candidate for this borough. He certainly has not the most remote chance of success; and the only object in view in proposing him appears to be to put the Reformers to expense and inconvenience. Should the Tories dare to go to a poll the electors of this great and important borough will return their late independent members by an overwhelming majority. **The electors of Finsbury never will so far disgrace themselves as to return a Tory, and, above all, a Tory of the cast of his Hanoverian Majesty** [emphasis added]."[589]

The prediction proved to be correct and the incumbents Thomas Wakley[590] (1795-1862) and Thomas Duncombe (1796-1861) were returned. However, Dudley had polled 2500 votes, 700 more than any previous Conservative candidate.[591]

In late 1841 and early 1842 Dudley was once again in the newspapers, this time in relation to his posts in the Treasury, first as an Assistant Controller and then as Deputy Comptroller. In the first instance he appeared in court as a witness in the "Exchequer Bill Affair", when a senior clerk Edward Beaumont Smith was accused of forging the signatures on Treasury Bills and attempting to market

---

[589] *Morning Chronicle* 19th July 1837; *The Examiner* 23rd July 1837 also included this in its description of the Finsbury preparations
[590] Medic and founder of *The Lancet*
[591] *The Times* 1st August 1837

them through an accomplice Ernest Rapallo in order to defraud the Treasury.[592] Rapallo turned Queen's evidence, Beaumont Smith was convicted and transported, and the Bills were repudiated.[593] In the second case a deposit by a Mr Tomkins as security for a loan was said to include a number of forged Bills that had only been detected subsequently. Tomkins had to repay the loan of £8000 and was charged £343 interest.[594] This judgement did not prevent him trying to recover his £11,000 deposit if he chose.

Maynooth and the Jew Bill

For Hoppen

"The first great outburst of anti-Catholicism after the Emancipation excitements of 1829 was generated in 1845 by Peel's proposal to [triple annual] state funding for the Catholic seminary at Maynooth ... and to place that funding on a more secure basis [i.e., make it permanent] ... The widespread agitation that ensued was orchestrated by Tories disturbed by Peel's refusal to trudge along the bigoted paths of yesteryear and by Evangelicals anxious to create a pan-Protestant alliance on terms congenial to themselves."[595]

Opposition to the likelihood of Peel's proposal began before this though. In January 1844 Dudley published his father's 1805 speech for the first time, amplifying it with an "illustrative appendix" as well as an introduction and notes.[596] Publication was allegedly motivated by watching O'Connell's "Monster-meetings" in Ireland for 'Repeal' of the established Church the year before.[597] Dudley's

---

[592] *The Times* 5th November 1841; *The Examiner* 6th November 1841; *Ipswich Journal* and *Bristol Mercury* 11th December 1841

[593] See www.users.globalnet.co.uk/~recb/chisoc/Medlam/ChisBell/chbh1.txt *The Times* on 5th January 1842 included a letter on the repudiated Bills.

[594] *The Examiner* 19th February 1842; *The Hull Packet* 25th February 1842

[595] Hoppen, 1998, op cit, p443

[596] Dudley Perceval, 'The Church Question in Ireland: Speech as Prepared by the Late Right Hon. Spencer Perceval for the Debate on the First Roman-Catholic Petition to the United Parliament (13th May 1805) ... with an Introduction, Illustrative Appendix, Notes and Comments to the Latter', London, William Blackwood & Sons, 1844

[597] Perhaps while visiting his father-in-law as Sir Richard Bourke had returned to his home at Thornfield, Castleconnell, Co. Limerick from Australia, was appointed High Sheriff of Limerick in 1839 and published the correspondence of Edmund Burke that he and Earl Fitzwilliam had edited in 1844.

view was that these meetings were designed to influence Parliament rather than foment riot by testing

"...the degree of success which the Popish Press had obtained in stimulating the people to hatred of the Church and the Protestants".[598]

Dudley retained his father's original language deliberately, even though he acknowledged that some of the terms were now thought abusive, in order, he claimed,

"... to arouse, if possible, the Churchmen of England, of *all* political parties, to a sense of their power, their rights and their responsibilities."[599]

Dudley asserted that "the real Roman Catholic question" was the overthrow of the Church in Ireland, and that his father had seen this would be the logical outcome of Emancipation forty years earlier when he claimed that

"'Emancipation' without Establishment would fail to conciliate Roman-catholic disaffection".[600]

According to Dudley, the Whigs had dismissed all Irish Church questions as party disputes with the Tories, while liberal Tories had been blind to the significance of the union between Church and State.[601] It was time for all politicians to wake up before

"... Roman-Catholic endowment ... ended in Roman-catholic ascendancy".[602]

But this was just an opening salvo in a protracted campaign. In 1845 Dudley developed his father's 1805 speech further in order to target Peel's proposals for Maynooth more specifically and to publish a 53-clause petition against the removal of Jewish

---

[598] Dudley Perceval, 1844, op cit, p v
[599] Ibid, p xi
[600] Ibid, p xiv
[601] Ibid, p xii
[602] Ibid, p x

207

disabilities.[603] In both instances Dudley argued that Christianity was at risk:

"In the one case (which is the case of the Maynooth Bill), no man with half Sir Robert Peel's intelligence can fail to see that ... If the nation has ceased to know which *is true Christianity*, the Common-law endowments for its maintenance ought to belong ... to all the sects which profess it. In the other case (which is the case of the Jew Bill) ... If the nation, the body politic, be grown indifferent to Christianity itself, the Common-law endowments for it are become an abuse - the political place and station of the Christian ministry an absurdity."[604]

The annual Maynooth grant had been increased to £13,000 by Grenville's Whig government of 1807, enough to educate 400 students. Spencer Perceval had returned it towards its historic level of £8,000 as Chancellor of the Exchequer from 1808. He said that this would be enough to produce 250 priests, and therefore sufficient for Ireland's requirements unless the aim was to establish the Roman Catholic Church. Peel's proposal went much further by both increasing the grant three-fold and making the endowment permanent. Dudley claimed to have had confidence for many years in Peel's

"... sound principles, ... gratitude for his patriotic labours from 1830 to 1841, and ... reverence ... for his unrivalled ability"

but no longer:

---

[603] Dudley Perceval, 'Maynooth and the Jew Bill: Further Illustrations of the Speech of the Right Hon. Spencer Perceval on the Roman Catholic Question in May 1805', London, William Blackwood & Sons, 1845 This was advertised in the *Morning Chronicle* on 12th April 1845 and published two days later on Monday 14th April. Dudley dedicated the pamphlet to Sir Robert Inglis (1786-1855), MP for Oxford University since defeating Sir Robert Peel at the 1829 by-election after the latter's resignation, as "... the man whose public and private character most nearly resembles ... that of Spencer Perceval". Inglis repaid the compliment in a Commons speech in 1851: "If such a man as the late Mr. Perceval - and in referring to that name, he could not but acknowledge the obligations which the cause of Protestantism, and of the Church of England owed in the present day to Mr. Dudley Perceval, a man worthy to bear the name of his great father ..." Gladstone was later to become Inglis' fellow MP for Oxford University from December 1847, but at this stage sat for Newark.

[604] Ibid, pp11-12 The Jewish Disabilities Bill was mainly concerned with civil and municipal offices. Jews were not admitted to Parliament until 1858.

"No man now but a willing dupe, or a thorough-paced parliamentary partisan, can fail to see what end these things [Bills] inevitably tend; - TO THE DEROGATION OF THE CHURCH; TO THE DESECRATION OF THE STATE; TO THE ENTHRONEMENT OF A BUREAUCRACY; AND TO THE NULLIFICATION AT LEAST, IF NOT TO THE ABROGATION, OF CONSTITUTIONAL MONARCHY IN ENGLAND." [605]

Perhaps because they affected him deeply, Dudley now resorted to emotional appeals, to prejudice and bigotry, instead of making the cogent arguments that had been a feature of his previous publications. It may be of course that he had run out of arguments that had not been countered already. On 23rd April 1845 the MP for Sheffield Sir Henry Ward (1797-1860) in opening the discussion of the Bill in the Commons said of Dudley's pamphlet:

"[He sought] to prove that there was only one true Christianity, and one true Church, of which the common and statute laws of England were intended to be the guardians. If that argument was to pass current, he could only say that Mr. Perceval's ghost was more formidable than was the living statesman himself." [606]

Gladstone resigned over the Maynooth affair[607] "after [spending almost] a year ... attempting to have the proposal reconsidered". [608] He could not reconcile the measure with his Anglican beliefs or his conscience. Disraeli thought that this signalled the end of his political career. But two months later Gladstone was to vote for the second reading of the Bill.[609] He objected to Peel's proposal to make the State responsible for the whole provision of the College,[610] as well as to the nature of the endowment:

---

[605] Ibid, p16 Capitals as in the original
[606] Hansard Parliamentary Debates, vol. LXXIX, 23rd April 1845, columns 1124-1230
[607] Morley, op cit, pp82-84
[608] Gladstone DNB entry
[609] W. E. Gladstone, 'Substance of a Speech for the Second Reading of the Maynooth College Bill in the House of Commons, on Friday, April 11, 1845', London, John Murray, 1845 On pp9-10 Gladstone praised Spencer Perceval as "... a man whose native honesty and candour led him thus frankly to recognise what he thought an obligation of good faith", despite his determination not to concede anything to the Roman Catholic Church, and " [he] regarded the grant ... as being a virtual portion of the legislative union with Ireland" in 1800.
[610] Ibid, p12 When the grant was first introduced in 1795 the intention had been to mix private support with that from the public purse.

"In conferring this increased endowment, do not let us attempt to conceal from ourselves that we are conferring new elements of power [towards Roman Catholic ascendancy]."[611]

But, so Gladstone said, he had been swayed by a number of factors. Firstly, he had found the arguments of the Bill's opponents to be very weak. Secondly, some (such as Dudley Perceval, though Gladstone did not name him) had argued from the basis that the country was Protestant, but for Gladstone communities do, **and must always**, cater for and contain diversity. This was a very sophisticated argument well ahead of its time, implying that there could not be a single conventional set of views. Thirdly, while some of the petitions received were against State funding of any religion at all, others found this acceptable for the Anglican Church but not the Roman Catholic one. These were incompatible, polar opposites, and as such they undermined both positions as far as Gladstone was concerned. In addition, the existing acceptance of the Presbyterian Church in Scotland showed that rigidity over Anglican establishment was not tenable. Finally, Gladstone concluded that, if there were no reasons for excluding Roman Catholics, their inclusion must be "a very great boon".[612] Not as a reward for past misbehaviour, therefore, or as a result of O'Connell's agitation:

"I am prepared, in opposition to what I believe to be the prevailing opinion of the people of England and of Scotland, in opposition to the judgment of my own constituents, from whom I greatly regret to differ, and in opposition to my own deeply cherished predilections, to give a deliberate and even anxious support to the measure."[613]

This perplexed his colleagues, but he had

"... he told J. H. Newman, 'clung to the notion of a conscience, in the state, until that idea has become in the general mind so feeble as to be absolutely inappreciable in the movement of public affairs'."[614]

---

[611] Ibid, p16

[612] Ibid, pp19-45 This may follow politically, but logically it does not.

[613] Morley, op cit, p85

[614] From H.C.G. Matthew's book, 'Gladstone 1809-1874', p69 referred to in Gladstone's DNB entry

Not everybody was convinced by his arguments, and some people interpreted them as those of a politician justifying his position. But Gladstone had recognised, even if he had not come to terms with, the reality of pragmatic politics where individual conviction sometimes had to be subordinated to party considerations, and may have decided that, in the scheme of things, this issue was less important than other matters. In order to change the latter, he would have to be less doctrinaire on the former.

The proposal was passed, but only by dint of Whig support since the Conservatives split 148 for and 149 against. This "prepared and perhaps ensured the great split of the following year" over the repeal of the Corn Laws.[615] The Maynooth vote had "roused protestants throughout the United Kingdom to a frenzy"[616] and in June 1845 the National Club was established by people such as Dudley who were greatly alarmed by the direction of events. The Chairman was the Duke of Manchester and the Vice-Chairmen comprised two Dukes, one Marquis, six Earls (including the 6th Earl of Egmont), three Viscounts and two other Lords. Some were from Ireland, as were a number of those on the fifty-three strong committee. Dudley Perceval was among them, as was Quintin Dick (1777-1858) who was then MP for Maldon, but had been replaced by Sir Robert Peel as MP for Cashel in Tipperary when Dick resigned in 1809. The principal aims of the National Club were

"To maintain the Protestant principles of the constitution ...
"To uphold a system of National Education based on Scripture and conducted by the ministers of religion.
"To preserve the Church of England and Ireland ..."[617]

These were the establishment and status quo causes that Spencer Perceval had espoused, including his insistence that the Church of England should provide education. Local associations were formed while a central meeting place was made available in London for campaigners. The "rabid"[618] National Club

---

[615] According to John Wilson Croker's DNB entry
[616] Sir Robert Peel's DNB entry
[617] *The Hull Packet and East Riding Times* 12th December 1845 Also advertised in *The Times* 6th December 1845
[618] M.G. Brock and M.C. Curthoys (eds.), 'The History of the University of Oxford', volume VI Nineteenth Century Oxford Part 1, Oxford, Clarendon Press, 1997, p324

"... campaigned against any alterations in the establishment of church and state and in the organisation of education which would, in its view, strengthen the position of the Roman Catholic Church in England and Ireland."[619]

Dudley's disaffection increased as the Conservatives were succeeded in government by the Whigs led by Lord John Russell in 1846 and the general election the following year failed to remove them. Dudley had been replaced as the Tory candidate in Finsbury, but this did not prevent various newspapers teasing him to support "the Protestant cause".[620] Gladstone performed another volte face on his return to Parliament in December 1847

"... support[ing] the removal of Jewish civil disabilities (which he had previously opposed); when given an honorary degree at Oxford on 5ᵗʰ July 1848, he was greeted in the Sheldonian Theatre by shouts of 'Gladstone and the Jew Bill'."[621]

In March 1848 Dudley and Gladstone were to correspond over the Bill, as they had done originally in 1845. Gladstone had been candid in his 7ᵗʰ March reply that

"I am not prepared to say that I can make up my mind to adopt the course you have suggested but I shall certainly think it my duty to give it mature consideration ..."

Despite Dudley's opening paragraph in his next letter on 17ᵗʰ March that Gladstone's response "made [him] reluctant to intrude upon you again", he then followed this with another thirteen and a half pages. Gladstone was not the man to be cowed by voluminous argument, and the weight of Perceval's letters failed to convince him.[622]

The National Club failed to make any appreciable difference in the short-term, and a disillusioned Dudley is supposed to have left the country for two years from 1847.[623] He may have rationalised

---

[619] See the papers held at the Bodleian library.
[620] *Liverpool Mercury* 20ᵗʰ July 1847 quoting the London *Standard*; *Preston Guardian* 24ᵗʰ July 1847
[621] Gladstone DNB entry from his Diaries for 5ᵗʰ July 1848
[622] British Library, Add. MSS 44367 ff.99,109; Add. MSS 49193, f.25
[623] *The Derby Mercury* 12ᵗʰ January 1853 says that "he quitted England for two years", while *John Bull* on 29ᵗʰ September 1856 states "during the next two years we find him absent from England, and abstaining from all participation in political movements". The latter is perhaps a clue that his absence was more apparent

this, even welcomed it, as a tactical withdrawal, and his previous arguments that the Maynooth and Jewish Disabilities Bills would "threaten the Queen's supremacy"[624] may have given him little option but to take a respite to recover his energies. Dudley was certainly not out of the country for all of the two years. He may simply have gone to ground, increasingly bewildered by the Chartist upheaval at home and the uprisings and revolutions that took place throughout Europe in 1848. Even if the family embarked on a continental tour,[625] they may have had to curtail it prematurely. They may have visited his father-in-law in Ireland, but probably only briefly as this was the middle of the famine years. Perhaps simply to demonstrate that they were taking practical steps to alleviate the poverty Dudley had highlighted in 1829, but possibly because they had seen for themselves the horrendous effects of the famine, Mary Jane (Mrs Dudley Perceval) was on the Committee of the Irish Work Society.[626] The sale of Limerick lace was one of the Society's prime objectives, and the Committee comprised people with Ireland connections as well as those with other links to the Percevals, such as Lord Monteagle and his wife. Limerick was one of the six most disturbed counties, and a special commission had been set up in January 1848 to examine agrarian offences in the counties of Clare and Limerick.[627] As might be expected of Sir Richard Bourke as High Sheriff, but also because he had been appalled previously by the impact of sectarianism, he was at the heart of events in Limerick. He had given evidence in 1845 (to the 1843-1845 Government Commission on the occupation of land in Ireland, otherwise known as the Devon Commission) on the disastrous impact of absentee landlords, but, as local examples demonstrated, competent agents could reduce their worst effects.[628] Limerick was very poor and, while wages were low, this did not mean that labour was cheap as often people were unable to perform the tasks

---

than real. There are several letters (including those to Gladstone already referred to) that indicate he remained at 16 Wilton Street for at least some of the time.
[624] Dudley Perceval, 1845, op cit, p28
[625] The son Charles Spencer was 18 that February, and admitted to Lincoln's Inn the following November, but did not matriculate at Trinity Hall, Cambridge until the end of 1848.
[626] *Freeman's Journal and Daily Commercial Advertiser* 15th May 1848; *The Times* 23rd May 1848
[627] K Theodore Hoppen, 'Elections, Politics and Society in Ireland 1832-1885', Oxford, Clarendon Press, 1984, pp348-349
[628] Joel Mokyr, 'Why Ireland Starved: A Quantitative and Analytical History of the Irish Economy, 1800-1850', London, George Allen & Unwin, 1983, p208

required of them. For example, one factory owner found that many people were so unfit and unwell that he could only find weavers capable of the coarsest work.[629] This was before the famine struck, bringing with it over a million excess deaths,[630] great suffering and injustice, as well as mass emigration that continued into the 1850s.

As a further illustration of his social conscience, in June 1848 Dudley contributed to the Society for Improving the Condition of the Labouring Classes, a fund set up to build model dwelling-houses for mechanics.[631] Dudley donated £2, as did many others so it was more than a gesture, while Queen Victoria headed the list of donors with £300.

In March 1849 Dudley returned to the fray, once again geeing up sympathetic MPs to adopt what in his view were the appropriate arguments in Parliament:

"My dear Mr Goulburn,
"Sir Robert Inglis being hors de combat, you are the Member of Parliament to whom one need make ... suggestions of Amendments to a Bill relating to the Church ..."[632]

This was the Clergy Relief Bill allowing people in Holy Orders to dissent from the established Anglican Church in England and Ireland. As he had attempted with Gladstone, Dudley wrote at length to Goulburn. His seven-side letter was accompanied by handwritten amendments on a draft of the Bill and, in addition, two sides on each of two of the clauses.[633] His letter concluded:

"With these **preliminary observations** [emphasis added], you will now readily understand the drift and purport of the amendments which I put into your hands, and press upon your adoption and advocacy."

Dudley no doubt thought he was assisting MPs and keeping them up to the mark; the experience from their side, even for sympathetic MPs, must have been of being beaten into submission. Even allowing for his father's views, and his increasing concern that

---

[629] Ibid, p221
[630] K Theodore Hoppen, 'Ireland Since 1800: Conflict and Conformity', London, Longman, 1999, p60
[631] *Morning Chronicle* 13ᵗʰ June 1848; *The Times* 14ᵗʰ June 1848
[632] British Library, Add. MSS 44162 f. 47
[633] Ibid f.55 and f.56

the Church was rapidly becoming a profession rather than a vocation, his attempt to be the Protestant conscience was increasingly heavy-handed. MPs such as Gladstone and Goulburn would not have been daunted, but many others would have, seeing him instead as an intimidating watchdog on a long leash, determined to repel all intruders regardless of whether they offered a real threat or not.

After his two years out of the limelight he seems to have contemplated taking further time out to write a life of his father. He had already organised many of his papers for earlier publications and now actively sought correspondence that would complement "a published life of [his] Admirable Father".[634] However, he never saw this project through as it was soon overtaken by other events that thrust him back into public prominence. He had already written to Henry Manning in 1850 about their different views of the Anglican Church. For Manning, their "divergencies [sic], if such there be" crystallised around Manning's belief that the Royal supremacy was contrary to the Lord's Will as expressed in the order of the Church:

"And after very long and painful deliberation I felt bound to release myself from the obligation to recognise it."[635]

Dudley had already campaigned against the 1847 circular of Henry Grey (1802-1894), 3rd Earl from 1845 and Colonial Secretary from 1846, that formally recognised the rank of Roman Catholic prelates and instructed that they were to be given "precedence immediately after the prelates of the Established Church".[636] Dudley's campaigning pamphlet rapidly went through three editions in two years, with his letter to Lord John Russell who had said Grey's instruction was of "no importance" published in January 1851 as a further postscript.[637] Although Dudley first published the

---

[634] See Mr P Mansel's November 1849 reply to Dudley's request for letters at British Library, Add. MSS 49193 f.27. Although he was unable to help, his sister was more obliging the following month (Ibid, f.30).

[635] British Library, Add. MSS 49193 f.31 Much younger than Robert James Carr, Manning arrived in Chichester after Carr had ceased to be Bishop there and moved to Worcester in September 1831. Manning was a friend of the Wilberforce family, and a relative by marriage as two of his wife Caroline's (?-1837) sisters married Samuel and Henry Wilberforce.

[636] Dudley Perceval, 'Earl Grey's Circular: A Memento', London, F & JH Rivington, 1849, p10

[637] *Morning Chronicle* 7th November 1850; *The Examiner* 18th January 1851; *The Times* 18th January 1851

pamphlet anonymously in 1849, including three unsigned articles in the *Morning Herald*,[638] he chose not to sustain this subterfuge in the adverts for the second and third editions.[639] He sent a copy to Manning, whose curious reply, perhaps demonstrating his own tortured state of anxiety in January 1851, was:

"It is the work of an acute but not of a deep mind: And strangely unconscious of facts. With much of it I heartily agree."[640]

Dudley interpreted events as popish aggression, a conclusion with which his fellow vestrymen at St George's, Hanover Square concurred in November 1850.[641] In January 1851 a larger meeting was convened by the Church of England at the Freemason's Tavern. Dudley put forward a motion calling for a re-instatement of the Royal licence for the Convocations at York and Canterbury.[642] This was an exclusionary tactic, aimed at ensuring that royal patronage for the one established, and Anglican, Church should be re-stated. Then, in a debate in the House of Commons on the Ecclesiastical Titles Assumption Bill on 20th March 1851, Henry Drummond launched an astonishingly abusive attack on Catholics as the number of conversions to the Roman Catholic Church increased. The Catholic newspaper *The Tablet* reported his speech as "The Drummond Infamy",[643] a reasonably restrained headline in the circumstances. Drummond had opened by asking

"Whether the Papists shall remain a tolerated sect under the dominion of the Queen? or, Whether the Queen shall become a licensed heretic under the dominion of the Pope?"

---

[638] *Morning Herald* 22nd August 1848, 23rd August 1848 and 19th February 1849
The first two articles argued against Grey's circular on points of form and principle respectively, while the third described it as "indefensible".
[639] *The Examiner* 14th December 1850 and 11th January 1851
[640] British Library, Add. MSS 49193 f.38 Manning was to be received into the Roman Catholic Church two months later on 6th April 1851.
[641] *The Times* of 15th November 1850 reported their meeting.
[642] *Lloyd's Weekly Newspaper* 19th January 1851; *The Derby Mercury* 22nd January 1851 provides a longer report
[643] *The Tablet* 29th March 1851

When he was upbraided by other MPs for describing nunneries as "either prisons or brothels", and for his language generally, his speech became even more vituperative.[644]

But 1851 was an inauspicious date for looking backwards. The Great Exhibition, and the census of religious attendances,[645] later that year were both to affirm that Britain and its empire were becoming increasingly diverse; a wider variety of religion was tolerated, even if political and military power remained concentrated in a few hands.

The Gladstone election

In his 1862 novel 'No Name'[646] Wilkie Collins observes at one point that

"On the small neutral ground of self-importance, the best men and the worst meet on the same terms."

He was not referring to the 1853 election at Oxford University, but he might have been. Although Dudley was a last minute candidate, and had not sought the position, the description is appropriate nevertheless. *The Examiner* was to dismiss him as "the faithful watchman", in contrast to the "able statesman" Gladstone.[647]

The Tory party had split in 1846 over the repeal of the Corn Laws. Sir Robert Peel's adherents, the Peelites, who had lined up behind his free trade arguments were opposed by the protectionist Conservatives led by Edward Stanley[648] (1799-1869), the 14th Earl of Derby from June 1851. Stanley felt that protectionism was a

---

[644] The full speech can be read at
http://hansard.millbanksystems.com/commons/1851/mar/20/ecclesiastical-titles-assumption-bill

[645] See, for example, Michael Watts, 'The Dissenters, Volume II: The Expansion of Evangelical Nonconformity', Oxford, Clarendon Press, 1995

[646] Wilkie Collins, 'No Name', London, Sampson Low, 1862 (OUP, Oxford World's Classics, 1986, p340)

[647] *The Examiner* 8th January 1853

[648] Like Dudley and Gladstone, Stanley attended Christ Church, Oxford (though unlike them his three years 1817-1820 ended without a degree) and like Spencer Perceval he is a forgotten Prime Minister. In 1824, according to his DNB entry, Stanley travelled to North America "accompanied by his Christ Church friends John Evelyn Denison (1800-1873), Henry Labouchere and John Stuart Wortley". These were to become familiar names again at the time of the 1853 election. Stanley had started in Parliament as a Tory MP on the liberal Canningite wing of the party, then joined the Peelite faction after Canning's death until 1846.

necessity if the empire, and the landed interest on which it depended, were to survive, but his over-riding objection to Peel's approach was that Peel had failed to shape opinion among Conservative MPs or take the party with him. As Angus Hawkins states in Derby's DNB entry:

"...he saw repeal as a betrayal of the mutual trust that should exist between a party leadership and its parliamentary support. 'Peel's great error', Stanley observed to Lord George Bentinck in October 1847, 'has always been disregarding the opinion of his party, whenever it did not exactly square with his own.'"

Derby was first asked to form a government in February 1851, but was unable to persuade the Peel faction to join him, and Lord John Russell's government staggered on for a further year until Russell resigned the following February. As had happened twelve months before, the Peelites again refused to join the government, but this time Derby managed to cobble one together from within the Conservative party. After the general election in July 1852 it remained a minority government,[649] but retained power until Disraeli's budget was roundly defeated in December 1852, largely as a result of Gladstone's opposition. Derby resigned the next day. George Gordon-Hamilton (1784-1860), the 4th Earl of Aberdeen, then formed a genuine coalition between the Peelite rump and the much larger group of Liberal MPs led by Lord John Russell. Although a joint ministry had first been mooted in 1851, it had failed to materialise at that point. The senior members of the new Cabinet, underlining that it was indeed a "ministry of all the talents", were Aberdeen as Prime Minister, Russell and Palmerston at the Foreign and Home Offices respectively, and Gladstone as Chancellor of the Exchequer. In early January 1853 the House of Commons adjourned until the 10th of February so that the new ministers could stand for re-election.

Most of the government were returned without opposition, with elections only being held for Gladstone's Oxford University seat and in Gloucester, Halifax and Southampton. After 7th January the

---

[649] Resulting in "299 Conservatives, 315 Liberals, Whigs and radicals, and 40 Peelites" according to Stanley's DNB entry, or 330 Conservative and Liberal Conservative (i.e., Peelite) and 324 Liberals according to Colin Rallings and Michael Thrasher (eds.), 'British Electoral Facts 1832-2006', Aldershot, Ashgate, 2007, pp6-7

Oxford University seat was the only one still to be polled.[650] Gladstone had offended some of the Fellows on several counts, but, whether the predominant issue was his stance on the Roman Catholic and Jewish religious issues, implying ultimately the separation of church and state, that had caused such grievance among High Church Anglicans, or his support for the future reform of Oxford University, moving it towards a professorial and educational model,[651] is beside the point. If someone could be found to oppose him, there was bound to be a close contest. Indeed, it was announced by those connected with the Conservatives and the Carlton Club[652] that the seat would be contested before it was decided who Gladstone's opponent would be. Lord Chandos[653] (1823-1889) was first put forward on 1st

---

[650] F.W.S. Craig (ed.), 'Chronology of British Parliamentary By-Elections 1833-1987', Chichester, Parliamentary Research Services, 1987, p30

[651] Like the Civil Service reforms of the 1850s, the intention was to move away from privilege and right towards places on the basis of merit. Anglican influence was also to be diluted so that the existing differentiation between religious Fellows and tutorial assistants would be removed. See, for example, W.R. Ward, 'Victorian Oxford', London, Cass, 1965, pp170-179 and E.G.W. Bill & J.F.A. Mason, 'Christ Church and Reform 1850-1867', Oxford, Clarendon Press, 1970.

Bill & Mason highlight the canker that the current approach now represented; a canker that had grown as society and education moved forward. It was of no benefit to the university, the feeder schools or to the (men only) students themselves:

"... early in the nineteenth century it [Westminster School, one of the main feeder schools for Christ Church] succumbed to rapid and protracted decay. It failed to absorb the lessons of Arnold's Rugby, its finances were weak, and successive cholera epidemics in London caused parents to prefer the salubrious conditions of the new schools rising in the country." (p27)

"... some of the causes of its decay [in the 1830s] also affected, though not in equal degree, other traditional nurseries of Christ Church, such as Eton and Harrow ..." (p28)

"The social elite came to Christ Church in great numbers ... but although many of them subsequently attained positions of eminence in public life, they rarely came for the sake of the academic advantages ... and ... it was not considered socially acceptable for [some of] them to compete for honours." (pp28/29) For example, it was not his intelligence that prevented Stanley from graduating; he was one of those who believed it beneath his status.

Edward Goodenough (Christ Church, and Stanley's, tutor, later headmaster of Westminster School and dean of Wells) referred to [the] aristocracy/Lords in 1815 as those "whose birth ... 'exempted them from a life of labour'." (p29)

[652] *The Guardian* 5th January 1853, p5

[653] MP for Buckingham from 1848-1857. His father, also named Richard Plantagenet Temple-Nugent-Brydges-Chandos-Grenville (1797-1861), second duke of Buckingham from 1839 when he inherited huge debts alongside his father's estate, was bankrupt by 1848 and forced to hand over control of his

January 1853, even though he had already made it clear that he was not prepared to stand. Chandos personally ensured that Gladstone was aware that it was a put up job; he had been proposed by "Dr C. Lempriere, DCL" without his consent and, indeed, after he had refused the candidature.

By 5th January the search for an alternative opponent had produced Dudley. He was proposed by George Denison (1805-1896), brother of John Evelyn (Stanley's fellow-traveller - metaphorically as well as literally) and Archdeacon of Taunton and Oriel College, who explained his reasons in the *Morning Chronicle*[654] and other papers, and thereby "severed a thirty year friendship"[655] with Gladstone. Gladstone had been nominated by the Provost of Oriel College. *The Morning Chronicle*, *The Examiner* and the *Liverpool Mercury* were among those papers that took a derisory view:

"Mr Perceval's pretensions to represent the University of Oxford will not stand a moment's serious investigation. The more we inquire into his qualifications, the more we admire the convenient morality of attempting to carry his election by 'a sudden assault'. We spoke yesterday of his belonging to a religious family remarkable for its 'crotchetiness'. ...

"... We do not say that Mr Dudley Perceval is absolutely wrong in all his views and opinions ... but we do say that nothing more is wanted to settle his claims to represent the University of Oxford than ... an attentive perusal of his publications."[656]

"We have looked into Mr Perceval's qualifications, and have discovered him to be a gentleman whose abilities it would be cruel to subject to public criticism.

"... [a] poor obscure person ... We know him by his friends. We know that he has been selected simply as the most conveniently empty vessel out of which the vials of a base wrath could be poured. No better man would consent to be taken up as an utensil for the purpose. ..."[657]

---

financial affairs to his son. Buckingham moved into lodgings in Wilton Street, the street Dudley lived in. Lord Chandos did stand against Gladstone for Oxford University in 1859 but lost by 200 votes.
[654] *Morning Chronicle* 5th January 1853
[655] *Hull Packet and East Riding Times* 7th January 1853
[656] *The Morning Chronicle* 6th January 1853
[657] *The Examiner* 8th January 1853

"The one [Gladstone] is a man whose public career has been, in some respects, one of the most brilliant in the present century; whose commanding talents, graceful eloquence, and high administrative capacities have raised him to the first rank of British statesmen. The other is Mr Robert [sic] Dudley Perceval, M.A.; and when we have said that, we have said all that we can learn about him, except, perhaps, that he is the reputed recipient of a patent place, with a salary of £600 per annum, for being kind enough to receive it. ... what possible claims he can have to represent the University of Oxford in Parliament, we are wholly at a loss to conceive."[658]

This was combative copy, as befitted Gladstone's home town paper, but it might at least have got Dudley's name correct. The *Derby Mercury*, perhaps to redress the balance, provided an uncritical, even positive, resume of his career the following day.[659]

The *Morning Chronicle* article on 6th January had described Dudley's pamphlet on Napier as "infantile", and questioned the sanity of Spencer junior and their Arden cousins Arthur and Charles, but the overwhelming impression is that the papers knew the election was not a foregone conclusion and were rattled. Aware of the possible outcome, *The Examiner* stressed in its article, not necessarily helpfully, that

"Mr Gladstone is too good a politician to continue a member of the Carlton Club, and ... too useful a man to continue to represent the University of Oxford. ... if Mr Gladstone be rejected at Oxford, the discredit of the result will attach to the University alone."

The Guardian had provided extensive coverage, starting with nearly seven pages on the 5th January, including leading articles on the election itself, "the church politics of conservatism" and the coalition cabinet, and, while they were not impressed with the way Dudley had been parachuted in by the Carlton Club, the reports did not descend to the abusive comments that had featured in some of the other papers.[660] It carried the following notice, no doubt at the behest of Gladstone's Committee, above the leading articles:

---

[658] *Liverpool Mercury* 11th January 1853
[659] *Derby Mercury* 12th January 1853
[660] *The Guardian* 5th January 1853, pp3-9

"Members of Convocation willing to support the re-election of Mr Gladstone are earnestly requested to go up to Oxford and record their vote without delay."

And, indeed, the election was close for a long while. At the end of the fourth day Gladstone's lead was only 56, 468 votes to Dudley's 412. The *Morning Chronicle* saw the increasing threat to Gladstone and re-iterated its abhorrence of the National Club and the extreme religious views Dudley represented.[661] On 15ᵗʰ January the *Preston Guardian* reported that the poll was continuing, but Gladstone was now bound to win. When the poll eventually closed at the final possible moment after twelve days of voting on the 20ᵗʰ January, Gladstone's majority was a slender 124, 1022 votes to 898. *The Guardian* analysed the results in detail on the 21ˢᵗ January, indicating that Gladstone had a five to one majority among professors, almost three to one among college residents, and carried Oriel and Christ Church colleges comfortably. He did less well at the Hebdomenal (governing) Board, however, where thirteen out of twenty college votes were cast for Perceval, with four colleges including Christ Church (which both Dudley and Gladstone had attended) remaining neutral.[662]

This edition of *The Guardian* was also the first to respond to the accusations of character assassination that Dudley directed at some of the papers after the election. Under the title of "A Needless Apology" it opened

"Mr Perceval's defence, addressed to Sir Brook Bridges,[663] will take the world by surprise. Nobody was aware that he had been attacked - attacked, that is, in any such sense as to call for a defence of himself. ... It has been, indeed, widely intimated that, though an amiable and well-intentioned man, he is somewhat eccentric, and that he is not sufficiently distinguished to represent the University of Oxford."[664]

The *Morning Chronicle* responded much more robustly and at length on the 29ᵗʰ January and 3ʳᵈ February.[665] In its view Dudley's

---

[661] *The Morning Chronicle* 8ᵗʰ January 1853
[662] *The Guardian* 21ˢᵗ January 1853
[663] Sir Brook Bridges (1801-1875), MP for Eastern Kent in 1852 and 1857-1868, and a fellow member of the National Club.
[664] *The Guardian* 21ˢᵗ January 1853
[665] *The Morning Chronicle* 29ᵗʰ January and 3ʳᵈ February 1853

letter demonstrated his overall incompetence to represent Oxford University, even arguing (which was certainly not true) that he could not construct a coherent moral argument. This was a particularly barbed judgement that Dudley would be unlikely to shrug off.

It is not recorded how he responded to the references in the Brasenose Ale song shortly afterwards.[666] Of course, he may not have been aware of them at all, but would probably not have interpreted them as flattering:

> "...'Twere easy, then, the inward change to note.
> How Dudley lost, how Gladstone gained a vote.
> Could rustic arguments long time prevail
> 'Gainst College eloquence and College Ale?

> "Oh, Dudley Perceval, thou fallen star.
> Whose only light shone from so very far,
> Why didst thou let them lead thee by the nose.
> To start two thousand voters from repose?
> Was it for thee inglorious to creep
> Amid the dirt which Chandos thought too deep?
> To try the treacherous ground where others slid,
> To do, in fact, what Dr. Marsham did ?
> Why didst thou trust the knave of "clubs" in town?
> Where was the host they promised to send down?
> "Lo, a troop cometh!" cried one bitter Rad:
> His hearers looked around—and saw but "G. A. D.,"

> "Enough of this: the warmth of either side
> Let us cool down and in the tankard hide;
> And drink to Alma Mater—drink to all
> Who would not see her Institutions fall.
> May she keep safe, when danger near her lurks,
> From Jews, John Russell, Infidels, and Turks."

Dudley's national profile petered out after the election, though he was still active in relation to the Society for the Propagation of the Gospel in Foreign Parts[667] and St George's Vestry.[668] In

---

[666] 'Brasenose Ale: A Collection of Verses annually presented on Shrove Tuesday by the Butler of Brasenose College, Oxford', Boston, Lincolnshire, 1878 "G.A.D." is George Anthony Denison.
[667] *Morning Chronicle* 22nd January 1853 and 23rd April 1853; *The Times* 9th May 1853

September 1855 he and Mary Jane holidayed at the newly fashionable Rhyl, staying at the prominent Queen's Hotel as did many of the well-known people of the time.[669]

A year later, three and a half years after the Oxford University election, Dudley was dead, a month before his fifty-sixth birthday. Of his siblings, only his oldest sister Jane died at a younger age. *John Bull* magazine, like the *Morning Herald*, was a Dudley supporter and its obituary paid him a longer and more fulsome tribute:

"Such a man, - one of the excellent of the earth, - a man who, though comparatively little known beyond the circle of his friends and personal acquaintances, nevertheless did good service to the State ...
"On this [the 1853 election], as on all occasions throughout the whole of his honourable career, [he] exhibited that gentlemanly bearing which was so eminently characteristic of him. Actuated by deep convictions, logically formed and religiously cherished, he was strenuous in the assertion of his principles ... His gentle disposition deprecated all violence of speech or action ... The loss of such a man [can only be reconciled by considering that] 'the righteous is taken away from the evil to come'."[670]

The conscience of duty, then, as Dudley believed was required of him; rather more than a "watchman", as personal considerations were subordinated to principles, but much less than a conscience of the nation, even a partisan segment of it.

---

[668] *Morning Chronicle* 31st March 1855 when Dudley was part of the Vestry deputation to the General Board of Health on the Metropolis Local Management Bill ; *Daily News* 20th November 1855 when Dudley was re-elected under the Metropolitan Management Act (as it became).
[669] *North Wales Chronicle* 8th September 1855
[670] *John Bull* 29th September 1856

9. ISABELLA (1801-1886) AND A HAPLESS HOME SECRETARY

As well as propelling certain people to bring about change, temperament and circumstance can also insulate others from the effects of a changing society. The oldest sister Jane had died in the first quarter of the nineteenth century when her father's successor Liverpool was still the Tory Prime Minister. Even if his government was no longer overtly pursuing Perceval's policies, this was too early for the impact of political and social change to be readily apparent. It would not have reached the closeted world of Felpham rapidly in any case. For Spencer and Frederick, the two oldest brothers, the predominant focus was necessarily on the immediate and personal, while Henry and Dudley actively resisted change - not just religious change, but frequently social change too. Frances and Maria were far from simple, though their expectations may have been straightforward. Maria showed herself to have a wide range of interests, and to be well-informed, intellectually rigorous and analytical, but she and Frances had grown up in a less complicated, pre-Reform world (they were 40 or close to it by 1832). Their early lives dated from pre-Waterloo times, when the characteristic attitude of the country was patriotism, looking outwards and directed away from, often ignoring, the situation at home. After 1843, and then the reminder of their own mortality provided by their mother's death the following January, they largely withdrew into the circumscribed, certain and safe society of Ealing. Louisa probably followed their example. Frederica took a more egalitarian and progressive view of the contribution she should make, but still informed by, even confined to, her past and place. By contrast, John and Ernest were to prove themselves almost radical in their determined drive for change. However, it was Isabella, inadvertently rather than actively or necessarily even consciously, whose life illustrates the transformation from the start of the century and a world of deference, from two social and economic classes of owner and labourer, and two political parties of Whigs and Tories, to a much more politically, economically and socially nuanced world by the time of her death in 1886. While events might still be characterised by confrontation rather than co-operation, a system that had previously recognised only polarities, indeed had been built on them, had begun to be replaced by more subtlety, by a third dimension that recognised shades of grey in a world that could no longer be seen or understood as black and white. History would still be written by the winners, but society was no longer just a zero-sum game. Other factions had found their voice, and were beginning to be heard as they increasingly sought to make others aware of the validity of their interpretation. Just as daylight included the full spectrum of colours, and evolution pre-supposed diversity, these social changes could be seen in a number of ways: managers interposed themselves between owners and workers; the middle class developed, as did the professions, alongside the aristocracy and the landless; religion and its forms expanded; education became more widely available and entitlement to it grew; political representation was enhanced and politics became more diverse: socialism began to develop as a third pattern of thought, and eventually as a third political perspective alongside liberalism and conservatism. Isabella was not overtly responsible for any of this, but it was her family that was to be at the centre of it.

Isabella was born a fortnight before Christmas 1801, the eighth surviving Perceval child and the fourth daughter. She was the last to marry (at the relatively late age of 33), and the only daughter to have children. Aged 10 when her father was assassinated, Gray records only her birth and one other collective reference.[671] As with her younger sisters Louisa and Frederica, there are no letters from her in the British Library. Indeed, Isabella Perceval is mentioned on only one occasion in newspapers before her marriage, when she attended the Queen's drawing room with her mother in April 1831.[672] As her older sister Jane and her brothers Henry and Ernest had done, she too was to marry a cousin - in her case Spencer Horatio Walpole (1806-1898), a man almost five years younger than herself. His mother Margaret (1769-1854) had been another of her father's sisters. While Spencer Horatio brought together the Perceval and Walpole connections in his name, his descent from Sir Robert Walpole was as indirect as it was junior in relation to the Egmont family. Nevertheless, the links first made over a hundred years before were forged afresh by their marriage. This pattern of inter-marriage was not unusual among families at this time, and reflected social opportunity and acquaintance, still limited for women, as much as it did other considerations.

Like Isabella's father and one of her brothers, Spencer Horatio had attended Trinity College, Cambridge and like them had then

---

[671] Gray, op cit, pp52 and 431
[672] *Morning Chronicle* 29th April 1831, and reported in *The Times* the day before.

gone on to Lincoln's Inn. He was still a lawyer when they married, practising in the Court of Chancery as had her father, and, although he lived long enough to become the senior QC,[673] did not become one until he was forty in 1846, the same year he became an MP. Somewhat surprisingly, Isabella's and Spencer Walpole's marriage (in Ealing, according to his DNB entry) on 6th October 1835 was not reported in the papers. Ten months later their first child Jane Margaret (1836-1874) was born in early August 1836 at Petersham, Surrey.[674] Their older son Spencer (1839-1907) was born two and a half years later, to be followed in December 1840 by their second daughter Isabella Margaretta Elizabeth (1840-1938) and a second son Horatio George in September 1843 (1843-1923).[675] As if to illustrate that a woman's public role was expected to be to bear her husband's children and ornament his career, Isabella next featured in the papers in 1849 and 1850 when she accompanied her husband, already a rising politician among the protectionist Conservatives, to Queen Victoria's court.[676] This impression was later to be reinforced by the brief notice of her death, barely an obituary, in the *Leeds Mercury*,[677] defining her almost exclusively in terms of her father and husband. The first sentence was unpromising ("**Some** interest attaches to the name of a venerable lady whose death we **have** to record ..." [emphasis added]) and it did not improve.

But there was one area in which Isabella was clearly the senior partner, pre-eminent in her marriage and at home, as her mother may have been. Gray reports that Caroline, Princess of Wales, commented that Perceval "was entirely governed by that silly woman his wife".[678] However, Caroline's motives for saying so were unlikely to be disinterested. There is ample evidence indicating that Isabella's dominance over her husband was much more apparent and acknowledged, both independently and by Walpole himself:

"Personally, Walpole is unambitious: but he is poor, has a family, the pension is an object, and Mrs Walpole, a daughter of Spencer

---

[673] Boase, op cit, p1174
[674] *Bristol Mercury* 13th August 1836
Horace Walpole's Gothic villa, Strawberry Hill, had been built in Petersham in the mid-eighteenth century. Jane died at the age of 38 on 6th September 1874 at the Walpole home in Ealing. The cause of death was given as rheumatic fever.
[675] *The Era* 17th September 1843
[676] *Daily News* 22nd May 1849 and 3rd May 1850
[677] *Leeds Mercury* 21st July 1886
[678] Gray, op cit, p429

Perceval's, who with her father's narrowness of mind has much of his ambition, never ceases to urge him on. (This he has told me himself.)"[679]

"But Mrs Walpole made an apparently decisive intervention [in 1867]: she sent a letter to the prime minister saying that her husband was not fit to continue. Hardy, who liked and admired Walpole, recorded him saying 'he was so overdone that he really was not fit for his work, and would persist in going out'."[680]

"The general importance of Mrs Walpole's influence is supported ... by his remark to Hardy of 19 June 1858: 'I have consulted my Prime Minister here at home' (Gathorne-Hardy, vol. 1, p123)."[681]

Moneypenny and Buckle point out that women such as Isabella could have an

"enormous, indeed decisive importance ... in directing and moulding the life of man, and particularly, political man".[682]

Walpole was one of the first prepared to acknowledge it openly.

Isabella and her husband moved out to the Hall at Ealing in 1844[683] in the hope that the country air would improve their older son's health. This remedy seemed to work, for a thirteen year old Spencer went to Eton in 1852, and though a nurse Leah Smith had been living with the family as late as 1851 to look after him, he was subsequently fit enough to take up rowing. The family employed three other servants at Ealing in 1851, a footman, a housemaid and a young lady's maid. In 1861 all the family still lived in Ealing, with the sons Spencer a clerk in the War Office and Horatio in his last

---

[679] John Vincent (ed.), 'Disraeli, Derby and the Conservative Party: Journals and Memoirs of Edward Henry, Lord Stanley 1849-1869', Sussex, Harvester Press, 1978, p187 in a diary entry for 3rd June 1862. This Edward Stanley was the 15th Earl and son of the Prime Minister Lord Derby.

[680] A.E. Gathorne-Hardy (ed.), 'Gathorne Hardy: First Earl of Cranbrook: A Memoir', 2 volumes, London, Longmans, Green & Co., 1910, vol. I, p215

[681] From Spencer Horatio Walpole's DNB entry by Derek Beales.

[682] William Moneypenny & George Buckle, 'The Life of Benjamin Disraeli', 2 volumes, London, John Murray, 1929, vol. II, p1426 in relation to Disraeli's career and his novel 'Endymion'.

[683] Given that Walpole was not well-off, it may be that Isabella's inheritance from her mother helped fund this purchase (and possibly contributed to the Pitzhanger Manor House one for her sisters too).

year at Eton. There were now four servants, a cook, footman and two housemaids, all of them different to the ones that had been with the family ten years before. Spencer Horatio and Isabella were away in Brighton on the 7th April (Census day in 1861), staying with his older sister Catherine (1804-1876) who was to marry the following day. She may have appreciated their support given her advanced years and that of her prospective husband Baron James de Teissier, who was about 67.[684] By 1871 the Ealing household included two footmen, a cook, two housemaids, and two other maids, seven servants in all to look after Isabella, her husband and their daughter Jane, who was now thirty-four and unmarried.[685] Another nurse was listed in the return, but she would have been accompanying Spencer and Marion Walpole (1842-1912), son and daughter-in-law, who were visiting with their ten-month old daughter.[686] In 1881 Spencer Horatio and Isabella were recorded at their home in London, 109 Eaton Square,[687] with their widowed daughter Isabella Heathcote, one of Walpole's brothers and his wife. One of the housemaids from 1871 was still with them, but eight other servants were different once again. For the first time they included a butler.

Spencer Horatio Walpole

Isabella's husband Spencer Horatio had been head boy at Eton in 1823 and it might be supposed that his illustrious name had played its part in this. It may also have contributed to his elevation into politics in 1846:

---

[684] Anne Shellim, personal communication, 26th March 2010
[685] The other three children were living elsewhere, having married by 1871: Spencer in 1867, Isabella in 1869 to George Parker Heathcote (1836-?) and Horatio in 1870 to his cousin, John Thomas' daughter Selina (1837-1935).
[686] Spencer and Marion Walpole had married at the British Embassy in Florence on 12th November 1867 according to the International Genealogical Index. Their first child Spencer Digby had died before reaching his second birthday in February 1871. Their infant daughter Maud Constance (1870-1947) had been born the previous May.
[687] This is just south of the Wilton Street area of Belgravia in which Dudley lived and is now bisected by that part of the King's Road between Sloane Square and the Royal Mews at Buckingham Palace. It was designed and built in 1827. "It was named after Eaton Hall, in Cheshire, the principal seat of the Duke of Westminster" according to www.british-history.ac.uk/report.aspx?compid=45218&strquery=Eaton+Square

"Mr Walpole lent to the new party, in a short while, his pleasant presence and his ready tongue."[688]

Ritchie's judgement was that

"As a scholar, a gentleman, and a lawyer, he has few, if any, equals on his own side of the House. In political consistency, and in the patient discharge of his duty, he is surpassed by none. For the rough work of the Home Office, it may be that he was too refined and feeling ... Be that as it may, no man in the House is held at this time in higher honour ..."[689]

In a diary entry for 19ᵗʰ March 1851, Lord Stanley records

"Walpole came up to me at the Carlton, began to discuss his own prospects, and those of the party, both in a tone of despondency: he thinks he is placed too high, is too old to take office for the first time, might have succeeded better if brought up to the profession of politics, etc. Walpole is not an unambitious man, but fear with him is stronger than hope, and principle than either."[690]

reflecting two months later that

"Walpole's character stands so high that he could not be attacked with any show of plausibility, except for his self-acknowledged tendency to vacillation."[691]

Walpole was part of the minority government Derby formed in 1852,[692] when the Conservatives were desperately short of talent and experience, adding to his established reputation as a lawyer by

---

[688] J Ritchie, 'op cit, p43 Walpole was one of four Conservatives Ritchie included, while another of his sketches was of the deceased MP Henry Drummond (one of nine deceased MPs, such as Palmerston and Bright). Ritchie refers to Drummond's originality and eccentricity, "... his speech was no index to his vote" (p398), as well as to his brevity and humour: "His object appeared to be simply to amuse and mystify the House."

[689] Ibid, p46 His future wavering, however, would suggest anything but Ritchie's judgement of "political consistency".

[690] Vincent, op cit, p57

[691] Ibid, p67 Diary entry for 2ⁿᵈ June 1851

[692] "Derby ... affords the only instance of a statesman who, on three occasions, has attempted to carry on the work of the government with only a minority of the House of Commons to support him." Spencer Walpole, 'The History of Twenty-Five Years', 5 volumes, London, Longmans, Green & Co., 1904-1908, vol. I, p150

giving up "a very lucrative practice at the bar",[693] thereby putting party interests before personal ones and reinforcing his standing as an MP of integrity:

"... devoid of political ambition, and disliking responsibility, [Walpole] at once offered to take any political appointment which he might be thought capable of filling. The post of Home Secretary was accordingly allotted to him."[694]

In Robert Stewart's judgement, perhaps echoing Ritchie, Walpole

"... was one of the party's few competent debaters, but apprehensive that he had been placed too high."[695]

His career as Home Secretary began by proposing to enfranchise the militia. This was a major blunder that

"... he announced one day from the Treasury Bench without having consulted any colleague or friend upon it. The surprise of the House was great: greater still the dismay of his brother ministers: and not less the amusement of both friends and enemies, when the plan was withdrawn as abruptly as it had been proposed."[696]

Greville described it as an "extraordinary and still unexplained escapade".[697] A few days later after another ill-advised speech by Walpole, this time against Maynooth, Greville concluded that

"Walpole, who was thought one of the most capable [Government ministers], has been a failure. He had the folly to make a strong anti-Catholic speech on the Maynooth grant, and he got into the

---

[693] Ritchie, op cit, p44
[694] Vincent, op cit, p49 Stanley diary note for 27th February 1851 when Derby failed to form a government, taking office a year later. It was the case, as Derby announced in the House of Lords, that he had failed in 1851 for "want of experience in public business", but for Malmesbury (1807-1889) the real cause was "the timid conduct of Mr Henley and Mr Herries" with the former feeling himself incapable of becoming the President of the Board of Trade. Earl of Malmesbury, 'Memoirs of An Ex-Minister: An Autobiography', 2 volumes, London, Longmans, Green & Co., 1884, vol. I, pp278-279 Diary note for 28th February 1851.
[695] Robert Stewart, 'The Foundation of the Conservative Party 1830-1867', London, Longman, 1978, p253
[696] Vincent, op cit, p71
[697] Strachey and Fulford, op cit, vol. VI, p338

ridiculous scrape about the votes to Militiamen, which he was forced so awkwardly to withdraw amidst a storm of ridicule from every quarter, the real history of which has never yet been explained."[698]

A year earlier in 1851 Greville had thought Walpole one of the best men in the party, not least because of the assessment of others that his speeches in parliament made him a strong candidate for high office in a Stanley government coupled with his apparent rejection of protectionism and any attempt to revive the Corn Laws.[699] Consequently, Greville must have been even more sorely disappointed by his performance in power.

Walpole had added to the evidence of his poor judgement in June 1852 when he had sought to revive an obsolete law of 1829 banning Roman Catholic processions. While Walpole's intention may have been to ensure that forthcoming elections were peaceful, the effect was quite the opposite.[700] In December that year Derby's minority government was replaced by Aberdeen's ministry of all the talents, with "Conservatism [having] been dragged down by Disraeli's budget".[701] Briggs endorses the comment in the *Edinburgh Review* that Derby's had been the first government which had

"... reduced inconsistency to a system, and want of principles to a principle".[702]

In March 1853 Walpole was to be offered the Chairmanship of the Commons Committee on Ways and Means - provided he would accept it. However,

"Walpole, with his usual vacillation, put off a positive reply, but with his usual uprightness of purpose, ended by a refusal ... although his position is that of a very poor man."[703]

It was not that he would not make up his mind (procrastination), but that he kept changing it (vacillation). This might be for various reasons, including that Isabella gave him advice at odds with his

---

[698] Ibid, vol. VI, p343 Greville diary entry for 7th July 1852

[699] Strachey and Fulford, op cit, vol. VI, p271

[700] Vincent, op cit, p73

[701] Stewart, op cit, p272

[702] Briggs, 2000, op cit, p364

[703] Vincent, op cit, p104 Stanley diary note for 24th March 1853.

instinctive response, but it would make him particularly difficult to deal with in situations where he was required to reach a decision and stick to it. On the other hand, it might be to his benefit as an arbitrator or chairman (as indeed he was to become of the Great Western Railway in 1855-1856,[704] and of Select Committees on Lunatics 1859, Boundary Commission revisions subsequent to the Reform Bill 1867[705] and Privilege 1879) required to see more than one point of view, or as a subordinate required to carry out somebody else's instructions. This might have been one reason why Derby found a place for him in three Cabinets, and why Isabella held sway at home.

This equivocation can be seen in his relationship with Gladstone. In May 1854 he expressed his admiration for him, thinking he had "more power than ever Peel had even at his highest tide".[706] Three years later Walpole worked with Gladstone and his fellow (but in this case Conservative) MP for Oxford University Sir William Heathcote[707] (1801-1881) to prolong the parliamentary session in August 1857, united by their opposition to the Divorce Bill. In between, however, while Heathcote supported Gladstone's 1854 Oxford University Bill, Walpole opposed the admission of Dissenters. After an initial division supporting this clause, Walpole pressed for a second to "neutralise the effects of the first".[708] As this was just a month after his initial expression of respect for Gladstone, it was clear that it only went so far.

Walpole first represented the constituency of Midhurst (in Sussex, and close to Cowdray Park) for ten years, then being invited to succeed Henry Goulburn as MP for Cambridge University on the latter's death in 1856. Walpole's election for the University was challenged on petition and his Conservative colleagues raised a special subscription to defray the expenses he incurred in fighting

---

[704] "... [He] resumed his directorship between 1859 and 1866, taking the chairmanship again in 1862–3" according to his DNB entry.

[705] Moneypenny & Buckle, op cit, vol. II, p381

[706] Strachey and Fulford, op cit, vol. VII, p38

[707] Heathcote's DNB entry states "On 8 November 1825 he married Caroline Perceval, youngest daughter of Lord Arden, and brother [sic] of Heathcote's schoolfriend, Arthur Perceval." Adding, "In 1854, after a short period as a director of the South Western Railway, he succeeded Sir Robert Inglis as one of the MPs for Oxford University; as such he quietly represented conservative opinion in the university, in marked contrast to ... Gladstone (whose earlier election he had supported as chairman of his London committee)."

[708] Strachey and Fulford, op cit, vol. VII, p44 Note of Greville diary entry 26th June 1854, where Greville applauds the finesse of Walpole's attempted manoeuvre.

this.[709] He was to remain an MP there until his retirement from Parliament in November 1882.[710] Goulburn was a follower of the older Spencer Perceval, held similar views on admitting Catholics to political power,[711] and was known to at least three of the sons (Spencer, Frederick and Dudley). Greville describes Goulburn and Walpole as great friends,[712] despite the twenty year difference in their ages, and this extended well beyond the political experience they shared in the Conservative party and as Home Secretaries.

There had been some talk of Walpole becoming Speaker at the start of the 1857 Parliament, but in the event his name was not put forward in case it upset Palmerston and his supporters on the Liberal benches opposite.[713] The Conservatives had been out of office for more than five years, during which time the Crimean War had been fought. Disraeli likened the disastrous war to the debacle of the Walcheren expedition in the Napoleonic Wars almost fifty years before in 1809,[714] the gallantry of the troops undermined by futility and incompetent leadership. Walpole wrote to him on October 25th 1854:

"I am as clear as you that the expedition to the Crimea was a great mistake. As long as we stood on the high moral grounds of right and justice, we were invincible; the moment we attempt either the humiliation or dismemberment of Russia, no one can conjecture to what extremities we might be driven."[715]

In February 1858 Walpole was once again Home Secretary in the returning Derby administration. Gathorne Hardy, an MP for three years, was Walpole's deputy at the Home Office and thought very highly of him:

---

[709] Stewart, op cit, p330

[710] Subsequently High Steward at Cambridge University from 1887 until his death. Boase, op cit, p1174

[711] Brian Jenkins, 'Henry Goulburn 1784-1856: A Political Biography', Liverpool, Liverpool University Press, 1996, p166

[712] Strachey and Fulford, op cit, vol. VI, p359 Greville diary entry for 31st August 1852

[713] Stewart, op cit, p344 This had been mooted as early as 1852, but not pursued: Moneypenny and Buckle, op cit, vol. I, p1196

[714] Gault, 2009 (a), op cit, pp141-145

[715] Quoted in Moneypenny and Buckle, op cit, vol. I, p1367.

"... [Gathorne Hardy] recognises the advantages he gained by being in a working office always under the public eye, and under Walpole, a gentle chief who gave him opportunities."[716]

"He found a warm friend and a kindly mentor in his official chief, Spencer Walpole, and was soon marked out as a future leader."[717]

At one point Hardy threatened to resign, piqued by a note from the Chief Whip, but Walpole dissuaded him:

"Stick to the Ship, my dear Hardy, and may you one day be its master."[718]

During 1858 the Government put together the Reform Bill that Disraeli, Leader in the House of Commons, was to introduce at the end of February 1859. For much of this time the Cabinet were at loggerheads over the detail,[719] and though the overall impact was moderate, Walpole resigned over the £10 county franchise even though Derby had sought to reason with him that this would simply reduce it to the existing borough level. Greville was surprised that Walpole had not resigned before.[720] A Cabinet member, though not always a fully informed one, Malmesbury concluded that

"Walpole and Henley have resigned on the Reform Bill; the former because we go too far, the latter because we don't go far enough."[721]

Walpole was succeeded as Home Secretary by Sotheron Estcourt (1801-1876), previously president of the Poor Law Board,

---

[716] Gathorne-Hardy, op cit, vol. I, p112

[717] Ibid, p116

[718] Ibid, p118 Walpole had promised to have a word with Derby at Cabinet on Hardy's behalf, pointing out that the Whip's letter was unwarranted. But, as Derby was ill, he was unable to do so. It was on this occasion that Walpole referred to Isabella as his PM at home, contrasting his reliance on her advice with Derby's absence.

[719] See, for example, Wilbur Jones, 'Lord Derby and Victorian Conservatism', Oxford, Basil Blackwell, 1956, pp247-251 As Malmesbury describes it, the Cabinet was split "so nothing was done". Malmesbury, op cit, vol. II, p145 Diary note for 3rd December 1858

[720] Strachey and Fulford, op cit, vol. VII, p398

[721] Malmesbury, op cit, vol. II, p152 Diary note for 28th January 1859. Also, Moneypenny & Buckle, op cit, vol. I, pp1589-1604.

who Hardy also found "an efficient and congenial chief".[722] By June 1859, however, the Derby administration had been replaced by Palmerston's government and began another extended period in opposition - this time for seven years. Greville noted that Walpole was now "null", particularly compared to Disraeli who was pre-eminent in the party in the Commons.[723] In one sense, though, his resignation enhanced Walpole's reputation as it had come just before he became entitled to a ministerial pension of £2000 p.a. (over £86,000 in 2009). On a matter of principle, therefore, he had given up both his present earnings as Home Secretary and his family's security for the future.

In 1862 Isabella's ambition for her husband came to the fore again, persuading him to withdraw a motion on the economy that he had put to the House before consulting her and which would be unlikely to benefit his progress (certainly as she intended it):

"... Mrs Walpole has entertained confident expectations of getting the Speakership from the Whigs: I know that he never acts without consulting her: as he, indeed, has more than once owned to me ..."[724]

Walpole withdrew his motion, making sure Palmerston and his Cabinet were aware before his own colleagues. Isabella's ambition had won out over his instinct, but it may be that she was correct in this instance and his approach would have proved fruitless in the short-term and counter-productive in the longer run (though in the event this was never tested).

In 1865 Gladstone was unseated as MP for Oxford University by Gathorne Hardy, who came second behind Heathcote. No doubt the voters of Oxford University were delighted with this outcome initially, but they soon realised that they had given up their best chance to keep Gladstone muzzled.[725] In 1866 the re-building of St Mary's Church, Ealing was completed. In addition to the gift of the baptistery windows already referred to, the font was presented by the Walpoles' older daughter Jane Margaret.[726]

---

[722] Gathorne-Hardy, op cit, vol. I, p134

[723] Strachey and Fulford, op cit, vol. VII, p446

[724] Vincent, op cit, p187 Stanley diary note for 3rd June 1862.

[725] Walpole, 1904, op cit, pp521-522

[726] 'St Mary's Church, Ealing: The restoration of a historic building as a centre for worship and outreach 1984-2003', undated

In June that year 1866, less than eight months after Palmerston's death the previous October, the government of his successor Lord John Russell (in the House of Lords as Earl Russell since 1861), with Gladstone the Leader in the Commons, was defeated over the issue of reform. Derby became a minority Prime Minister for the third time, with Walpole Home Secretary again[727] and Gathorne Hardy now President of the Poor Law Board. The Reform League continued to agitate, demanding to hold a mass meeting in Hyde Park. When this was refused by the government, they went ahead anyway "and three days and nights of intermittent scurmishing [sic] followed".[728] Order was only restored when Walpole accepted the offer of the Reform League to intervene. It is said that Walpole was so overcome that he broke down in tears during the meeting. The Reform League sought to exploit the situation by claiming that Walpole had permitted them to hold another rally in Hyde Park two days later. Walpole denied it, but the overall impression created was one of weakness.[729] Derby described it as "This fiasco of Walpole's".[730]

Far from disappearing the pressure for reform increased, and to add to the challenges the government was confronted by economic depression, a cholera outbreak and increasing Fenian atrocity in Ireland by the end of the year. Most of these had repercussions for the Home Office in one way or another. Walpole had failed to grapple with sanitary reform as Home Secretary previously, again leaving it to his successors, but in 1867 he

"... brought in two bills which extended the coverage of the Factory Acts to many more trades and to workshops, thus affecting, he claimed, 1.4 million women and children."[731]

---

[727] Given Derby's reservations this was to ensure Walpole became eligible for a pension.

[728] Royden Harrison, "The 10th April of Spencer Walpole: The problem of revolution in relation to reform, 1865-1867", *International Review of Social History*, 1962, vol. VII, pp351-399
The date referred to is 10th April 1848 which was to have been the day on which the Chartists launched their most vigorous uprising against the establishment and the constitution. But their "monster meeting" on Kennington Common failed to live up to expectations, with the government's preparations ensuring the Chartists presented their petition to Parliament peacefully.

[729] Vincent, op cit, p261 Stanley diary note for 26th July 1866. In comparison, Malmesbury's diary notes for 22nd July to 27th July seem only partially informed. Malmesbury, op cit, vol. II, p362

[730] Moneypenny & Buckle, op cit, vol. II, p186

[731] Walpole's DNB entry

By the time the Acts were passed, however, he had again resigned as Home Secretary. The Reform League, in order to press their demands for universal manhood suffrage and vote by ballot, planned another public meeting in Hyde Park on Monday 6th May 1867. Walpole banned it on the 1st. On Friday 3rd May the House of Commons debated the government preparations, which, as in 1848, included the recruitment of more than 12,000 special constables and the deployment of troops. Yet on 4th May *The Times* reported that

"Nearly all the proclamations issued by Mr Walpole and posted all over London have been either torn down or defaced."[732]

In contrast to the Chartists in 1848, the Reform League was defiant, determined not only that the demonstration would go ahead, but that the use of force by the authorities should be met in kind. The alternatives were to submit to the establishment once more by calling the meeting off "... or to destroy the present political fabric".[733] For Charles Bradlaugh (1833-1891), subsequently MP for Northampton from 1880 but already well-known as a radical and a member of the Reform League executive,

"... we shall have to gather there as a People's Parliament, denying that you (the Commons) are the parliament of the nation; and we will gather there with or without your permission for it is our right."[734]

By 6.30pm on the 6th May about 150,000 people[735] were inside Hyde Park, and the police and army had made no attempt to prevent them or to break up the demonstration. It was apparent that the government had been defeated and Walpole humiliated, but the real victory was that the reform cause had triumphed, a victory accentuated by the people's dignified conduct of the demonstration. Whereas in 1866 the Reform League

---

[732] *The Times* 4th May 1867
[733] *Working Man* 4th May 1867, cited by Harrison, op cit, p362
[734] Charles Bradlaugh, "Reform or Revolution", undated pamphlet but probably 1867, cited by Harrison, op cit, p363
[735] *Daily News* 7th May 1867 As Harrison points out, estimates varied from more than 20,000 to less than 500,000.

"... had shown that the Government could not preserve order without its help; now it had demonstrated that it was able to impose its will upon the Government."[736]

As Howard Whitbread (1858-1944), a great-grandson of the Whig MP Samuel Whitbread (1764-1815) and a Liberal MP himself, was to say memorably at an election meeting in 1892:

"The whole path of history is marked out by a series of barren poles from which hang the tattered remnants of the colours which the Tories have nailed to the mast."[737]

Authority had proved to be impotent in the face of the people, but the power of wider society was clearly a difficult message for the establishment to accept, and it was Walpole who was blamed in the immediate aftermath for not acting. "Thus, 6th May 1867 became the 10th April of Spencer Walpole."[738] "We now date constitutional history from the WALPOLE period" trumpeted the *Saturday Review*,[739] but the establishment had yet to share this view, avoiding the implications by focussing on the smaller picture - a classic displacement strategy in the face of the unpalatable. Raised expectations have often proved the precursor to social change, hence, for example, the view that

"... one should always beware of those who have a bit, because ... it is they who push upward."[740]

This was to prove no different, and Isabella's life from 1801 to 1876 encompassed this change from one world to another, with her husband at the heart of it. In the short term, however, Walpole's resignation was accepted and he was replaced as Home Secretary on 17th May by Gathorne Hardy, an appointment with which Walpole was delighted:

---

[736] Harrison, op cit, p365
[737] Sam Whitbread, 'Plain Mr Whitbread: Seven Centuries of a Bedfordshire Family', Dunstable, The Book Castle, 2007, p76
[738] Harrison, op cit, p365
[739] *Saturday Review* 11th May 1867
[740] Ryszard Kapuscinski, 'The Emperor: Downfall of an Autocrat', London, Penguin, 2006, p113

"... Walpole ... came in to tell me that he had resigned; he wished me to feel, that if his place were offered me it was the very thing he desired, and that I was to have no scruple in taking it."[741]

Walpole remained in the Cabinet without portfolio,[742] retiring just after Derby on 28th February 1868 when he refused to serve under Disraeli, the new Prime Minister, who he felt had failed to support him over the Hyde Park rally and indeed had effectively driven him from office.[743]

"Walpole wishes to retire, saying that his position in the cabinet without office, is anomalous, which is true, but the reason is that he is influenced by his wife, who hates Disraeli."[744]

Walpole's warmth and kindness as a colleague extended to his private life, and accounts in part for the high regard in which he was held as a church estates commissioner and in a range of other appointments, including as President of the Literary Society for over thirty years.

There had been many attempted Reform Bills in the 1850s and 1860s, including Russell's in 1852, Aberdeen's in 1853/54, Palmerston's in 1860, Gladstone's in 1866, as well as Derby's previous attempt in 1858, often "single-barrelled"[745] in Malmesbury's words. In some cases they were mounted to give the illusion of action, while ensuring that, whatever the outcome, little or no change could result. For a long time the Derby/Disraeli one in 1867 was touch-and-go and it was only Derby's persistence that saw it enacted. At first his determination showed itself in maintaining the Cabinet's discussion

"Several Cabinets [all May and during June] on the Reform Bill, which each time became more Radical [relatively speaking]."

and then in driving it through, despite opposition in parliament

---

[741] Gathorne-Hardy, op cit, vol. I, p215 Gathorne Hardy diary entry for 9th May 1868.

[742] "Derby did not want to drop him, recognizing that the cabinet was at fault and not wishing to make him a scapegoat" according to Walpole's DNB entry.

[743] As reported by his son Spencer Walpole in Walpole, 1904, op cit, vol. II, pp199 & 287

[744] Vincent, op cit, p330 Stanley diary entry for 26th February 1868

[745] In other words, they did not deal fully with the issues of representation, including seats and their distribution, as well as the franchise itself.

"After many vicissitudes, the Reform Bill came up to the House of Lords, and Lord Derby moved the second reading ... without a division, saying it was 'a leap in the dark'. Peers on our [Conservative] side were averse to it, but, at a meeting of them, Lord Derby said he would resign if it was rejected."[746]

It was far from the last word, being only a modest contribution to change, but nevertheless it was another step on the path to reform. As Hobsbawm, makes clear, it was the start of a long haul rather than the precursor of immediate upheaval:

"In the decade 1867-1875 the industrial middle class had more or less completed its reform programme - as usual, borne upon the back of a great popular agitation, and as usual with the result of having to face a newly enfranchised working class whose political demands were bound to clash with its own."[747]

A few years later in 1882 there was a brief period of contentment between the economic upheavals with which the previous decade ended and those which would characterise the middle of the 1880s. Demands for change were no longer prominent at this time - or as the *Spectator* put it:

"Britain as a whole was never more tranquil and happy. No class is at war with society or the government: there is no disaffection anywhere, the Treasury is fairly full, the accumulations of capital are vast."[748]

Isabella continued the Perceval tradition of longevity, dying in her eighty-fifth year in 1886. Her husband Spencer Horatio was a widower for twelve years to 1898. Both are buried at St Mary's Ealing, the church they had attended for much of their married life and which Isabella had known from her youngest days.

---

[746] Malmesbury, op cit, vol. II, pp365-371 "The Leap in the Dark" is the title Asa Briggs gives to the final chapter in 'The Age of Improvement', op cit, covering this event.

[747] Hobsbawm, 1947, op cit, p306

[748] Spectator, summer of 1882 cited in Margaret Cole, 'The Story of Fabian Socialism', London, Heinemann, 1961, p1

10. JOHN PERCEVAL (1803-1876)

John Thomas (the name by which he was usually known, and which he used himself to distinguish him from other John Percevals, not least several of the Earls of Egmont) was aged nine at the time of his father's assassination. It may be that he was the young boy who, so Gray recounts, saw his father's body not long afterwards in the Speaker's office at the House of Commons.[749] A year earlier his father had revived the regency after George III's second bout of madness started in October 1810. It is not clear what effect these events may have had on John Thomas' own mental health in later life, but for Gray he was "ill-fated".[750]

Army and asylums

In 1822, the year after he left Harrow, John Thomas was involved in a carriage accident with his mother Jane Carr on 22nd May. They were almost certainly on a final trip together, perhaps for some last minute items, before he joined the army. She was taken to court that November by a man called Wayte, who had been injured in the accident and was seeking compensation for the poor driving of her coachman.[751] This aside, John Thomas first came to public attention in 1838 when he published his 'Narrative', an account of his madness from 1830 and his incarceration in two private asylums from January 1831 to early 1834.[752] He followed this up by publishing a second version in 1840.[753]

On 23rd May 1822, the day after the accident, John Thomas entered the army as an ensign in the 1st Regiment of Foot Guards, the Grenadiers.[754] He had previously been receiving half-pay from the 2nd Dragoon Guards, but the posting in the Grenadiers, the

---

[749] Gray, op cit, p459 n1

[750] Ibid, p52 & p431

[751] *The Times* 30th November 1822 and 24th January 1823

[752] John Thomas Perceval, 'A Narrative of the Treatment Experienced by a Gentleman, During a State of Mental Derangement', London, Wilson, 1838

[753] Gregory Bateson brought the two parts together and re-published them with an introduction as 'Perceval's Narrative: A Patient's Account of his Psychosis 1830-1832', Stanford, Stanford University Press, 1961 Bateson's book was reviewed in the British Medical Journal in October 1962 by R. Hunter & I. Macalpine, "John Thomas Perceval (1803-1876) patient and reformer", *British Medical Journal*, 1962, pp391-395

[754] F.W. Hamilton, 'The Origin and History of the First or Grenadier Guards', 3 volumes, London, John Murray, 1874, vol. III, p482

senior infantry regiment, was his first authentic commission. When he joined up, Frederick the Duke of York (1763-1827) was both the Colonel of the Grenadiers and commander-in-chief of the army. On his death in 1827 both positions passed to the Duke of Wellington (1769-1852), who remained the Colonel of the Grenadier Guards on becoming Prime Minister in 1828, but had to give up the overall army command.[755] John Thomas was in the First battalion and was posted to Ireland twice, the first time in 1822-1823 when Habeas Corpus was suspended to help maintain order and the country was in the grip of a famine; the second in 1828-1829 as the Catholic Emancipation Act was being debated. On both occasions the battalion was there to keep the peace, being garrisoned in Dublin on each occasion.[756] In between, John Thomas had been promoted on 8th April 1826 (though whether to Captain or Lieutenant is not clear from Hamilton's listing)[757] and was with the battalion when they were sent first to Spain in December 1826, and then Portugal. George Canning had despatched

"a British force to Lisbon to protect the constitutional party in Portugal against the intrigue of the Powers"[758]

in accordance with old treaty obligations. The battalion returned to England at the end of April 1828.[759] John Thomas resigned his commission in the Grenadier Guards on 11th June 1830 as his mental health difficulties increased "to prepare himself for his doom" as he described it. He then spent a term at Magdalen Hall, Oxford University,[760] went to Scotland to search out the Irvingites and by Christmas 1830 was insane. Bateson provides more details, but John Thomas then found his way to Dublin, was brought back by his brother Spencer and was committed to Brislington House in Bristol in January 1831. He was not quite 28.

It is possible to speculate about why John Thomas went to Dublin at this time, but it may be that it was simply a place with which he was familiar, just as he would have been aware of the

---

[755] Ibid, vol. III, pp89-91 & 104
[756] Ibid, vol. III, pp80-82 & 106
[757] Ibid, vol. III, pp482 His entry in the Harrow School Register, op cit, says his rank was Captain, while 'The United Service Journal and Naval and Military Magazine', London, Colburn & Bentley, 1830, Pt II, p122 says that he "retired Lieutenant".
[758] C.R. Fay, 'Life and Labour in the Nineteenth Century' (4th edition), Cambridge, Cambridge University Press, 1947, p8
[759] Hamilton, op cit, vol. III, pp85-87 & 105
[760] Foster, 1888, op cit, vol. III, p1097

Irvingites in Scotland. A battalion of the Grenadier Guards was sent there again in 1831 and this may have added to Dublin's primacy for John Thomas. Ireland was perhaps at the forefront of his mind in any case because he was attempting to reconcile his father's views on Roman Catholics, his own misgivings and Wellington's role as Prime Minister when the Emancipation Act was passed. Wellington's hero status may have been even more apparent in the Grenadiers than in other regiments, and consequently his subsequent political about-turn on Catholics even harder to accept. Equally, though, it may have been John Thomas' experience of war, and the horrors of poverty and ill-treatment in Ireland, that added to an already unstable mind, tipping him over the edge.

John Thomas was fortunate that Brislington House was a private asylum. Well-run ones were less reliant on restraint than the public asylums such as Bethlem and offered patients and families some anonymity. Standards of care were considerably higher and the approach more enlightened. In some circumstances, according to Porter, servants were even permitted.[761] Bateson says that a private asylum could be afforded because of the £50,000 capital grant Parliament had settled on the children after their father's assassination, but his mother was well enough off to ensure that he received this care in any case.

In May 1832 John Thomas was transferred to Ticehurst asylum in Sussex where he remained until he was well enough to be discharged in early 1834. He married Anna Gardner almost immediately on 31st March 1834, possibly in Holborn. Gray says that the marriage was "quite out of his station in life",[762] but it is not clear whether she and John Thomas knew each other previously or whether they met at Brislington or Ticehurst.[763] Gray's comment would suggest that, if the latter, she was not another patient, but may have worked at one of the asylums or lived locally. They left soon after for Paris, though whether for a particular purpose or whether they were just keen to get away from England, starting a new life in a new country, is not clear. The first two of their four

---

[761] Roy Porter, "Madness and its institutions", pp. 277-302 in A. Wear [ed.], 'Medicine in Society: Historical Essays', Cambridge, Cambridge University Press, 1992
[762] Gray, op cit, p52 n5
[763] They may have first met in Ireland. Although this is unlikely, it might account for the fact that, while her father's name Thomas is known, no other details have survived of him or her mother. It might also help explain why John Thomas fled to Dublin in 1830.

daughters were born in Paris in April 1835 and June 1836. The oldest daughter Jane Beatrice (1835-1893) and the youngest Fanny (1845-1862) never married, but Alice Frederica (1836-1921) and Selina Maria did, the latter to her cousin Horatio George, Isabella's younger son.

John Thomas' account of his illness in his 'Narrative' reinforces the importance of a patient helping themselves and being given the time to recover. Self-help and understanding were critical in this case. John Thomas took the view that, as the patient knows most about his mental health, his views should not be discounted nor his behaviour penalised by restraint. He says nothing of his parents' or siblings' actions to account for his feelings of inadequacy - though he did write to his mother as "Lady Carr" when he wished to upset her. Bateson comments that schizophrenia can provide its own cure in time; this has been recognised since, but was first identified by John Thomas. Bateson also posits treatment similarities between the 1830s and 1961 that reinforce the patient's sense of isolation and lack of control. These reinforced John Thomas' delusions initially. But, as he became more aware of their inappropriateness, so he became angry at them. He was beginning to recover. The speed with which he married after his discharge would suggest that Anna had played her part in this.[764]

Mental health reformer

From that point to his death in 1876 he dedicated himself to improving mental health treatment, and "the care and conditions of the insane". He described himself as "the attorney-general of all Her Majesty's madmen". His legacy as a mental health reformer has lasted to the present day and has been influential throughout Europe.

Gray says that in 1838 "he fell foul of the home office for distributing pamphlets 'calculated to inflame the lower orders'".[765] This seems to be a euphemism for agitation against the introduction of the new poor law, including a Huddersfield poster. This was an issue to which he would return in 1843 as "Guardian of the Parish of Kensington", the same role that his brother Henry had assumed in Elmley Lovett. For John Thomas, however, it was to be anything but "low-key".

---

[764] Parts of this paragraph appeared in my article first published in *The Psychologist*. Gault, 2008(a), op cit

[765] Ibid The reference is to Home Office papers (HO 40/40).

In 1839 and 1840 he wrote five letters to *The Satirist* magazine about the mistreatment that resulted from the lunacy laws and the inhuman conditions in which people were often held in asylums. The magazine's subtitle was *The Censor of the Times*, and it had already taken up this cause under the title of 'The Madhouse System', adopting a quote from Jeremy Bentham as its slogan: "Publicity is the soul of justice". John Thomas' first letter, number 22 in the magazine's series, was written from Paris in August 1839:

"... I trust that the information I have been able to obtain, relative to the state of this [lunacy] law in France, may be sufficiently interesting to your readers to find a place in ... your fearless journal.
"Having had the pleasure of meeting with one of the *Juges de Premiere Instance* of Amiens, I related to him the atrocious case of my friend, Mr. Paternoster,[766] and others of that nature, which had occurred in England, at which he was greatly surprised, and assured me that such an abuse of authority was, if not impossible, very difficult in France. He informed me that previous to the imprisonment, or, as it is termed, the interdiction of a person of unsound mind, there must be a *conseil de famille*, and, after that, the decree of a tribunal where the individual is always examined, together with the witnesses to acts of folly. *Three* physicians are also appointed by the tribunal to examine the patient. **This is very different from the interested examination of mad doctors paid by the relatives, as in England.** [emphasis added] ...
"... I shudder when I reflect upon what I have witnessed myself of the conduct of the female keepers in Lunatic Asylums in England, towards ladies of the utmost modesty and refinement; when I recollect the indelicate nature of the treatment, the cruelty, the violence that I myself ... was subjected to, and know that women are abandoned by their relations to the same treatment, and exposed to the rude grasp of such ruffians as those by whom I was surrounded, I feel ... that this subject ... is hardly fit for public discussion; **but without an exposure of the evil, what hope can we entertain of reform?** [emphasis added] ..."[767]

---

[766] Paternoster had already provided evidence of the mistreatment women were subjected to in asylums, and in *The Satirist* of 25ᵗʰ October 1840 listed thirty-two people who had been incarcerated in Finch's madhouse at the same time as him, often with no justification, and subjected to "every abuse and atrocity in the foul catalogue of madhouse crimes".
[767] *The Satirist* 22ⁿᵈ September 1839

Perceval had in his sights both the families who "abandon[ed] their nearest and dearest kindred to such disgusting treatment" and the government who, rather than protecting the vulnerable, permitted it. Women were often raped and, even if they were not, it would be suspected that they had been. People were discharged, perhaps ejected might be a better word, without any help or support, let alone the skills or even references that might assist them to gain employment.

John Thomas followed up with a letter in February 1840 (from Kensington) referring to the trial Paternoster had brought against Finch and his madhouse, and the assault and false imprisonment that he alleged he had been subject to. Perceval highlighted the true lunacy of the situation, in other words the court procedures:

"... the ridiculous costume of the judge and counsel ... the vain and captious quibbling [of the lawyers] ...
"... the business of the court conducted with so little courtesy and decent respect to the rights of others ...
"...The truth is the whole system is one of gross hypocrisy..."[768]

The Commissioners of Lunacy had taken Finch's side, acting "*for the defendant*" rather than undertaking an impartial examination. Like the Commissioners, the Attorney General was aware of the flaws in the 1832 law, but had done nothing to remedy it. For Perceval even Paternoster's disability, walking "occasionally with a thick stick", had been made to count against him, as had his Roman Catholicism and, of course, his letters to *The Satirist*. As the magazine stated in its next issue a week later, while it was not surprising that Paternoster's charges had been dismissed, of more concern was that the public had been hoodwinked: the defendant and his witnesses had not been cross-examined, the abuses remained hidden and the principles of humane treatment had not been tested.[769]

One of the defences asylum licensees mounted was that, because they often lived off the premises, they could not be held accountable for the abuses that took place in their asylums. Perceval highlighted such a case in the same issue of *The Satirist*, in which a young woman had died the year before from the injuries she received in an asylum near Southampton. While the licensee

---

[768] *The Satirist* 16th February 1840
[769] *The Satirist* 23rd February 1840

might have been reprimanded by the magistrates, the law as it currently stood could not prevent that person continuing to run the asylum. Not only did the law need changing, but Perceval was amazed that the church and the local Bishop, who would have been aware of the cruel treatment once it had been reported, had not put the government under pressure to do so.

In October 1840 John Thomas's fifth letter reflected on the circumstances of his brother-in-law Edward's suicide at Denham Park asylum earlier that year.

"... it was reported that my unfortunate cousin, who met a violent death by throwing himself from a window at Denham-park, had been confined in a room at the top of the house, and had opened the window to execute his purpose, taking advantage of the absence of one of the attendants.

"This statement I felt at the time reflected discredit to some degree upon the family, for want of proper care, and undue discredit upon the institution at Denham-park; but I have been unwilling hitherto to notice it. Now, however, I [wish] to correct it ...

"... my cousin ... [was] placed in a drawing-room on the second floor ... the windows of which *were fastened down*, so that he could not open them. The situation was chosen for him with great anxiety by his brothers, after he had himself assented to and repeatedly requested to be placed under observation. ... [At Edward's request, the wire blinds on the windows were eventually removed.] It was thought that he was so far recovered (and he was evidently so much recovered in health)[770], that he might be trusted; but he availed himself of this relaxation of precaution, in a moment of delusion or phrenzy [sic], to throw himself, being of very small stature, *through one of the panes of glass* - a thing almost incredible, and hardly to be expected, even by those who conduct such institutions."[771]

While John Thomas was keen to give credit to the enlightened, if over-solicitous, consideration his cousin had been shown at Denham Park, he was equally determined to draw attention to instances of bad practice that highlighted the rotten system and the doctors, owners and commissioners who colluded in it. For example, John Bright (1780/81-1870), not the well-known MP but

---

[770] In other words, this confirms a physical dimension to his disability as well as a mental one.
[771] *The Satirist* 25th October 1840

originally a physician, became "one of the commissioners for regulating madhouses" appointed by the Royal College of Physicians. "From 1828 to 1845 Bright served as one of five ... metropolitan commissioners in lunacy",[772] and John Thomas was one of the patients he visited. Bright was already considered "negligent, incompetent, and ignorant" by fellow medics, and a member of an underpowered and inadequate Commission, but Perceval's criticisms of him were scathing.[773]

In 1843 he had written to Sir James Graham (1792-1861), Sir Robert Peel's Home Secretary from 1841. His letter (copied to *The Times*) highlighted the iniquity of a Kensington parishioner denied poor relief and sent to the workhouse.[774] It was the start of a campaign, with all his letters to Graham being published in 1846.[775] He also wrote eleven letters to Peel himself over the same period.[776] In May 1845 Lord Normanby (1797-1863) drew attention on John Thomas' behalf to the latter's demand for a committee to examine the Lunacy Commission.[777] Perceval's determination was buoyed up by his certainty that his principles were born out of experience; they were entirely appropriate and he was indefatigable in their pursuit.

There were others who shared the same views and John Thomas helped found the Alleged Lunatic's Friends Society on 7th July 1845, first as one of the Directors and a Trustee, and then becoming its Honorary Secretary as well the following year. The list of vice-presidents published in the first report[778] in 1846 included several MPs, of whom the most prominent was perhaps one of the Finsbury MPs, Thomas Slingsby Duncombe. Dudley Perceval had

---

[772] Bright's DNB entry by Jonathan Andrews
[773] John Thomas Perceval, 'A Letter to the Secretary of State for the Home Department upon the unjust and pettifogging conduct of the Metropolitan Commissioners on Lunacy, in the Case of a Gentleman lately under their surveillance', London, Effingham Wilson, 1844 The letter was printed and advertised for sale in *John Bull* magazine on 27th July 1844 and *The Satirist* the following day at a price of 1/6.
[774] *The Times* 3rd August 1843
[775] John Thomas Perceval, 'Letters to Sir J. Graham ... upon the reform of the law affecting the treatment of persons alleged to be of unsound mind', London, 1846 These letters were also printed and advertised in *The Times* on 30th April 1846, again at a price of 1/6.
[776] British Library, Add MSS 40426-40597 passim
[777] *The Times* 21st May 1845 Normanby had been Home Secretary in Melbourne's government for the two years before Peel became Prime Minister in 1841.
[778] The Alleged Lunatic's Friends Society, 'First Report of The Alleged Lunatic's Friends Society', London, McDowall, 1846

stood against him as the Conservative candidate for Finsbury in 1837, but was roundly defeated in this radical borough for which Duncombe was an MP for twenty-seven years from 1834 to his death in 1861.[779] Duncombe was to take up a number of anti-establishment causes over the years, including the Ten Hours Bill, Chartism and the rights of religious dissenters and Jews. He was also to clash with James Graham over other issues.

In the preamble to its 1846 report, the Society drew attention to the help already available to the poor, dumb and blind, even the "crooked of limb". By contrast alleged lunatics, the crooked of mind, "were wickedly dealt with by their fellow creatures", although "society's peace is based on that of the individual and the individual's on that of society". The Society referred to two people it had already helped who had been "entombed alive in the confinement of a Lunatic Asylum", and would assist others who were discharged without any means of support or obtaining employment.[780] Subscriptions (five guineas for life membership or ten shillings annually) could be sent to the Society's bankers, its offices or to John Thomas at his home, Campden Cottage, Notting-hill Square (re-named as Campden Hill Square after 1893). The Society shrewdly offered free membership to any clergyman who preached on the Society's behalf or devoted their church to that purpose. It was clearly aware that, given the uphill nature of its task, marketing and the influence of the clergy would be critical. Ostensibly to celebrate the Society's first anniversary, but also to promote its existence, it offered very generous essay prizes to coincide with a festival on 7th July 1846.

The Society was the first mental health advocacy organisation, beginning today's self-help and advocacy movements.[781] Four days before it was founded, Duncombe attempted in the Commons on the basis of Perceval's petition to establish a Committee on asylum and Commission abuses, and failing that to defer the proposed Bill introduced by Lord Ashley to the next session.[782] Duncombe's amendment was heavily defeated. One of the Society's first campaigns was to increase Parliamentary opposition to the 1845 Acts (Lunacy and Regulation of Lunatic Asylums). The Society

---

[779] See Chapter 8 above Duncombe was six years older than John Thomas, but like him had been to Harrow School and then joined the army.
[780] The Alleged Lunatic's Friends Society, op cit, pp5-11
[781] D. Brandon, "A friend to alleged lunatics", *Mental Health Today*, October 2007, pp37-39
[782] *The Times* 3rd July 1845

spent nearly £135 (about £7000 today) in fighting this, a sizeable proportion of its first year income of £403 (about £20,000). The first report listed the amendments it had achieved in the Act and others it had unsuccessfully sought.[783]   The former required asylum proprietors to reside on the premises, the grounds for insanity to be recorded on the committal certificate, and extended the time people could bring an action to twelve months after confinement. These were significant steps forward, but the Society had failed to ensure that people could cross-examine witnesses who had proclaimed them insane. It recognised that there was still a long way to go - not least in changing society's attitudes so that the stigma and repulsion of "lunatic" and "insanity" were removed and people were not incarcerated without proper legal authority. Too often certification was used as a convenient way of getting hold of another person's assets while they were still alive. The Society aimed to end this, ensuring that the vulnerable could depend on "the shield of the law's protection".[784]

In 1859 John Thomas gave evidence on the operation of asylums to the Select Committee chaired by Spencer Horatio Walpole, his brother-in-law. One of the proposals was to transfer medical visitors from the Court of Chancery to the Lunacy Commissioners on the grounds that this would eliminate duplicate visits. Another campaigner against this, with similar views to John Thomas, was John Bucknill, President of the Association of Medical Officers of Asylums and Hospitals for the Insane, who followed up his appearance before the Committee by letter.[785] He argued that these were separate roles, the medical visitors assessing individuals and the Commissioners inspecting institutions. It would not be cost-effective to combine the two other than where visits overlapped.   On the contrary, alleged lunatics should receive increased and independent assistance, with, for example, solicitors attending all inquisitions on their behalf.   Bucknill also drew attention to the anomaly whereby 7000 people deemed insane were in workhouses rather than asylums "contrary to law, justice and humanity".[786]   This needed tackling.   The Select Committee reported in 1860, recognising the significance of increased liberty and the rights of "lunatics" - though more in principle than in

---

[783] The Alleged Lunatic's Friends Society, op cit, pp24-25
[784] Ibid, pp30-32
[785] John Bucknill, 'A Letter to the Right Hon. Spencer Horatio Walpole MP, Chairman of the Select Committee on Lunatics', 1860
[786] Ibid, p12

practice. John Thomas had campaigned on both issues, arguing that continuing to see friends and family could be an important step on the road to recovery. This pre-figures subsequent developments in mental health, such as care in the community, as well as some of the entitlements to normal life enshrined in the UN Declaration of Human Rights.

In 1861 the family was living at 3 High Street, Herne Bay, the house in which Frederick's family had lived previously and his son Charles had been born in 1848, and for which James Dolman held the freehold by 1853.[787] John Thomas and Anna may have hoped that the sea air would benefit their youngest daughter's health - but to no avail, as she died the following year aged 17. In January 1862 John Thomas wrote from this address to *John Bull* magazine highlighting the cruelties in lunatic asylums:

"In your paper of the 4th of January ... you allude to the horrible treatment of a paralysed patient in the county asylum at Hanwell. I am sorry to have to remind you that this is not a solitary instance ... for a few months ago inquests were held on another patient in that asylum who had died after receiving very dreadful injuries, as well as on one who was accidentally scalded to death. And only lately ... two keepers were tried for the murder of a patient at Colney Hatch, who had died with eleven of his ribs fractured, their ligatures separated, his breast bone broken in, and his liver ruptured[788] ... When I gave my evidence to the Select Committee ... in 1860, the Committee were surprised by my assuring them that ... this was still the normal treatment of two classes of patients, the very violent and the very weak and troublesome, in both our private and public asylums ... This opinion was founded on the complaints and on the information which the ... Alleged Lunatic's Friends Society were constantly receiving ..."[789]

Perceval's letter went on to point out that, though the Select Committee report barely reflected his evidence, no sooner had it been printed than other instances of abuse became known. One husband, concerned over his wife's treatment, had previously been

---

[787] See Chapter 6 above

[788] Though the keepers were not convicted because some of the evidence was ruled inadmissible and the jury felt unable "to rely on the evidence of two of the patients who had been present in the ward at the time of the ill-treatment of the deceased".

[789] *John Bull* 25th January 1862

a keeper himself in the Surrey County Asylum at Wandsworth. He was therefore aware of the possibilities:

"... it was all very well for the magistrates to lay down rules for the humane treatment of patients, yet, 'when we were alone, we treated them as we thought proper'."[790]

For John Thomas "the whole system of dealing with lunatic patients is ... radically defective" and their management and government "vicious in principle". Churches of all denominations were found wanting, though whether through "apathy, timidity or from ignorance" Perceval was not clear. He was ahead of his time too in speaking out against the vast warehouses of inhumanity that many asylums were, making containment the primary objective and enlightened medical care and individual attention well-nigh impossible.[791] Not for nothing were most of the staff called "keepers". The safety of those outside was the over-riding rationale, not the rehabilitation of those inside. But John Thomas was equally conscious that the Society was having little impact on public opinion and not raising sufficient funds to do more than scratch the surface. It was only the few individual success stories that kept the Society going.

Six years later on 29th March 1868 John Thomas wrote to Gladstone,[792] arguing for the separation of church and state in Ireland, allowing people to judge for themselves whether to be Catholic or Protestant on the basis of education rather than propaganda. As Perceval had argued previously, his view was that Church rates should be paid according to personal preference, with the non-aligned (i.e., those who did not profess any religious affiliation) having the option to see their payments used for general welfare and education. Any surplus funds should be used to revive the Irish language and culture. The Act of Union in 1801 between England and Ireland had made Catholics less than citizens in their own country, and it should be dissolved if only "from sympathy with the national feelings of Irishmen and with their sufferings and

---

[790] Ibid

[791] Yet it would be the 1970s before closure of the huge mental health hospitals began and the 1990s before the programme was concluded. Learning disability hospitals have been closed even more recently.

[792] John Thomas Perceval, 'A Letter to the Right Hon. W.E. Gladstone, MP on the Separation of the Irish Church from the State, and In Favour of a Dissolution of the Union Between England and Ireland', London, Truelove, 1868

poverty".[793]   Roman Catholic priests should be treated like foreign medics, allowed to minister to those in England who believed in them.

This was a humanist perspective, very different to the usual approach of lumping people into categories and responding to them on the basis of assumed characteristics.   In other words, people were to be seen as individuals rather than just as members of the mob or as figures in the crowd.   Needless to say, this was at odds with a society that depended on the exploitation of the masses at home and abroad, and their unquestioning subjugation, but it chimed exactly with Perceval's approach to mental health reform.

It was because Gladstone was to present a motion to the House of Commons the following day, 30th March 1868, for a Committee on Church and State separation in Ireland that Perceval had appealed to him.   John Thomas knew that, while Gladstone might be sympathetic, in all probability the majority of the House of Commons would not.   It was too soon after the threats to the establishment the previous July.   Nevertheless, John Thomas wished to assure Gladstone - perhaps especially as a son of Spencer Perceval - that religious freedom was vital, underpinning a range of other freedoms and human happiness as a whole.   But, as he probably expected, the debate at the end of March was the start of a process rather than its conclusion.   Gladstone had a majority of 56 for a Committee, but Disraeli and Queen Victoria led the opposition.   For Disraeli the importance of the Irish church was as an "outwork of the Church of England".   If it was disestablished, there might be a domino effect that could threaten the "divine right of Government ... the keystone of human progress" in Disraeli's view.[794]   Besides, the 1867 Reform Bill had yet to be fully implemented, and in these circumstances, the opposition argued, disestablishment was not only premature but might prove destabilising.   John Thomas added another sixteen pages to the fifteen of his original Gladstone letter by 9th April, and then published the whole in the hope that it would add to the overall pressure for change.

John Thomas died on 28th February 1876 aged 73.   His death was noted by *The Times* and *John Bull* on one side of the political divide, by the *Pall Mall Gazette* on the other, but there was no

---

[793] Ibid, p4
[794] Moneypenny & Buckle, op cit, vol. II, p364

obituary, either in these publications or elsewhere.[795] A week later on 5th March he was buried in Kensal Green cemetery, as his fellow reformer Thomas Duncombe had been fifteen years earlier. The Perceval grave had been purchased on 19th November 1862, originally for the youngest daughter Fanny who had died a week earlier.[796] Seven years after John Thomas' death, Anna Perceval was buried alongside her husband and daughter on 27th January 1883.

---

[795] *The Times* 2nd March 1876; *Pall Mall Gazette* 2nd March 1876; *John Bull* 4th March 1876

[796] The grave cost 15 guineas and could accommodate six coffins (copy of the invoice from the General Cemetery Company, personal communication, 26th January 2010). The invoice had been sent to John Thomas at 3 High Street, Herne Bay.

11. ERNEST PERCEVAL (1807-1896)

Harrow and Hussars

The youngest child Ernest was not quite five years old when his father was assassinated. Ernest may have been aware of the changed atmosphere in the household, and his father's absence, but the event would have had less lasting significance for him than for the older children. As Gray says, "... baby Ernest ... [was] still scarcely out of the nursery"[797] and was only seven when his mother re-married in January 1815. He went to Harrow in 1817, remaining there until 1824.[798] Even John Thomas had managed to become a prefect at the School, but the Harrow School Register does not indicate that Ernest was one. Rather it records that the highlight of Ernest's school career was when he won the champion racket. Rackets was a game in its own right rather than a development from real tennis and rapidly evolved into the sport of squash:

"... in the early 19th century at Fleet Prison ... the inmates took to hitting a ball against a wall to keep themselves amused. The game of Rackets was soon developed from this pastime, which rather surprisingly soon found its way into Britain's growing band of public schools and by 1830 the first game of squash was being played at Harrow School."[799]

Ernest, like his older brother Frederick, was the only other Perceval son not to go to university - even if John Thomas did so but briefly and belatedly. In keeping with the active reputation he had acquired at Harrow, Ernest entered the army on 22nd April 1824 as a cornet in the 15th (the King's) Hussars. Little more than a year later he became a lieutenant in July 1825 and by the end of 1826 had progressed to the rank of Captain by purchase.[800] His step-father Henry Carr had taken nearly two years to attain the rank of Captain in a foot regiment (see Table 3 in Chapter 2 above), while

---

[797] Gray, op cit, p431

[798] Harrow School Register 1800-1911, op cit, p80

[799] www.worldsquash2008.com/the-championships/history-of-squash.aspx

[800] H.C. Wylly, 'XVth (The King's) Hussars 1759 to 1913', London, Caxton, 1914, p443 Also, *Morning Chronicle* 20th December 1826 from *London Gazette* 19th December 1826: "15th Regiment of Light Dragoons [though re-named as the Hussars from 1806] - Lieutenant Ernest Augustus Perceval to be Captain by purchase".

John Thomas had required almost four in the premier infantry regiment. Ernest had done so in half the time in the cavalry, but then remained a Captain before retiring from the army when he sold his commission on 31st May 1833.

In late summer 1829 Ernest had travelled alone throughout Europe, though more it seems as an adventure than on holiday. Certainly, it was not a conventional "grand tour". He got as far as Hungary, and on his way back on 4th October he wrote from Dresden to his mother Lady Carr at Ealing:

"If I happened to arrive at a Port about 12 o'clock which is the time they dine in Hungary the people of the town would always make me sit down with them and not expect any money. At other times they would give me fruit and wine. They all expressed their surprise at my undertaking so long a journey alone, ..., and it should seem that they considered it dangerous to travel by myself as they used to say ah "das ist gefaulich [sic]" when I told them I was going to travel all night. However, I never found the least obstruction ..."[801]

The 15th Hussars did not fight a battle between Waterloo in 1815 and the Second Afghan War in 1878-1880,[802] and therefore missed the Crimean War entirely. They were engaged in policing at home as election riots in Nottingham and Manchester threatened up to 1832, and were sent to Ireland for a second tour of duty in May 1833.[803] Later that year they were moved to Cork in case they were required to embark for Portugal, but in the event were not, and Bombay in 1839 proved to be their next taste of foreign service. According to Peter Burroughs:

"Guards battalions seldom went on foreign service and most cavalry regiments remained in Britain, though some served in India."[804]

---

[801] British Library, Add. MSS 49195, f.52

[802] Arthur Swinson (ed.), 'A Register of the Regiments and Corps of the British Army', London, The Archive Press, 1972, p41; C.B. Norman, 'Battle Honours of the British Army 1662-1901', Newton Abbot, David & Charles, 1971

[803] Wylly, op cit, pp271 & 250

[804] Peter Burroughs, "An unreformed army? 1815-1868", p164 in Chandler, D.G. & Beckett, I. (eds), 'The Oxford History of the British Army', Oxford, Oxford University Press, 2003 This might suggest that John Thomas Perceval's service with the Grenadier Guards in Spain and Portugal was unusual (see Chapter 10 above), but it refers to foreign service within the Empire (i.e., colonial service).

Had Ernest joined the army primarily to parade rather than fight (though there is no suggestion that this was his intention), it might be thought that he had found a compatible and comfortable berth. The former may have been correct, but the latter certainly was not. In 1832

"... Lord Brudenell did achieve a command: he bought the lieutenant-colonelcy of the 15th Hussars, at a cost, it was stated in *The Times*, of between £35,000 and £40,000."[805]

This is the equivalent of almost £2m today.[806]

James Thomas Brudenell (1797-1868) had been at Harrow briefly at the same time as Henry Perceval, two years his junior, but is better known as the 7th Earl of Cardigan, the man who led the 11th Hussars, the Light Brigade, into "the valley of death" at Balaclava, largely because he disputed, or wilfully misinterpreted, the orders of his brother-in-law, John Bingham the 3rd Earl of Lucan (1800-1888). When Brudenell assumed command of the 15th Hussars in 1832, he was taking over one of the most highly thought of regiments in the army, whose previous Colonel, Joseph Thackwell (1781-1859), had worked his way up the ranks since joining them in 1800 and had been a respected officer in their Peninsular War campaign and at Waterloo. As Colonel he had been a stern disciplinarian but a humane one:

"... the defaulters' list was short, and floggings and court-martials were rare".[807]

The inexperienced Brudenell lacked any military credibility and soon adopted a different approach, taking command in a typically arrogant and contemptuous manner:

"Though the 15th was a notably efficient regiment, the new commanding officer viewed it with disgust. He demanded more

---

[805] Cecil Woodham-Smith, 'The Reason Why', London, Penguin Books, 1953, p36
[806] Saul David, 'The Homicidal Earl: The Life of Lord Cardigan', London, Little Brown, 1997, p60 says that Brudenell "exchanged commissions with Lieutenant-Colonel Joseph Thackwell". Wylly, op cit, p382 says much the same, while Thackwell's DNB entry states "In November 1831 he arranged to exchange to half pay with Lord Brudenell, who reportedly paid between £35,000 and £40,000 for command of the 15th."
[807]Woodham-Smith, op cit, p37

glitter, more dash, and he set to work to drill, polish, pipeclay, reprimand and discipline the 15th to within an inch of their lives."[808]

Even before the regiment went to Ireland in May 1833, a year after Brudenell had joined them, his

"... regime was arousing, in the words of the regimental history, a good deal of discontent."[809]

Ernest's retirement was preceded a month earlier in April 1833 by that of Major Frederick Buckley (?-?), who had joined the 15th Hussars in 1817, became a major at the end of 1827, and led the troops deployed to deal with the Nottingham riots in 1831, being commended for the manner in which he did so. His experience of the regiment was almost entirely under Thackwell's command and he was clearly unable to stomach the change to an inexperienced yet authoritarian Brudenell. Buckley was one of the regiment's two majors, the other being Sir Walter Scott (1801-1847) the novelist's son, and had organised Thackwell's leaving gift in 1832,[810] writing to him on behalf of the other officers regretting his departure and thanking him for his many acts of kindness.[811] Buckley sold his commission to one of Ernest's fellow captains Courtenay Philipps (?-?), while one of the regiment's Lieutenants purchased Ernest's captaincy. It must be assumed that both these promotions were acceptable to Brudenell, thereby consolidating his regime.

Even if Ernest had other reasons for retirement, and may have wished to avoid service in Ireland and overseas, he and Buckley must have been relieved that they evaded subsequent events in Ireland:

"Brudenell's talent for mis-managing men would be seen to more explosive effect before too long."[812]

In less than two years since taking command, Brudenell's harsh and unbending approach had generated pro- and anti-Brudenell factions among the officers, depending on whether he was thought to be

---

[808] Ibid, p40

[809] David, op cit, p61

[810] Wylly, op cit, p278

[811] H.C. Wylly, 'The Military Memoirs of Lt. Gen. Sir Joseph Thackwell', London, John Murray, 1908, p105

[812] David, op cit, p61

motivated by the best military intentions or by malice. This split undermined the regiment's morale and the deterioration escalated as Lady Brudenell's wife[813] was snubbed by other officers' wives offended by her reputation for adultery and scurrilous behaviour. Brudenell's underhand and inconsistent treatment of some officers, including the surreptitious recording of conversations, sealed the decline in discipline:[814]

"His overbearing manner and violent temper brought frequent clashes with regimental officers. He twice put Captain Augustus Wathen (c1805-1843) under arrest..."[815]

on spurious charges, prevented a desperate Wathen from exchanging or selling his commission and then had him court-martialled. But this went badly wrong for Brudenell and Wathen was found not guilty. The King approved the not guilty finding, exonerated Wathen and ordered that Brudenell be removed from command of the 15th Hussars. As the *United Service Gazette* and *The Times* pointed out, the case had highlighted the most abhorrent implications of the purchase system, a system that must be abolished if the army was to be reformed:

"Feeling all the enormity of the tyranny of Lord Brudenell's persecution of Captain Wathen, we are willing to give him the

---

[813] Previously Elizabeth Johnstone (1797–1858) who married Brudenell after her divorce from Mr Johnstone in 1826. Brudenell had been cited by her husband for "criminal conversation with his wife", but the case resulted in damages rather than a duel. Brudenell's reputation as a Lothario was frowned upon but just about socially acceptable for a man. Elizabeth and Cardigan were estranged before her death and in 1857 he began an affair with Adeline De Horsey (1824-1915) who he married in 1858.

[814] David, op cit, pp62-83; Woodham-Smith, op cit, pp40-49

[815] Cardigan's DNB entry by John Sweetman, which adds "...when a court-martial vindicated Wathen, [Brudenell] was removed from command, returning to the half-pay list on 21 March 1834. Thoroughly incensed, Brudenell lobbied furiously for another regiment. ... he subjected senior politicians and influential officers to personal pressure. The military secretary at the Horse Guards, Lord Fitzroy Somerset (later Lord Raglan), after one of many confrontations, remarked: 'Lord Brudenell favoured me with another of his disagreeable visits yesterday'. Brudenell's offensive paid off: on 30 March 1836 he obtained command of the 11th hussars for some £40,000, joining his new regiment in India shortly before it returned to England."

benefit of negative exoneration, which his infirmity of temper and incompetency of command may be supposed to afford."[816]

It would be 1871 before the purchase system was eliminated, when Cardwell's army reforms followed those that had already taken place in the civil service and the universities. The secret electoral ballot was introduced a year later in 1872. Although the changes in church and basic education had been about access and entitlement, the overall move towards a more egalitarian society, where merit rather than wealth was the primary determinant of place and influence (as with the expansion of the franchise development previously), was gathering pace.

The Trevelyans

On 13th May 1830 Ernest married his cousin Beatrice Trevelyan (1809-1898) "fourth daughter of Sir John Trevelyan, bart" at St George's, Hanover Square.[817] The service had been conducted by the Lord Bishop of Bristol and, as *Freeman's Journal* explained, the bride's father had estates both at Nettlecombe Court, Somerset and in Wallington, Northumberland.[818] Describing the wedding as a 'Marriage in High Life' may have been standard practice for such newspaper articles, but was appropriate for this society event, the marriage of a Captain in the 15th Hussars and a baronet's daughter.

Ernest and Beatrice were to emulate their parents and have a large family themselves of twelve children (six boys and six girls) in the eighteen years from July 1831 to May 1849, of whom nine survived into adulthood.[819] The first two children were born in Nottingham and Manchester where the 15th Hussars were stationed in 1831 and 1832, with the other ten all being born in Somerset. After Ernest had left the army in 1833, their next three children were born between 1834 and 1836 at Oakhampton House, near

---

[816] *United Service Gazette* 11th January 1834; also *The Times* 30th January 1834
[817] 'Annual Register for 1830', London, Baldwin & Cradock, 1831, p227 This was the same Sir John Trevelyan who, at the age of 80, was with his sister-in-law, Ernest's mother Jane Carr, at Elm Grove in 1841 - see Chapter 2 above.
[818] Beatrice had been born at the latter and she and Ernest were to be buried at Nettlecombe. *Freeman's Journal and Daily Commercial Advertiser* 21st May 1830
[819] The oldest child Beatrice died before her first birthday in 1832, Hugh Spencer (1840-1849) died at the age of nine and their eleventh child Edmund Dudley Spencer (1848-1868) died before his twenty-first birthday.

Wiveliscombe, a property they had leased temporarily.[820] They included the oldest boy, also called Ernest Augustus (1835-1924), who joined the 88th Foot, was decorated for his service in the Crimean War[821] and retired as a Captain in 1864,[822] and an older sister, another Beatrice (1834-1915), who was a boarder at a house in Hove, "living on her own means" as the 1891 Census described her, dying more than twenty years later in Bristol.[823] Between 1838 and 1844 another five children were born at Bindon House, another rented property they had moved to in the nearby village of Milverton, also in the Vale of Taunton Deane.[824]

Sir John Trevelyan died in 1846, and his obituary featured in the 'Annual Register for 1846', underlining his aristocratic credentials:

"At Nettlecombe Court,[825] Somersetshire, aged 85 ... the fifth Baronet of that place, and of Wallington, Northumberland (1661-2).
"... [he] succeeded to the Baronetcy April 1828 ... In 1798 he raised 'the Wallington and Kirkdale Volunteer troop of Cavalry,' of which he was constituted Captain commandant, and in 1830 served the office of Sheriff of Northumberland. ...[he] married, in August 1791, Maria, daughter of Sir Thomas Spencer Wilson, of Charlton ..."[826]

When Spencer Perceval had been Prime Minister, Sir John had drafted a latter asking him for a peerage but had not sent it,

---

[820] The Oakhampton Manor Estate including Oakhampton House was put up for sale in 1920 by Lt Col H.E. Norton. The sale particulars describe Oakhampton House as a Georgian residence of fourteen bedrooms built in 1734 and set in 40 acres. The estate comprised another 304 acres and two farms. A map of the estate is included. A picture of the House in about 1908 is available as an old postcard at www.oldpicturepostcards.co.uk/wiveliscombe.htm

[821] Burke's Peerage, op cit, p1288

[822] *Daily News* and *Morning Chronicle* 25th August 1860; *Freeman's Journal* 27th August 1860; *Daily News* 21st September 1864

[823] The house in Hove might have been the same one that her aunt Frederica, always close to Ernest, subsequently bequeathed in 1900 - see Chapter 5 above.

[824] Bindon House is now a hotel set in seven acres of grounds, so was clearly another substantial residence in 1840.

[825] 'Victoria County History of Somerset', vol. V, London, Oxford University Press, 1985 contains many references to Nettlecombe Court, as it does to the Trevelyans, Milverton and Wiveliscombe. An 1839 map of the Nettlecombe estate is included on p112, while the house is mapped on p114 and pictured on p109. The photograph shows a huge property (apparently being used as a school at this point), while the map of the estate shows the church next to the house.

[826] 'Annual Register for 1846', London, F & J Rivington, 1847, obituaries for 23rd May 1846

deciding instead to await his inheritance on his father's death.[827] Trevelyan's death, not long after Jane Carr's, enabled Ernest's family to settle down, moving out of rented property and purchasing a house in Chapel Cleeve where the youngest two children were born in 1848 and 1849. They were to live there until 1866. Trevelyan's heir was Beatrice's oldest surviving brother Sir Walter Calverley Trevelyan (1797-1879), another product of Harrow School and of Oxford University. He married twice, refurbishing Wallington and developing Seaton in Devon as a seaside resort with his first wife, but died childless.[828] He bequeathed Wallington to his cousin Charles Edward Trevelyan (1807-1886), the man who in 1854 with Sir Stafford Northcote (1818-1887) wrote the report[829] that led to Gladstone's far-reaching reforms of the civil service, substituting

"... the patronage system of civil service appointments and recommend[ing] open examination and promotion by merit ..."[830]

From 1858 Charles Trevelyan returned to India spending much of the remainder of his administrative career there. He did find time to argue against the purchase of army commissions, advocating reform based on merit in his evidence to a committee of inquiry and then publishing a book on the subject in 1868 in order to underline the issue.[831] These were just three of his many publications, including previously on the Irish crisis and the famine in 1848, and subsequently on India, education, medical relief, charity visits to the

---

[827] Somerset Record Office DD/WO/54/11/20

[828] Walter Trevelyan's DNB entry

[829] 'Report on the organisation of a permanent civil service', London, Eyre & Spottiswoode, 1854 - known as the Northcote–Trevelyan report

[830] Charles Trevelyan's DNB entry Like Spencer and Isabella Walpole his London address was in Eaton Square.
Stafford Northcote had been Gladstone's private secretary in 1842, and was initially a Whig MP, but joined the Conservatives in 1858 at Disraeli's request, eventually becoming his successor as Leader in the House of Commons in 1880. The Trevelyan interest in Seaton may have arisen in part because of Northcote's background as a Devon landowner, estates Northcote inherited as Earl of Iddesleigh in 1885.

[831] Charles Trevelyan, 'Money or merit: The army purchase question considered with especial reference to the recent commission of inquiry', London, C.J. Skeet, 1857; Charles Trevelyan, 'The Army purchase question and report, and minutes of evidence of the Royal Commission considered, with a particular examination of the evidence of Sir Charles Trevelyan', London, James Ridgway, 1858; Charles Trevelyan, 'The British Army in 1868', 4th edition, London, Longmans, Green & Co., 1868

poor and child labour. He pursued the principles of access, entitlement and merit with a vengeance, both as a practical administrator and as a campaigner for change.

Personal and public affairs: Family and the Home Office

The family

Beatrice Perceval, therefore, had family links to some of the more enlightened thinking in mid-nineteenth century Britain, while Ernest Perceval had been at the receiving end, personally and professionally, of blind arrogance and blinkered prejudice - from Brudenell and Bellingham to name but two, though which was which is a matter of choice. He may have been conservative by background, but the Trevelyans were natural Whigs, and Ernest was to demonstrate at the Home Office that his conservatism was of the one-nation Derby model.

The 1841 Census records Beatrice and Ernest at Mount Terrace, Seaton, possibly on holiday from Bindon House, and perhaps living in one of the Trevelyan family's substantial seaside properties, with their six oldest surviving children and six servants. The children were aged one to eight and their parents would have been reliant on the servants, three of whom were fifteen year-old girls effectively acting as nursery nurses, to look after them for much of the time.

In their forties in 1851 Ernest and Beatrice were visiting and supporting Beatrice's aged and widowed mother (Ernest's aunt) Dame Maria Trevelyan (?-1852) at Hartford Hall, her home at Bedlington near Morpeth in Northumberland. She and Sir John had married sixty years before in 1791 and she was to die the following year. Ernest was still described on the Census form as a Captain in the army, though he had long since ceased to be. Their children, ten of whom were still living at this time, were not with them but remained at Chapel Cleeve with their governess and a maiden aunt Julia Trevelyan (1798-?). In the late 1840s Beatrice's youngest sister Helena (c1815-1898) had caused a major sensation by divorcing her husband and marrying a younger cousin. This was unheard of and the reverberations continued into the 1850s.[832]

The 1861 Census recorded the family at their home, Chapel Cleeve House at Old Cleeve near Watchet and close to the

---

[832] Somerset Record Office DD/WO/58/4/12

Somerset coast, with Ernest described on the return as a retired cavalry officer for the first time.   The Victoria County History includes many references to Chapel Cleeve and Old Cleeve.[833] Old Cleeve is within the Freemanors hundred that had passed to the Earls of Egmont, and was still held by them in Ernest's time.[834] Seven of the children, now aged 11 to 28, lived with them at Chapel Cleeve, while the oldest son Ernest was away serving with the 88th Foot and a 17 year-old Alfred was in his last year at Radley School.[835]   A thirteen year-old Edmund was elsewhere. A young governess, the 26 year-old Margaret le Reidereal (who despite her name had been born in Royston) was now helping the 59 year-old Isabella Maynard, who had been the sole governess ten years before in 1851, and even though the youngest child Cecil was now aged 11. The family required in addition, and the house was large enough for, five maids and a groom.[836]

An 1835 map[837] shows that Ernest and Beatrice's three homes in Somerset, and the Trevelyan estate of Nettlecombe, were all in close proximity to, and within easy reach of, each other to the north-

---

[833] 'Victoria County History of Somerset', op cit, vol. V, pp39-54 The nearby Brendon Hills provided the prime site for Ernest's second son Spencer George (1838-1922) to collect geological specimens. He donated these to Taunton Museum, and subsequently sent the catalogue to Cambridge University (where he had attended Trinity Hall) in 1909. See 'Catalogue with Preface of a Collection of Minerals in the Taunton Museum from the Brendon Hills and Other Localities in West Somerset', 1909. He lived at Clifton in Bristol and in 1922 his son gave his scrapbook to the University. He considered that Taunton Museum had not displayed the collection properly and some of the cuttings concern his campaign for improved museum displays.

[834] Ibid, pp8-9 for a map of the hundred and p11 for the Egmont connection

[835] All four of the sons who might benefit from a public school education were sent to Radley School: Alfred (1843-1935) for seven years from 1854-1861; the oldest son Ernest Augustus for three years previously from 1850-1853; the next oldest Spencer George was there with Alfred for three years in 1854-1857; and the youngest Cecil Henry (1849-1920) from 1864-1867. See 'St Peter's College, Radley - Register 1847-1962', Aldershot, Radleian Society, 1965, pp8, 18, 52. That Ernest sent his children to Radley rather than Harrow is likely to be significant. Radley is just south of Oxford and therefore closer to Somerset, but this may not have been the only reason. In 1857-1863 the future 7th Earl of Egmont, Charles (1845-1897) was also sent to Radley. His father the Rector of Calverton (see Chapter 3 above), also called Charles George Perceval, had been to Harrow, and it may be that it was partly on Ernest's advice that the more local Radley was preferred.

[836] 'Victoria County History of Somerset', op cit, vol. V, p45 for a picture of the house

[837] 'Smith's Map of the County of Somerset', London, C Smith, 1835

west of Taunton. Nettlecombe Court, for example, was on the turnpike route from Wiveliscombe to Watchet.[838]

Ten years later Ernest and Beatrice, now in their sixties and described as landowners, were in their fifth year at Severn House, Henbury, Gloucestershire to the north of Bristol. Chapel Cleeve had proved too large a house once several of the children moved away and Henbury was within striking distance of Clifton where their sons Spencer George and Alfred lived.[839] Three unmarried daughters still lived with them, as did a cook, three maids and a groom. A gardener and his family lived separately but in the grounds.

The Home Office

Ernest was private secretary in the Home Office on three occasions. The first two of these were in 1852-1853 and 1858-1859 when his brother-in-law Spencer Horatio Walpole was Home Secretary in Derby's first two governments. Walpole was Home Secretary again in 1866-1867, but on this occasion it was his son Spencer Walpole, already a civil servant in his late twenties, who acted as his private secretary.[840] This would have been good experience for the younger Walpole and Ernest may have been relieved not to be required; indeed, he may have been offered the post first and turned it down, perhaps because he and Beatrice had recently moved to Henbury, a convenient justification if the real reason was that he could no longer square his brother-in-law's reactionary views on electoral reform with his and the Trevelyan opinion.

In keeping with Spencer Horatio Walpole's disappointing performance as Home Secretary in 1852-1853, no records have been found of Ernest's time as private secretary for this period. On the second occasion in 1858-1859 Walpole spent much of his time arguing against the Reform Bill and Ernest was left to handle the administrative burden of the department. In contrast to Hardy's spell as Home Secretary ten years later, much of this was

---

[838] 'Victoria County History of Somerset', op cit, vol. V, p108

[839] Indeed, Spencer George gave Severn House as his address in an 1866 article "On the Discovery of A Bed of Devonian Corals at Withycombe, West Somerset" to the *Geological Magazine*. The draft deeds are held at Somerset Record Office DD/CCH/2/3. There are no relevant Perceval records held in either the Bristol or Gloucestershire Record Offices, though Bristol has a plan of Severn House 35749/88.

[840] Sainty, op cit, pp33 and 57 The second time Ernest was appointed it was reported in *John Bull* magazine on 6th March 1858.

routine.[841] The examples at Hertfordshire Record Office include an application for interment under a church in Ely. The applicant was not deterred by "Mr Walpole['s] regrets that he cannot impinge upon the rule" of not undertaking burials in such vaults, and Ernest brought the matter to a conclusion by referring to a

"... similar application lately made by one of the Cabinet members, and ... refused".

In August 1858 Ernest wrote on embossed Home Office paper to a Mr Higgins in the Colonial Office

"My dear Higgins,
"I forward at the request of my nephew Mr Spencer Perceval, an application for another vacancy which he has heard of in a Judgeship at Corfu, and should be much obliged to you if you could bring it favourably before Sir Lytton Bulwer. If Sir Lytton entertains his request, and wishes to refer it to Mr Walpole, he will be ready to answer any questions with reference to this application."[842]

The Spencer (1828-1890) referred to was the eldest son of Ernest's brother Spencer, had trained as a barrister and was now almost 30. A month later another brother Frederick wrote to Bulwer-Lytton directly, suggesting an agricultural studentship for his son Spencer Frederick.[843] It would not be surprising if Bulwer-Lytton had been confused. It is worth noting that Ernest was prepared to use his position in this way, though perhaps it would be naïve to expect him not to, and he clearly did not make a habit of it.

Ernest backed up his support for his nephew by writing in a personal capacity on Christmas Eve 1858 from his home at Chapel Cleeve:

"My dear Wolfe,
"The writer of the enclosed is a talented young Barrister, practising at the Chancery Bar, but whose health makes him anxious for a more genial climate than this. He applied to the late Colonial Sec. [presumably Bulwer-Lytton's predecessor] for a Colonial Judgeship

---

[841] For example, Hertfordshire Record Office D/EK/026/148/1, D/EK/026/148/2, D/EK/026/148/4

[842] Hertfordshire Record Office D/EK/026/148/3 Walpole was this Spencer's uncle as well of course.

[843] See Chapter 6 above

and had Mr Walpole's goodwill, who would I know be glad to back this application, for which however I do not wait in order to save time.

"If you would be so kind as let me know if the vacancy he attends to is still open, and if there would be any chance of his success were he to make a more proper and formal application I shall be much obliged to you."[844]

Perhaps this was the first opportunity Ernest had to follow it up, at home and away from the demands of the office. The time of year, mid-winter and close to Christmas, may have brought Spencer to mind again for both family and health reasons.

When Gathorne Hardy replaced Walpole as Home Secretary on 17th May 1867, Ernest became private secretary for the third time. Walpole applauded Hardy as his successor[845] and may have recommended Ernest as private secretary, though Hardy would have been aware in any case of his skills from previous occasions and welcomed, perhaps was in need of, his experience. Ernest's and Beatrice's son Edmund was to die a few months later in February 1868, but this had been expected for some time and Ernest may have appreciated the distraction, even though the post was no sinecure. It must have been particularly challenging at this time for a number of reasons, but especially for somebody who had turned 60.

Gathorne Hardy wasted no time, appointing Ernest the same day he took up post himself[846] and introducing him to the Prince of Wales at a royal levee the following month.[847] The Metropolitan Board of Works had been set up in January 1856,[848] charged with improving public heath in London. The Board's engineer Joseph Bazalgette (1819-1891) oversaw the construction of London's drainage and sewer systems to divert raw sewage from the Thames through 1300 miles of sewers - though the most visible effect may have been the three and a half miles of river embankment built in the late 1860s and 1870s.[849] However, if public health was an issue

---

844 Hertfordshire Record Office D/EK/O26/148/5
845 See Chapter 9 above
846 *The Times* 18th May 1867 The references in Sainty confirm that this was Ernest rather than his son.
847 *The Times* 20th June 1867; *Daily News* 20th June 1867
848 This was a provision of the Metropolitan Management Act of 1855 under which Dudley Perceval was re-elected.
849 Bazalgette's DNB entry

in London, it was equally if not more so elsewhere.   Edwin Chadwick had helped alert the authorities in the 1840s, but little had been done, partly because, with the recent exception of London, action depended on voluntary initiatives rather than public requirement.   There were no formal local sanitary or government structures beyond the Poor Law Boards, and urban parishes were too small to tackle the issues on their own.   Living conditions could be grim, hospitals were often dirty and unhealthy, antiseptics were not widely understood or used until the 1880s,[850] and the basics of clean air, food and water were not generally available in the urban areas in which most people lived.   In four cholera outbreaks in the middle third of the nineteenth century, there were 32,000 deaths in England in 1831-1832, 62,000 in 1848-1849, 20,000 in 1853-1854, and 14,000 in 1866-1867.[851]   The impact of cholera was dramatic, "a shock disease" with a high mortality rate (as well as topical in 1867), while other "fevers such as typhus focussed attention on filth and poverty".[852]

This was not just political propaganda that happened to fit the Victorian ideals of self-improvement and public development, or a growing socialism.   Rather, such belief systems were generated by, and consequent on, increased questioning of social conditions and the society and values that permitted them.[853]   It was not that myths were treated as facts, but that real-world observations led to the conclusion that impact would depend on state action and could no longer be left as before to enlightened individual philanthropy or company responsibility.   This had proved a recipe for inconsistency and haphazard implementation at best, for inaction and exploitation at worst.

As President of the Poor Law Board previously, Hardy may have appreciated, and been frustrated by, some of the limitations of

---

[850] Hoppen, 1998, op cit, p327

[851] R. Morris, 'Cholera 1832 - The Social Response to an Epidemic', London, Croom Helm, 1976, p79. Cited by Wohl, 1983, op cit, pp118-125.
According to Wohl, part of the fear induced by the 1832 outbreak in which Spencer Perceval junior played such a prominent part (see Chapter 4 above) was that cholera had crossed the Channel, or "god's moat" as it was described.

[852] Wohl, 1983, op cit, pp119 & 125

[853] Friedrich Hayek in his introduction to 'Capitalism and the Historians', London, Routledge, 1954 claims that increasing immiseration of the poor was a myth; in his view, conditions were better than before for the majority of people and it was capitalism and the industrial revolution that had fostered this. What had changed were the expectations of a growing population. "Economic suffering both became more conspicuous and seemed less justified, because general wealth was increasing faster than ever before." (p18)

this disjointed approach. John Simon (1816-1904) and other public health visionaries influenced the Royal Sanitary Commission set up in 1868 to recommend

"... the reorganizations of public health institutions that were carried out in a series of Acts between 1871 and 1875",[854] with the

"Local Government Act of 1871 and the Public Health Act of 1872 creat[ing] a national network of rural and urban sanitary authorities."[855]

According to Wohl, the rich were aware that they neglected the poor at peril to themselves and their own health, while for reformers such as Dickens slum clearance and sanitary reform were the necessary precursors of educational and social improvements. Although public health reform could proceed initially without raising wider questions about social structure and general living standards, by the 1880s these would be unavoidable.[856]

Besides putting the Commission in train, Hardy's time at the Home Office was taken up with Ireland. He and Ernest were confronted with Fenian outrages that threatened the mainland, and possibly the monarchy itself, in pursuit of a separate state. The Fenian atrocities were no longer confined to Ireland and Hardy's "first year was a year of universal terror".[857] A police sergeant Brett was murdered in Manchester as his prisoner was rescued by fellow Fenians. Brett's alleged killers were apprehended and imprisoned in Clerkenwell under sentence of death. John Bright (1811-1889), previously Radical MP for Manchester but now for Birmingham, wrote to Hardy on 15th November 1867 encouraging him to commute the death sentences:

"We have a large Irish population in these towns, and ... mercy will have a far better effect than severity in this case ..."[858]

---

[854] Simon's DNB entry

[855] www.thornber.net/medicine/html/phealth.html According to Cole, op cit, p11 "... much more could have been done [in the field of public health] had the Local Government Board created in 1871 been given into the hands of enlightened experts such as Sir John Simon rather than those of the mandarins of the Poor Law".

[856] Wohl, 1983, op cit, pp6-9

[857] Gathorne-Hardy, op cit, vol. I, pp216-217

[858] Ibid, pp229-231

Three days later, after Hardy had refused to receive a deputation of Fenian supporters, they forced their way into the Home Office itself:

"Picture my surprise and indignation when on hearing voices I gradually woke to the fact that they were in the next room making speeches. Perceval ... came to tell me they had passed ... [the messenger] who unfortunately did not resist more than by word. We sent for police, and, on a second summons ... at my direction, they went away, but met the police, so they saw what was meant for them."[859]

A week later

"Perceval sent warning of some strange fellow who had been trying to get admission to 109 Eaton Square, as the residence of the Home Secretary. Nothing is known of him here, but [there were] reports ... of some desperado from Dublin with bad intentions towards the Prince of Wales."[860]

Gathorne-Hardy reports this as though the "desperado" had mistaken the address, for his father lived at 35 Eaton Square, but 109 Eaton Square was the home of Isabella and Spencer Horatio Walpole, the previous Home Secretary. Fenian intelligence may have been slightly out of date, but it was clearly extensive.

On 13th December 1867 a huge bomb went off at Clerkenwell prison even though the authorities had prior intelligence of when it was likely to be planted. The prisoners had been moved as a precaution, but houses opposite the prison wall were destroyed and several people killed or maimed. St Paul's Cathedral and other public buildings had to be protected in case the Fenian campaign became even more bloodstained, but the government found it difficult to persuade Queen Victoria to behave more cautiously. On 8th January 1868 she wrote dismissively of four previous assassination attempts; she was wary of being "knocked on the head", as had happened once before, and of an assailant carrying a knife, but argued that the best protection against shooting was to remain a moving target. This strategy had served her well on three earlier occasions.[861]

---

[859] Ibid, p231 Gathorne Hardy diary entry for 18th November 1867.
[860] Ibid, p233 Gathorne Hardy diary entry for 25th November 1867.
[861] Ibid, pp239, 242-245 and 251

Gladstone's Irish Church Bill in March 1868 did not lead to the government's immediate resignation as the Reform Act was still to be fully implemented in Scotland and Ireland,[862] and, in addition, Queen Victoria argued that her Coronation Oath would have to be negated before the Irish church could be disestablished. With no Cabinet ready for government, Gladstone was prepared to wait.[863] The dissolution of Parliament took place on the 11th November, three months after it had been prorogued, with the subsequent general election resulting in a Liberal majority of 112. Rather than be dismissed by the new House of Commons in January 1869, Disraeli set a precedent when his government resigned, accepting the inevitable on 28th November 1868. Hardy had been re-elected unopposed for Oxford University, but was out of office for the next five years. Ernest returned to private life in Henbury. By the time Hardy was next required in a Disraeli government as Secretary for War in February 1874, Ernest would be nearly 67 and too old to be called on. No matter what regrets he may have had that he was no longer required as a public servant, he must have been relieved as well.

Final days

In August 1869 *Trewman's Exeter Flying Post* carried an advertisement from the solicitors who had acted for Sir Walter Calverley Trevelyan in the court of Chancery in relation to the Trevelyan estates (primarily in Somerset, though there were smaller holdings in Devon and Cornwall).[864] Parts of the Nettlecombe family estate, as it was collectively known, were to be leased to the Ebbw Vale Steel, Iron and Coal Company Ltd to quarry iron and other ores. The Company would have to act in accordance with various Acts of Parliament passed in relation to mining and quarrying in 1857, 1858 and 1864, satisfy Ernest Augustus Perceval and Spencer Horatio Walpole as trustees, and protect the rights of the Trevelyan family (including Beatrice Perceval and her sister Helena), but subject to these conditions the Company was given the opportunity to exploit the mineral wealth of the area. This prospect may have been another reason why a move out of the area to Henbury in 1866 was attractive for Ernest and his family.[865]

---

[862] See Chapter 10 above
[863] Gathorne-Hardy, op cit, vol. I, pp272-275
[864] *Trewman's Exeter Flying Post* 25th August 1869
[865] One of the most prominent mines was located in the Brendon Hills.

Like many of his siblings, Ernest made several donations to charities, of which one in particular is worth noting. In 1871 he subscribed £5 to the fund set up to help peasant farmers in France.[866] This had the very practical aim of sending feed for them and their animals so that famine would not follow their country's disastrous defeat in the Franco-Prussian War. This aim would have struck a chord with a practical man such as Ernest who was a landowner himself.

In 1881 Ernest, Beatrice and the two daughters still living with them were on holiday in Tenby, accompanied by their two youngest surviving sons Alfred and Cecil. Alfred was to marry that July at the age of 38, while Cecil was 45 before he married in January 1895.[867] A lengthy report of Alfred's wedding featured in the *Ipswich Journal* in September, referring to Ernest of "Severn House, Clifton" and "Longwitton Hall, Northumberland".[868] Ernest was publicly acknowledged as a man of substance in his own right.

Neither Ernest nor Beatrice was listed in the 1891 Census.[869] A reference in the National Archives for 1890 identifies an Ernest Perceval at Wonford Asylum[870] at Heavitree, near (and now part of) Exeter, but it is not clear if this refers to Ernest or his son and, if the latter, whether he was visiting as an inspector or living there as a resident. Ernest would have been 83 and his son 65.[871] However,

---

[866] *The Times* 6th February 1871

[867] *Liverpool Mercury* 19th July 1881; *Bristol Mercury and Daily Post* 26th January 1895

[868] *Ipswich Journal* 17th September 1881

[869] For England, Wales, Isle of Man or the Channel Islands - either as Perceval or mis-spelt as Percival.

[870] National Archives C211/62
Wonford had been opened in 1869 "for the reception of lunatics of the middle and upper classes" at a cost of £30,000 (£1.4m today) and could accommodate 93 patients. The medical superintendent of Wonford was Dr Rees Philipps, who reported on the operation of the asylum and acted for the Lunacy Commissioners, both inspecting other establishments in the area, particularly where they were thought to infringe the lunacy laws, and advising on the sanity of individuals.
British Medical Journal (*BMJ*), 24th July 1869; Daniel Hack Tuke, 'Chapters in the History of the Insane in the British Isles', London, Kegan Paul, Trench & Co., 1882, pp490 & 556
The *BMJ* 19th January 1884 reports on one such inspection of premises at Crediton in Devon where a farmer Mr Strong had seven lunatics living at his farmhouse even though a licence for six patients had previously been refused.

[871] It is worth noting that the son's place of death has not been established. The 1898 Visitation does not refer to him after his service in the Crimea, even though he was not to die for more than sixty years until 1924 (International Genealogical Index and Burke's Peerage).

most sources indicate that Ernest died at his home Severn House on 19th January 1896. These include the 1898 Visitation of England[872] signed off by his son Cecil who was also the executor of his Will. Ernest's entry refers to a brass in his memory in Henbury Church and confirms that he was buried at Nettlecombe. Although his confinement and death at Wonford Asylum as a chancery lunatic would provide the story with symmetry, his death at Henbury fits better with the brief press notices that appeared at the time.[873] At the end of January 1896 *The Bristol Mercury and Daily Post* reported a meeting of the Henbury Association in connection with the local Thornbury Conservatives.[874] This mourned Ernest's passing, "a prominent member of the Association". At the Chairman's instigation

"A vote of condolence was passed sympathising with Mrs Perceval and family in their bereavement."

---

[872] Jackson and Crisp, op cit, p96
[873] *Pall Mall Gazette* 24th January 1896; *Bristol Mercury and Daily Post* 25th January 1896
[874] *Bristol Mercury and Daily Post* 31st January 1896

12.   SHAPING THE CENTURY

George Eliot's novel 'Silas Marner' was published in 1861.[875]   Her lifestyle was unconventional, but her book affirmed many of the dilemmas and themes that affected this generation of the Percevals and similar families in the nineteenth century.   An overwhelming obsession with wealth and place was in the process of being tempered by a growing acknowledgement of principles that emphasised individual tolerance and respect, and the importance of community.   A move towards a humanitarian and humanist society was later to be described as socialism, not least to distinguish it from the crudest examples of capitalism to which it was opposed.   The term did not automatically imply, nor was it yet confused with, communism.   As the century progressed, inter-denominational religious dispute often became redundant, being replaced by a world-view that was more sophisticated and depended on debate rather than dispute.   It was difficult to condemn your neighbour or fellow worker, no matter how different their background or views, the better you knew them, and particularly if your well-being and safety depended on them.   But removing such prejudice was never straightforward and often sectarian rivalry endured.   Birth and background need not bring with it a fixed place in society, and the growth of education and the professions meant that people (for which, read "men" in nearly all cases) could be judged on their abilities rather than on an implied and immutable set of characteristics.   There was still a different set of criteria for women, but, though exceptional, George Eliot and others like her showed that society was changing and that the accepted mores could be challenged.

Those who adapted most readily to the increasing emphasis in some quarters on equality, access, entitlement and merit could take advantage of the opportunities.   If adaptation was impossible, it might be prudent to adjust as best one could, especially in the absence of a safety net, in case events passed you by and times moved on without you.

This generation of the Percevals was born in one world, but the longest lived saw another dawn.   An establishment based almost exclusively on the accepted hierarchy of wealth and family background was to be moderated in the last third of the century by other values.   The more conservative Percevals, and particularly

---

[875] George Eliot, 'Silas Marner', Edinburgh, William Blackwood & Sons, 1861

those who defined themselves by their allegiance to the Anglican Church, would have been threatened by this. Jane died too young, while Frederick appeared resigned to his fate and seemed to have few expectations by the end. In earlier years, however, he had sought to capitalise on his family connections. Henry lived outside the mainstream of society, except for occasional forays that sought to preserve the existing order, while Dudley, though he may have mellowed in his final years, had died in any case before many of the changes began to be felt. Spencer junior died soon after, but he had also decided on a life beyond the mainstream of politics and religion. Eventually, he may have turned towards Catholicism as the best way of adhering to the objectives he had set himself and the values with which he felt most comfortable. Isabella may have come to the conclusion that, ambitious though she had been in terms of place and politics for her husband in earlier years, family influence was as attractive and rewarding in the long-run. In any case both her sons were marking their mark in the world, as did her younger daughter, and the £20,000 her husband had inherited from the 6th Earl of Egmont in 1874, along with his pension, would have diminished the necessity for her ambition. The other four sisters, Frances, Maria, Louisa and Frederica continued to seek conventional outlets that did not challenge the accepted norms. John Thomas and Ernest, from different personal and political perspectives, welcomed the increasing emphasis on meritocracy, equality and individual rights.

Figure 7 illustrates some of the relationships between the Percevals and the handful of other families most closely linked to them. A similar diagram could be drawn in terms of places such as Ealing, Worcester, Somerset and Herne Bay, or institutions, particularly law, politics, church, mental health, army, school and Oxbridge. It leaves out of account families such as Macleod and Bourke, and people such as Shaftesbury, Manning and Newman.[876] Nevertheless, it is worth noting that, while the monarchy and aristocracy were particularly relevant for their parents' generation, some of the Perceval children had begun to move in wider, less restricted and restrictive circles as well. Inevitably, their connections tended to be well-connected themselves, often through politics, the church or educational background, but not all of the Percevals sought to trade on this to their own advantage. Indeed,

---

[876] As well as connections of the older generation such as Canning, Castlereagh and Harrowby.

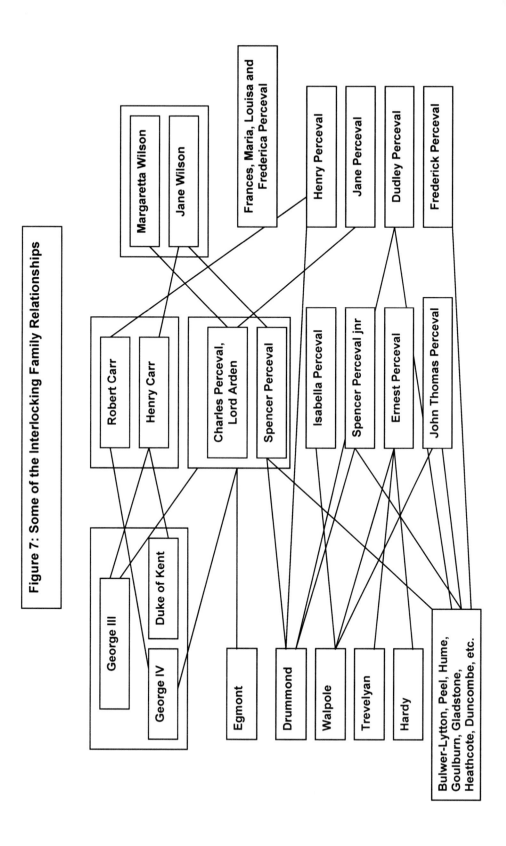

Figure 7: Some of the Interlocking Family Relationships

the younger ones would have found it abhorrent and inimical to their principles.

The three Reform Acts of 1832, 1867 and 1884 took place over more than fifty years, half a century. George Eliot's 'Felix Holt the Radical'[877] was based on the first Reform Act in 1832 and published the year before the second. While universal manhood suffrage eventually resulted, there was little of the nineteenth century left by the time the third had been implemented. Even after this, though, half the adult population did not have the vote; society was still male-oriented and men-dominated. Women would have to stage a lengthy campaign of militant civil disobedience themselves before the vote was eventually secured by those over 30, and women were able to become MPs, in 1918. It was another ten years before the Equal Franchise Act was passed in 1928, and twenty years after that before plural voting was eliminated in 1948, with the 1950 general election the first to be held under these conditions. Nineteenth century equality, while it might have appeared radical at the time, was less so in retrospect and only went so far, but it is salutary to recall that these impediments were only removed within living memory.

The nineteenth century was therefore not a period of untrammelled progress. Particular dilemmas included ensuring that:

- as the existing theocracy and establishment were replaced, not least by a move towards democracy and merit, this was not choked off by the intrusion of another oligarchy. This has often been the fate of socialism, particularly in its later Marxist and communist forms.
- the potential tension between individual freedom and society's development did not degenerate into a stalemate. Rather that the state was able to set the conditions for human development within boundaries that resulted in benefits for the whole community (as in modern France and Germany) - in other words, concentrating on the many not the few, and certainly not on advantages to some at the expense of others.

---

[877] George Eliot, 'Felix Holt the Radical', Edinburgh, William Blackwood & Sons, 1866 (Oxford, Clarendon Press, 1980)

As a counterpoint to Keynes' view with which this book opened, Hayek's 'Road to Serfdom'[878] highlights the potential (or alleged) pitfalls of socialism from a conservative viewpoint, while the current economic crisis is a reminder that the lessons of the past have not always been heeded, or at least that they can soon be forgotten when confronted by more elemental human instincts. Progress can be haphazard and crab-like, circular and cyclical rather than linear, a situation that was as characteristic of the nineteenth century as it remains in the twenty-first.

In 'An Unsocial Socialist' Bernard Shaw has the eponymous Sidney Trefusis comment on the prevailing order that applied for much of the nineteenth century:

"May your ladyship's goodness sew up the hole which is **in the pocket where I carry my character, and which has caused me to lose it so frequent. It's a bad place for men to keep their characters in; but such is the fashion. And so hurray for the glorious nineteenth century! [emphasis added]**"[879]

Some of the Percevals would not have understood the dangers of this perspective, conditioned, limited and in some cases imprisoned as they were, by the conventions in which they had been brought up. Others, however, anticipated the risks and saw beyond it, recognising that this outlook was, and should be treated as, an illusion. Those who lived longest proved themselves the most adaptable, or perhaps the explanation should run the other way round. While it remains arguable whether the century had more impact on those who found themselves in harmony with change, or on those who felt threatened by it, both groups helped shape the century.

---

[878] Friedrich Hayek, 'Road to Serfdom', London, Routledge, 1944
[879] Bernard Shaw, op cit, pp40-41

BIBLIOGRAPHY

Adams, Max, 'The Firebringers: Art, Science and the Struggle for Liberty in Nineteenth Century Britain', London, Quercus, 2009

Adolphus, John, 'The Last Days, Death, Funeral Obsequies, &c. of Her Late Majesty Caroline …', London, Jones & Co., 1822

The Alleged Lunatic's Friends Society, 'First Report of The Alleged Lunatic's Friends Society', London, McDowall, 1846

'Annual Register for 1783', London, J Dodsley, 1785

'The Annual Register or a View of the History, Politics and Literature for the Year 1809', London, Otridge et al., 1811

'Annual Register for 1814', London, Baldwin, Cradock & Joy, 1815

'Annual Register for 1818', London, Baldwin, Cradock & Joy, 1819

'Annual Register for 1821', London, Baldwin, Cradock & Joy, 1822

'Annual Register for 1830', London, Baldwin & Cradock, 1831

'Annual Register for 1832', London, JG & F Rivington, 1833

'Annual Register for 1846', London, F & J Rivington, 1847

'Annual Register for 1859', London, J & FH Rivington, 1860

'List of the Society of Antiquaries in 1833'

Aspinall, A (ed.), 'Later Correspondence of George III', 5 volumes, Cambridge, Cambridge University Press, 1970

Bateson, Gregory, 'Perceval's Narrative: A Patient's Account of his Psychosis 1830-1832', Stanford, Stanford University Press, 1961

The Belfast News-Letter 27th November 1891

Besant, Arthur Digby, 'Our Centenary: Being the History of the First Hundred Years of the Clerical, Medical and General Life Assurance Society', London, Clerical, Medical and General Life Assurance Society, 1924

Bill, E.G.W. & Mason, J.F.A., 'Christ Church and Reform 1850-1867', Oxford, Clarendon Press, 1970

Birmingham Daily Post, 4th November 1861; 1st June 1884; 20th September 1892

Boase, Frederic, 'Modern English Biography', vol. II, Truro, Netherton & Worth, 1897

Booth, Charles, 'Life and Labour of the People in London', London, Macmillan, 1902

Boulger, Demetrius, 'The History of Belgium 1815-1865', London, Pitman, 1913

Bourne, George, 'The History of the British and Foreign Bible Society From Its Institution in 1804 to the Close of Its Jubilee in 1854', 2 vols., London, Bagster & Sons, 1859

'Boyle's Court Guide', London, Eliza Boyle, January 1816 & 'April 1818

Bradlaugh, Charles, "Reform or Revolution", undated pamphlet but probably 1867

Brady, Alexander, 'William Huskisson and Liberal Reform', (2nd edition), London, Frank Cass & Co, 1967

Bragg, Rosemary, 'The Anglican Church in Ghent', Maidenhead, Bragg for St John's Church Ghent, 1980

Brandon, D., "A friend to alleged lunatics", *Mental Health Today*, October 2007

'Brasenose Ale: A Collection of Verses annually presented on Shrove Tuesday by the Butler of Brasenose College, Oxford', Boston, Lincolnshire, 1878

'Brasenose College Register 1509-1909', 2 volumes, Oxford, Blackwell, 1909

Briggs, Asa, 'The Age of Improvement: 1783-1867', 2nd edition, Harlow, Longman, 2000

Briggs, Asa review of 'The Victorian World Picture' by David Newsome, *The Times Higher Education Supplement*, 19th September 1977

Bristol Mercury, 13th August 1836; 11th December 1841; 3rd February 1844

Bristol Mercury and Daily Post, 26th January 1895; 25th January 1896; 31st January 1896

British Library, Add. MSS 38251, f.266; Add. MSS 40414, f.103, f.182; Add. MSS 40426-40597 passim; Add. MSS 40494, f.173; Add. MSS 40543, f.82; Add. MSS 44162 f.47, f.55, f.56; Add. MSS 44367 f.99, f.109; Add. MSS 47140, ff.94-97; Add. MSS 49188, f.70, f.84; Add. MSS 49191, f.1-4, f.5, f.7, f.11, f.15, f.17, f.37, f.41, f.80, f.82, f.86, f.88, f.92, f.120, f.121, f.129, f.134; Add. MSS 49192, including f.139; Add. MSS 49193, f.1, f.4, f.21, f.22, f.25, f.27, f.31, f.38; Add. MSS 49195, f.52

Brock, M.G. and Curthoys, M.C. (eds.), 'The History of the University of Oxford', volume VI, Nineteenth Century Oxford Part 1, Oxford, Clarendon Press, 1997

(Lord) Broughton, John Cam Hobhouse, 'Recollections of a Long Life', 2 volumes, London, John Murray, 1909

British Medical Journal, 24th July 1869 & 19th January 1884

Bryant, Kenneth, 'The Spencer Perceval Memorial Church of All Saints, Ealing Common', Leominster, Orphans Press, 2005

Bucknill, John, 'A Letter to the Right Hon. Spencer Horatio Walpole MP, Chairman of the Select Committee on Lunatics', 1860

Burford, Beverley (ed.), 'Images of Charlton House: A Pictorial History', London, Greenwich Council, 2002

'Burke's Peerage and Baronetage', Wilmington, Delaware, Burke's Peerage & Gentry, 2003

Burnett, Bishop ,'A Reply to the "Report of the Commissioners of Inquiry at the Cape of Good Hope, Upon the Complaints Addressed to the Colonial Government and to Earl Bathurst by Mr Bishop Burnett"', London, Sherwood, Gilbert & Piper, 1826

Burroughs, Peter, "An unreformed army? 1815-1868" in D.G. Chandler & I. Beckett (eds), 'The Oxford History of the British Army', Oxford, Oxford University Press, 2003

Burton, Anthony, 'Thomas Telford', London, Aurum Press, 1999

Caledonian Mercury, 11th April 1831 & 1st February 1844

Canton, W., 'History of the British and Foreign Bible Society', 5 volumes, London, John Murray, 1904

Chadwick, Edwin, 'Report on the Sanitary Condition of the Labouring Population of Great Britain', London, W. Clowes & Sons, 1842

Christ's College, Cambridge Archives:
'Conveyance of the Advowson of Elmley Lovett to the College and Abstract of Title', April 1840
Letter from Reverend John Lynes to Reverend Bryan Sneyd Broughton re the Conveyance of the Advowson of Elmley Lovett, 29th September 1836
Letter from Bryan Sneyd Broughton to Christ's College's solicitors, October 1840
Will of John Lynes 1831

Clarke, John, 'The Price of Progress: Cobbett's England 1780-1835', London, Granada Publishing, 1977

'The Clergy List for 1841', London, Cox, 1841

'Clerical Guide', 2nd edition, London, FC & J Rivington, 1822

Cockburn, Henry, 'Memorials of His Time', London, T.N. Foulis, 1909 (originally A&C Black, 1856)

Cole, Margaret, 'The Story of Fabian Socialism', London, Heinemann, 1961

Collins, Wilkie, 'No Name', London, Sampson Low, 1862 (OUP, Oxford World's Classics, 1986)

Colquhoun, Patrick, 'Treatise on Indigence', London, Hatchard, 1806

Cooper, Charles Purton, 'A Brief Account...of the Court of Commissioners of Bankrupt', London, J. Murray, 1828, pp242-402

Cooper, James Fenimore, 'Excursions in Italy', 2 volumes, London, Richard Bentley, 1838

Courier, November 1814 - January 1815

The Court Magazine & Monthly Critic, 1st May 1844

Cracroft, Bernard, 'The analysis of the House of Commons, or indirect representation', pp 155-190 in G.C. Brodrick (ed.), 'Essays on Reform', London, Macmillan, 1867

Craig, F.W.S. (ed.), 'Chronology of British Parliamentary By-Elections 1833-1987', Chichester, Parliamentary Research Services, 1987

Crammer, John, 'Asylum History: Buckinghamshire County Pauper Lunatic Asylum - St John's', London, Gaskell for Royal College of Psychiatrists, 1990

Crockford's Clerical Directories 1841-1890, London, Church House

Croker, John Wilson, 'The Croker Papers: The Correspondence and Diaries of ...', (edited by Louis Jennings in 3 volumes), London, John Murray, 1884

Daily News, 22nd May 1849; 3rd May 1850; 2nd June 1853; 20th November 1855; 27th September 1859; 25th August 1860; 21st September 1864; 7th May 1867; 20th June 1867; 6th January 1874; 14th May & 26th June 1900

Dale, Antony, 'Fashionable Brighton 1820-1860', Newcastle, Oriel, 1967

Davenport, Rowland, 'Albury Apostles', Birdlip (Glos.), United Writers, 1970

David, Saul, 'The Homicidal Earl: The Life of Lord Cardigan', London, Little Brown, 1997

Dean, Ptolemy, 'Sir John Soane and London', London, Lund Humphries, 2006

The Derby Mercury, 1st August 1827; 30th March & 31st August 1831; 10th June 1835; 22nd January 1851; 12th January 1853

Dickens, Charles, 'Sketches by Boz', February 1836 (London, Penguin, 1995)

Disraeli, Benjamin, 'Sybil, or The Two Nations', London, Henry Colburn, 1845

Donkin, Sir Rufane, 'A Letter on the Government of the Cape of Good Hope, and on certain events which have occurred there of late years, under the administration of Lord Charles Somerset: Addressed most respectfully to Earl Bathurst', London, Carpenter & Son, 1827

Dowden, Richard, 'Africa: Altered States, Ordinary Miracles', London, Portobello Books, 2008

Drummond, 'Histories of Noble British Families', vol. 2, London, William Pickering, 1846

Drummond, Andrew Landale, 'Edward Irving and His Circle', London, Clarke, 1937

'Ealing Parish Magazine', numbers 1 to 39, January 1860 to March 1863

The Economist 28th February 1891

Egmont, John Perceval, Earl of, 'Things As They Are', Dublin, S. Powell, 1758

Eliot, George, 'Felix Holt the Radical', Edinburgh, William Blackwood & Sons, 1866 (Oxford, Clarendon Press, 1980)

Eliot, George, 'Silas Marner', Edinburgh, William Blackwood & Sons, 1861

Engels, Friedrich, 'The Condition of the Working Class in England', (English translation 1892), London, Penguin, 1987

The Era, 22nd March 1840; 3rd & 17th September 1843; 26th October 1845

Esdaile, Charles, 'The Peninsular War: A New History', London, Allen Lane, 2002

The Examiner, 23rd July 1837; 6th November 1841; 19th February 1842; 14th December 1850; 11th and 18th January 1851; 8th January 1853

Fay, C.R., 'Life and Labour in the Nineteenth Century' (4th edition), Cambridge, Cambridge University Press, 1947

Fay, C.R., 'Huskisson and His Age', London, Longman Green & Co, 1951

Fay, C.R., 'Round About Industrial Britain 1830-1860', Toronto, University of Toronto Press, 1952

Flegg, Columba Graham, 'Gathered Under Apostles: A Study of the Catholic Apostolic Church', Oxford, Clarendon Press, 1992

Fletcher, Anthony, 'Growing up in England: The Experience of Childhood 1600-1914', London, Yale University Press, 2008

Foster, Joseph, 'Alumni Oxonienses: The Members of the University of Oxford 1715-1886', 4 volumes, Bristol, Thoemmes Press, 2000 (reprint of Oxford, Palmer and Co., 1888)

Fraser, Flora, 'The Unruly Queen: The Life of Queen Caroline', London, Macmillan, 1996

Freeman's Journal, 13th January 1831; 31st January 1844; 27th August 1860

Freeman's Journal and Daily Commercial Advertiser, 21st May 1830; 15th May 1848; 4th October 1849

Garden Court Chambers, '57-60 Lincoln's Inn Fields, London', Open House London handout, undated

Garvin, Tom, 'Preventing the Future: Why Was Ireland So Poor For So Long?', Dublin, Gill & Macmillan, 2005

Gathorne-Hardy, A.E. (ed.), 'Gathorne Hardy: First Earl of Cranbrook: A Memoir', 2 volumes, London, Longmans, Green & Co., 1910

Gault, Hugh, '1809: Between Hope and History', Cambridge, Gretton Books, 2009 (a)

Gault, Hugh, 'An expert by experience', *The Psychologist*, vol. 21, May 2008 (a), pp462-463

Gault, Hugh, 'Spencer Perceval: Private values and public virtues', *The Historian*, Number 98, Summer 2008 (b), pp6-12

Gault, Hugh, 'The enigmatic Mr Carr: A life less ordinary', (unpublished), May 2009 (b)

The Gentleman's Magazine, 1859, vol. II, December, pp653-654

Gibbs, Vicary, 'The Complete Peerage', vol. 5, London, St Catherine Press, 1926

Gladstone, W. E., 'Substance of a Speech for the Second Reading of the Maynooth College Bill in the House of Commons, on Friday, April 11, 1845', London, John Murray, 1845

Glover, Michael, 'The Peninsular War 1807-1814: A Concise Military History', London, David & Charles, 1974

Gould, Sheila, 'Felpham Matters: The Growth of a Sussex Coastal Village from 1800-1914', Felpham, Gould, 1996

Grant, I.F., 'The Macleods: The History of a Clan 1200-1956', London, Faber and Faber, 1959

Grant, James, 'Sketches in London', London, W.S. Orr & Co., 1838

Granville, A.B., 'The Royal Society in the Nineteenth Century', London, Churchill, 1836

The Graphic 10th January 1874

Gray, Denis, 'Spencer Perceval. The Evangelical Prime Minister 1762-1812', Manchester, Manchester University Press, 1963

The Guardian, 5th & 21st January 1853

Gwynn, Denis, 'Father Dominic Barberi', London, Burns Oates, 1947

Hamilton, F.W., 'The Origin and History of the First or Grenadier Guards', 3 volumes, London, John Murray, 1874

Hampshire Telegraph and Sussex Chronicle, 26th January 1824; 23rd May 1825

Hanrahan, David, 'The Assassination of the Prime Minister: John Bellingham and the Murder of Spencer Perceval', Stroud, Gloucestershire, Sutton Publishing, 2008

Hansard House of Commons Debate, vol. 24, 19 February 1813, cc655-6

Hansard Parliamentary Debates, vol. 39, 16th March 1819, columns 1021-1023; vol. 41, 6th December 1819, columns 798-800

Hansard Parliamentary Debates (new series 2), vol. 13, 27th May 1825, columns 903-909; 16th June 1825, columns 1166-1173; 22nd June 1825, columns 1274-1275; 5th July 1825, columns 1483-1485; vol. 15, 19th May 1826, columns 1277-1282; vol. 16, 7th December 1826, columns 303-313; 8th December 1826, columns 320-321; vol. 17, 17th May 1827, columns 883-895; 8th June 1827, columns 1168-1175; 29th June 1827, columns 1427-1438; vol. 18, 28th February 1828, columns 828-829; vol. 19, 8th May 1828, columns 432-436; vol. 20, 6th February to 30th March 1829; vol. 21, 22nd May 1829, column 1555

Hansard Parliamentary Debates (new series 3), vol. III, 9th March 1831, columns 256-268; vol. IX, 17th January 1832, column 580; vol. IX, 26th January, 1832, columns 895-903; vol. IX, 31st January 1832, columns 1030-1048; vol. XI, 19th March 1832, columns 577-581 & 2nd April 1832, column 1244; vol. LXXIX, 23rd April 1845, columns 1124-1230

Harrison, J.F.C., 'The Early Victorians 1832-1851', London, Weidenfeld & Nicholson, 1951

Harrison, Royden, "The 10th April of Spencer Walpole: The problem of revolution in relation to reform, 1865-1867", *International Review of Social History*, 1962, vol. VII, pp351-399

'Harrow School Register 1571-1800', (ed W.T.J. Gun), London, Longmans Green, 1934

'Harrow School Register 1800 to 1911', 3rd edition (ed. by M.G. Dauglish and P.K. Stephenson), London, Longmans Green & Co., 1911

Harrowby MSS, vol. VIII, fol. 146

Hayek, Friedrich, 'Capitalism and the Historians', London, Routledge, 1954

Hayek, Friedrich, 'Road to Serfdom', London, Routledge, 1944

Hazlitt, William, 'The Spirit of the Age' (2nd edition), London, H. Colburn, 1825

Hearth and Home 1st October 1891

Hertfordshire Archives and Local Studies:
    Letters from Ernest Perceval D/EK/026/148/1, D/EK/026/148/2, D/EK/026/148/4, D/EK/026/148/3, D/EK/026/148/5
    Letter from Fred Perceval to Edward Bulwer-Lytton, 21st September 1858, D/EK 026/149/1
    Letter from Fred Perceval to Edward Bulwer-Lytton, 25th November 1858, D/EK 026/149/2

Hilton, Boyd, 'A Mad, Bad and Dangerous People?: England 1783-1846', Oxford, Clarendon Press, 2006

Hinde, Wendy, 'Catholic Emancipation: A Shake to Men's Minds', Oxford, Blackwell, 1992

Hinde, Wendy, 'George Canning', London, Collins, 1973

Hobsbawm, Eric, "Bernard Shaw's Socialism", *Science and Society*, 1947, vol. XI, pp305-326

Hoppen, K Theodore, 'Elections, Politics and Society in Ireland 1832-1885', Oxford, Clarendon Press, 1984

Hoppen, K Theodore, 'Ireland Since 1800: Conflict and Conformity', London, Longman, 1999

Hoppen, K Theodore, 'The Mid-Victorian Generation 1846-1886', Oxford, Clarendon Press, 1998

Hudson, Tim & Hudson, Ann (eds.), 'Felpham by the Sea: Aspects of History in a Sussex Parish', Bognor, Hudson, 1988

The Hull Packet, 25th February 1842

The Hull Packet and East Riding Times, 12th December 1845; 12th October 1849; 7th January 1853

The Hull Packet and Humber Mercury, 8th April 1828

Hunt, Tristram, 'Building Jerusalem: The Rise and Fall of the Victorian City', London, Weidenfeld & Nicolson, 2004

Hunter, R. & Macalpine, I., "John Thomas Perceval (1803-1876) patient and reformer", *British Medical Journal*, 1962

Ipswich Journal, 12th January 1828; 11th December 1841; 17th
    September 1881

Jackson, Joseph & Crisp, Frederick (eds.), 'Visitation of England
    and Wales', vol. 6, privately printed, 1898
Jackson's Oxford Journal, 24th May 1823; 17th January 1824; 1st
    April 1826; 12th March 1831; 24th March 1832; 13th June 1835
Jalland, Pat, "Death, grief and mourning in the upper-class family,
    1860-1914", p183 in Ralph Houlbrooke (ed.), 'Death, Ritual and
    Bereavement', London, Routledge, 1989
Jenkins, Brian, 'Henry Goulburn 1784-1856: A Political Biography',
    Liverpool, Liverpool University Press, 1996
Jessup, Frank W, 'A History of Kent', London, Phillimore, 1974
John Bull, 30th July 1827; 19th August 1833; 28th August 1843; 27th
    July 1844; 6th October 1849; 29th September 1856; 6th March
    1858; 25th January 1862; 19th February & 26th November 1870;
    3rd October 1874; 4th March 1876
Jones, Wilbur, 'Lord Derby and Victorian Conservatism', Oxford,
    Basil Blackwell, 1956

Kaminsky, Arnold P., 'The India Office 1880-1910', London,
    Mansell, 1986
Kapuscinski, Ryszard, 'The Emperor: Downfall of an Autocrat',
    London, Penguin, 2006
Kensington and Chelsea Local Studies:
    1841 Census returns
    1841 Rate Book
Kent Archives, Centre for Kentish Studies:
    Electoral Registers 1840/41 to 1848/49 and 1853/54 to 1858/59
    List of Justices of the Peace, Q/JC 66-67
    Melville's Directory 1858
    Pigot's Directory 1826/27
    Poll Books for East Kent for 1832, 1852 (Feb and July), 1857
    Post Office Directory 1851
Keynes, John Maynard, 'The Economic Consequences of the
    Peace' (Royal Economic Society edition, originally 1919),
    London, Macmillan, 1971
Keynes, John Maynard, 'The Political Doctrines of Edmund Burke',
    Keynes Papers at King's College, Cambridge, 1904

The Lady's Newspaper, 6th October 1849

Langton, John & Morris, R.J. (ed.), 'Atlas of Industrialising Britain', London, Methuen, 1986

Leary, Emmeline, 'Pitshanger Manor', London, Pitshanger Manor Museum, 1990

Leeds Mercury, 21st March 1840; 3rd February 1844; 20th May 1882; 21st July 1886

Leonard, Dick, 'Nineteenth-Century British Premiers: Pitt to Rosebery', Basingstoke, Palgrave Macmillan, 2008

Liverpool Mercury, 25th January 1828; 20th July 1847; 11th January 1853; 19th July 1881

Lloyds Banking Group Archives:
Clerical Medical Minute Books Nos. 1-10
Letters from Frederick James Perceval, 6th November 1826 and 29th August 1827, LD0299, items 19 and 23

Lloyd's Weekly Newspaper, 7th October 1849; 19th January 1851

London Gazette, 23rd May 1815; 1818; 12th February & 15th July 1820; 2nd January 1821; 19th December 1826

London Gazette Supplement, 3rd January 1815; 19th February 1820

Macleod, R.C., 'The Book of Dunvegan II 1700-1920', Aberdeen, Third Spalding Club, 1939

McPherson, R.G. (ed.), 'Journal of the Earl of Egmont: Abstract of the Trustees Proceedings for Establishing the Colony of Georgia 1732-1738', Athens, Georgia, University of Georgia Press, 1962

Malmesbury, Earl of, 'Memoirs of An Ex-Minister: An Autobiography', 2 volumes, London, Longmans, Green & Co., 1884

Manchester Times, 13th September 1856

Maxwell, Herbert (ed.), 'The Creevey Papers: A Selection from the Correspondence and Diaries of the Late Thomas Creevey', London, John Murray, 1905

Mayhew, Henry, 'London Labour and the London Poor', 2 volumes, London, George Woodfall & Son, 1851

'Memoirs and Services of the 83rd Regiment, County of Dublin, 1793 - 1807', London, Rees, 1908

Mokyr, Joel, 'Why Ireland Starved: A Quantitative and Analytical History of the Irish Economy, 1800-1850', London, George Allen & Unwin, 1983

Moneypenny, William & Buckle, George, 'The Life of Benjamin Disraeli', 2 volumes, London, John Murray, 1929

Montgomery, John, '1900: The End of An Era', London, George Allen & Unwin, 1948

Monroe, Horace, 'Elmley Lovett and the Moules of Sneads Green', London, Mitchell, Hughes and Clarke, 1927

Morley, John, 'The Life of Gladstone' (abridged and with a preface by CFG Masterman), London, Hodder & Stoughton, 1927

Morning Chronicle, April - June 1813; November 1814 - January 1815; 27th December 1819; 20th December 1826; 29th April 1831; 19th July 1837; 12th April 1845; 13th June & 21st July 1848; 7th November 1850; 5th, 6th, 8th, 22nd and 29th January, 3rd February, 12th March, 23rd April & 4th June 1853; 31st March 1855; 19th September 1859; 25th August 1860

Morning Herald, 22nd & 23rd August 1848; 19th February 1849

Morris, R., 'Cholera 1832 - The Social Response to an Epidemic', London, Croom Helm, 1976

Muir, Ramsay, 'A History of Liverpool', Liverpool, University Press of Liverpool, 1907

(Lord) Munster in 'Portugal and Spain campaign', 1831, i, pp145-146

Namier, Lewis and Brooke, John, 'History of Parliament: The House of Commons 1754-1790', 3 volumes, London, Secker and Warburg, 1985

National Archives, ACC/0503/083; ACC/0503/101-104; HO 40/40; C211/62

Negus, Victor, 'History of the Trustees of the Hunterian Collection', London, E&S Livingstone Ltd., 1966

The Newcastle Courant, 2nd February 1828; 24th January 1829; 7th January 1832; 2nd February 1833

Noake, John, 'Noake's Guide to Worcestershire', London, Longman, 1868

Norman, C.B., 'Battle Honours of the British Army 1662-1901', Newton Abbot, David & Charles, 1971

Norman, E.R., 'Church and Society in England 1770-1970: A Historical Study', Oxford, Clarendon Press, 1976

[Northcote–Trevelyan report] 'Report on the organisation of a permanent civil service', London, Eyre & Spottiswoode, 1854

North Wales Chronicle, 8th September 1855

O'Connell, Maurice R, 'Daniel O'Connell: The Man and His Politics', Dublin, Irish Academic Press, 1990

Owen, Robert, 'A New View of Society and Report to the County of Lanark', edited and with an introduction by Vic Gatrell, London, Pelican, 1970

'Oxford Dictionary of National Biography', Oxford, Oxford University Press, 2004

'Oxford English Dictionary', (2nd edition), Oxford, Oxford University Press, 1989

Pakenham, Thomas, 'The Scramble for Africa', London, Abacus, 1992

Pakenham, Thomas, 'The Year of Liberty: The Story of the Great Irish Rebellion of 1798', London, Abacus, 2004

Pall Mall Gazette, 2nd March 1876; 8th April 1885; 24th January 1896

Parissien, Steven, 'George IV: The Grand Entertainment', London, John Murray, 2001

Pearce, John, 'The Artizans', Labourers and General Dwellings Company Limited: A statement addressed to the shareholders', London, 1877

Pearse, G.E., 'The Cape of Good Hope 1652-1833', Pretoria, JL Van Schaik Ltd., 1956

Pellew, Jill, 'The Home Office 1848-1914: From Clerks to Bureaucrats', London, Heinemann, 1982

Pelling, Henry, 'A History of British Trade Unionism' (5th edition), London, Penguin, 1992

Pepys, Henry, 'A Charge Delivered to the Diocese of Worcester by Henry Pepys, D.D., Bishop of Worcester', London, 1845

Perceval, Dudley, 'The Church Question in Ireland: Speech as Prepared by the Late Right Hon. Spencer Perceval for the Debate on the First Roman-Catholic Petition to the United Parliament (13th May 1805) ... with an Introduction, Illustrative Appendix, Notes and Comments to the Latter', London, William Blackwood & Sons, 1844

Perceval, Dudley, 'Earl Grey's Circular: A Memento', London, F & JH Rivington, 1849

Perceval, Dudley, 'Maynooth and the Jew Bill: Further Illustrations of the Speech of the Right Hon. Spencer Perceval on the Roman Catholic Question in May 1805', London, William Blackwood & Sons, 1845

Perceval, Dudley, 'Remarks on the character ascribed by Colonel Napier to the late Right Hon. Spencer Perceval', (2nd edition), London, James Fraser, 1835

Perceval, Dudley, 'Quietus Optabilissimus: or, The nature and necessity of real securities for the United Church, with a liberal and lasting settlement of the Catholic question', London, Ridgways, 1829

Perceval, Edward, 'Remarks on a late publication, entitled, "An essay on the principle of population, or, A view of its present and past effects on human happiness, by T.R. Malthus, A.M. Fellow of Jesus College, Cambridge"', London, Bickerstaff, 1803

Perceval, John Thomas, 'A Letter to the Right Hon. W.E. Gladstone, MP on the Separation of the Irish Church from the State, and In Favour of a Dissolution of the Union Between England and Ireland', London, Truelove, 1868

Perceval, John Thomas, 'A Letter to the Secretary of State for the Home Department upon the unjust and pettifogging conduct of the Metropolitan Commissioners on Lunacy, in the Case of a Gentleman lately under their surveillance', London, Effingham Wilson, 1844

Perceval, John Thomas, 'Letters to Sir J. Graham ... upon the reform of the law affecting the treatment of persons alleged to be of unsound mind', London, 1846

Perceval, John Thomas, 'A Narrative of the Treatment Experienced by a Gentleman, During a State of Mental Derangement', London, Wilson, 1838

Perceval, Spencer George, "On the Discovery of A Bed of Devonian Corals at Withycombe, West Somerset", *Geological Magazine*, 1866

Perceval, Spencer George, 'Catalogue with Preface of a Collection of Minerals in the Taunton Museum from the Brendon Hills and Other Localities in West Somerset', 1909

Philippart, John (ed.), 'The Royal Military Calendar or Army Service and Commission Book', 3rd edition, 5 volumes, London, Egerton, 1820

Pool, Bernard (ed.), 'The Croker Papers 1808-1857', London, Batsford, 1967

Porter, Roy, "Madness and its institutions", pp. 277-302 in A. Wear [ed.], 'Medicine in Society: Historical Essays', Cambridge, Cambridge University Press, 1992

Post Office London Directory, London, Kelly, 1841

Preston Chronicle, 3rd February 1844

Preston Guardian, 24th July 1847

'St Peter's College, Radley - Register 1847-1962', Aldershot, Radleian Society, 1965

Rallings, Colin & Thrasher, Michael (eds.), 'British Electoral Facts 1832-2006', Aldershot, Ashgate, 2007

Rand, Benjamin, 'Berkeley and Percival', Cambridge, University Press, 1914

Ritchie, J. Ewing, 'British Senators: Or, Political Sketches, Past and Present', London, Tinsley Brothers, 1869

Robson, Ann P. & Robson, John M. (eds.), 'The Collected Works of John Stuart Mill, Volume XXII - Newspaper Writings December 1822 - July 1831 Part I', London, Routledge and Kegan Paul, 1986

Rousseau, Jean-Jacques, 'The Social Contract', Amsterdam, Chez MM Rey, 1762

Rubinstein, W.D., 'The end of "Old Corruption" in Britain 1780-1860', *Past and Present*, 101 (1983), pp55-86

Rubinstein, W.D., 'The Victorian middle classes: Wealth, occupation and geography', *Economic History Review*, 30 (1977 (a)), pp602-623

Rubinstein, W.D., 'Wealth, elites and the class structure of modern Britain', *Past and Present*, 76 (1977 (b)), pp99-126

Ruotsila, Markku, 'The Catholic Apostolic Church in British politics', *Journal of Ecclesiastical History*, 56 (2005), pp75-91

'St Mary's Church, Ealing: The restoration of a historic building as a centre for worship and outreach 1984-2003', undated

Sainty, John, 'Home Office Officials 1782-1870', London, IHR/Athlone Press, 1975

The Satirist, 22nd September 1839; 16th, 23rd February & 25th October 1840; 28th July 1844

Saturday Review, 11th May 1867

Saye, Ruth & Saye, Albert "John Percival, First Earl of Egmont" in Horace Montgomery (ed.), 'Georgians in Profile: Historical Essays in Honor of Ellis Merton Coulter', Athens, Georgia, University of Georgia Press, 1958, pp1-16

Sedgwick, Romney, 'History of Parliament: The House of Commons 1715-1754', 2 volumes, London, HMSO, 1970

Shaw, Bernard, 'An Unsocial Socialist', London, Swan Sonnenschein, 1887 (reprinted London, Virago, 1988)

Skidelsky, Robert, 'John Maynard Keynes 1883-1946: Economist, Philosopher, Statesman', London, Macmillan, 2003

'Smith's Map of the County of Somerset', London, C Smith, 1835

Smith, E.A., 'The Affair of Queen Caroline', Stroud, Sutton, 1993

Somerset Record Office:
DD/CCH/2/3
DD/WO/54/11/20
DD/WO/58/4/12

Southey, Robert, "On the state of the poor", 1812, collected in 'Essays, Moral and Political', 2 volumes, London, John Murray, 1832

Squibb, G. D., 'Doctors' Commons: A History of the College of Advocates and Doctors of Law', Oxford, Clarendon Press, 1977

Stannard, Martin, 'Evelyn Waugh: The Early Years 1903-1939', London, Dent, 1986

Stephen, J., 'The Clapham sect', *Edinburgh Review*, 80 (1844), pp251–307

Stewart, Robert 'The Foundation of the Conservative Party 1830-1867', London, Longman, 1978

Strachey, L. & Fulford, R. (ed.) 'The Greville Memoirs', 1814–1860, 8 vols., London, Macmillan, 1938

Swinson, Arthur (ed.), 'A Register of the Regiments and Corps of the British Army', London, The Archive Press, 1972

Sykes, Christopher, 'Evelyn Waugh: A Biography', London, Collins, 1975

The Tablet, 29th March 1851

Thane, Pat, 'Old Age in English History: Past Experiences, Present Issues', Oxford, Oxford University Press, 2002

Thompson, F.M.L. (ed.), 'Cambridge Social History of Britain 1750-1950: Volume 1 Regions and Communities', Cambridge, Cambridge University Press, 1990

Thompson, F.M.L. (ed.), 'Cambridge Social History of Britain 1750-1950: Volume 3 Social Agencies and Institutions', Cambridge, Cambridge University Press, 1990

Thompson, F.M.L., 'English Landed Society in the Nineteenth Century', London, Routledge and Kegan Paul, 1963

Thompson, F.M.L., 'The Rise of Respectable Society', London, Fontana, 1988

Thorne, R.G. (ed.), 'The House of Commons 1790-1820', 5 volumes, History of Parliament Trust, Secker & Warburg, 1986

The Times, 5th May 1815; 24th February & 10th November 1819; 7th March 1820; 30th November 1822; 24th January 1823; 9th February 1829; 21st December & 29th December 1830; 6th January & 29th April 1831; 4th January & 18th April 1832; 30th

January 1834; 5th December 1835; 8th October, 19th October & 13th December 1836; 1st August 1837; 28th August 1840; 22nd August & 5th November 1841; 5th January 1842; 3rd August & 28th August 1843; 13th July 1844; 21st May, 3rd July & 6th December 1845; 30th April 1846; 23rd May & 14th June 1848; 15th November 1850; 18th January 1851; 10th January, 12th March & 9th May 1853; 8th April 1854; 3rd May 1856; 17th April 1858; 8th October 1859; 17th January 1863; 4th May 1867; 18th May 1867; 20th June 1867; 6th February 1871; 2nd March 1876; 20th January 1885; 8th April 1885; 15th June 1894; 2nd November 1903; 2nd November 1905

Totman, Sidney, 'A History of the Manor and Parish of Burgh, including Burgh Heath, Nork, Preston and Tattenham', Beaconsfield, Totman, 1970

Trevelyan, Charles, 'Money or merit: The army purchase question considered with especial reference to the recent commission of inquiry', London, C.J. Skeet, 1857

Trevelyan, Charles, 'The Army purchase question and report, and minutes of evidence of the Royal Commission considered, with a particular examination of the evidence of Sir Charles Trevelyan', London, James Ridgway, 1858

Trevelyan, Charles, 'The British Army in 1868', 4th edition, London, Longmans, Green & Co., 1868

Trewman's Exeter Flying Post or Plymouth and Cornish Advertiser, 4th October 1849; 25th August 1869

Troup, Edward, 'Home Office', London, GP Pitman & Sons, 1925

Tuke, Daniel Hack, 'Chapters in the History of the Insane in the British Isles', London, Kegan Paul, Trench & Co., 1882

'The United Service Journal and Naval and Military Magazine', London, Colburn & Bentley, 1830

United Service Gazette, 11th January 1834

Valentine, Alan, 'The British Establishment 1760-1784', Norman, University of Oklahoma Press, 1970

Venn, John, 'Biographical History of Gonville and Caius College 1349-1897', vol. II (1713-1897), Cambridge, Cambridge University Press, 1898

Venn, J.A., 'Cambridge University Alumni Cantabrigienses', Pt. II from 1752-1900, vol. V, Cambridge, Cambridge University Press, 1953

Victoria County Histories:

'Ealing and Brentford: Churches: Ealing', A History of the County of Middlesex: Volume 7: Acton, Chiswick, Ealing and Brentford, West Twyford, Willesden, 1982

'Ealing and Brentford: Other estates', A History of the County of Middlesex: Volume 7: Acton, Chiswick, Ealing and Brentford, West Twyford, Willesden, 1982

Essex, vol. II, London, Dawson & Sons, 1977

Kent, vol. III, London, Dawsons, 1974

'Putney', The Environs of London: volume 1: County of Surrey, 1792

Somerset, vol. V, London, Oxford University Press, 1985

Sussex, vol. II, London, Dawsons, 1973

Sussex, vol. IV, London, Dawsons, 1973

Sussex, vol. VII, London, Dawsons, 1973

Warwickshire, vol. II, London, Dawsons, 1965

Worcester, vol. III, London, Dawsons, 1971

Worcester, vol. IV, London, Dawsons, 1971

Vincent, John (ed.), 'Disraeli, Derby and the Conservative Party: Journals and Memoirs of Edward Henry, Lord Stanley 1849-1869', Sussex, Harvester Press, 1978

Wade, John, 'The Black Book, or Corruption Unmasked on Places, Sinecures, Pensions and Reversions', London, Fairburn, 1820

Walpole, Horace, 'Memoirs of King George II', (J. Brooke, ed.), 3 volumes, New Haven, Yale University Press, 1985

Walpole, Horace, 'Memoirs of the Reign of King George III', (D Jarrett, ed.), 4 volumes, London, Yale University Press, 2000,

Walpole, Spencer, 'The Life of the Right Honourable Spencer Perceval', 2 volumes, London, Hurst and Blackett, 1874

Walpole, Spencer, 'The History of Twenty-Five Years', 5 volumes, London, Longmans, Green & Co., 1904-1908

Walvin, James, 'Victorian Values', London, Andre Deutsch, 1987

Ward, W.R., 'Victorian Oxford', London, Cass, 1965

Warwickshire County Record Office:
    '1860 Rate Book, St Nicholas parish, Warwick', CR1618/W33/61-89
    'Warwickshire Directory 1860', C910 KEL

Watts, Michael, 'The Dissenters, Volume II: The Expansion of Evangelical Nonconformity', Oxford, Clarendon Press, 1995

Westminster Archives:
    '1841 Rate Book, St George's, Hanover Square', C660, 2291

Whitbread, Sam, 'Plain Mr Whitbread: Seven Centuries of a Bedfordshire Family', Dunstable, The Book Castle, 2007

Wilcox, Renee, 'A history of the parish of St Paul, Nork, Banstead, Surrey', 1985

Winch, Donald, 'Riches and Poverty: An Intellectual History of Political Economy in Britain 1750-1834', Cambridge, Cambridge University Press, 1996

Wohl, Anthony S, 'Endangered Lives: Public Health in Victorian Britain', London, Dent, 1983

Wohl, Anthony S, 'The Eternal Slum: Housing and Social Policy in Victorian London', London, Edward Arnold, 1977

Woodham-Smith, Cecil, 'The Reason Why', London, Penguin Books, 1953

Worcestershire County Record Office:
'A History of Worcestershire Churches'
Bishop Carr's Visitation Act Book 1833-1839, 802/2609
Bishop Pepys' Visitation Act Book 1841-1878, 716.011/2657
'Bishop's Register', Kidderminster Deanery, Elmley Lovett institution folios f.25-f.40, 716.093/2648/12b/ii f.40
Elmley Lovett 1835 entries in 'Curate's Memo Book and Parochial Visitor's Guide', Oxford, JH Parker, 1833 850/9845/5 (i)
'Elmley Lovett Vestry Minute Book 1824-1887', 850/9845/5(ii)

'Words of Truth and Trust: being addresses at the meetings of the Association of Female Workers held after the Mildmay conference', London, SW Partridge & Co, 1874

Working Man, 4th May 1867

Wormald, Audrey, 'Hillingdon Church and Parish 1770-1999', May 2008

Wylly, H.C., 'The Military Memoirs of Lt. Gen. Sir Joseph Thackwell', London, John Murray, 1908

Wylly, H.C., 'XVth (The King's) Hussars 1759 to 1913', London, Caxton, 1914

Young, Arthur, 'Tours in England and Wales', LSE Economic and Political Science Tracts, Reprint 14, London, Lund Humphries, 1932

Young, G.M. (ed.), 'Early Victorian England 1830-1865', volume 2, Oxford, Oxford University Press, 1934

Young, Urban C.P., 'Life and Letters of the Venerable Father Dominic Barberi, C.P., Founder of the Passionists in Belgium', London, Burns Oates & Washbourne Ltd., 1926

WEBSITES

hansard.millbanksystems.com/commons/1851/mar/20/ecclesiastical
-titles-assumption-bill

www.allsaintsealing.org

www.archive.org/details/christscollege00peiluoft

www.archive.org/stream/visitationenglan06howa

www.british-history.ac.uk/report.aspx?compid=45253

www.british-history.ac.uk/report.aspx?compid=22578

www.british-history.ac.uk/report.aspx?compid=51394

www.british-history.ac.uk/report.aspx?compid=42998

www.british-history.ac.uk/report.aspx?compid=45218

www.coronersociety.org.uk/wfBriefHistory.aspx

www.familysearch.org/eng/Search/frameset_search.asp

www.historyhome.co.uk/peel/refact/refmod2.htm

www.oldpicturepostcards.co.uk/wiveliscombe.htm

www.opcdorset.org/WeymouthMelcombeFiles/MelcombeSM-
Burs1851-1860.htm

www.rcpe.ac.uk/library/history/reprints/improving-insane.pdf

www.thornber.net/medicine/html/phealth.html

www.twickenham-museum.org.uk/house_detail.asp?HouseID=26

www.users.globalnet.co.uk/~recb/chisoc/Medlam/ChisBell/chbh1.txt

www.victorianlondon.org/dickens/dickens-r.htm

www.visionofbritain.org.uk/

www.worldsquash2008.com/the-championships/history-of-
squash.aspx

INDEX

Principal references are in **bold** type. Some minor references, entries in the 19th century Chronology on pages 22-39 and individual Perceval grandchildren are not indexed.
Sub-entries are in alphabetical order. n preface refers to the notes; it is followed by the note (rather than page) number.

Aberdeen, George Gordon-Hamilton, 4th Earl of 126, 218, 232
Adams, John Quincy 81-82
Addington, Henry 48, 50, 53, 59
agriculture 2, 6
Albury, Surrey 133, 134
All Saints Church, Ealing 16, 157-158
Alleged Lunatic's Friends Society 18, **249-253**
Althorp, Lord *see* John Charles Spencer
America, Britain at war with 160-161
Anglican(s)/Anglican religion 49, 73, 133-138, 141, 142, 156, 196, 203, 205, 209, 210, 214, 215, 216, 219, 276 *see* Evangelical Anglicans
Arden, Lord 12, 13, 45, **48-58**, 64, 68, 71, 98, 107, 112, 134
re-marriage of sister-in-law Jane (Perceval) Wilson 77-79, 83, 96-97
Arlington Street, London 79, 80, n191, 91, n567
army 1, 114, 238, 276
15th Hussars *see* Ernest Perceval
83rd Foot 90 *see* Sir Henry William Carr's military career *and* Peninsular War

Grenadier Guards *see* John Thomas Perceval
army commissions, abolition of purchase n32, 260-261, 263
Artizans Dwellings Acts 1868-1882 154
Artizans, Labourers and General Dwellings Company 153-156
Ashley, Lord *see* Shaftesbury, 7th Earl of
asylums *see* mental health for general *and* named asylums
Australia 11, n597

Barberi, Father Dominic 141
Barker, Mary 16, 160, 163-165
Basrelli, Father 140-141
Bathurst, Earl 199-201, n567
Beaumont Smith, Edward 205-206
Bedford Row, Holborn 65, 66, 94
Belgium 141, 156, 161, n448
Bellingham, John 61, 69, n151, 153, 264
Belsize House, Hampstead 13, 66, 67, n144, 94
Bennett, Hugh 184
Bentham, Jeremy 130, 246
Berkeley, Bishop 41
Billericay, Essex 159, 160, 162
Bindon House, Somerset 262, 264
Birmingham 8, 10, 12, 16, 159, 166, 270 *see* Frederick Perceval
Black Book 1820 50, 51, 54, 56, n126, 58 *see* sinecures
Boer War 11, 18
Bognor, Sussex 100, 101
Bombay 128, 257
Bourke, Mary Jane 17, 201, 213, 224
Bourke, Sir Richard n60, 199-201, n579, 204-205, n597, 213
Bradlaugh, Charles 238